BRITISH ARMY HANDBOOK
1914–1918

BRITISH ARMY
HANDBOOK
1914–1918

ANDREW RAWSON

SUTTON PUBLISHING

First published in the United Kingdom in 2006 by
Sutton Publishing Limited · Phoenix Mill
Thrupp · Stroud · Gloucestershire · GL5 2BU

British Library Cataloguing in Publication Data
A catalogue record for this book is available from the British Library.

ISBN 0-7509-3745-9

Typeset in 9.5/12pt New Baskerville.
Edited and designed by Donald Sommerville.
Printed and bound in England by
J.H. Haynes & Co. Ltd, Sparkford.

Pages ii–iii: As the whistles blow, Canadian troops head into no man's land to raid German trenches on the Ancre Heights in October 1916. *(IWM CO876)*

CONTENTS

ACKNOWLEDGEMENTS

When I started work on this book, I never realized what a journey of discovery I was embarking on; many people have helped me along that journey. Dr John Bourne, Director of the Centre for First World War Studies at Birmingham University, has been a constant help, clearing up a host of queries and pointing me towards useful sources.

Many of the photographs come from the Imperial War Museum's Department of Photographs where the staff's friendly and professional guidance aided me in my arduous search for relevant illustrations. Countless members of staff at libraries across the north of England, including Leeds City, Leeds University, Manchester and Bradford City Libraries have patiently sought out material. Without their assistance my work would have been impossible.

Finally, I would like to thank Nick Reynolds of Sutton Publishing Ltd and Donald Sommerville for guiding me, seemingly effortlessly, through the writing and preparation of this book.

I hope that this book increases the understanding of what the men and women endured between 1914 and 1918 and it is dedicated to my son Alex; let us hope that his generation learns from their experiences.

CHAPTER ONE

BACKGROUND

A CENTURY OF PEACE?

The year 1815 marked the end of Great Britain's involvement in European campaigns for nearly a century (with the brief exception of the Crimean War). While political and military struggles flared across the continent, the British Empire expanded round the world. Private enterprise conquered territories in the search for new resources while the Army followed and the Royal Navy patrolled the oceans, protecting the shipping routes.

China was a source for opium and tea while Burma was a major supplier of teak but, after complaining about trading, both were forced to submit to British rule; China handed over Hong Kong while Burma was totally annexed.

India was Britain's main concern but attempts to secure the North-West Frontier in 1838 to protect against a feared Russian invasion ended in disaster; fifty years of skirmishing followed before the Afghans accepted a British envoy in Kabul. There was trouble in Lahore in 1848 when the Sikhs invaded the British East India Company's territories and in 1857 Indian Sepoys mutinied, massacring British garrisons before they were suppressed. After quelling the uprisings the Army took control of the East India Company's area, starting the era of the British Raj and peace in India. A final uprising by Chitral tribesmen at the end of the century resulted in the annexation of the area.

Tensions with Russia flared in 1854 and Britain sent 30,000 troops to the Crimea as part of an alliance with France, Turkey and Sardinia to prevent the Russians extending their influence over Turkey. The Army suffered setbacks at Balaclava and Inkerman, while thousands died of sickness during the siege of Sevastopol. A new medal, the Victoria Cross, was introduced as the highest award for valour during the war and, when the French captured a key position in the Sevastopol fortress the following year, the Russians withdrew and made peace.

In Africa, Britain had annexed the Cape Colony from the Dutch East India Company as early as 1814, establishing a toehold at the southern tip of the continent, but further colonization was delayed by the threat of malaria. The annexation caused tension with the Boers and they withdrew into the Transvaal and the Orange Free State to retain their independence.

The discovery of quinine in 1850 allowed travellers to explore more readily and, once they returned with news of vast untapped riches, European traders with private armies staked their claims. Professional armies soon followed to protect the new provinces. The British Army pursued an aggressive occupation policy, annexing Basutoland, the Gold Coast, the Transvaal and Zululand (where British troops suffered a humiliating defeat at Isandlwana). An invasion of Natal in 1881 resulted in the First Boer War and stirred the Boers to arm themselves with modern rifles and guns bought from Europe.

British troops landed in Ashanti in 1896, extending the Empire's hold on the west coast of Africa.

Great Britain had staked its claims in North Africa by purchasing the Egyptian share in the French Suez Canal project, and then took over the Sudan in 1882 after crushing a rebellion by the Mahdists and the Dervishes. General Gordon's attempt to rescue isolated garrisons ended in disaster and his force was cut off and massacred in Khartoum. General Kitchener finally regained control of the Sudan after the Battle of Omdurman in 1898.

Germany, a late starter in the colonization of Africa, claimed rights to German South-West Africa (now Namibia), Kamerun (Cameroon), Togo and German East Africa (Tanzania), stirring protests among the other European powers. The German chancellor,

Otto von Bismarck, held a conference in Berlin in 1884 where the European powers agreed to divide Africa up to avoid conflict in Europe. It did not mean peace for the natives, however. Soon after Cecil Rhodes' small army occupied Matabeleland with the help of the new Maxim machine gun, renaming the area Rhodesia.

Trouble again flared in South Africa when gold was discovered in the Transvaal in 1886, sparking an influx of settlers eager to stake their claim. An abortive raid in 1896 stirred resentment and when the British failed to secure rights for their citizens in 1899, the Boers retaliated by invading the Cape Colony, besieging the towns of Ladysmith, Mafeking and Kimberley. The British Army responded with huge task forces but setbacks at places such as Colenso and Spion Kop showed that it was lacking in many areas when British soldiers were confronted by determined men armed with modern weapons. It was the start of a new learning curve, one that would stand the British Army in good stead for the war in Europe a decade later.

Overwhelming numbers and an aggressive resettlement policy, in which families were imprisoned in concentration camps, forced the Boers to roam the *veldt* as guerrillas and, when supplies dwindled, they eventually sued for peace. The annexation of the Transvaal and the Orange Free State meant that one-third of Africa was now British.

REORGANIZATION OF THE ARMY

Between 1899 and 1902 the British Army was engaged in its first major campaign of the twentieth century, facing the well equipped and highly motivated Boers in South Africa. The experience was a rude awakening for the War Office and high command; it was time to reform all areas of the armed services.

A report was published in 1903 and the Commander-in-Chief, Field Marshal Lord Roberts, implemented many of the recommendations but the Cabinet refused to sanction conscription and plans to expand the Army had to be scrapped.

Lord Esher's committee strengthened the Committee of Imperial Defence and set up the Army Council to replace the post of commander-in-chief in February 1904. Members reported to the Secretary of State for War on a wide range of military, civil and financial matters. Before long they had authorized the establishment of a General Staff and its three main branches, setting up directorates to improve training, staff work and operational planning.

Many of the changes were in place before 1914, the majority implemented during a major reorganization in 1908. The following were the most noteworthy:

EXPEDITIONARY FORCE

Regular units across the United Kingdom were made ready to mobilize as an Expeditionary Force of 6 infantry divisions and 1 cavalry division.

2.5-inch muzzle-loading mountain guns were ideal during campaigns such as the one against the Pathans in 1897, but they proved to be no match for the modern armaments used by the Boers.

The khaki drill uniform and webbing used in South Africa would soon be replaced by a modern version as part of the sweeping reforms of the Army.

ARMY CORPS

There had been no plans to operate a corps structure in the field but on mobilization the decision was taken to correspond with the French command system. Corps staff at Aldershot were joined by 2 improvised corps staffs, each controlling 2 divisions.

STAFF

Staff officers were trained at the Staff College, Camberley, while the Administrative Staff were trained at the London School of Economics; Indian Army Staff attended Quetta Staff College.

OFFICERS

Volunteer Corps at the universities and public schools were transformed into the Officers' Training Corps to ease the pressure on the Sandhurst and Woolwich Military Colleges. Sandhurst waived the entry examination for candidates with exemplary records to speed up their training schedule.

CAVALRY

A census of horses available across the country was taken and requisition powers were introduced.

ARTILLERY

Field batteries were armed with quick-firing field guns equipped with shock absorbers to reduce the amount of recoil after each shot. The divisional field artillery was grouped into 3 x 18-pounder and 1 x 4.5-inch howitzer brigades, each with 3 x 6-gun batteries, and ammunition columns were introduced to manage the distribution of shells. The general reserve of artillery had doubled to 81 batteries by 1912 and the Garrison Artillery Militia was trained and made ready to be mobilized as a Special Reserve.

INFANTRY

Steps were taken to balance the numbers of battalions at home and overseas, with each regiment having a battalion in Great Britain and another serving abroad. The numbers were eventually set at 84 home battalions and 73 in overseas garrisons. Command in the infantry battalions was streamlined by reducing the number of companies from 8 to 4. The infantry were issued with the new Short

Magazine Lee-Enfield rifle and marksmanship training with rapid fire was improved.

ARMY SERVICE CORPS

Subsidies were offered to private vehicle owners providing they would make them available during a national emergency. Specially designed military vehicles were introduced for private sale and again listed for requisitioning. Divisional transport was re-organized in 1912, grouping all but the first-line transport into companies. A fleet of lorries was allocated to each division to bring forward supplies and evacuate the wounded.

ROYAL ARMY MEDICAL CORPS

Bearer companies and field hospitals were reorganized and each division received a self-contained field ambulance unit. Clearing hospitals were organized to treat casualties evacuated from the battlefield.

CIVILIAN MEDICAL SERVICES

Plans were put in place to use hospitals and voluntary aid in the United Kingdom (allowed under the 1906 Geneva Convention) while the Army Nursing Service was given official recognition.

RESERVES

Steps were also taken to provide a pool of reserves to reinforce the Regular Army.

THE NATIONAL RESERVE

A register of officers and men with military experience was started in 1910 and by 1914 it had 350,000 members.

SPECIAL RESERVE

The Militia was renamed the Special Reserve.

THE TERRITORIAL FORCE

Individuals and units of the Volunteer forces were invited to become Territorial troops or disband and the Territorial Associations (not the War Office) were given responsibility for organizing and maintaining the Territorial Force. The Territorial infantry formed 14 divisions along the same lines as the Regular divisions while the Yeomanry was reorganized into 14 brigades as the second line of cavalry. Although numbers were far below the establishment of 316,000 in 1914, retired Territorials were expected to re-enlist during a national emergency.

IMPERIAL MILITARY FORCES

In 1907 staff officers were sent out to the Dominion staff colleges to teach new candidates. Dominion forces also agreed to standardize their organizations in line with the British Army but they reserved the right to abstain from Britain's conflicts.

BRITAIN'S STANDING ARMY

The Regular Army numbered 247,000 men in August 1914; 129,000 were stationed across Great Britain, while the rest were serving with the Indian Army or at other overseas postings across the Empire.

DISPOSITIONS AT THE OUTBREAK OF WAR

Six infantry divisions and 4 cavalry brigades were stationed as follows:

1st Division: Aldershot.
2nd Division: 1 brigade in London and Windsor and 2 brigades at Aldershot.
3rd Division: Southern Command area along the south coast.
4th Division: Eastern Command area on the south-east coast.
5th Division: Deployed across Ireland.
6th Division: 1 brigade in Northern Command, 2 brigades in southern Ireland.
Cavalry: 4 cavalry brigades were stationed at Aldershot, Tidworth, south-east England and Ireland; they assembled as the Cavalry Division when war was declared.

ENLISTING

Men joined the Regular Army for a variety of personal and financial reasons, but the majority were looking for a steady job with a regular income. Minimum requirements were 5 feet 3 inches in height, and age between 19 and 38; and once at the regimental depot or a recruiting office the potential soldier had to pass a series of physical tests. A new recruit enlisted for 7 years' service and he would be kept on the National Reserve for 5 years after he was discharged.

TRAINING

The *Combined Training* manual was released in 1902 drawing on lessons learnt in South Africa and it was quickly renamed *Field Service Regulations*. An updated version was released in two parts in 1909: *Part I (Operations)* and *Part II (Organization and Administration)*.

The annual training cycle began with physical exercise, drill and route marching while the recruits learnt basic skills including musketry, hand-to-hand fighting, signalling and scouting. The winter months were spent on education and rifle drill, with unit training beginning in the spring, starting with company, squadron and battery exercises, working through combined arms training up to large-scale manoeuvres by the end of the summer.

Those wishing to be commissioned as Royal Artillery and Royal Engineer officers attended the Royal Military Academy at Woolwich, while those seeking commissions in the cavalry, infantry, Indian Army and Army Service Corps went to the Royal Military Academy, Sandhurst. Rather than attend Sandhurst, a third of infantry and cavalry officers had trained with the Officers' Training Corps at the universities and public schools or had previous experience with the Militia; only a handful of men were commissioned from the ranks.

Infantrymen did bayonet training with padded jackets and rifles armed with spring-loaded plungers while the Musketry School at Hythe focussed on training the men to deliver a high rate of aimed fire with the rifle. Instructors taught the recruits to concentrate on short bursts of rapid fire. Recruits were expected to be able to fire between 12 and 15 rounds a minute. Individual firing was recommended and platoon volleys were rarely used. Commands were restricted to starting and ending firing, with officers stepping in if the firing was getting out of hand.

Cavalrymen had the extra responsibility of caring for their horse and tack; artillery drivers had two horses to look after. After completing basic riding skills, troopers learnt the art of attack riding, fencing with blunted swords and musketry.

PAY AND PROMOTION

New recruits started on one shilling (1s – £0.05) a day but numerous deductions were made for food and equipment. However, soldiers could earn extra pay by increasing their skills or gaining promotion and a senior non-commissioned officer (NCO) could earn around 6s a day. Soldiers received field allowances if they were serving overseas. They were paid in local currency, at around 25 francs to £1 in France.

A well-behaved private could expect to be promoted to lance-corporal after two years and might make corporal after four; few reached the rank of sergeant unless they re-enlisted. A few sergeants were promoted to colour sergeant (or staff sergeants in some arms) and senior NCOs and warrant officers usually stayed with the Army for the full 21 years' service.

New subalterns received 7s 6d a day while those with specialized skills earned more. Army officers bought their own uniforms but received a uniform grant of £50 towards the cost. A part-time Territorial infantry subaltern earned 5s 3d a day while his lieutenant-colonel received 18s.

ACCOMMODATION

Purpose-built barracks had been erected in the garrison towns across Great Britain towards the end of the nineteenth century. While the officers and sergeants had comfortable messes and a higher standard of accommodation, the other ranks lived in barrack rooms with 20–40 beds. There were married quarters but men had to be 26 years old and have served at least 5 years before applying for permission to marry. A man could marry without the Army's consent but he had to support his wife, paying for her lodgings

A machine-gun crew train with their Maxim gun.

outside the barracks; many opted to stay single and visit the prostitutes living nearby.

THE TERRITORIAL FORCE

The previously-existing local Militia and Volunteer units were reorganized into the Territorial Force during the 1908 reforms, creating 14 Territorial infantry divisions and 14 Yeomanry cavalry brigades modelled on the Regular Army formations. Units recruited locally to form a full range of units with strong ties to the local community.

Infantry battalions were affiliated to line regiments. While most county regiments had 2 Territorial battalions, 4 had just 1 Territorial battalion (and no Regulars) to begin with (Cambridgeshire, Herefordshire, Hertford-

shire and Monmouthshire); the London Regiment was also all-Territorial with 24 battalions grouped into 2 divisions.

LIFE IN THE TERRITORIAL FORCE

The minimum age was 18 but the physical standards on joining were the same as for the Regulars. Men trained one or two evenings a week at local drill halls and they were often called the Saturday Night Soldiers or the Terriers. The annual summer camp was the highlight of the calendar where the men took part in large-scale exercises; over 250,000 Territorial soldiers were on annual manoeuvres when war was declared on 4 August 1914.

Territorials agreed to full-time service if war was declared and they could be posted

7

anywhere in the United Kingdom. Overseas service in times of conflict was optional but over 17,000 signed the Imperial Service Obligation before the outbreak of the First World War.

The principal role of the force during a war was supposedly home defence, and the Territorials were intended to protect the ports and coastline after the Expeditionary Force left for the Continent.

ORGANIZATION

The Territorial infantry divisions had 3 infantry brigades, each of 4 battalions. The artillery had 4 field artillery brigades and 1 battery of heavy artillery per division, but the brigades only had 4-gun batteries. Support services included 2 Royal Engineer field companies, a signals company, a divisional train, 3 field ambulance units and a clearing hospital. The divisions needed ammunition columns, cyclist companies and an extra engineer field company to bring them up to full establishment.

The Territorial Army was 47,000 (all ranks) short of the establishment of 316,000 in August 1914; the deficit was soon made up.

DIVISIONS AND RECRUITING AREAS

Divisional, brigade and support arms numbers were issued in May 1915 when the first Territorial divisions were deployed in France. Divisional numbers and regional titles are given opposite.

THE INDIAN ARMY

The Army in India numbered 236,000 soldiers, including 74,600 British officers and men serving with British Army units and another 2,300 British officers commanding 159,100 Indian officers and men. Indian Army recruits enlisted for 21 years and had an option to stay on for another 4 years or serve in the reserve to receive a pension. Another 40,000 men served in the auxiliary forces, providing internal security, and there were 34,000 men serving with the frontier militias and military police.

In 1913 the Army in India began to re-organize into 10 divisions and 5 cavalry brigades so that it could better defend the Afghanistan border and maintain internal security. On the outbreak of war in Europe, Indian Army units would deploy overseas to support the British Expeditionary Force and help protect other British territories. Two infantry and 2 cavalry divisions would head for France, while 6 infantry brigades garrisoned the Suez Canal in Egypt; 1 infantry division would also head to the Persian Gulf to look after British interests there.

The Indian Army formed 2 armies:

NORTHERN ARMY

1st (Peshawar) Division: Afghanistan border.
2nd (Rawalpindi) Division: Reserve for the North-West Frontier.
3rd (Lahore) Division: Lahore area.
7th (Meerut) Division: Delhi area.
8th (Lucknow) Division: Lucknow area.

SOUTHERN ARMY

4th (Quetta) Division: Persian Frontier.
5th (Mhow) Division: North of Bombay.
6th (Poona) Division: Bombay area.
9th (Secunderabad) Division: Southern India.
Burma Division: Burma–China border.

INDEPENDENT BRIGADES

Kohat, **Bannu** and **Derajat Brigades** held posts along the North-West Frontier.

CAVALRY BRIGADES

Five cavalry brigades.

ORGANIZATION
INFANTRY DIVISION

Infantry: 3 infantry brigades, each with 1 British battalion and 3 Indian battalions. A pioneer battalion was later added to the division.

Indian battalions had 13 British officers, 17 Indian officers (junior to all British officers) and 723 other ranks; embarkation strength was increased to 840 all ranks in preparation for the inevitable losses through casualties or illness. In 1917 the number of other ranks

TERRITORIAL DIVISIONS AND RECRUITING AREAS

East Lancashire Division (42nd)	Manchester, Salford and East Lancashire
1st Wessex Division (43rd)	Hampshire, Somerset, Dorset, Wiltshire, Devon, Cornwall
Home Counties Division (44th)	Surrey, Middlesex and Kent
2nd Wessex Division (45th)	Raised in September 1914 in the same area as 1st Wessex Division (included as its numbering falls in the 1st Line series)
North Midland Division (46th)	Staffordshire, Lincolnshire, Leicestershire, Nottinghamshire
2nd London Division (47th)	London boroughs
South Midland Division (48th)	Warwickshire, Gloucestershire, Worcestershire, Oxfordshire, Buckinghamshire, Berkshire
West Riding Division (49th)	West Riding of Yorkshire
Northumbrian Division (50th)	Northumberland, North and East Ridings of Yorkshire
Highland Division (51st)	Highlands of Scotland, north of the Firth of Forth
Lowland Division (52nd)	Glasgow, Edinburgh and Lowlands of Scotland
Welsh Division (53rd)	Cheshire, North Wales and Welsh Borders
East Anglian Division (54th)	Essex, Norfolk, Suffolk, Bedfordshire, Northamptonshire
West Lancashire Division (55th)	Lancashire west of the River Lune, including Liverpool
1st London Division (56th)	London boroughs

MOUNTED TERRITORIAL UNITS

In August 1914 two mounted divisions were formed from Territorial Yeomanry and Cyclist battalions for home defence:

1st Mounted Division	Notts and Derbyshire, South Midlands, Eastern Counties
2nd Mounted Division	Formed from surplus Yeomanry and Cyclist battalions
74th (Yeomanry) Division	Formed in Egypt from dismounted Yeomanry units in 1918

increased to 962 and embarkation strength rose to 1,030. Battalions were originally organized into 4 double companies, subdivided into companies and half-companies, but they adopted the British 4-company system in May 1915; it took two years to complete the reorganization. Companies were recruited from the same religious group.

Divisional cavalry: 1 regiment organized into 4 squadrons, each with 3 troops. Nine British and 18 Indian officers led 536 other ranks.

Artillery: The division had 2 artillery brigades: 1 brigade manned by British regulars and organized into 3 field batteries modelled on British battery organization; 1 Indian mountain brigade with 2 batteries, each armed with 6 x 10-pounder guns; these were crewed by 5 British officers, 3 Indian officers and 235 other ranks.

Engineers: Two Indian field companies, named Sappers and Miners. Four British officers and 4 Indian officers led 202 other ranks.

The strength of a division grew from around 12,300 to 14,310 men.

GUARDING THE EMPIRE

'The sun never set on the British Empire' by the end of Queen Victoria's reign and the same could be said of the British Army. While the Navy patrolled the high seas, 118,000 Regular soldiers guarded the Empire's territories. Over 30 battalions served as an integral part of the Indian Army divisions; a similar number were stationed at outposts across India and Burma. The trade route through the Mediterranean and the Suez Canal was important and 12 battalions were stationed at Gibraltar, Malta and Egypt; 2 more protected the South African ports. The Army garrisoned many of the Royal Navy's refuelling depots around the world, including Hong Kong, Tientsin and Singapore in the Far East and outlying stations such as Bermuda, Aden and Mauritius.

IRISH HOME RULE – THE CURRAGH INCIDENT

During the nineteenth century, the people of Ireland formed an increasing desire for self-government and the Home Rule movement gained momentum during the agricultural depression of the 1880s. Prime Minister William Gladstone proposed to give certain powers to an Irish parliament in 1886 but dissent increased after two bills failed to pass through the London parliament, resulting in the formation of a new political party, Sinn Féin, dedicated to gaining support for Irish freedom.

A third Home Rule Bill was passed in 1912, but the decision to hand over control of the police to the Irish was greeted with outrage by the Protestants who formed the majority of the population of Ulster. In the summer of 1914 parliament eased tensions by excluding Protestant-dominated Ulster from the changes for six years but, as the situation on the Continent deteriorated, Great Britain was focussed on the threat of an Irish civil war.

The government ordered the Army to take action and on 20 July 1914 Brigadier-General Hubert Gough was ordered to deploy the cavalry brigade stationed at the Curragh. Gough refused and he was dismissed but every officer of the 16th Lancers resigned in protest while other senior officers voiced their support. Faced with internal dissension in the Army at a time when the political situation in Europe was threatening to explode, the government reversed its decision and re-instated the officers. Several senior Army officers immediately resigned as a result.

THE WAR BOOK

The British and French general staffs started to meet in 1911 and drew up plans to land a British Expeditionary Force (BEF) in France, assembling it near the Belgian border on the French Army's left flank. However, the plan was only an obligation of honour and not part of any formal treaty, being designed to protect Belgium's neutral stance if Germany decided to invade.

At the same time, the Committee of Imperial Defence compiled the current defensive plans and circulated them to the Army and government departments. This collection of documents was known as the War Book. Updated circulars were issued so departments could act on new initiatives. Heads of department met occasionally under the title of the Coordination Sub-Committee but the Secretariat of the Committee of Imperial Defence coordinated the development of the War Book.

Each department had a chapter summarizing action to be taken, both during the build-up to war (the Precautionary Stage) and on the declaration of war (the War Stage). Simultaneous and corresponding actions taken by other departments were outlined so there was no confusion; large departments, including the Army, had an internal War Book detailing what each branch, arm and service was expected to do.

When war threatened, prepared telegrams and despatches were taken from files, signed

Barracks were sparse and luxuries were few for soldiers at the turn of the century. These new recruits are subject to a company sergeant-major's eagle eye while preparing for a kit inspection. *(IWM Q30061)*

and issued without delay. The number of telegrams required would block the country's telegraph system so non-urgent messages were written out in advance ready to be delivered by post. Steps were also taken to notify headquarters across the Empire at any hour of the day or night.

On the declaration of war, departments referred to their War Book as soon as the telegrams and messages reached their headquarters. It meant that the first units of the BEF were ready to sail in a few days while Territorial units were already deploying along the coast.

THE COUNTDOWN TO WAR

As Great Britain focussed on Ireland, the rest of Europe was teetering on the brink of war. Throughout the later part of the nineteenth century and the early part of the twentieth the major powers of Europe had formed two alliances. France and Russia were the Entente while Germany and Austria-Hungary were the Central Powers. Great Britain had long before signed a treaty to protect Belgium and had developed an *entente cordiale* with France and Russia, among other things to protect British interests in India and the Persian Gulf.

On 28 June 1914 members of a Serbian nationalist secret society, the Black Hand, assassinated Archduke Franz Ferdinand, heir to the Austro-Hungarian throne, during a visit to Sarajevo. Three weeks later Austria-Hungary demanded custody of the assassins, expecting a refusal that would give grounds for a limited war against Serbia.

Serbia had strong Slavic ties with Russia and Austria-Hungary was anxious for Germany's support in case Russia responded by declaring war. Germany agreed, encouraging Austria-Hungary's warlike stance. As expected, Serbia responded unfavourably to the ultimatum and Austria-Hungary declared war on Serbia on 28

TIMELINE OF BRITISH OPERATIONS ON THE WESTERN FRONT

1914

23 August	Battle of Mons (BEF)
24 August	Start of the retreat from Mons (BEF)
26 August	Battle of Le Cateau (II Corps)
5 September	End of the retreat from Mons (BEF)
7–10 September	Battle of the Marne (BEF)
12–15 September	Battle of the Aisne (BEF)
4–10 October	Defence of Antwerp (IV Corps)
early October	BEF transferred from the Aisne to Flanders
10 October–2 November	Battle of La Bassée (II and Indian Corps)
12 October–2 November	Battle of Messines (Cavalry Corps)
13 October–2 November	Battle of Armentières (III Corps)
19 October–22 November	First Battle of Ypres (I and IV Corps)
26 December	First Army forms on the Lys and Second Army forms in the Ypres Salient

1915

10–13 March	Battle of Neuve Chapelle (First Army)
22 April–25 May	Second Battle of Ypres (Second Army)
9 May	Battle of Aubers Ridge (First Army)
15–25 May	Battle of Festubert (First Army)
13 July	Third Army forms on the Somme
25 September–13 October	Battle of Loos (First Army)

1916

5 February	Fourth Army forms on the Somme and Third Army moves to the Arras sector
22 May	Reserve Army forms on the Somme
2–13 June	Battle of Mount Sorrel (Second Army)
1 July–18 November	Battles of the Somme (Third, Fourth and Reserve Armies)
30 October	Reserve Army renamed Fifth Army

July, provoking an immediate military response from Russia.

Germany began to mobilize, fearful of the threat posed by Russia's huge armies to Germany's eastern territories. The German mobilization plan (named the Schlieffen Plan after the Chief of Staff who first proposed it) called for a pre-emptive attack on France with the bulk of the German Army, intended to secure the Western Front in less than six weeks; Germany could then turn against the Russians with its whole force.

Germany declared war on Russia on 1 August, and invaded both Belgium and Luxembourg on the same day. France responded two days later, and on 4 August, following unsuccessful attempts to get Germany to withdraw behind its borders, Great Britain declared war on Germany and Austria-Hungary. Countries across the Empire, including Australia, Canada, India, New Zealand and the Union of South Africa also pledged their support for the British cause. The Great War had begun.

1917

11 January–13 March	Operations on the Ancre (Fifth Army)
14 March–5 April	German retreat to the Hindenburg Line (Third, Fourth and Fifth Armies)
9 April–4 May	Battle of Arras (First and Third Armies)
3–17 May	Battle of Bullecourt (Fifth Army)
7–14 June	Battle of Messines (Second Army)
21 June–18 November	Operations on the Flanders Coast (Fourth Army)
31 July–10 November	Third Battle of Ypres (Second and Fifth Armies)
15–25 August	Battle of Hill 70 (First Army)
20 November–3 December	Battle of Cambrai (Third Army)

1918

German Offensives

21 March–5 April	First Battles of the Somme (Third and Fifth Armies)
9–29 April	Battle of the Lys (First and Second Armies)
27 May–6 June	Battle of the Aisne (IX Corps under French command)

The Advance to Victory – The 100 Days

20 July–2 August	Battles of the Marne (XXII Corps under French command)
8–11 August	Battle of Amiens (Fourth Army)
18 August–6 September	The Advance in Flanders (Second and Fifth Armies)
21 August–3 September	Second Battles of the Somme (Third and Fourth Armies)
26 August–3 September	Second Battles of Arras (First and Third Armies)
12 September–9 October	Battles of the Hindenburg Line (First, Third and Fourth Armies)
9–12 October	Pursuit to the River Selle (First, Third and Fourth Armies)
28 September–11 November	Final Advance in Flanders (Second Army)
2 October–11 November	Final Advance in Artois (Fifth and First Armies)
17 October–11 November	Final Advance in Picardy (First, Third and Fourth Armies)
11:00 a.m. 11 November	Armistice

The Territorials were on their annual summer camp when war was declared; within days they were deployed at their war stations along the coast after working to the strict timetables laid down in the War Book.

THE BEF'S SECTOR

The BEF grew ten-fold in size between August 1914 and November 1918 and the length of its sector increased accordingly, expanding and contracting according to circumstances. Major changes were:

September 1914: Holding a 16-mile sector on the Aisne.
October 1914: Holding a 24-mile sector between Ypres and Armentières.
Spring 1915: Front extended south to Loos, covering 36 miles.
July 1915: Third Army took over a 30-mile sector on the Somme from the French.
February 1916: Fourth Army took over the Somme front while Third Army took over the Arras sector from the French, giving the BEF a continuous 90-mile sector.
Winter 1916–17: The sector extended to 110 miles.
March 1917: The German withdrawal to the Hindenburg line shortened the line by 15 miles.
Winter 1917–18: The British sector increased to 123 miles.
Spring 1918: The French took over 40 miles of front from the BEF during the German offensives on the Somme and Lys.
August 1918: The BEF's front had extended to 100 miles.
Autumn 1918: Front gradually shortened to 64 miles during the Advance to Victory.

CHAPTER TWO

MOBILIZATION AND TRAINING

DEPLOYING THE BRITISH EXPEDITIONARY FORCE

In the last days of peace, the British government committed 6 infantry divisions and 1 cavalry division to France as the British Expeditionary Force. The General Officer Commanding-in-Chief of the BEF in 1914 was Field Marshal Sir John French. The first 4 divisions to land formed 2 corps.

I CORPS

1st and 2nd Divisions; sailed on 11 August under General Sir Douglas Haig.

II CORPS

3rd and 5th Divisions; followed over the next two days under General Sir James Grierson. Grierson died of a heart attack on 17 August and General Sir Horace Smith-Dorrien took his place.

Men of the 11th Hussars gather on the deck of their ship to view the coast of France; they would be in action near Mons a week later. *(IWM Q51128)*

CAVALRY

The Cavalry Division with 4 brigades followed and joined the BEF near Mons. A fifth independent cavalry brigade operated with the BEF and the cavalry was reorganized as 2 divisions on 13 September.

III CORPS

This formation was established in France on 31 August under General Sir William Pulteney. 4th Division had remained in Eastern Command to protect the coast from invasion; it sailed for France on 21 August and came under III Corps on the 31st. 6th Division left for France on 7 September and joined III Corps.

THE OLD CONTEMPTIBLES

Kaiser Wilhelm II of Germany poured scorn on the British Expeditionary Force and on 19 August, four days before the first battle at Mons, he gave the order to: '. . . address all your skill and all the valour of my soldiers to exterminate first the treacherous English; walk over General French's contemptible little army.' The name stuck and the men who served during the retreat from Mons, the advance to the Aisne and the First Battle of Ypres were referred to as the Old Contemptibles.

RECALLING THE OVERSEAS GARRISONS

As early as 5 August the authorities decided to recall trained Regulars from overseas garrisons to form new divisions, and replace them with partially trained Territorial battalions and Indian troops. A month later India agreed to release 32 British Regular and 20 Indian battalions in exchange for 42 Territorial battalions. In all 57 battalions were recalled from overseas postings; they reached Britain between September 1914 and March 1915 and assembled as 5 new Regular divisions:

INDIA

29 battalions came from India and 3 from Burma (battalions serving with the Indian Army divisions remained with them throughout the war).

MEDITERRANEAN

2 battalions from Gibraltar, 5 each from Malta and Egypt.

SOUTH AFRICA

4 battalions.

FAR EAST

2 battalions from Hong Kong, and 1 each from Tientsin and Singapore.

OTHER GARRISONS

1 battalion each from Bermuda, Aden and Mauritius. Ex-soldiers who had emigrated to Canada formed a battalion, Princess Patricia's Light Infantry; 3 independent Regular battalions and a Territorial battalion completed the 5 divisions.

ASSEMBLING THE GARRISON BATTALIONS

The first group of garrison battalions returned (mainly from the Mediterranean and South Africa) at the end of September 1914 and formed 2 divisions.

A force was assembled at the beginning of October to help the Belgian Army secure the Flanders coast. **7th Division** was formed at Lyndhurst with independent units in Britain and battalions from overseas garrisons. A **3rd Cavalry Division** was formed from unallocated cavalry units in Britain. These two divisions were grouped under General Rawlinson's IV Corps and sailed to Zeebrugge and Ostend on 6 October. **8th Division** formed at Southampton and joined the BEF in November.

A total of 36 battalions and 9 artillery brigades (assembled from batteries stationed in Britain or recalled from India) were joined by Territorial engineers, field ambulances and trains; they formed three new Regular divisions over the winter of 1914–15.

27th Division: Assembled at Winchester in November 1914 and sailed to France in December 1914.

28th Division: Assembled at Winchester in December 1914 and sailed to France in January 1915.

En route to the assembly areas, three officers of the 11th Hussars stretch their legs when their train stops in Rouen. *(IWM Q51151)*

29th Division: Assembled at Leamington in March 1915 and immediately sailed for Gallipoli.

RESERVISTS

One condition of joining the Army was to be available for 5 years on the Reserve. Men were liable to be called up in a national emergency and they had to attend 12 days' refresher training a year; in return they received a weekly payment. By August 1914 the Reserve numbered 145,000 men, organized into three sections.

ARMY RESERVE
SECTION A
Limited to 6,000 men with preference given to soldiers who had had overseas service. Men had to be available to support the Regular Army during a civil emergency. They joined for 1 year, with an option to extend to 2 years, and they were paid 7s a week.

SECTION B
The rest of the officers and men were put on the Section B Reserve List when they left the Army. They would be recalled in the event of a war and put to work manning facilities across Great Britain. Basic pay was 3s 6d a week. Section B Reservists could transfer to Section A if there was a vacancy within 6 months of their discharge.

There was no Section C in August 1914.

SECTION D OR SUPPLEMENTAL RESERVE
A man could extend his term on the Reserve for an extra 4 years, receiving a payment of 3s 6d a week in return. Section D Reservists would be called up if Section B had been exhausted.

The Regulars and Reservists marched mile after mile during the opening weeks of the war, either being chased by, or chasing the German armies across the French countryside. *(IWM Q60734)*

On the declaration of war many Reservists reported to their depots and, while willing Section A and B Reservists were posted to Regular battalions, the rest joined Special Reserve battalions. Others preferred to join one of Kitchener's New Army units.

SPECIAL RESERVE

Men wanting to try Army life, without giving a full commitment, could join the 64,000-strong Special Reserve. They enlisted for 6 years with an option to extend another 4. After 6 months' training they returned to their jobs, attending 4 weeks' training a year. They could be called up if there was a general mobilization. They had to re-enlist on an

annual basis and were only paid if they were called up.

By August 1914 there were 100 Special Reserve and Extra Reserve battalions (the different types of battalions are explained further in Chapter 5) based at the regimental headquarters. They served as regimental administrative bases and were run by 8 officers, a regimental sergeant-major, 38 NCOs, and 50 men. These battalions also acted as recruiting centres. The 3 Special Reserve cavalry regiments, the North Irish Horse, the South Irish Horse and King Edward's Horse, all served in France and Flanders.

The Special Reserve was split into two sections:

SECTION A

4,000 men liable for 12 months' overseas service.

SECTION B

Skilled men were particularly valuable and they were split into three categories:

Category A: Artillery, Engineers and other services, South Irish Horse, King Edward's Horse.

Category B: Territorial soldiers who had agreed to the Special Reserve conditions, known as the Imperial Service Obligation.

Category C: Army Service Corps Transport drivers.

The Special Reserve of Officers was for civilians with a desire to be an army officer.

THE NATIONAL RESERVE

The Territorial Force county associations kept a register of 215,000 men with military experience who had no Reserve obligation. They were divided in three classes.

Class I: Under 42 years in age.

Class II: Home service men; officers and senior ranks under 55 years of age, junior ranks under 50.

Class III: Medically unfit.

The National Reserve was organized in Protection Companies and attached to Territorial battalions in October 1914. The men were invited to help guard railways and important locations across the country but a month later they were instructed to present themselves for enlistment; the overwhelming majority joined up. The Protection Companies were renamed Supernumerary Companies in March 1915 but, as the number of men joining up started to fall, the fit men were transferred in July 1915:

Category A: Posted to Service battalions.

Category B: Formed the 18th to 24th Battalions of the Rifle Brigade.

Category C: Posted to Provisional battalions.

Those incapable of marching 10 miles were transferred to the new Royal Defence Corps.

By November 1914 the Reservists had been deployed and although the Special Reservists had been drafted, some were unfit, elderly or unwilling; most were transferred to the six Special Reserve siege and railway companies during the first winter of the war.

THE TERRITORIAL FORCE

Once the Expeditionary Force had left for France, the defence of the British Isles was left to the Territorial Force and the Special Reserve. Pre-arranged mobilization plans made sure that Special Reserve infantry and the Territorial Force artillery were guarding the ports by 9 August while the 14 Territorial divisions were in position along the coast by the 18th. General Sir Ian Hamilton controlled the 200,000-strong Central Force and the men continued their training while on coastal duty. When it was time for the 1st Line Territorial divisions to leave for France, 2nd Line Territorial divisions took their place.

OVERSEAS COMMITMENT

Over 17,500 Territorial soldiers had already committed themselves to overseas service by signing the Imperial Service Obligation, and on 15 September the rest were given the opportunity to volunteer. Battalions would be designated 'General Service' if over 60% of the men volunteered and came under War Office control when new recruits had increased the numbers to 25% over establishment. The enthusiasm of the 'Terriers' meant that every unit met the criteria.

Battalions were split into two. General service men stayed with the 1st Line battalions while the home service men joined new recruits in 2nd Line battalions. Sometimes there were enough volunteers to make a second General Service battalion and a 3rd Line battalion was organized for the home service men and recruits.

RECRUITMENT IN THE TERRITORIAL ARMY

The Secretary of State for War, Lord Kitchener, wanted the New Armies to take

Men crowd towards the gangplank as their ship docks in Boulogne harbour. The camouflage paint was used to break up the vessel's silhouette. *(IWM Q7252)*

DEPLOYMENT OF THE TERRITORIAL DIVISIONS

Many units in the 14 infantry divisions were on their annual summer camp when war broke out and immediately deployed to their war stations.

A new headquarters, GHQ Central Force, was formed on the outbreak of war to control home defence. It was divided into First, Second and Third Armies and with 8 divisions moved to the coast; the remainder gathered in southern England.

COASTAL PROTECTION

Lowland Division (52nd): Firth of Forth defences in Scotland.
Northumbrian Division (50th): Tyne defences around Newcastle.
West Riding Division (49th): Yorkshire and Lincolnshire coast.
East Anglian Division (54th): Norfolk, Suffolk and Essex ports.
Home Counties Division (44th): Kent and East Sussex ports.
1st Wessex Division (43rd): Somerset, Devon and Cornwall.
2nd Wessex Division (45th): Replaced the 1st Wessex Division when it sailed to India.
West Lancashire Division (55th): Lancashire coast, covering Liverpool.

CENTRAL FORCE

North Midland Division (46th): Luton area.
2nd London Division (47th): St Albans area.
South Midland Division (48th): Chelmsford area.
Highland Division (51st): Bedford area.
Welsh Division (53rd): Northampton area.
1st London Division (56th): London area.

The Northumbrian (50th) and West Riding (49th) Divisions were also part of Central Force. 2nd Wessex (45th) Division, a duplicate of 1st Wessex (43rd) Division, was formed quickly and is usually classed as a 1st Line Territorial division but can be considered as a 2nd Line division (*these terms are discussed below*).

precedence over the Territorial divisions so they did not reduce the public and private support for the pals battalions (*described below*). The Territorials suffered as they were called upon to release officers and NCOs to instruct their rivals.

The decision meant that there was no surge of volunteers for the Territorials during the opening weeks of the war. However, the county associations continued to attract recruits for the 2nd and 3rd Line battalions and the number of Territorial Force soldiers had more than doubled by the end of 1914; the first appeal for new volunteers did not appear until the autumn of 1915. The cautious approach to recruitment allowed the battalions to form at a steady rate, preventing many of the frustrations felt in the New Armies.

OVERSEAS GARRISONS

Territorial battalions were quickly deployed to overseas garrisons, releasing Regular battalions for service in Europe. Eighteen were sent to protect the Mediterranean supply line in September 1914; the Home Counties Division sent 2 battalions to Gibraltar, the 1st London Division sent 4 battalions to protect Malta while the East Lancashire Division sent all 12 of its battalions to man the Suez Canal defences in Egypt (the division would move to Gallipoli in May 1915). The Army then replaced Regular battalions in India with Territorial battalions. Twenty-four battalions of the 1st Wessex and Home Counties Divisions were despatched in October; the 2nd Wessex Division followed in December.

WINTER CHANGES

During the winter of 1914–15 steps were taken to prepare the Territorials for overseas service but the lack of facilities made training difficult. The North Midland Division moved to Essex to train; the Welsh Division spent the winter in billets around Cambridge before moving to Bedford in May 1915; the East Anglian Division moved to St Albans at the same time. Meanwhile, 29 battalions were sent to France between November and March to bolster the strength of the Regular divisions. These were as follows: Highland Division 6 battalions; Lowland Division 3; Welsh Division 6; East Anglian Division 3; West Lancashire Division 9; 1st London Division 2. The West Lancashire Division and 1st London Division were disbanded in April 1915; they would be re-formed in France at the start of 1916.

The first complete territorial division to leave for France was the North Midland Division at the end of February 1915. The 2nd London and South Midland Divisions followed in March and by the end of April the West Riding, Northumbrian and Highland Divisions were all engaged on the Western Front.

The Lowland Division left in May 1915 to reinforce the landings at Helles on Gallipoli while the Welsh and East Anglian Divisions left in July to take part in new landings on the peninsula at Suvla.

Captain Bruce Bairnsfather drew many cartoons depicting trench life and the caption to this one sums up the attitude of long-serving soldiers to new arrivals:

Up last draft: 'I suppose you 'as to be careful 'ow you looks over the parapet about 'ere.'

Out since Mons: 'You needn't worry, me lad; the rats are going to be your only trouble.'

MOUNTED DIVISIONS

1st Mounted Division formed in Norfolk and Suffolk in August 1914 and **2nd Mounted Division** formed on 2 September in Suffolk. They were deployed on coastal duties.

INDEPENDENT MOUNTED BRIGADES

The **Highland Mounted Brigade** and the **South-Western Mounted Brigade** acted independently.

2ND LINE TERRITORIAL DIVISIONS

After the Home Service men had been identified, they were organized into 2nd Line battalions and on 31 August authority was given to form 14 duplicate 2nd Line divisions, one for each 1st Line division (they were numbered in April 1915):

2nd Wessex Division (45th)
2nd West Lancashire Division (57th)
2nd/1st London Division (58th)
2nd North Midland Division (59th)
2nd/2nd London Division (60th)
2nd South Midland Division (61st)
2nd West Riding Division (62nd)
2nd Northumbrian Division (63rd)
2nd Highland Division (64th)
2nd Lowland Division (65th)
2nd East Lancashire Division (66th)
2nd Home Counties Division (67th)
2nd Welsh Division (68th)
2nd East Anglian Division (69th)

Recruiting began in earnest in September 1914 and the divisions began to form in November 1914 though the men continued to live at home during the winter months. The divisions had reached full establishment by the spring of 1915 and replaced the 1st Line divisions in Central Force or along the coast.

COASTAL DEFENCES

62nd Division: Yorkshire and Lincolnshire.
63rd Division: Tyne defences.
64th Division: Firth of Tay defences.
65th Division: Firth of Forth defences.

CENTRAL FORCE

First Army: 61st, 68th and 69th Divisions in Suffolk and Northamptonshire.
Second Army: 57th and 67th Divisions in Surrey and Kent; 66th Division joined in August.
Third Army: 59th and 60th Divisions in Hertfordshire and Essex; 61st Division transferred from First Army in April and 58th Division joined in August.

The government decided to send some of the divisions to France and another selection was made in August 1915; 3rd Line units were

Kitchener's imposing figure enticed many young men to join the New Armies. *(IWM Q48378)*

formed for Home Service men and recruits. During training men were continuously drafted overseas to join 1st Line divisions and units struggled to keep up to strength.

Third Army disbanded over the winter of 1915–16 and 3 divisions moved to Salisbury Plain to complete their training; 60th and 61st sailed to France in June.

REORGANISING HOME DEFENCE

By March 1916 seven of the 2nd Line Territorial divisions were preparing to leave England, requiring a reorganization of Central Force. It was split into Northern and Southern Armies; reporting to Field Marshal Sir John French, now the Commander-in-Chief of Home Forces.

NORTHERN ARMY

58th, 62nd and 64th Divisions covered the east coast as far south as Norfolk.

SOUTHERN ARMY

65th, 66th and 67th Divisions covered the Suffolk, Essex and Kent coast.

In April 1916 59th Division was posted to Ireland to suppress the Easter Rising (65th Division took its place in September). Two divisions were based at Aldershot and Salisbury Plain during the second half of 1916 as an Emergency Reserve while a third division formed the General Reserve for Home Forces.

Five divisions (57th, 58th, 59th, 62nd and 66th) left for the Western Front at the start of 1917, leaving 3 divisions covering the Norfolk, Suffolk and Essex coasts (they reported to XXIII Corps after February 1918); they remained in England until the end of the war.

HOME SERVICE DIVISIONS

In November 1916, 71st, 72nd and 73rd Divisions (there was no 70th Division) were formed from a mixture of Provisional, Garrison and 2nd Line Territorial battalions. Two guarded the south coast while the third covered the Lancashire coast. The Provisional battalions were affiliated to line regiments in April 1917 and the divisions joined Southern Army. Graduated battalions (made up of new conscripts) of the Training Reserve replaced some battalions but the Home Service divisions were disbanded in 1918.

KITCHENER'S RECRUITMENT CAMPAIGN

On 5 August 1914 Field Marshal Earl Kitchener was appointed Secretary of State for War and the following day the House of Commons authorized the Regular Army to treble in size, aiming to add 500,000 men between the ages of 19 and 30. The announcement overturned Viscount Haldane's plans to use the county associations for recruitment. Kitchener was one of the few leaders who believed that the war would not be over by Christmas and he therefore wanted to raise 70 new divisions over the next 3 years; it was going to need the full mobilization of British manpower.

Kitchener wanted to create a New Army avoiding the traditional class conditions of the Regular Army. He believed that the Territorial Force did not have the appropriate structure or facilities to cope with the expansion and was concerned that the home service restrictions would complicate recruitment. His New Army was for volunteers signing up for 3 years' overseas service or for the duration of the war.

A massive propaganda campaign started on 11 August, calling for 100,000 men. The public responded immediately to the call 'Your King and Country Need You', and thousands of men flocked to recruiting offices.

The reasons why men volunteered for the Army were many, not least that the British people had not been involved in a major overseas conflict since 1815. Daily reports of the heroic deeds of the BEF at Mons and on the retreat to the Marne helped to inspire many men while others were swayed by popular propaganda. Peer pressure and the desire to join with friends or to attract the ladies persuaded others to volunteer. Many men had a genuine ambition to escape their humdrum lives, and wanted to see the world; others wanted to escape family or financial troubles.

Temporary recruiting offices were kept busy as hundreds of men queued up to take their turn filling in the forms and passing a medical examination. After the new recruit had sworn the oath and taken the King's Shilling (the recruiting sergeant was awarded sixpence per man) the new recruit returned home to wait for his travel warrant and instructions.

Men with previous Army service could re-enlist up to the age of 45 but some volunteers lied about their age to avoid rejection. Many under-age boys and over-age men were also encouraged to sign up by the eager recruiting sergeants.

Volunteers were normally assigned to units of the New Armies and most were allowed to choose which branch of the service they wanted to serve in. Thousands enlisted in local units, many of them raised by dignitaries or organizations, while others travelled miles to join a particular regiment or corps.

By the middle of September 1914, 500,000 men had volunteered, forcing the Army to introduce a temporary increase in physical standards to reduce the number of recruits. Numbers had topped a million by February 1915 and 1.5 million in September 1915.

THE NEW ARMIES

Thirty New Army divisions, grouped into 5 New Armies, eventually saw overseas service. The New Army infantry divisions (there were no New Army cavalry divisions) were organized along the same lines as the Regular divisions.

FIRST NEW ARMY: K1

Following Parliament's agreement to add 500,000 men to the Army on 6 August 1914, a proclamation was issued on 11 August 1914 asking 100,000 volunteers aged between 19 and 30 to sign up for General Service. Enough troops for 6 divisions had been signed up by the end of the month and as they assembled at their training grounds across the United Kingdom an Army Order authorized their formation into divisions, numbering them 8th to 13th (8th was renumbered 14th when the 8th Regular Division formed). The First New Army of 6 divisions was constituted on 21 August 1914.

Infantry battalions were given consecutive numbers in their regiments following the Territorials, with the word Service after the unit number. Most line infantry regiments raised one K1 battalion but some raised two.

The divisions were as follows:

9th (Scottish) Division: Assembled on Salisbury Plain in September 1914.
10th (Irish) Division: Moved to Basingstoke in England in May 1915.
11th (Northern) Division: Spent the winter around Grantham, moving to Aldershot in April 1915.

A grim-faced sergeant looks on as the officer leans on his crutches to hear new recruits swear the oath on the Bible. *(IWM Q30071)*

12th (Eastern) Division: Assembled around Colchester; winter weather forced the men into billets around Hythe; the division reached Aldershot in February 1915.

13th (Western) Division: Gathered on Salisbury Plain, then spent the winter in billets around Chiseldon, Cirencester and Basingstoke; returned to Salisbury Plain in February 1915.

14th (Light) Division: Assembled at Aldershot, moved into winter billets across Surrey and reassembled at Aldershot in February 1915.

The 9th, 12th and 14th Divisions sailed to France in May 1915; 10th, 11th and 13th Divisions sailed to Egypt, heading for Gallipoli, a month later.

SECOND NEW ARMY: K2

Six K2 divisions were authorized by Army Order 382 on 11 September and formed over the weeks that followed:

15th (Scottish) Division: Assembled at Aldershot in November and moved to Salisbury Plain.

16th (Irish) Division: Formed in camps at Fermoy, Buttevant and Tipperary in September.

17th (Northern) Division: Trained in camps across Dorset, billeted across the county during the winter months.

18th (Eastern) Division: Assembled around Colchester.

19th (Western) Division: Camped on Salisbury Plain; poor weather then scattered the men into billets across south-west England.

20th (Light) Division: Camped at Aldershot, and billeted across Surrey during the winter.

17th Division completed its training near Winchester while the rest of Second Army prepared on Salisbury Plain. Most divisions left for France in June–July 1915 but 16th Division fell behind its training timetable and stayed in Ireland until September; it eventually reached France in December 1915.

THIRD NEW ARMY: K3

The news that British troops had been in action at Mons and were on the retreat, created a new surge of volunteers and a third group of 6 divisions was assembled in September 1914. Divisions recruited in certain areas of the country but they had no titles:

21st Division: Recruited in the north-east of England and assembled in the Aylesbury area; it spent the winter months in billets across Buckinghamshire.

22nd Division: Recruited in the north-west of England, it trained at Eastbourne, billeting in the area during the winter.

23rd Division: Recruited in the north-east of England and spent its first six months around Aldershot.

24th Division: Recruited in the south-east of England and trained in the Sevenoaks area.

25th Division: Recruited in the north-west of England and assembled on Salisbury Plain; the men spent the winter billeted in the Bournemouth area.

26th Division: Recruited across England and Scotland and assembled on Salisbury Plain before moving into winter billets across the south of England.

Brigade training resumed at the original camps in April 1915 and four weeks later 26th Division moved to Salisbury Plain while the rest of Third Army assembled around Aldershot. Third New Army crossed the Channel between the end of August and the end of September 1915.

FOURTH NEW ARMY: K4
(OCTOBER 1914–APRIL 1915)

On 8 October the order was given to form Service battalions, organized in 6 divisions numbered 27th to 32nd (renumbered 30th to 35th after the 27th–29th (Regular) Divisions were formed). Fourth Army was broken up in April 1915 and the 6 divisions were split into 18 Training Reserve brigades to provide reinforcements for the first three New Armies; the support units were distributed across the rest of the New Army divisions. The battalions were converted into Training Reserve battalions in September 1916, losing their regimental titles.

FIFTH NEW ARMY
(FOURTH ARMY AFTER APRIL 1915)

Local benefactors and dignitaries encouraged towns and organizations to form units and before long friends and colleagues were parading together as 'pals' or 'chums' battalions. They received little help while the War Office concentrated on the Territorials and New Armies but, with the help of fund-raising efforts and local subscription, accommodation and supplies were found. Fifth New Army was created on 10 December 1914 with 6 divisions, numbered 37th–42nd. It was renamed Fourth Army the following April and the divisions were renumbered 30th–35th.

30th Division: The Earl of Derby raised 4 Liverpool and 8 Manchester Pals battalions.

31st Division: 4 Hull Pals, 2 Bradford Pals and 2 Barnsley Pals battalions and 1 each from Sheffield, Leeds, Durham and Accrington.

32nd Division: 3 Birmingham, 3 Salford and 3 Glasgow Pals battalions and one each from Bristol and Newcastle and the Lonsdale battalion.

33rd Division: 5 Public Schools battalions, the Empire battalion, Kensington and West Ham Pals, the Church Lads Brigade, 2 Sportsmen's and a Football battalion.

34th Division: A Tyneside Scottish and a Tyneside Irish Brigade, 2 Pals battalions from Edinburgh and 1 each from Grimsby and Cambridge.

35th Division: Bantam battalions from across the country.

Recruitment began in September 1914 and troops lived in their own homes or in temporary camps; the winter weather forced the latter into billets. Brigade training and musketry training began in June 1915. The 31st, 32nd, 34th and 35th Divisions were stationed in the North Riding of Yorkshire and 30th and 33rd Divisions were based in Nottinghamshire. Fourth New Army gathered on Salisbury Plain in August for final training and left for France over the winter of 1915–16 (31st Division spent the winter on the Suez Canal in Egypt).

BANTAMS

In August 1914 the Member of Parliament for Birkenhead, Alfred Bigland, was given permission by the War Office to form a battalion of undersize, yet physically fit, men. Over 3,000 men, many of them miners, volunteered in a short time (the bantam is a small cockerel, both aggressive and hardy).

SIXTH NEW ARMY (FIFTH NEW ARMY AFTER APRIL 1915)

The units were predominantly locally raised pals battalions:

36th (Ulster) Division: Formed in September from the Ulster Volunteer Force.

37th Division: Army troops from first three armies (originally 44th Division).

38th (Welsh) Division: Welsh pals battalions; on 29 September 1914 the Welsh National Committee was appointed to raise a Welsh Army Corps; it was later reduced to a division (originally 43rd Division).

39th Division: Raised by mayors across London and along the south coast.

40th Division: Another Bantam division; many volunteers were unfit and rejected; 4 battalions from 39th Division brought the division up to strength.

41st Division: Raised in the spring of 1915 by the London mayors.

The War Office adopted the 6 divisions in April 1915. 37th Division was already on Salisbury Plain and it left for France in July 1915. The remaining divisions were still at an early stage of training and, while 38th Division gathered near Winchester, the rest assembled around Aldershot. 36th Division was the first to leave for France in October 1915 and 38th and 39th Divisions followed over the winter; 40th and 41st Divisions were the last to leave in May 1916.

THE TRAINING RESERVE

In April 1915 the 75 battalions of the Fourth New Army were converted into 2nd Reserve battalions to train reinforcements. The 6 divisions were broken up and the Fifth New Army was renamed Fourth New Army. The

These new recruits for the Lincolnshire Regiment practise with old Lee-Enfields in their civilian clothes while a handful of uniformed NCOs look on. *(IWM Q53286)*

divisions raised by local subscription (36th–41st) raised another 68 Reserve battalions, organized in 24 Training Reserve brigades.

Officers in the Training Reserve wore regimental uniforms and badges but other ranks had a General Service button mounted on a red disc on their cap; a numbered coloured patch on the sleeve denoted the battalion. Shoulder titles were discontinued in June 1917 and from December 1917 red battalion numbers on the cap replaced the sleeve numbers.

PREPARING THE NEW ARMIES

It took 11 months to train a man from basic drill to divisional exercises during peacetime with the Army's full facilities to hand but Kitchener hoped to achieve the same results in 6 months despite the lack of instructors and equipment. The Regular divisions had the pick of Special Reservists, time-expired and re-enlisted soldiers and despite enormous efforts to prepare the men for war the New Armies would be a shadow of the original Expeditionary Force.

ACCOMMODATION

The Army could accommodate 174,800 single men in various barracks at the time of mobilization. Although the number was increased to 262,000 by using empty buildings and moving families out of married quarters, the space available still fell far short of requirements. Over 500,000 men were billeted at home, in private lodgings or public buildings, while new encampments were built.

Contractors were working on hutted encampments when the weather broke in October 1914, making the temporary tented camps uninhabitable. Men were forced to sleep in tents on the wet ground and train on parade grounds covered in ankle-deep mud.

Many men had to crowd into the partially finished camps, sleeping 50 to a hut designed for 20, while the rest were moved into churches, cinemas and church halls.

The camps were ready by the spring of 1915 and many units gathered for brigade training and musketry for the first time. Three months later the divisions began assembling around Aldershot and on Salisbury Plain for three months of final training.

TRAINING

Makeshift divisional and brigade staffs were assembled with a mixture of retired officers, convalescing officers and officers without assignments (many on leave from India). Only a few trained officers and non-commissioned officers were available, and they included many Reserve officers who were behind the times.

Selected university candidates, warrant officers and non-commissioned officers were commissioned while Territorial officers were attached to the Officer Training Corps. The Royal Military College and Royal Military Academy abolished their fees, increased the number of candidates and reduced the length of their courses; 33 new officer training schools were also set up.

Battalions often started with a couple of experienced officers and a handful of veteran NCOs while the rest were chosen from the assembled mob. Civilian occupations were a useful guide and many New Army officers were white-collar workers with the necessary literacy skills. Blue-collar workers with man-management skills were made NCOs while trained craftsmen were transferred to the engineers.

There was a shortage of instruction manuals and training started with basic drill and physical exercise to toughen the men. Route marches were commonplace and the men

Uniforms were issued when they became available and men were sometimes forced to parade in a hybrid mixture of clothing. *(IWM Q30069)*

carried iron weights (known as Kitchener's chocolate) in their pockets to simulate carrying a loaded pack. Trench warfare was first mentioned at the start of 1915 and, although troops practised digging short stretches, practical training was mostly carried out in France.

UNIFORMS

The Army only had a limited reserve of clothing and equipment and established firms could not cope with the flood of new contracts. Men were paid half a sovereign to provide their own suit, greatcoat and boots. As the weeks passed clothing turned into rags and as boots lost their soles men practised slow marching on grass.

Second-hand clothing contractors provided spare clothing, and supplies from the United States and Canada alleviated the pressure on British contractors. A national shortage of khaki mean that uniforms were made in a wide array of colours and styles. Some 500,000 civilian greatcoats were purchased and 500,000 blue serge uniforms were manufactured from Post Office stocks; red coats, grey uniforms, canvas suits, emergency forage caps, old pattern water bottles and white haversacks were also used. Uniforms had no unit badges or means of identifying rank and battalions adopted unofficial markings, including coloured cloth patches, armbands or cords on the shoulder.

Private contributions or fund-raising for the pals battalions allowed units to buy uniforms, blankets and greatcoats privately. The 38th (Welsh) Division was provided with uniforms made out of a local grey cloth (called *Brethyn Llwyd*) while private enterprises paid for 10,000 uniforms for the 36th (Ulster) Division.

Men left their windswept camps in the pouring rain when the weather broke in October 1914, and resembled 'a nomad tribe on the move' as they headed for their winter billets. The first issue of khaki uniforms, issued one to a platoon, arrived in the spring; a division's full complement of uniforms, webbing and other personal equipment soon followed.

INFANTRY WEAPONS

The New Armies had no arms or equipment to begin with and items arrived in small quantities throughout the winter; a division's full issue of equipment was often delivered after the order to travel overseas was given.

The first issues of weapons were small quantities of out-dated Lee-Metford and Lee-Enfield magazine rifles, supplemented by supplies of worn and defective rifles. The rest of the men drilled with wooden rifles and machine-gun sections practised with dummy weapons or obsolete Maxim guns. Canadian Ross and Japanese Arisaka rifles were issued as training aids but a shortage of small arms ammunition meant men were forced to practise shooting on miniature ranges with .22-calibre ammunition. Small quantities of Mark III Lee-Enfields began to arrive in the spring of 1915 but the full complement of rifles did not reach many divisions until two weeks before embarkation.

ARTILLERY WEAPONS

The artillery found it harder to find trained officers and 2nd lieutenants led some brigades to begin with. Crews trained with 'Quaker guns' (dummy guns made from timber) while the horse teams practised limbering with poles and hooks mounted on pairs of old wheels. A variety of obsolete guns arrived during the winter months of 1914–15 and the field artillery practised with British 15-pounder and French 90mm breech-loading guns while the howitzer batteries used obsolescent 12-pounder breech-loaders.

As soon as new field guns and howitzers left the factory they were sent to join the divisions on Salisbury Plain and at Aldershot. However, gun sights, directors, range tables and telephones were often in short supply and the crews had to practise with dummy items.

HORSES

The peacetime establishment of horses for the British Army was 25,000, enough to mount the cavalry and keep a minimum number at each barracks, and a similar number of potential remounts were registered. However,

Uniforms and boots have arrived but, with equipment in short supply, these men are forced to practise marching around Wembley. *(IWM Q53274)*

as soon as the BEF went to war the number required leapt to 165,000, with the additional horses being needed to bring the infantry divisions up to establishment, to keep the supply chain moving and to replace casualties. Remount commissions across the United Kingdom and North America made up the deficit.

It took time to procure horses and new riders and drivers had to practise mounting and dismounting with wooden horses. Many animals were undernourished and unshod when they arrived and stabling was in short supply. Harnesses and saddles arrived much later and the first stocks were a mixture of regulation, civilian and colonial designs.

MEDICAL CLASSIFICATION

Kitchener's call for volunteers heralded a short period of unrestricted enlistment that overwhelmed the facilities for examining men. The Army was used to 50,000 recruits a year but there were 500,000 in September 1914 alone. Medical inspectors supervised RAMC officers as they carried out examinations but the latter were soon withdrawn to serve with the BEF. Civilian examiners were paid 2s 6d for each recruit and, with too many volunteers and too few examiners, many unfit men were admitted.

The Army limited recruiting at the end of 1914 and examiners were restricted to 40 examinations a day; fees were withheld if a recruit turned out to be unfit. Volunteers were given the choice of enlisting immediately, returning to their work until the Army had a posting, or deferring enlistment to a later date.

Standards continued to be inconsistent and a series of classifications was introduced in March 1915:

Class A: Fit for service at home or abroad.
Class B: Temporarily unfit for service abroad.
Class C: Fit for service at home only.
Class D: Unfit for service at home or abroad.

Medical boards carried out inspections and issued classifications while travelling medical boards, with two senior medical officers and a senior officer from another regiment or corps, checked standards and re-examined unfit men after July. The recruit's medical officer carried out a final examination when he reached his posting. The travelling boards also assessed unfit and convalescing soldiers; those who would recover were sent to a command depot to receive treatment.

Lord Derby was appointed Director-General of Recruiting in October 1915 and he introduced revised classifications to cover different standards of fitness:

(1) Fit for general service.
(2) Fit for field service at home.
(3) Fit for garrison service
    (a) abroad
    (b) at home.
(4) Fit (a) for labour
    (b) for clerical work.
(5) Unfit for any military service.

Medical classification was extended to convalescing men in June 1916. A training programme was also introduced (known as hardening):

First week: March one mile without arms twice a day.
Second week: March two miles quick march twice a day.
Third week: Doubled to four miles twice a day.
Fourth week: Full duty and ready at the end of the week.

The classification system was revised at the same time:

CATEGORY A
Fit for general service.
    (i) Trained and physically fit for overseas service. (Regular and New Army soldiers in this category were posted to Reserve battalions; Territorials to command depots.)
    (ii) Physically fit but needed training to become A(i).
    (iii) Convalescing men expected to be fit in three months. (Sent to the regimental depot for light duties and for hardening.)

    (iv) Young men who would be A(i) or A(ii) when they were 19.

CATEGORY B
Fit for service abroad on lines of communication.
    (i) Garrison or provisional units; able to march, good eyesight and hearing.
    (ii) Labour units or garrisons; able to walk, reasonable eyesight and hearing.
    (iii) Sedentary work.

CATEGORY C
Fit for garrison duty at home.
    (i) Garrison or provisional units; able to march, good eyesight and hearing.
    (ii) Labour units or garrisons; able to walk, reasonable eyesight and hearing.
    (iii) Sedentary work.

CATEGORY D
Temporarily unfit for Categories A, B, or C.
    (i) In command depots.
    (ii) In regimental depots under treatment.
    (iii) In any unit or depot under or awaiting treatment.

During the initial rush of volunteers, medical officers were over-worked and many unfit men were accepted by the New Armies; standards improved as the months passed. *(IWM Q30067)*

CATEGORY E

Unfit for service and not likely to be within 6 months.

Examiners also had to assess a man's anticipated state of health after 4 months' training. Convalescents expected to recover went to a command depot for light duty. Convalescents unlikely to recover fully went to a Reserve or Provisional battalion

Medical appeal boards were introduced in October 1916 to deal with over 400 re-examinations a month. From November examiners worked in groups of five and rotated work as follows: eyes, ears, nose and throat; limbs and joints; external parts of the body; chest and internal organs. Nearly a million exempted men were recalled under the Military Service Act and re-examined to catch fraudsters and rectify the earlier mistakes.

FINAL CLASSIFICATION

A final classification of recruits was introduced when the National Service Ministry took over responsibility for examining potential recruits:

Grade I: Fit for general service; would become Category A when called up.

Grade II: Likely to improve with training; Category B(i) or C(i) when called up.

Grade III: Only fit for labouring duties or a sedentary occupation. Recruit distribution battalions put men in this category through physical training and re-graded them.

Grade IV: Permanently and totally unfit for any form of military service.

An attempt to comb the country for recruits was started in November 1917 and the country was divided into ten recruiting regions, sub-divided into county and city areas. Travelling medical boards visited factories and collieries to search for men who could be released from reserved occupations (known as badged or starred men). National Service Medical Boards examined around 2,400,000 men.

Further improvements included replacing the Medical Appeal Boards with physicians or surgeons while permanent discharge centres determined if men were fit for the reserve or had to be discharged. Hospital Invaliding Medical Boards also assessed patients when

After months of training in civilian clothes and with obsolete weapons, a Kitchener's service battalion proudly parades for a visiting dignitary. *(IWM Q33353)*

Bayonet practice on straw dummies at one of the huge training camps on the French coast. *(IWM Q33340)*

they left hospital; the two boards were merged in August 1918 to avoid duplication of work. After discharge civilian medical boards assessed a man to see if his health had deteriorated in service and forwarded the information to the Pensions Board.

DENTISTRY

Many physically fit volunteers had to be rejected because of poor teeth and 70% of the recruits needed some type of dental treatment. Standards were lowered at the start of the war but they were soon raised when the number of soldiers reporting sick with dental problems began to rise. From February 1915 recruits could be passed as fit subject to dental treatment and dentists across the country volunteered their services, treating men for free.

Twelve dentists were sent to France in November 1914 but the main problem was still at home as the number of soldiers needing treatment before they could go overseas rose to over 130,000 a month. By the time of the Armistice the number of dentists in France had risen to 849 and the state of the men's teeth had improved dramatically as dentistry

became recognized as part of the military medical organization.

EYESIGHT

From March 1915 a soldier with poor eyesight was issued with two pairs of spectacles before he sailed overseas; the issue was extended to every soldier liable for active service in November 1915.

COMPULSORY SERVICE

The introduction of conscription in early 1916 ended the system of local Reserve battalions.

THE NATIONAL REGISTRATION ACT

The National Registration Act was introduced on 15 July 1915 by when the numbers of new recruits had begun to fall. A month later a new propaganda campaign was launched and recruiting staffs began canvassing men between the ages of 18 and 41.

Men and women between the ages of 15 and 65 had to register to comply with the Act, stating their occupation and ability to work, and they were issued with a registration card. It gave the government a list of potential recruits and a survey of industries at the same time. Workers in reserved occupations had their cards starred; the medically unfit also had their cards starred. The number of people with starred cards rose to over 2.5 million by the end of the war.

THE DERBY SCHEME

Lord Derby was appointed Director-General of Recruiting on 11 October 1915 and immediately introduced a system of volunteering known as the Derby Scheme. Men were allowed to enlist immediately but the majority attested with an obligation to come if called up. Attesters wore an armband to show their willingness to serve and were paid 2s 9d a week; a War Pension to support dependants was also introduced. Derby Men were organized into 46 groups:

Groups 1–23: Single men aged between 18 and 41, one group per year.
Groups 24–46: Married men aged between 18 and 41, one group per year.

Results were disappointing but when the War Office announced that conscription would be introduced, recruitment offices were overwhelmed with men wishing to be attested. Between 23 October and 15 December 1915, 2,184,979 men attested and 215,431 men enlisted for immediate service. However, over 650,000 single men had still not volunteered for service.

CONSCRIPTION

The government introduced the National Military Service Act in January 1916 and conscription started on 2 March 1916. Every male British resident (except in Ireland) who was between 18 and 41 years of age on 15 August 1915 and unmarried or a widower was liable for General Service (unless he had a dependent relative or child to support). Conscripts were categorized into classes (a new term to distinguish between volunteers and conscripts); Classes 1–23 were for single men aged 18 to 41, one class per year of age. The Conscription Act was extended to married men on 25 May 1916. New conscripts

could be assigned to any branch and had no choice of unit unless they wanted to join the Navy; the Senior Service had first call on conscripts.

Between January and June 1916 the 92 groups and classes were called up in the following order:

Groups 1–23 (single Derby men): between 25 January and 28 March.
Classes 1–23 (single conscripts): between 3 and 28 March.
Groups 24–46 (married Derby men): between 7 March and 13 June.
Classes 24–46 (married conscripts): between 3 and 24 June.

The Conscription Act produced only 43,000 new recruits; 1,433,827 men were starred men in a reserved profession or trade. Four exemption badges were issued to men engaged in war work: Admiralty Badge, War Service badge issued by the Ministry of Munitions, War Office Badge (issued before the War Service badge came into existence) and the War Munitions Volunteer Badge.

In all 748,587 men claimed exemption due to ill-health, financial hardship or domestic problems. There was a small number of conscientious objectors, including political opponents of the war, pacifists and followers of some religions (some agreed to serve with non-combatant units such as the Royal Army Medical Corps).

Around 2,000 local tribunals held hearings across the country to examine each application. Some claims were certified justified while other claimants were sentenced to prison for refusing to be conscripted. Appeals were dealt with by 73 Appeal Tribunals. Military representatives provided by a Central Tribunal assisted with complex cases. Over 93,000 men failed to attend their hearing and the police were used to round up absentees.

MAINTAINING THE BRITISH ARMY

The Army in France had been below establishment since August 1914, only

Lewis gun teams of the 28th (Western Australia) Battalion practise drill at Renescure in September 1917. A few days later these men were in action near Polygon Wood, east of Ypres. *(IWM E(AUS)683)*

reaching full strength by June 1916. The staff estimated a requirement for 200,000 replacements during the Somme Offensive but the number of casualties was more than double that figure, leaving the Army 165,000 men below strength by the end of the year. As recruiting sergeants combed industries for suitable men, stricter exemption conditions were imposed to make up the shortfall. The Training Reserve took over putting new conscripts through basic training to speed up the process.

A shortage of manpower following the extensive campaigns of 1917 called for a reduction in the number of battalions per British infantry division from 12 to 9 at the start of 1918; over 150 battalions were disbanded, amalgamated or transformed into entrenching battalions (Canadian divisions remained at 12 battalions). The German Spring Offensives of 1918 created a new shortage and the minimum age of conscription was lowered to 18 on 10 April 1918 to make up numbers.

AUSTRALIAN IMPERIAL FORCE (AIF)

Australia offered 20,000 volunteers on 7 August 1914 and organized them as the 1st Australian Division and the 1st Australian Light Horse Brigade. Numbers far exceeded expectations and over 30,000 men sailed from Albany in Western Australia on 1 November. The AIF spent the winter training in Egypt and the first two battalions saw action along the Suez Canal on 3 February 1915.

In all 416,809 Australians served.

1ST AUSTRALIAN DIVISION

Organized in the same way as British divisions. Infantry battalions had 32 officers and 991 other ranks in 8 companies; they were reorganized into 4 companies in January 1915.

The division was short of artillery; the 36 guns were grouped in 9 x 4-gun batteries. The division first saw action in the landings on Anzac Beach, Gallipoli, on 25 April 1915.

2ND AUSTRALIAN DIVISION

The Australian government offered 3 more infantry brigades in the spring of 1915 and they joined the artillery brigades in Egypt in July. The division landed at Gallipoli in August 1915.

EXPANSION OF THE AIF

Australia offered another 50,000 men in November 1915 but a plan to send 9 infantry brigades to France was shelved after the heavy losses at Gallipoli.

3RD AUSTRALIAN DIVISION

Formed in Australia in March 1916 and reached Britain in July. Replacements for casualties suffered by other units on the Somme had to be sent to France, delaying deployment until December 1916.

4TH AUSTRALIAN DIVISION

Formed in Egypt in February 1916 with 4th Australian Brigade from the ANZAC Division and 2 new brigades. It took time to train the artillery and the division left for France in June 1916.

5TH AUSTRALIAN DIVISION

8th Brigade was formed in Australia and it joined 2 new brigades in Egypt in February 1916. Again it took time to train new artillerymen and the division left for France in June 1916.

6TH AUSTRALIAN DIVISION

Plans to form a 6th Division were shelved due to a shortage of reinforcements; the Australian parliament voted against introducing conscription.

AUSTRALIAN AND NEW ZEALAND MOUNTED DIVISION

The division was formed in Egypt in March 1916 with the 1st, 2nd and 3rd Australian Light Horse Brigades and the New Zealand Mounted Rifles Brigade. It served in Egypt and Palestine.

IMPERIAL MOUNTED DIVISION

The division formed in Egypt in January 1917 with the 3rd Australian Light Horse Brigade, 5th and 6th Mounted Brigades. After serving in Palestine it was renamed the Australian Mounted Division in July 1917.

NEW ZEALAND EXPEDITIONARY FORCE (NZEF)

On 7 August 1914 New Zealand offered an Expeditionary Force of 8,000 men, comprising a divisional headquarters, an infantry brigade, a mounted rifles brigade and artillery. Each of the country's 4 military districts, Wellington, Otago, Canterbury and Auckland, provided an infantry battalion with 33 officers and 977 other ranks and a mounted rifles regiment with 26 officers and 523 men. A composite battalion occupied German Samoa and remained there until April 1915.

New Zealand introduced conscription at the end of 1916, the only dominion to do so. Over 220,000 New Zealanders served, over 100,000 of them overseas.

NEW ZEALAND AND AUSTRALIAN (ANZAC) DIVISION

8,459 men set sail in October, reaching Alexandria at the beginning of December. They were joined by the 1st Australian Light Horse Brigade and the 4th Australian Brigade and formed as the New Zealand and Australian Division (ANZAC Division) under the New Zealand Headquarters. The two mounted brigades were left behind when the division landed at Anzac Cove on Gallipoli on 25 April 1915; they would fight dismounted on the peninsula after May 1915. The 3rd Australian Light Horse Brigade served with the division from May 1915. The division withdrew from Gallipoli on 20 December 1915 and returned to Egypt where it was disbanded. The 1st and 3rd Australian Light Horse and New Zealand Mounted Rifles Brigades went to form the Mounted Division; 4th Australian Brigade joined 4th Australian Division.

NEW ZEALAND DIVISION

The decision was taken to form a New Zealand Division in February 1915. Drafts formed 2nd Brigade and 3rd Rifle Brigade was formed with volunteers from the Samoan occupation force. The division reached France in April 1916 and joined II ANZAC Corps. A 4th New Zealand Brigade joined the division in May 1917; it was disbanded in February 1918.

CANADIAN EXPEDITIONARY FORCE (CEF)

On 7 August 1914 the Canadian government offered to send 20,000 men to the United Kingdom while the Royal Canadian Regiment relieved the British garrison on Bermuda. The Permanent Force (Canada's regular army) provided administrative staffs for 4 brigades as 30,500 volunteers with previous military experience assembled at Valcartier, near Quebec. Provisional battalions (the

A New Zealand battalion prepares to move up to the line in September 1916. On the 15th the men would advance alongside tanks past the village of Flers on the Somme. *(IWM Q1244)*

Provisional title was soon dropped), based on Canada's provinces, were each organized into 8 companies. The Expeditionary Force sailed for Britain on 3 October.

In all 418,035 Canadian soldiers eventually served overseas from a total of 628,964 who enlisted.

1ST CANADIAN DIVISION

The battalions, each with 30 officers and 996 men, were reorganized into 4 companies on Salisbury Plain. Bad weather hampered training and the men lived under canvas while contractors completed hutted encampments. The division sailed to France in February 1915 with 3 brigades; 4th Brigade was disbanded.

2ND CANADIAN DIVISION

Canada offered another 20,000 men in October 1914. They spent the winter training at local depots and sailed to Britain in May 1915. The division completed its training at Shorncliffe and went to France in September 1915.

3RD CANADIAN DIVISION

The British asked for more troops in June 1915 and 3rd Canadian Division assembled in France in December 1915 using the following troops already serving overseas: **7th Brigade:** Two battalions of the Royal Canadian Regiment serving in Bermuda and Princess Patricia's Canadian Light Infantry previously serving with a British division; **8th Brigade:** the Canadian Mounted Rifles recalled from Egypt and converted into infantry, plus 2 further battalions from unallocated units in Britain and France; **9th Brigade:** did not join until February 1916; 3rd Indian (Lahore) Division provided the artillery until Canadian crews joined in July 1916.

4TH CANADIAN DIVISION

The British government asked Canada to provide 12 battalions for Egypt at the end of 1915. The Canadian government suggested forming the 10th, 11th and 12th Training Brigades stationed at Shorncliffe into a new division. It assembled at Bramshott in April 1916 and sailed to France 4 months later with the artillery of 3rd Indian (Lahore) Division; Canadian artillery joined in May 1917.

5TH CANADIAN DIVISION

As the strength of the Canadian Army peaked at 300,000 in May 1916, a 5th Canadian Division was proposed. However, the Somme battles soon drew heavily on replacements at the same time as recruiting started to fall in Canada. The Canadian government approved a 5th Canadian Division for home defence in the United Kingdom in January 1917 but casualties at Arras caused further manpower shortages. The artillery and engineers joined Canadian Corps troops in France in August 1917. The division was broken up in February 1918 and the machine gun companies joined Canadian Corps troops.

CANADIAN CAVALRY BRIGADE

The Royal Canadian Dragoons, Lord Strathcona's Horse and the Royal Canadian Horse Artillery Brigade formed Canada's Permanent Mounted Force. They left for England with the 1st Canadian Division and the Canadian Cavalry Brigade formed when 2nd King Edward's Horse joined in February 1915. The brigade crossed to France in May and served dismounted as Seely's Detachment with the 1st Canadian Division until September. 1st and 2nd Canadian Mounted Rifles Brigades were attached to the Cavalry Brigade in September–December 1915. The Canadian Cavalry Brigade Machine Gun Squadron joined and the Fort Garry Horse replaced 2nd King Edward's Horse in February 1916. The brigade was attached to the 3rd Cavalry Division from April 1916, transferring to the 2nd Indian (later 5th) Cavalry Division in June 1916; it returned to the 3rd Cavalry Division in March 1918.

EAST AFRICAN DIVISIONS AND SOUTH AFRICAN TROOPS

A **South African Brigade** was sent via Egypt to France in April 1916 and it joined the 9th (Scottish) Division at the end of the month;

Canadian soldiers pause for a welcome break while attempting to dig a drainage channel in their trench.
(IWM CO286)

---

it served on the Western Front until the Armistice. In all 74,196 South Africans served in campaigns abroad from a total 136,070 in arms.

1st East African Division

Two infantry brigades and a mounted brigade had been raised in Nairobi by the end of 1914. The name Magadi Division was soon changed to 1st East African Division and it advanced into northern German East Africa.

2nd East African Division

Formed in January 1916. It advanced into the northern part of German East Africa, east of Kilimanjaro. Operations ended in March 1916 and the division was reorganized as a South African formation. Disease took its toll while the division guarded the Central Railway; it was disbanded in December 1916.

3rd East African Division

Formed with the 2nd South African Brigade in March 1916. 2nd South African Mounted Brigade took its place in May (2nd South African Brigade became 1st East African Division's reserve) and served in the northern territories of German East Africa. Again disease took its toll and the division was withdrawn and returned to South Africa; it was disbanded in September 1916.

The Indian Army

On the outbreak of war the War Office asked for 2 divisions and a cavalry brigade to serve in France. 3rd (Lahore) and 7th (Meerut) Divisions and the Secunderabad Cavalry Brigade were chosen; the request was subsequently increased to 2 cavalry divisions.

The gas alert is on. A South African sentry braces himself against the cold while keeping an eye on the weather vanes; a change in wind direction could signify a gas attack. *(IWM Q1712)*

Although the Lahore Division sailed at the end of August 1914, the rest of the Indian Expeditionary Force was delayed by a lack of shipping. Several other Indian Expeditionary Forces served in other theatres.

In all 1,524,187 troops from the Indian subcontinent served during the Great War.

EXPEDITIONARY FORCE A: TROOPS SENT TO FRANCE

3RD (LAHORE) DIVISION

Sailed to Egypt and, while the 9th (Sirhind) Brigade reinforced the Suez Canal defences for a time, the rest of the division reached France at the end of September 1914.

7TH (MEERUT) DIVISION

Sailed to Egypt but was diverted to France, arriving in October 1914.

1ST INDIAN CAVALRY DIVISION

Assembled in October 1914 and sailed for France where deployment was delayed until December by horse-sickness.

2ND INDIAN CAVALRY DIVISION

Sailed for France in November 1914 and reached the front in January 1915.

Indian cavalry brigades were known by their geographical rather than numerical titles in France to avoid confusion with British brigades. The two divisions were renamed 4th and 5th Cavalry Divisions on 26 November 1916. They were disbanded in March 1918 and the Indian elements sailed to Egypt where they reformed as the 1st and 2nd Mounted Divisions. They were again named 4th and 5th Cavalry Divisions on 22 July 1918.

OTHER EXPEDITIONARY FORCES

EXPEDITIONARY FORCE B

The Bangalore (27th) and Imperial Service Brigades served in East Africa.

EXPEDITIONARY FORCE C

Five battalions were sent to East Africa and deployed along the Uganda Railway.

EXPEDITIONARY FORCE D

Mesopotamia. 6th (Poona) Division was mobilized for service in Europe but it was diverted to Mesopotamia in October 1914. It surrendered at Kut al Amara on 29 April 1916.

EXPEDITIONARY FORCE E

The original Egyptian Expeditionary Force.

EXPEDITIONARY FORCE F

Reinforcements sent to Egypt.

EXPEDITIONARY FORCE G

Troops sent to Gallipoli.

GUARDING INDIA

The two armies in India were renamed commands in January 1918 and were deployed as follows:

NORTHERN ARMY, LATER NORTHERN COMMAND

1st (Peshawar) Division: Afghanistan border.
2nd (Rawalpindi) Division: Reserve for the North-West Frontier.
8th (Lucknow) Division: Lucknow region; it reported to Army HQ after January 1918.
3rd Lahore Divisional Area: Formed in September 1914, disbanded in May 1917.
7th Meerut Divisional Area: Formed in September 1914, renamed Meerut Division in June 1917.

16th Indian Division: Formed in December 1916 and took over 3rd Lahore Divisional Area in May 1917.
Kohat, **Bannu** and **Derajat Brigades** manned posts along the North-West Frontier.

SOUTHERN ARMY, LATER SOUTHERN COMMAND

4th (Quetta) Division: Persian Frontier.
5th (Mhow) Division: North of Bombay.
6th Poona Divisional Area: Formed in October 1914, renamed 6th Poona Division in June 1917.
9th (Secunderabad) Division: Southern India.
Burma Division: Burma–China border.

EXPANDING THE INDIAN ARMY

The Reserve numbered 34,700 men but most were elderly or infirm. Before long the system of sending replacements overseas broke down, with the caste system complicating matters. The problems delayed the expansion of the Army until 1916; eventually 826,900 Indians enlisted.

Increased pay and improved conditions boosted recruiting, while regimental depots grouped together to develop improved training facilities. Second battalions were formed but they did not always follow the same class structure as was customary in the first battalions.

Eight new Indian infantry divisions (10th–12th and 14th–18th; 13th Division was never established) were formed between December 1914 and January 1918, with Punjabi Muslims providing 40% and the Sikh community providing 25% of new recruits.

10TH INDIAN DIVISION

Formed in Egypt in December 1914. It served on the Suez Canal until it was disbanded in March 1916 to provide replacements for France.

11TH INDIAN DIVISION

Formed in Egypt in December 1914. It served on the Suez Canal and provided replacements for France. The division was broken up in May 1915 but the brigades continued to operate on the Canal.

Indian troops follow their instructor's orders during bayonet practice. *(IWM Q33336)*

12TH INDIAN DIVISION

Formed in Mesopotamia in April 1915. Units joined 6th (Poona) Division's advance on Baghdad. They went on to serve in the unsuccessful Kut Relief Force and the division disbanded in March 1916.

14TH INDIAN DIVISION

Formed in May 1916 in Mesopotamia from the unsuccessful Kut Relief Force. For the remainder of the war the division fought in Mesopotamia.

15TH INDIAN DIVISION

Formed in May 1916 on the Euphrates Front and served for the rest of the war in Mesopotamia.

16TH INDIAN DIVISION

Formed in December 1916; took over responsibility for 3rd Lahore Divisional Area in May 1917.

17TH INDIAN DIVISION

Formed in August 1917 to protect the Mesopotamian lines of communication.

18TH INDIAN DIVISION

Formed in Mesopotamia in January 1918 from units stationed in India.

Several British divisions were Indianized in 1918 by replacing British battalions with Indian battalions. A total of 22 Indian battalions joined British divisions in Egypt while 40 battalions joined British divisions in Macedonia.

POST-WAR ENGAGEMENTS

Four divisions, the 1st (Peshawar), 2nd (Rawalpindi), 4th (Quetta) and 16th, fought in Afghanistan during May 1919. The 17th Indian and 18th Indian Divisions occupied Iraq and suppressed a rebellion in 1920.

SMALLER DOMINIONS AND COLONIES

Men from across the rest of the Empire also served, including over 9,000 from Newfoundland (not then part of Canada), twice that number from the West Indies and another 31,000 from minor dominions and colonies.

CHAPTER THREE

THE HIGHER DIRECTION OF THE WAR

THE WAR COUNCIL

Before the war the Committee of Imperial Defence, a small group of Cabinet members and military advisors, considered strategic issues and directed war preparations; they reported directly to the Prime Minister.

On 5 and 6 August 1914 ministers and the staffs of the Navy and Army held a council of war to discuss preparations for the war in Europe, concentrating on the strength of the Expeditionary Force, the recalling of overseas garrisons and the Indian Army involvement.

Prime Minister Asquith (third from right) watches men adjusting shell fuses during a visit to the Somme in August 1916. *(IWM Q4188)*

Lord Kitchener was appointed Secretary of State for War on 5 August 1914 and immediately began issuing orders to the Army Council which in turn instructed the Commander-in-Chief of the British Expeditionary Force. One of Kitchener's major contributions was to set in train the mobilization of British manpower with his call to arms for volunteers; this resulted in the formation of the New Armies.

The Cabinet handed over control of strategy to the War Council, a streamlined version of the Committee of Imperial Defence with Sir Maurice Hankey as secretary, on 25 November 1914. The Cabinet continued to be responsible for policy but the Council assessed and reported on developments. Following the defeat of the Asquith government on 25 May 1915, the new coalition government renamed the War Council the Dardanelles Committee (Great Britain's principal theatre of operations during the summer of 1915) on 7 June. A month later the first Inter-Allied Military Conference took place at Chantilly, the first of many. Since the French Army was still very much larger than the BEF French views dominated proceedings and, with large areas of France under enemy occupation, they naturally pressed for offensive action on the Western Front. This eventually dictated the date and place of the BEF's offensive at Loos in September.

The Dardanelles Committee was re-organized with fewer members on 30 October 1915 and renamed the War Committee. The British and French prime ministers agreed to a mixed committee to coordinate their actions when they met in Paris on 17 November 1915. Military representatives from Russia, Italy and Serbia attended the second Inter-Allied Military Conference held at Chantilly on 2 December 1915; it was the start of regular meetings to direct war policy.

On 5 June 1916 Lord Kitchener was lost at sea when HMS *Hampshire* was sunk en route to Russia; David Lloyd George took his place as Secretary of State for War.

The members of Prime Minister Lloyd George's War Cabinet pose in Downing Street for the camera. (*IWM Q27968A*)

THE WAR CABINET

Lloyd George replaced Herbert Asquith as prime minister in December 1916 and immediately streamlined the War Council, renaming it the War Cabinet. Lloyd George led the Cabinet, assisted by the Earl of Derby, Secretary of State for War, and a small number of dedicated members. The original members were Earl Curzon, Viscount Milner, Andrew Bonar Law and Arthur Henderson.

The War Cabinet controlled the British involvement in the war until the Armistice, calling on the General Staff and other experts for advice; the Chief of the Imperial General Staff attended meetings regularly. A sub-committee, the Imperial War Committee, gave the dominions representation and the first meeting of this committee was held in March 1917.

CABINET COMMITTEE ON MUNITIONS AND THE MINISTRY OF MUNITIONS

Kitchener chaired the first Cabinet Committee on Munitions on 12 October 1914 to investigate the armaments industry. The private armaments industry would take time to reach targets and in the meantime, contracts were placed with companies in the USA.

The Ministry of Munitions, led by Lloyd George, was formed on 1 July 1915 to co-ordinate the armaments industries. It introduced the Munitions of War Act to tie men to their jobs, restrict profits and ban industrial action; it also investigated bringing women into the industry. An amendment in January 1916 extended the Act to cover construction, the power industry and electricity suppliers.

It still took time to meet the Army's demands and, although annual shell production rose from 5 million in 1914 to 53 million in 1916, General Haig believed that shell stocks were inadequate until the summer of 1916. Production peaked at 87.5 million in 1917 but the Army had to wait until 1918 before the artillery had unlimited stocks.

Over 2.5 million men and 750,000 women eventually produced 162 million shells at 5,000 factories.

QUALITY CONTROL

The expansion of the munitions industry led to quality control problems as the new workforce came to terms with new designs and makeshift plants. Mills bombs and rifle grenades were issued with defective fuses while poorly made phosphorus bombs spontaneously combusted. Shell production climbed rapidly but fuses were always in short supply and by August 1916 some 25 million 18-pounder shells were waiting for fuses.

THE SUPREME WAR COUNCIL

After the costly campaigns of 1916 and 1917 Lloyd George began to promote a combined Allied strategy in the autumn of 1917, in part to restrain the attacking strategies of the C-in-C of the BEF, Field Marshal Haig, and the Chief of the Imperial General Staff, General Sir William Robertson. The Austro-Hungarians and Germans overran the Italian front at Caporetto in October 1917, prompting a crisis in the Allied command; unless cooperation was assured, the war could be lost.

Lloyd George advocated a Supreme War Council at the Rapallo Conference of 5–7 November 1917 and it was inaugurated on 1 December at Versailles, near Paris, with Marshal Ferdinand Foch as the President. The Council's principal representatives, a leading military figure from Britain, France, Italy and the USA, met regularly and Lloyd George's choice, General Sir Henry Wilson, effectively bypassed Haig and Robertson in the policy-making process.

The British section of the council had the following members:

Prime Minister: David Lloyd George
Cabinet Minister: Viscount Milner
Earl of Derby (Secretary for War after April 1918)
Military Representative:
General Sir Henry Wilson
Major-General Sir Charles Sackville-West from February 1918

General Sir Henry Rawlinson was a temporary member at the first meeting in February 1918.

Chief of Staff: Maj-Gen Sackville-West Brigadier-General Herbert Studd after February 1918
War Cabinet Secretary: Sir Maurice Hankey
Foreign Office Representative: Sir George Clerk

The Chief of Staff controlled four branches: Allied and Neutral Branch, Enemy and Neutral Branch, Material and Manpower Branch, Maps and Camp Commandant.

On 3 February 1918 the British government announced the enlargement of powers of the Supreme War Council at Versailles and the CIGS, General Robertson, soon resigned in protest. He was replaced by General Sir Henry Wilson.

Ineffective cooperation between the British and French military during the German Somme offensive in March resulted in the appointment of Marshal Ferdinand Foch as the supreme commander of Allied forces in France on 14 April 1918.

The Supreme War Council considered various aspects of Allied strategy but its chief role in the final months of the war was to consider armistice terms with Germany and Austria-Hungary. It then continued to meet to deal with the peace treaty settlements, reparations and the treatment of the Kaiser.

THE ARMY COUNCIL

British Army policy and organization were controlled and managed by the Army Council which had been established in 1904. The Secretary of State for War (as the Army minister in the government was then known) was the President and the Council had six further members, four senior officers and two civilians. These were the Chief of the Imperial General Staff (CIGS), the Adjutant-General, the Quartermaster-General, the Master-General of the Ordnance, the permanent secretary at the War Office and a financial secretary. The Chief of the Imperial General Staff advised the Council on operational matters.

CHIEF OF THE IMPERIAL GENERAL STAFF (CIGS)

The CIGS was the Army's main contact with the politicians and he was expected to meet the War Council or later War Cabinet on a regular basis, briefing them on military matters, forthcoming operations, new technology and commitments to various theatres. In turn he would put forward the Army's plans and requirements.

The first CIGS of the war, General Sir Charles Douglas, aided Field Marshal French during the retreat from Mons and the Battle of the Aisne; he died in October 1914. Lieutenant-General Sir James Murray

As Chief of the Imperial General Staff, General Sir William Robertson had the difficult task of explaining the Army's needs to the politicians. *(IWM Q69626)*

struggled to contend with Kitchener's interference and, after disasters in the Dardanelles and on the Western Front, Lieutenant-General Sir Archibald Murray replaced him in September 1915. Murray's appointment was terminated when General Sir Douglas Haig became the BEF's new Commander-in-Chief.

Lieutenant-General Sir William Robertson was chosen as CIGS in December 1915 because of his ability to deliver clear and decisive reports to the civilian politicians, leaving the military-minded, but inarticulate, General Haig to concentrate on affairs at GHQ in France.

Robertson accepted the post after negotiating his own terms, making him the only authority allowed to give the government advice on operational matters, ending the Secretary of State for War's interference. A month after his appointment Robertson was made 'responsible for issuing the orders of the Government in regard to military operations'. The CIGS's new status stopped Kitchener giving contradictory advice on overall strategy. Robertson also revived the General Staff.

The Haig–Robertson partnership lasted until February 1918. Robertson resigned in protest at the undermining of his position by the military advisor on the Supreme War Council. He was replaced by the military advisor himself: Lieutenant-General Sir Henry Wilson.

HOME DEFENCE FORCES

In peacetime the British Army was split into Home Commands, responsible for housing, training and organizing the units in their area. The Irish Command was also kept busy maintaining civil order across Ireland.

London District: Central London
Aldershot Command: Aldershot
Northern Command: York
Southern Command: Salisbury
Eastern Command: Central London
Western Command: Chester
Scottish Command: Edinburgh
Irish Command: Dublin

On 5 August 1914 GHQ Central Force was mobilized under General Sir Ian Hamilton and immediately set to work giving support to the Expeditionary Force as well as organizing the troops stationed across Great Britain on coastal defence. Central Force headquarters was organized along the same lines as the GHQs operating overseas and the staff coordinated the work of their offices with the civilian authorities.

The Major-General General Staff and GSO1 coordinated staff work while the Director of Army Signals operated the communications systems across Great Britain. The Deputy Adjutant-General and Deputy Quartermaster-General organized the acquisition of supplies, transport, equipment and ammunition aided by Assistant Directors of Supplies, Transport and Ordnance. The Deputy Director of Railway Transport and the Embarkation Commandants coordinated movement of troops around Great Britain and across the Channel while the Deputy Director of Medical Services made arrangements for distributing the wounded across the country. The Assistant Director of Veterinary Services made similar arrangements for animals.

Central Force split the country into three areas, all based in the southern half of England, where the majority of troops were stationed:

First Army: Bedford
Second Army: Aldershot
Third Army: Luton

One of the first concerns was coastal protection. The War Book had laid down orders for 9 Territorial divisions, 10 mounted brigades and 4 cyclist battalions to patrol the coast. The units immediately moved to their war stations and completed their training while on coastal defence duties. 2nd Line Territorial and New Army divisions took over when the 1st Line Territorial divisions headed overseas.

Over the months that followed home commands continued to work with the various regimental headquarters on recruitment, supervising 2nd Line Territorial and New Army units through the early stages of their

Field Marshal Sir Douglas Haig and his staff gather on the steps of GHQ to greet the King in August 1918. *(IWM Q9232)*

training. They assembled as divisions under one of the 3 armies and completed their final training, usually at Aldershot or on Salisbury Plain. General Sir (Henry) Leslie Rundle took over when General Hamilton left to take command of the Mediterranean Expeditionary Force in March 1915.

As the number of divisions in Great Britain started to dwindle, steps were taken to revise the Army's home organization under its new commander. Field Marshal Viscount French took command in December 1915, as Central Force was renamed GHQ Home Forces; Third Army was disbanded at the same time. The following spring First and Second Armies were reorganized into Northern Army and Southern Army. Northern Army, led by General Sir Bruce Hamilton, was based at Mundford before moving to Norwich. Southern Army was based at Brentford under General Sir Arthur Paget. 59th Division had to move to Ireland in the spring of 1916 to restore order after the Easter Rising in Dublin

(a division was kept there until the spring of 1918). Field Marshal French's command was renamed GHQ Forces at Home in June 1916.

The two armies were broken up on 16 February 1918 and General Sir William Robertson took command in May 1918 (his command was renamed GHQ Forces in Great Britain in August 1918). A few 2nd Line Territorial divisions remained in Great Britain on coastal duty until the end of the war.

GENERAL HEADQUARTERS, BRITISH EXPEDITIONARY FORCE
COMMANDER-IN-CHIEF

Field Marshal Sir John French became Commander-in-Chief of the BEF on 4 August 1914 and led it through the retreat to the Marne and the advance to the Aisne, before moving north to defend the Ypres Salient. After the offensives of 1915 failed to break through the German lines the poor handling of the reserves during the Battle of Loos in September became controversial. General Sir Douglas Haig, First Army's commander, blamed French for this, though many historians assert that Haig was far more at fault. However, Haig used his influential contacts to ensure that he replaced French as Commander-in-Chief of the BEF on 15 December 1915.

General Haig (promoted to Field Marshal on 1 January 1917) led the BEF through the drawn-out campaigns on the Somme in 1916 and at Arras and Ypres in 1917. On 14 April 1918, during the tense days of the German spring offensives, he was forced to report to the new generalissimo, Marshal Foch. Despite the spring setbacks, Haig continued in command, leading the BEF during the Advance to Victory until the Armistice on 11 November.

THE STAFF

Four senior officers reported directly to the Commander-in-Chief:

Chief of the General Staff (CGS)
Quartermaster-General (QMG)
Inspector General of Communications (IGC)
Adjutant-General (AG)

Holders of these posts and the important position of Military Secretary are shown in the table below.

The number of staff officers with GHQ's 1st and 2nd Echelons rose from 53 to 101 during the war. However, the number of General Staff officers only increased from 22 to 30 and the

---

CHIEFS OF THE GENERAL STAFF

Lieutenant-General Sir Archibald Murray	from 4 August 1914
General Sir William Robertson	from 25 January 1915
Lieutenant-General Sir Launcelot Kiggell	from 22 December 1915
Lieutenant-General Hon Sir Herbert Lawrence	from 24 January 1918

QUARTERMASTERS-GENERAL

Lieutenant-General Sir William Robertson	from 4 August 1914
Lieutenant-General Sir Ronald Maxwell	from 27 January 1915
Lieutenant-General Sir Travers Clarke	from 23 December 1917

INSPECTORS-GENERAL OF COMMUNICATIONS

Lieutenant-General Frederick Robb	from 5 August 1914
Lieutenant-General Ronald Maxwell	from 19 September 1914
Lieutenant-General Frederick Clayton	from 27 January 1915
Lieutenant-General (Joseph) John Asser	from 2 December 1916

General Asser was known as the **Commander, Lines of Communications Area**

ADJUTANTS-GENERAL

Lieutenant-General Sir Cecil Macready	from 4 August 1914
Lieutenant-General Sir George Fowke	from 22 February 1916

MILITARY SECRETARIES

Colonel Hon W. Lambton	from 5 August 1914
Brigadier-General H. Lowther	from 6 September 1915
Brigadier-General Duke of Teck	from 27 December 1915
Major-General William Peyton	from 8 May 1916
Major-General Harold Ruggles-Brise	from 22 March 1918

Engineer-in-Chief's staff was enlarged from 1 officer to 9. The number of staff officers with GHQ's 3rd Echelon at the base increased from 28 to 36 and clerical establishments expanded to serve the staff. The number of officers connected with other supporting services rose from 45 to 129.

THE GENERAL STAFF

The CGS led the General Staff branch. The Major-General General Staff, the Major-General Royal Artillery, and the Engineer-in-Chief reported to him. The CGS ran operations and intelligence, covering planning and coordination of the Army's branches, intelligence-gathering and training.

A **Major-General General Staff** assisted the CGS but the post was known as the **Sub-Chief** or **Deputy Chief of the General Staff** between January 1915 and February 1918 at General Robertson's insistence. A **Brigadier-General General Staff (Intelligence)** coordinated information collected by various intelligence agencies. A **Brigadier-General General Staff (Operations)** or Oa was added in November 1914 to cover operational planning; he also summarized the state of the British order of battle. A **Brigadier-General General Staff (Intelligence)** or Ob was added in July 1915 to coordinate information on the German order of battle and troop movements.

A **Major-General Royal Artillery** controlled artillery operations along the Western Front; an Assistant Director was added in November 1916 and a Brigadier-General RA in April 1918. An **Assistant Director (Anti-Aircraft)** coordinated air defence after November 1917.

The **Engineer-in-Chief** supervised and coordinated engineering works. An **Inspector of Mines** was appointed in January 1916 to coordinate tunnelling operations. A **Director of Gas Services** was appointed at the same time to organize the Special Brigade and anti-gas measures.

Training became increasingly important and a **Brigadier-General General Staff (Training)** joined the staff in January 1917; an **Inspector-General of Training** coordinated training after July 1918. An **Inspector of the**

Machine Gun Corps was appointed in March 1918.

QUARTERMASTER-GENERAL

The QMG ran the Quartermaster-General's branch assisted by a Deputy Quartermaster-General. This branch dealt with the movement of supplies forward, the evacuation of the wounded and communications. The Directors of Army Signals, Medical Services, Supplies and Transport reported to the QMG.

The **Director of Army Signals** dealt with communications and after December 1914 he supervised deputy directors on army staffs.

The **Director of Supplies** dealt with the movement of food and equipment, maintaining adequate stocks and monitoring consumption. The engineers delivered their stores straight to their parks and a **Director of Engineering Stores** was appointed to organize the distribution in June 1918.

The **Director-General of Medical Services** coordinated the operations of the casualty clearing stations as well as the stationary and base hospitals along the coast. A Deputy Director-General Medical Services assisted.

The **Director of Transport** made sure that there were enough horses, wagons and vehicles to keep the Army supplied and the casualties moving to the rear.

INSPECTOR GENERAL OF COMMUNICATIONS

The IGC's staff maintained the lines of communications, making sure that there were enough roads and railways for the Quartermaster-General's wagons and lorries to move on. They also supervised the bases along the coast at Boulogne, Calais, Le Havre, Rouen and Marseilles; advanced bases were set up when the front line stabilized. Directors of Railways, Works, Remounts, Veterinary Services and Ordnance Services reported to the IGC. The Postmaster-General also came under this branch.

A **Director of Railways** supervised train movements. The British Army started to use the French canals for moving supplies and wounded in December 1914 and the **Director** of **Inland Transport** controlled these operations.

The British Army's lines of communications broke down during the 1916 Somme Offensive. A civilian expert, (Honorary) Major-General Sir Eric Geddes, was offered the post of **Director-General (Transportation)** and he joined on 20 October 1916. He immediately appointed a **Director of Roads** and a **Director of Docks** to rectify the problems. The post of Director of Railways was known as Director of Transport after February 1917 and it was again renamed Director of Railway Traffic in March 1918. The Director-General of Transportation reported to the Quartermaster-General after June 1918.

A **Director of Works** supervised construction work along the lines of communication and a **Controller of Labour** was appointed in December 1916 to make sure manpower was used effectively. A **Director of Forestry** had also been appointed in May 1916 to co-ordinate operations with the French government.

A **Director of Remounts** procured horses and supervised their training, while the **Director of Veterinary Services** controlled the animal medical services.

A **Director of Ordnance Services** controlled the purchase and delivery of weapons, ammunition, equipment and clothing. A **Controller of Salvage** was added in February 1918 to coordinate the collection and repair of clothing, weapons and equipment.

A **Director of Army Postal Services** ran the postal system, covering both official and private mail.

ADJUTANT-GENERAL

The AG's branch dealt with the personnel and financial aspects of the Army, covering payment of the men and the purchase of food and equipment. A Deputy Adjutant-General stationed at the base assisted him.

The **Paymaster-in-Chief** dealt with internal financial matters and a **Director of Hirings and Requisitions** was added in January 1915 to control financial dealings with the French and Belgians. A **Brigadier-General Personnel**

For three years Château de Beaurepaire, close to Montreuil, served as General (later Field Marshal) Haig's headquarters. *(IWM Q3645)*

Services was added in September 1917; a further brigadier-general was appointed a year later to deal with demobilization.

MILITARY SECRETARY

The Military Secretary was responsible for appointments and promotions of officers, considering recommendations by their superiors. He also dealt with honours.

LIAISON WITH THE FRENCH

A British mission joined the French General Headquarters (GQG) on 18 August 1914. Following the German breakthrough on the Lys in April 1918, a second mission joined the Armies in France HQ to coordinate operations with French troops moving into the British sector at Mont Kemmel, south-west of Ypres.

THE ARMIES

First and Second Armies were formed on 26 December 1914 and an official establishment was defined in March 1915. Third Army was added on 13 July 1915 and Fourth Army on 5 February 1916. Reserve Army was formed on

The heavy artillery came under army control. This crew of a 15-inch howitzer prepare to fire their weapon during Third Army's attack east of Arras in April 1917. Note the size of the shell on the left and the length of the ramrod on the right. *(IWM Q1990)*

---

22 May 1916 and was renamed Fifth Army on 30 October.

To begin with each army controlled an average of 3 corps, 2 in the front line and 1 in reserve. An army held its front with an average of 7 divisions, 4 at the front and 3 in reserve. Numbers could increase to as many as 6 corps, 4 in the front line and 2 in reserve and a maximum of 24 divisions, during offensives.

Dozens of units reported to the various branches of the army staff and they were referred to as army troops; for example an army field artillery brigade reported to the Major-General Royal Artillery.

COMMAND AND STAFF

A general usually commanded an army; a staff of 31 officers and 106 other ranks assisted him. Eleven senior officers ran the main branches of the staff:

MAJOR-GENERAL GENERAL STAFF (M-GGS)

This officer was the chief of staff and the head of the operations section. His subordinates controlled several areas of staff work: monitoring the status of troops under the army's command; planning and coordinating offensive operations and defensive schemes; assessing the enemy's strength; arranging training facilities for officers and men.

MAJOR-GENERAL ROYAL ARTILLERY (M-GRA)

Heavy, medium and then field artillery brigades were brought under army control and by the time of the Armistice the M-GRA was responsible for up to 900 medium and heavy artillery pieces in army artillery brigades. He also coordinated the field artillery operated by the corps and divisions under his command. A number of machine-gun battalions and motor machine-gun battalions reported directly to the M-GRA.

DEPUTY ADJUTANT AND QUARTERMASTER-GENERAL (D-A & QMG)

A major-general, he coordinated the movement of arms, ammunition, clothing, food and water to the front and casualties to the hospitals with the help of two assistants.

DEPUTY DIRECTOR SUPPLIES AND TRANSPORT (D-DS & T)

A colonel (brigadier-general after October 1917), he controlled the Army Service Corps transport units, including trains, horse-drawn and motorized transport. He ran a supply column, an auxiliary (horse) company, an auxiliary (petrol) company and an auxiliary (omnibus) company. Reserve parks held fleets of spare vehicles and mechanical transport mobile repair units carried out field repairs.

DEPUTY DIRECTOR ORDNANCE SERVICES (D-DOS)

A colonel, he ran the ordnance workshops and maintained stocks of equipment. He also ran the workshops servicing and repairing weaponry, and the salvage units.

CHIEF ENGINEER (CE)

The role of the CE (a major-general) increased with the onset of trench warfare and his span of responsibility grew to cover four areas: **military engineering** – building and maintaining trench systems and mapping them while tunnellers waged an underground war; **infrastructure** – building and maintaining roads, railways, bridges, water pipelines, encampments and dumps; **maintenance and repair** – parks kept a supply of materials, equipment and a fleet of vehicles while workshops carried out maintenance and repairs; and **specialized units**.

SPECIALIZED UNITS

After September 1915 Special Brigade companies carried out gas attacks; a meteorological unit at GHQ monitored weather conditions. Flash-spotting sections and a sound-ranging section coordinated observation of German batteries for the artillery.

COMMUNICATIONS

A Deputy Director of Signals (a colonel) maintained army communications to GHQ and the corps. The army also had pigeon lofts and horses for staff orderlies.

DIRECTOR MEDICAL SERVICES (DMS)

Each army was responsible for maintaining the movement of wounded from the front-line units to the base hospitals along the coast. During an offensive an army controlled more than a dozen casualty clearing stations and a stationary hospital; 4 motor ambulance convoys were kept on stand-by for busy periods.

DEPUTY DIRECTOR REMOUNTS

A colonel or lieutenant-colonel organized the accommodation, training and supply of replacement horses for units in the army rear area. Two colonels managed the transport horses and maintained numbers.

DEPUTY DIRECTOR OF VETERINARY SERVICES (D-DVS)

A colonel or lieutenant-colonel controlled a casualty clearing chain for horses.

ANTI-AIRCRAFT DEFENCE

A number of RFC squadrons reported directly to army headquarters and balloon sections were also used for observation. An anti-aircraft commander was added in November 1916. This lieutenant-colonel controlled 10 anti-aircraft sections and 5 searchlight companies; anti-aircraft gun workshops maintained the guns.

SECURITY

Garrison battalions and garrison companies carried out guard duties in the army's rear area while military police coordinated traffic movements behind the lines.

PRINTING AND STATIONERY

An army had photographic and printing sections to print forms, orders, training leaflets and general stationery.

ARMY INSIGNIA

Armies adopted recognizable insignia for their vehicles and shoulder patches for the men.

First Army: Painted a white line down the back of its vehicles.
Second Army: Transport personnel used a red-black-red armlet marked with the Roman numeral II.
Third Army: Transport personnel used a similar armlet marked with a bull's-eye.

Fourth Army: Displayed the boar's head.

Fifth Army: Used a red fox while General Gough was in command; General Birdwood replaced it with a red-black-red brassard marked with a five-pointed star.

The cavalry were hard pressed during the BEF's retreat to the Marne and these men of the 11th Hussars make the most of a short break. *(IWM Q51200)*

ARMY OPERATIONS

BRITISH EXPEDITIONARY FORCE
1914

The BEF crossed to France under the leadership of Field Marshal Sir John French and assembled around Wassigny and Landrecies on 17 August before moving north into Belgium to take up positions on the French Army's left flank.

Mons and Le Cateau: The first contact with the Germans was at Mons on 23 August. Despite holding its positions the BEF had to fall back to comply with French movements. Heading south-west, II Corps made another stand at Le Cateau on the 26th with similar results; III Corps joined a few days later.

Retreat to the Marne: The retreat continued in earnest, sometimes covering over 20 miles a day, as the Germans harried the 3 corps. South of St Quentin they crossed the River Aisne and went through the forests of Compiègne and Villers-Cotterets before crossing the River Marne east of Paris.

Advance to the Aisne: The retreat finally ended on 5 September after the tired men of the BEF had covered over 200 miles in 13 days. The 3 corps headed north, crossing the Marne west of Château-Thierry, on 9 September, and the Germans fell back. The advance crossed the Aisne east of Soissons on the 13th and found the Germans dug in on the hills overlooking the river. After travelling many miles a day, the men had to fight for every yard; it was the start of trench warfare.

Race to the Sea: On 1 October the BEF withdrew from the line and moved north by train to Flanders. II Corps detrained at Abbeville on the 9th and encountered the Germans east of Béthune. III Corps arrived at St Omer and Hazebrouck on the 11th and came into contact with the enemy east of Armentières.

Antwerp Operations: Meanwhile, an expeditionary force had landed at Ostend to assist the Belgians at Antwerp. Their attempt was in vain and the force (later known as IV Corps) fell back, joining I Corps as it moved to Ypres.

Battles of Armentières and First Ypres: Fighting erupted all along the front and the BEF was forced on the defensive in the face of overwhelming numbers. Although driven back in places, the men held on until the attacks subsided on 22 November.

With new divisions expected, the BEF split into **First** and **Second Armies** on 26 December; both reported to Sir John French's GHQ.

FIRST ARMY
1914

Formed on 26 December, under the command of General Sir Douglas Haig; it took over the right of the BEF's line between **Cuinchy** and **Bois Grenier**.

1915

I Corps was engaged at **Givenchy** and **Cuinchy** in January and February.

Battle of Neuve Chapelle: IV Corps advanced north of the village and the Indian Corps advanced to the south on 10 March. Further attacks failed to exploit the success.

Battle of Aubers Ridge: IV Corps' northern pincer failed to break through to Fromelles while the Indian Corps and I Corps faced similar difficulties around Neuve Chapelle.

Battle of Festubert: The Indian Corps and I Corps advanced south-west of Neuve Chapelle on the night of 15 May. I Corps' right flank entered the German trenches east of Festubert the following day. No more advances were made and the attack was called off on the 25th.

IV Corps' attack west of **Givenchy** on 15 June failed completely.

First Army extended its line south to **Grenay** in June.

Battle of Loos: I Corps captured Hohenzollern Redoubt and advanced towards Cité St Elie and Hulluch on 25 September while IV Corps captured Loos and Hill 70. Subsidiary attacks by the Indian Corps and III Corps in the Lys area failed. First Army's offensive had stalled by 27 September and it had lost the Hohenzollern Redoubt by 1 October when XI Corps took over the sector; a final attack on 13 October failed.

General Haig was promoted to Commander-in-Chief of the BEF on 22 December; General Sir Henry Rawlinson took his place.

1916

Rawlinson transferred to Fourth Army on 4 February and was replaced by General Sir Charles Monro. I Corps attacked the **Hohenzollern Redoubt** in March and the Germans retaliated in April and May north of **Loos**.

German Attack on Vimy Ridge: IV Corps lost part of its trenches on 21 May.

At the end of June First Army was holding the line from **Aubers Ridge** to **Souchez**, south-west of Lens.

Attack at Fromelles: XI Corps' attack on 19 July failed to secure any part of the German line.

Monro left for India on 7 August and was temporarily replaced by Lieutenant-General Sir Richard Haking; General Sir Henry Horne took over on 30 September.

1917

Battle of Arras: I Corps held the line opposite Liévin on 9 April while the Canadian Corps captured Vimy Ridge; XIII Corps was inserted on the right of First Army's front on the 12th. The Germans soon withdrew from Liévin, Vimy and Bailleul and First Army followed up. XIII Corps captured Gavrelle on 23 April but elsewhere along the front the attack failed; another attack on the 28th failed; Fresnoy and Arleux were finally taken on 3 May.

First Army probed the German line west and south of **Lens** throughout June; the Canadian Corps captured Avion while XIII Corps cleared Oppy Wood.

Battle of Hill 70: The Canadian Corps captured Hill 70, east of Loos, and cleared the northern suburbs of Lens on 15 August.

1918

First Battles of the Somme: XIII Corps repulsed a German attack east of Arras on 28 March.

Battle of the Lys: The German attack on 9 April overran XI Corps' and part of XV Corps' line between Bois Grenier and Festubert; I Corps held on to Givenchy. As the two corps fell back towards the Nieppe Forest, I Corps extended its front along the Aire Canal. By 12 April the crisis had passed on First Army's front and XV Corps was handed over to Second Army.

Advance to Victory: First Army initially held a 22-mile sector between Arras and Béthune.

Advance in Flanders: I Corps followed the German withdrawal towards La Bassée at the end of September.

Second Battles of Arras: The Canadian Corps and XXII Corps attacked astride the River Scarpe on 26 August, pausing in front of the Canal du Nord ten days later.

Battles of the Hindenburg Line: The two corps

First Army's line was broken during the Battle of the Lys in April 1918 and only heroic rearguard actions at barricades like this stopped the Germans from capturing Hazebrouck. *(IWM Q6531)*

crossed the canal on 27 September and advanced towards Cambrai, reaching the River Selle by 12 October. I Corps and VIII Corps on the left followed up the German withdrawal and reached the Sensée Canal on the same day.

Final Advance: The left wing crossed the canal on 17 October and moved in line with the right, north of Denain. The Canadian Corps replaced I Corps in the centre of the army front and a general advance began on the 20th. XXII Corps and the Canadians reached the Schelde Canal at Valenciennes by 23 October and VIII Corps reached the Canal du Jard two days later. First Army renewed its advance on 4 November and quickly pushed east on either side of the Condé Canal beyond Mons.

SECOND ARMY

1914

Second Army was formed on 26 December under General Sir Horace Smith-Dorrien; it took control of the line from **Bois Grenier** to **Vierstraat**.

1915

V Corps extended the line north to **St Eloi** in February and then to **Hill 60**; it was engaged at both places in March and April before extending its sector to cover the east side of the Ypres Salient.

Second Battle of Ypres: The Germans used gas on 22 April, exposing V Corps' left flank. It fought to restore the line for the next two weeks but it was forced to retire to a smaller salient on 4 May. General Sir Herbert Plumer took over command of Third Army three days later. German attacks east of Ypres continued until 25 May, forcing further withdrawals.

V Corps fought for **Hooge** during June–August and attacked the same area with VI Corps on 25 September.

1916

In February V Corps was engaged at the **Bluff**,

south-east of Ypres. It tried to improve its positions around **St Eloi** at the end of March and the Canadian Corps continued the fight 4–16 April. The Canadians were engaged at **Mount Sorrel**, east of Ypres, 2–13 June. By the end of June Second Army's line extended from Boesinghe, north of Ypres, to Aubers Ridge.

1917

Battle of Messines: Nineteen mines were detonated below the German trenches on 7 June. X Corps cleared the northern part of Messines Ridge, IX Corps captured Wytschaete and II ANZAC Corps cleared the area around Messines. The ridge was secured by 14 June.

Third Battle of Ypres: Following Fifth Army's failure to clear the Gheluvelt plateau, Second Army took over the Westhoek sector at the end of August. I ANZAC Corps cleared Polygon Wood between 20 and 26 September while IX and X Corps advanced towards Gheluvelt.

Second Army then took over a larger sector. II ANZAC Corps captured Gravenstafel on 4 October and I ANZAC Corps took Broodseinde but further attacks on 9 and 12 October were hampered by the appalling conditions. The Canadian Corps replaced the ANZACs and made repeated attacks against Passchendaele; the village was taken on 10 November. Second Army Headquarters immediately transferred to **Italy** with Plumer as C-in-C of the British Force in Italy.

1918

General Plumer returned to the Ypres Salient on 13 March 1918; his command was renamed Second Army.

Battle of the Lys: The Germans captured Messines Ridge from IX Corps on 10 April, forcing it to abandon Armentières. As the retreat continued through Neuve Eglise and Wulverghem Second Army took over XV Corps' sector. As II and XXII Corps pulled back, VIII Corps withdrew from the Ypres Salient, releasing troops for the Lys area. Bailleul fell on 17 April but the line soon stabilized. French troops took over the

Hopes for a quick breakthrough during Second Army's attack east of Ypres on 31 July 1917 were dashed as heavy rain turned the Flanders fields into a sea of mud; even mules struggled to find a route through the waterlogged craters. *(IWM Q5940)*

Dranoutre sector on 21 April but they lost Mont Kemmel on the 25th, forcing XXII Corps to fall back from Wytschaete. Second Army finally held a line between Ypres and the Nieppe Forest.

Advance in Flanders: The Germans started to withdraw south of Ypres on 18 August and by 6 September XV Corps was facing Armentières while X Corps had reached Messines Ridge.

Final Advance: Second Army attacked east of Ypres on 28 September with II Corps and XIX Corps. X and XV Corps followed up, reaching the River Lys by 3 October. The left flank renewed the offensive on 14 October and Menin fell on the 16th. After XV Corps cleared Tourcoing and Roubaix a pursuit to the River Schelde followed and by 30 October all 4 corps had reached the river. They crossed it on 9 November and advanced to the River Dendre.

THIRD ARMY
1915

Formed on 13 July under General Sir Charles Monro and took over a 15-mile sector between **Hébuterne** and the **River Somme** from the

French a few days later. General Sir Edmund Allenby took command in October

1916

Third Army transferred to a 20-mile sector east of **Arras** in March.

Vimy Ridge: XVII Corps lost part of its front-line trenches to the Germans on 21 May.

Gommecourt Salient: VII Corps' subsidiary attack at the start of the Somme Offensive on 1 July failed.

Third Army held the line covering **Arras** until the following spring.

1917

German Withdrawal to the Hindenburg Line: Between 17 and 19 March VII and XVII Corps advanced towards Neuville Vitasse.

Battle of Arras: XVII Corps advanced along the north bank of the River Scarpe to Fampoux on 9 April while VI Corps advanced east of Arras, capturing Monchy-le-Preux by the 12th; VII Corps cleared the Hindenburg Line around Neuville Vitasse on the army's right flank, taking Wancourt ridge by the 15th. The 3 corps advanced over half a mile on 23 April but further attacks on the 28th and 3 May made little progress.

Actions on the Hindenburg Line: VII and IV Corps continued to probe the line between 20 May and 16 June. General Sir Julian Byng replaced Allenby on 9 June.

Battle of Cambrai: With 324 tanks leading, IV Corps advanced through Havrincourt, and Graincourt to the outskirts of Bourlon Wood while III Corps captured Marcoing and Masnières on 20 November. Flesquières, Cantaing and Noyelles were taken the following day but Bourlon Wood did not fall until the 28th. The Germans counter-attacked on 30 November, taking Villers-Guislain and Gonnelieu from VII Corps. V Corps relieved IV Corps the following day and by 6 December Third Army had withdrawn to the Flesquières line.

1918

First Battles of the Somme: The German attack on 21 March struck IV Corps and VII Corps

north and south of the Flesquières Salient and by the end of the second day Third Army was on the retreat. Reinforcements strengthened XVII and VI Corps' line south-west of Arras, but the rest of the army fell back to the west bank of the Ancre, north of Albert. Over six days Third Army retreated up to 22 miles in places.

Advance to Victory: By 21 August Third Army held a 17-mile sector between Neuville Vitasse and Albert with VI, IV and V Corps.

Second Battles of the Somme: The army's left flank advanced towards Bapaume on 21 August and the right followed two days later as XVII Corps came under Third Army; a German withdrawal to the Canal du Nord began on 3 September. IV and V Corps crossed the canal on Third Army's right flank on 4 September.

Battles of the Hindenburg Line: Over the next two weeks Third Army pushed slowly beyond Havrincourt, finally breaking through the Hindenburg Line on 27 September. When XVII and VI Corps crossed the St Quentin Canal south of Cambrai, the Germans withdrew to the River Selle at Solesmes.

Final Advance in Picardy: IV Corps crossed the Selle on 20 October and Third Army followed up the German withdrawal towards Le Quesnoy. After a brief pause, XVII and VI Corps cleared the area south of Valenciennes before IV and V Corps moved through the Mormal Forest. Maubeuge was captured on 4 November and Third Army was across the Belgian border by the 11th.

FOURTH ARMY
1916

Formed on 5 February under General Sir Henry Rawlinson and took over Third Army's sector between the **River Somme** and **Hébuterne** a month later with XIII and X Corps. VIII and XV Corps joined the army during the spring as the sector extended north of the River Ancre.

Battle of the Somme: XV Corps captured Mametz and XIII Corps took Montauban on 1 July but the rest of the army suffered heavy losses in no man's land. Reserve Army took

Fourth Army's long-awaited attack on 1 July 1916 ended in disaster; 60,000 British troops were killed or wounded on the first day of the four and a half month Somme campaign. Men of 7th Division are silhouetted against the chalk lines marking the trenches covering Mametz. *(IWM Q87)*

over VIII and X Corps on 4 July as Fourth Army focussed its attentions on Bazentin Ridge. III Corps fought its way through La Boisselle and Contalmaison as XV Corps battled for Fricourt and Mametz Wood; XIII Corps cleared Bernafay and Trônes Woods.

XV Corps captured the Bazentin villages and XIII Corps reached Longueval in a night attack on 14 July but for the next two months piecemeal attacks on High Wood, Delville Wood, Ginchy and Guillemont failed to gain ground. XIV Corps took over the Ginchy sector on 16 August.

The deadlock was broken on 15 September as III Corps captured Martinpuich and XV Corps took Flers with the help of tanks; XIV Corps also made progress towards Lesboeufs. Ten days later XV Corps entered Gueudecourt while XV Corps reached Lesboeufs and Morval. Although Fourth Army continued to attack until 5 November it made little progress. It extended its line south to Rosières over the winter.

1917

German Withdrawal to the Hindenburg Line: The withdrawal began on 17 March and III Corps crossed the River Somme to occupy Péronne the following day; IV Corps crossed on the 20th. In the north XIV and XV Corps crossed the Canal du Nord and advanced to the St Quentin Canal north of St Quentin.

Fourth Army transferred to the **Flanders coast** on 21 June in the hope of exploiting a breakthrough at Ypres; it never came and the army took over responsibility for the Ypres Salient in November.

1918

General Rawlinson left on 21 February to represent Britain on the Supreme War Council in Versailles and General Sir William Birdwood held the post temporarily until General Plumer returned from Italy on 13 March; a few days later Fourth Army was renamed Second Army.

First Battles of the Somme: General Rawlinson formed a new Fourth Army on 2 April and took over Fifth Army's troops (XIX Corps) holding the line east of Amiens.

The Advance to Victory: Fourth Army initially held a 16-mile sector east of Amiens with the Canadian, the Australian and III Corps.

Battle of Amiens: The Australians and Canadians attacked on 8 August and by the 11th had advanced 15 miles east of Amiens.

Second Battles of the Somme: III Corps captured Albert on 22 August while the Australians advanced astride the River Somme. Six days later the Germans withdrew, allowing the right flank to advance to the river south of Péronne. The left followed up and III Corps crossed the Canal du Nord on 2 September. The Germans then fell back towards the Hindenburg Line north of St Quentin.

Battles of the Hindenburg Line: An attack on 29 September broke through the Hindenburg Line and IX Corps and the Australian Corps crossed the St Quentin Canal (with the help of American troops). XIII Corps took over the Vendhuile sector on 1 October and by the 6th the Beaurevoir Line had been cleared; the Germans then fell back to the River Selle south of Le Cateau as II American Corps joined the pursuit.

Final Advance in Picardy: IX and XIII Corps crossed the Selle on 17 October and reached the Sambre Canal on the 24th. IX Corps cleared the Mormal Forest on 4 November while XIII Corps crossed the canal; a general pursuit to the Belgian border followed.

RESERVE ARMY, FIFTH ARMY FROM 30 OCTOBER 1916

The Reserve Corps formed in April 1916 under Lieutenant-General Sir Hubert Gough and a month later it was expanded to an army headquarters behind the Somme front.

Battle of the Somme: Reserve Army took over Fourth Army's left flank on 4 July and, while VIII Corps held its positions astride the River Ancre, X Corps cleared Ovillers. At the end of July, I ANZAC Corps took over the Pozières sector while II Corps entered the Thiepval sector; XIV Corps held the north bank of the Ancre briefly before handing over to V Corps.

The Canadian Corps relieved the Australians at the beginning of September and captured Courcelette on 15 September with tanks; II Corps finally took Thiepval on the 26th. The Reserve Army made little progress across the Ancre Heights during October and, as II Corps took over the Courcelette sector, Reserve Army was renamed Fifth Army on the 30th. A final attack by V Corps on 13 November cleared Beaumont-Hamel and Beaucourt.

1917

Operations on the Ancre: The Germans started a slow withdrawal from the Ancre on 17 February and by the 28th Fifth Army was close to Bapaume.

German Withdrawal to the Hindenburg Line: The withdrawal began in earnest on 17 March and over the next few days II Corps, V Corps and I ANZAC Corps moved up to the Hindenburg Line on either side of Bullecourt. I ANZAC Corps repulsed an attack on Lagnicourt on 15 April.

Battle of Bullecourt: V Corps and I ANZAC Corps were engaged in the village during 3–17 May; they continued to make limited attacks against the Hindenburg Line until the end of the month.

Third Battle of Ypres: On 31 July XIV Corps advanced towards Langemarck, XVIII Corps attacked through St Julien, XIX Corps moved towards Zonnebeke and II Corps advanced towards Gheluvelt. Poor weather stalled the advance and, although Langemarck fell on 16 August, little progress was made elsewhere. Second Army took over the principal role in the campaign at the end of August, leaving Fifth Army holding a line between Langemarck and Westhoek.

V Corps took over XIX Corps' sector at the beginning of September and advanced towards Poelcapelle and Zonnebeke on the 20th; V Corps reached Zonnebeke on 26 September while Poelcapelle fell to XVIII Corps on 4 October. The Germans soon withdrew towards Houthulst Forest and Fifth Army's campaign ended on 12 October; it transferred to the Somme in November and took over the front south of Cambrai.

1918

The army's front was extended south to the River Oise in February.

Battles of the Somme: The German attack on 21 March overran XIX and XVIII Corps north of St Quentin and forced III Corps to retire behind the Crozat Canal. Fifth Army fell back

Two Highlanders dash through ruins on the look-out for snipers during Fifth Army's chaotic retreat across the Somme in March 1918. *(IWM Q10915)*

across the Somme Canal and III Corps retired across the River Oise, becoming separated from the rest of the army. The Germans crossed the Somme Canal in XVIII Corps' sector and Fifth Army fell back in disarray along the south bank of the river towards Villers-Bretonneux.

General Sir Henry Rawlinson replaced Gough at the end of March and the command was renamed Fourth Army. A new Fifth Army was formed under General Sir William Birdwood on 23 May and it took over the XI and XIII Corps' sectors north of Béthune, on First Army's left flank, on 1 July.

Advance in Artois and in Flanders: The two corps followed up the German withdrawal across the Lys Plain starting on 18 August, reaching a line between Fleurbaix and Loos by 6 September. Fifth Army took command of I Corps astride the La Bassée Canal at the end of the advance.

Final Advance in Artois: Followed up the German withdrawal towards the Haute Deule Canal, crossing on the 15th; Lille fell two days later. Fifth Army advanced quickly to the River

Schelde, reaching it on 21 October. Troops crossed the river on 9 November, clearing Tournai and Antoing before pushing east to Ath on the River Dendre.

THE CORPS

Corps (or to give them their full title army corps) were a new level of command for the British Army, introduced in August 1914 to correspond with French Army methods. To begin with each corps had 2 divisions but the corps developed into an elastic formation, with the number of divisions changing. It had four roles:

ASSAULTING THE ENEMY LINE

Each corps would control a sector of the front around 3 miles long and carry out the long-term planning of operations. Typically a corps had 2 or 3 divisions in the front line and 1 or 2 in reserve.

HOLDING THE LINE

The length of a sector varied from 5 to 15 miles.

SUPERVISING AN ARMY'S REAR

Each army had one or two corps in reserve during offensive operations, marshalling divisions into the battle zone.

TRAINING AND CONSTRUCTION

Several corps supervised units working on lines of communication and defensive lines during 1918. One corps ran training schools for conscripts and the US Army.

Corps operating in the Mediterranean were smaller and usually reported directly to the theatre GHQ; in some cases they were the highest level of command in a theatre.

COMMAND AND STAFF

There was the cadre of staff for 1 corps at Aldershot but the rest of the staff for the 2 corps initially established (and the many others formed later) had to be assembled from scratch.

A howitzer crew wait for orders under their camouflage netting; they have a large stock of shells ready to fire at the German positions. *(IWM Q6460)*

Each corps was usually commanded by a lieutenant-general. He reported directly to GHQ to begin with and to the relevant army after December 1914 when this level of command was introduced. Headquarters staff began with 18 officers and 71 other ranks, expanding to 50 officers and 141 other ranks by 1918.

The four branches were represented by four senior officers with the following roles:

Brigadier-General General Staff: Planned operations and assessed intelligence.
Deputy Adjutant and Quartermaster General: Dealt with logistics.
Brigadier-General Royal Artillery: Coordinated the artillery batteries.
Chief Engineer: Supervised fortifications and infrastructure.

A **Commander of Corps Heavy Artillery** was added in the spring of 1916 and took command of the medium and heavy batteries.

Supporting services were organized in three departments:

Assistant Director Signals: Maintained communications.
Deputy Director Medical Services: Organized casualty clearing stations.
Assistant Director Veterinary Services: Supervised facilities for the horses.

Corps were identified by Roman numerals and the number on the Western Front peaked at 21 in 1917, including 2 ANZAC and 1 Canadian (an Indian corps also served in France throughout 1915); other corps controlled operations in the Mediterranean.

A corps rarely moved and it was the lowest

level of command concerned with the long-term conduct of a campaign or defensive measures in its sector. The staff would become familiar with their area, briefing divisions as they rotated through it.

CORPS TROOPS

Corps troops consisted of a signals cable section in 1914 but they expanded to over 2,000 men by the end of the war as the role of the corps increased. By 1918 a corps commander could expect to have the following units working directly for his staff:

CORPS ARTILLERY TROOPS

Medium and heavy artillery brigades operating under corps control were organized into heavy artillery groups led by the Commander of Corps Heavy Artillery, after the spring of 1916. Shells were stored at the corps ammunition parks and 3 ammunition columns kept the batteries stocked. A motor transport company kept the vehicles moving and 2 mobile ordnance workshops serviced the batteries.

CORPS ENGINEER TROOPS

The signals section was expanded to a company as the front line stabilized and, while the air-line section erected overhead lines, several cable sections installed underground lines. The tunnelling companies operating in the corps' sector reported to the corps' chief engineer. Army troops companies and an area employment company supervised labourers working in the corps' area.

SECURITY

A cavalry regiment and a cyclist battalion maintained security in the corps' area.

SPECIALIST TROOPS

A battery of motor machine guns and a battery of heavy trench mortars could be deployed if necessary.

AERIAL OBSERVATION

A detachment of the Royal Flying Corps was attached to each corps headquarters for observation duties.

CORPS OPERATION ORDERS

Each corps was responsible for planning operations in its sector, briefing divisions as they moved up to the front line. Corps' orders identified the overall objectives of an attack and described each division's role, outlining objectives and providing marked-up maps (showing objectives, trenches, villages and enemy positions). They would provide the schedule for the artillery's preliminary bombardment and the timetable for the infantry and the artillery. After the summer of 1915 corps headquarters took responsibility for the medium and heavy artillery, later extending this control to all artillery. Arrangements for communications were detailed and reserves would be identified along with arrangements for moving them forward to relieve the assault troops.

CORPS INSIGNIA

The standard corps insignia was a red-white-red brassard (armlet) but corps also adopted recognizable insignia for their vehicles and shoulder patches for the men:

Cavalry Corps: Female head wearing a hat; later changed to St George and the Dragon.
I Corps: Monogram A1.
II Corps: Corps armlet, red-white-red, with a six-pointed star.
III Corps: Equilateral triangle with red, white and black sides (the racing colours of General Pulteney, the first commander).
IV Corps: Corps armlet with the number 4 in the centre (numbers were later banned and it was covered with a black patch).
V Corps: White five-pointed star.
VI Corps: British bulldog.
VII Corps: Polar bear and the seven stars of *Ursa major.*
VIII Corps: Hunter's horn (after General Hunter-Weston).
IX Corps: Bow and arrow (from General Hamilton-Gordon's crest).
X Corps: An unadorned red-white-red brassard.
XI Corps: Gold eleven-pointed star adorned with a red circle and white cross.

XII Corps: No corps symbol, deployed in Macedonia.

XIII Corps: Double horseshoes placed back-to-back, one white and one red.

XIV Corps: Blue and white chequerboard (signal code flag for the letter N, 14th in the alphabet).

XV Corps: Letter Y drawn to resemble three Vs (totalling 15 in Roman numerals).

XVI Corps: No corps symbol, deployed in Macedonia.

XVII Corps: Rectangle with green on top and white below.

XVIII Corps: Letter M and crossed axes (a pun on General Maxse's name).

XIX Corps: Three question marks (a pun on General Watts's name).

XX Corps: A pyramid with a scarab at its base (served in Palestine).

XXI Corps: Four-leaved shamrock (veins on three leaves shaped as VII, a total of 21).

XXII Corps: A foxhound.

OTHER THEATRES

EGYPT

The British Army was dependent on the Suez Canal as the supply route to India and Mesopotamia. From October 1912 Major-General Julian Byng had led the troops protecting the waterway: a small force of 4 infantry battalions, a cavalry regiment and 2 artillery batteries.

The Egyptian Camel Corps took over the canal defences at the end of August 1914 when the Regular Army garrison battalions returned home and Lieutenant-General Sir John Maxwell took over as an Indian infantry brigade joined. The arrival of the East Lancashire Division a month later secured the canal.

General Sir Charles Monro took command of the **British Force in Egypt** on 27 October 1914 as diplomatic relations were severed with Turkey; war was declared eight days later. When more Indian troops arrived, they were organized into the 10th and 11th Divisions and an Australian and New Zealand contingent arrived in December.

Over the next 12 months Turkish attacks failed to threaten the waterway and General Sir Archibald Murray took over as GOC in January 1916 when troops returned from Gallipoli. He reorganized the Mediterranean Expeditionary Force and British Force in Egypt into the **Egyptian Expeditionary Force** on 20 March. Two months later Murray formed the **Western Frontier Force** to crush Senussi uprisings in the Western Desert. It was renamed the **Delta and Western Force** on 6 March 1917 and disbanded on 21 March 1918.

In October 1916 Murray withdrew his headquarters to Cairo, leaving Lieutenant-General Sir Charles Dobell in command of **Eastern Force** east of the Suez Canal. He then began organizing logistical support for future operations into Palestine, building a railway and water pipeline; the **Desert Column** under Lieutenant-General Sir Philip Chetwode protected the work.

GALLIPOLI

The **Mediterranean Expeditionary Force** formed on 11 March 1915 under General Sir Ian Hamilton and over the weeks that followed troops assembled on the islands of Lemnos and Mudros. The Gallipoli landings began on 25 April at Helles, at the southern tip of the peninsula, and at Anzac Cove on the west coast. Part of the Royal Naval Division made a demonstration in the Gulf of Saros to the north to pin down reserves while French troops landed at Kum Kale on the opposite side of the Gallipoli straits.

Battle of Helles: 29th Division led VIII Corps' attack and pushed 3 miles inland alongside French troops, linking all of its landing beaches by 28 April. Another attack on 6 May captured the Turkish front line covering Krithia but further attacks failed to make headway.

Battles of Anzac: 1st Australian Division and the New Zealand and Australian Division pushed inland onto the mountains but were unable to cross the peninsula. A stalemate followed and costly attacks in May and June were unable to break the deadlock.

Battles of Suvla: IX Corps landed north of

Anzac on 6 August and although 10th (Irish) and 11th (Northern) Divisions captured the high ground overlooking the bay, they were unable to link up with the Anzac beachhead. Attacks against Chocolate Hill, Scimitar Hill and W Hills in August failed to break the deadlock and attempts to take Sari Bair, Lone Pine and Russell's Top overlooking Anzac Cove were also unsuccessful.

Lieutenant-General Sir William Birdwood took over as temporary commander on 17 October and he was replaced by General Sir Charles Monro ten days later; Monro took command of all forces in the Eastern Mediterranean on 23 November, including Egypt, Salonika and Gallipoli. The forces on Gallipoli were renamed the **Dardanelles Army** under the command of General Birdwood.

The Evacuation: As the weather deteriorated, the War Cabinet decided to abandon the Dardanelles campaign and withdraw troops to Egypt. Troops left Anzac and Suvla beachheads with minimum interference on the night of 19 December and Helles was evacuated on the night of 7 January 1916 bringing the campaign to a close and, with it, the end of the Dardanelles Army.

PALESTINE

When Lloyd George took over as Prime Minister in December 1916, he immediately looked for results in the Mediterranean. The Australian and New Zealand Mounted Division began by driving the Turks back over the Palestine border, paving the way for an invasion.

Although General Murray was ready to invade Palestine at the start of 1917, he was ordered to suspend operations to allow troops to be withdrawn for the Arras offensive on the Western Front. Sensing that an early success might rout the Turks, he attacked Gaza and Beersheba with the troops to hand.

Gaza: The first assault on the Gaza position on 26 March 1917 was driven back by Turkish counter-attacks and a second attack east of the town on 19 April also failed. General Sir Edmund Allenby took command at the end of June and disbanded the Desert Column and

Machine-gunners keep a look-out along the Suez Canal during the long stand-off with the Turks. *(IWM Q24276)*

the Eastern Force to concentrate on the invasion of Palestine.

A third attack on Gaza was launched on 28 October and the Desert Mounted Corps attacked Beersheba on the inland railway. With the help of a naval bombardment, Gaza fell on 6 November and within days the Egyptian Expeditionary Force had advanced over 30 miles.

Jerusalem and Jericho: On 17 November Allenby turned his attentions inland to Jerusalem, capturing it on 9 December; Jericho was taken on 21 February 1918.

Battle of Megiddo: The final offensive in Palestine began on 19 September 1918. XXI Corps broke through the Turkish lines on the coast north of Jaffa and mounted troops advanced inland, reaching Haifa and Nazareth, over 50 miles away, a few days later. Meanwhile, the Arab Northern Army harried Turkish troops, raiding the Damascus railway.

Damascus fell on 1 October and over the next four weeks mounted troops, again aided by the Arabs, pursued the Turkish Army as it fell back towards Aleppo. The town was occupied on 26 October and the armistice with Turkey came into force five days later.

Gallipoli. Men of the 2nd Royal Naval Brigade practise an attack on the island of Imbros in June 1915. The real attempts to advance on Helles ended with high casualties and failure. *(IWM Q13324)*

BRITISH SALONIKA ARMY

10th (Irish) Division reached Salonika in October 1915 and sent a mobile force to Lake Dojran to pave the way for the invasion of Serbia. Lord Kitchener placed General Sir Charles Monro in command on 4 November but the War Office did not recognize the arrangement and continued to communicate with 10th Division's commander. Lieutenant-General Sir Bryan Mahon replaced Monro on 15 November and formed a new army headquarters with XII Corps' staff. Three weeks later 10th Division was forced to retire to Dojran, leaving many prisoners in enemy hands.

XVI Corps reached Salonika in January 1916 and dug in on either side of Lake Dojran. Lieutenant-General George Milne replaced Mahon on 9 May but attempts to capture positions at Horseshoe Hill in August and Machukovo a month later failed. A series of attacks in the Struma Valley started on 30 September, and the Karajaköis hills, Mazirko and Yeniköi were taken over the next few days. Bairakli Jum'a fell at the end of October but

attacks on Tumbitza Farm, south-east of Serres, in November and December failed.

XII Corps attacked Bulgarian positions south and south-west of Dojran on the night of 24 April 1917; no trenches were held and a repeat attack on the night of 8 May also failed. Ferdie and Essex Trenches near Bairakli Jum'a were taken in May and Homondos, Bairakli and Kumli were captured in October. A year-long stalemate followed.

XVI Corps' final assault on the Salonika front began on 18 September 1918 and within days the Bulgarians were falling back towards the Strumica Valley. British troops crossed the Serbia–Bulgaria border on 25 September and an armistice was declared five days later.

BRITISH FORCE IN ITALY

After the Austro-German offensive broke through the Italian positions in the Julian Alps on 24 October 1917, French and British troops were sent to shore up the line and XIV Corps' headquarters opened at Pavia on 6 November 1917. General Sir Herbert Plumer assumed command of the **British Force in Italy**, reporting to the Italian Commando Supremo. XIV Corps took over the Montello sector on the Piave front at the beginning of December and a month later XI Corps reached the Arcade sector.

The crisis in Italy had passed by March 1918 and XI Corps was recalled to France. XIV Corps moved to the Asiago Plateau on the Piave front where it was renamed **British Forces in Italy** under General the Earl of Cavan.

Battle of the Piave: British troops held off an attack on the Asiago Plateau on 15 June.

Cavan became the leader of a new Italian **Tenth Army**, comprising XIV Corps and Italian XI Corps on 9 October.

Battle of Vittorio Veneto: The final offensive in Italy began on 24 October and British troops reached the River Piave two days later. The River Tagliamento was crossed on 3 November and the armistice with Austria was declared the following day.

MESOPOTAMIA

The discovery of oil by the Anglo-Persian Oil Company (British Petroleum) in 1908 had made the Persian Gulf important to the Royal Navy which was beginning to change from coal-fired to oil-fired engines for its ships. British warships moved into the Gulf on the outbreak of war to protect the oil installations, raising Turkish protests. At the beginning of October 1914 a brigade from the 6th (Poona) Indian Division landed and occupied Abandan, repulsing Turkish attacks against the Ahwaz oil field before driving them out of Basra and up the River Tigris.

The Gulf was secure but the 6th Indian Division was over-stretched and facing a strong Turkish force including local Arabs. 12th Indian Division arrived in April 1915, and after securing Basra headed up the Tigris through Amara towards Kut al Amara, plagued as it went by bad weather and sickness.

On 28 September Major-General Charles Townshend's force captured Kut and moved up the river, finding the Turks entrenched at Ctesiphon, 20 miles south of Baghdad. An attack on 22 November failed to break the

Salonika. A mule carries two Argyll and Sutherland Highlanders down a mountain road. *(IWM Q31798)*

Turkish lines and 6th Indian Division fell back to Kut where 15,000 troops and followers were surrounded.

Although Turkish attacks at the end of the year were beaten off, Townshend's men could not raise the siege. Lieutenant-General Sir Fenton Aylmer, India's Adjutant-General, was sent to Mesopotamia to command a new Tigris Corps forming with 2 Indian divisions, ready to advance to relieve Kut.

The first attempt started on 4 January 1916 but once again bad weather and sickness delayed the advance, forcing Aylmer to wait for the 13th (Western) Division. With only enough food to last until the middle of April, time was running out for Townshend. As rains flooded the Tigris valley, the relief attempt started on 7 March but, although Hanna and Fallahiya had been taken by 5 April, the advance was stopped at Sanniyat, 10 miles short of Kut. Major-General Sir Frederick Gorringe replaced Aylmer in command for the final attack on 22 April but when it failed the garrison capitulated, leaving over 13,000 soldiers and followers in Turkish hands.

Mesopotamia. A Lewis gun section of the 7th Staffordshires engages Turkish troops in the open during 13th (Western) Division's advance on Baghdad. *(IWM Q24670)*

Major-General Stanley Maude took over from Gorringe in July and, although he was ordered to protect the oil pipelines, was intent on avenging the loss of the Kut. He divided the Tigris Corps into I and III Indian Corps, and his troops advanced up the Tigris on 13 December. After a prolonged fight his men bridged the river north of the town on 24 February 1917, forcing the Turks to withdraw towards Baghdad with cavalry and gunboats in pursuit. They crossed the River Diyala east of the city, entering the capital on 11 March.

Maude sent columns up the Rivers Tigris and Diyala to secure his position but by April the campaign had been relegated to a secondary role as attention turned to Palestine. Maude died of cholera in November 1917; Major-General Sir William Marshall took his place.

A year later columns again headed north along the Tigris and Diyala, coordinating with the advance in Palestine. The armistice with Turkey was announced on 31 October 1918.

Allied casualties during the four-year campaign in Mesopotamia were 92,500 men; many had succumbed to the variety of diseases rife in the area.

GERMAN EAST AFRICA

Three battalions of the King's African Rifles were spread across East Africa, Uganda, and Nyasaland in August 1914. Three Indian brigades joined them but attempts to capture Tanga failed. A brief stalemate followed as the British-led forces were compelled to deploy to protect the Uganda Railway.

Two infantry brigades and a mounted brigade were raised in the Nairobi area and grouped together as the Magadi Division at the end of the year. It was renamed the 1st East African Division and advanced into northern German East Africa.

After a disappointing campaign the South African troops were withdrawn in March 1916 and the remaining British, Indian and African troops headed once more towards Kilimanjaro in 3 columns in May 1916. Again the result was inconclusive. Although 1,500 German troops had been rounded up by November 1917 the remainder fought on. As sickness took its toll, African troops took over the lion's share of the fighting. Eventually 22 King's African Rifles battalions were raised. The final pockets of German troops surrendered after the Armistice.

CHAPTER FOUR

ARMS, CORPS AND REGIMENTS

ARMS OF THE SERVICE

The branches of the Army were called the Arms of the Service and the fighting branches were collectively known as 'The Arms'. The administrative branches were known as 'The Services'. Together these had the following order of precedence:

THE ARMS

Household Cavalry
Royal Horse Artillery
Line cavalry
Yeomanry and Special Reserve cavalry
Royal Field Artillery
Royal Garrison Artillery
Royal Engineers
Foot Guards
Line infantry regiments

THE SERVICES

Army Service Corps
Army Ordnance Corps
Royal Army Medical Corps
Army Veterinary Corps
Army Pay Corps
Military Provost Staff Corps
Intelligence Corps
Army Chaplains Department

PRECEDENCE

In detail the regimental order of precedence was:

MOUNTED TROOPS

1st Life Guards
2nd Life Guards
Royal Horse Guards (The Blues)

Royal Horse Artillery

1st (King's) Dragoon Guards
2nd Dragoon Guards (Queen's Bays)
3rd (Prince of Wales's) Dragoon Guards
4th (Royal Irish) Dragoon Guards
5th (Princess Charlotte of Wales's) Dragoon
  Guards
6th Dragoon Guards (Carabiniers)
7th (The Princess Royal's) Regiment of
  Dragoon Guards
1st (Royal) Dragoons
2nd Dragoons (Royal Scots Greys)
3rd (King's Own) Hussars
4th (Queen's Own) Hussars
6th (Inniskilling) Dragoons
7th (Queen's Own) Hussars
8th (The King's Royal Irish) Hussars
9th (Queen's Royal) Lancers
10th (Prince of Wales's Own Royal) Hussars
11th (Prince Albert's Own) Hussars
12th (Prince of Wales's Royal) Lancers
13th Hussars
14th (King's) Hussars
15th (The King's) Hussars
16th (The Queen's) Lancers
17th (Duke of Cambridge's Own) Lancers
5th (Royal Irish) Lancers
18th (Queen Mary's Own) Hussars

19th (Queen Alexandra's Own Royal) Hussars
20th Hussars
21st (Empress of India's) Lancers

Badges of the cavalry regiments are shown on pages 71–3.

YEOMANRY REGIMENTS

Yeomanry regiments saw active service on the Western Front and at Gallipoli and Salonika, usually in a dismounted role. They were useful in Egypt and Palestine where there was scope for mounted operations. In 1918 some regiments were converted into infantry or machine-gun units.

Wiltshire
Warwickshire
Yorkshire Hussars
Nottinghamshire
Staffordshire
Shropshire
Ayrshire
Cheshire
Yorkshire Dragoons
Leicestershire
North Somerset
Duke of Lancaster's Own
Lanarkshire
Northumberland
South Nottinghamshire Hussars
Denbighshire
Westmoreland and Cumberland
Pembroke
Royal East Kent
Hampshire
Buckinghamshire
Derbyshire
Dorset
Gloucestershire
Hertfordshire
Berkshire
1st County of London
Royal 1st Devonshire
Suffolk
Royal North Devon
Worcestershire
West Kent
West Somerset

Oxfordshire
Montgomeryshire
Lothians and Border
Lanarkshire
Lancashire Hussars
Surrey
Fife and Forfar
Norfolk
Sussex
Glamorgan
Welsh Horse
Lincolnshire
City of London (Rough Riders)
2nd County of London (Westminster Dragoons)
3rd County of London (Sharpshooters)
Bedfordshire
Essex
Northamptonshire
East Riding of Yorkshire
1st Lovat's Scouts
2nd Lovat's Scouts
Scottish Horse

SPECIAL RESERVE CAVALRY

The regiments of the Special Reserve were irregular units that were among the first to join the Regular army in France.

North Irish Horse
South Irish Horse
King Edward's Horse

INFANTRY REGIMENTS

The order of precedence of the infantry regiments and the number of battalions each raised in the course of the war in the various categories (Regular, Territorial, Service, etc.) are shown in the table on pages 74–9. The table includes the Welsh Guards, first formed in 1915.

Badges of the infantry regiments are shown on pages 80–6.

ARTILLERY, ENGINEERS, NEW CORPS AND SUPPORT SERVICES

Badges and further details of these corps are given in Chapters Six and Seven.

1st Life Guards

2nd Life Guards

Royal Horse Guards
(The Blues)

1st (King's) Dragoon Guards

2nd Dragoon Guards
(Queen's Bays)

3rd (Prince of Wales's)
Dragoon Guards

4th (Royal Irish) Dragoon
Guards

5th (Princess Charlotte of
Wales's) Dragoon Guards

6th Dragoon Guards
(Carabiniers)

7th (The Princess Royal's)
Dragoon Guards

1st (Royal) Dragoons

2nd Dragoons
(Royal Scots Greys)

3rd (King's Own) Hussars

4th (Queen's Own) Hussars

5th (Royal Irish) Lancers

6th (Inniskilling) Dragoons

7th (Queen's Own) Hussars

8th (The King's Royal Irish) Hussars

9th (Queen's Royal) Lancers

10th (Prince of Wales's Own Royal) Hussars

11th (Prince Albert's Own) Hussars

12th (Prince of Wales's Royal) Lancers

13th Hussars

14th (King's) Hussars

15th (The King's) Hussars   16th (The Queen's) Lancers   17th (Duke of Cambridge's Own) Lancers   18th (Queen Mary's Own) Hussars

19th (Queen Alexandra's Own) Hussars   20th Hussars   21st (Empress of India's) Lancers

INFANTRY REGIMENTS

In precedence order	Recruiting area
The Grenadier Guards	Based at Wellington Barracks, London
The Coldstream Guards	Based at Chelsea Barracks, London
The Scots Guards	Based at Tower of London
The Irish Guards	Based at Wellington Barracks, London
The Welsh Guards	Based at White City, London
The Royal Scots (Lothian Regiment)	Edinburgh and Lothian
The Queen's (Royal West Surrey) Regiment	Guildford and Croydon, Surrey
The Buffs (East Kent Regiment)	East Kent
The King's Own (Royal Lancaster Regiment)	North Lancashire
The Northumberland Fusiliers	Newcastle and Northumberland
The Royal Warwickshire Regiment	Warwickshire and Birmingham
The Royal Fusiliers (City of London Regiment)	London area
The King's (Liverpool Regiment)	Liverpool area
The Norfolk Regiment	Norfolk
The Lincolnshire Regiment	Lincolnshire
The Devonshire Regiment	Devonshire
The Suffolk Regiment	Suffolk
Prince Albert's (Somerset Light Infantry)	Somerset
The Prince of Wales's Own (West Yorkshire Regiment)	York, Leeds and Bradford
The East Yorkshire Regiment	East Riding of Yorkshire
The Bedfordshire Regiment	Bedfordshire
The Leicestershire Regiment	Leicestershire
The Royal Irish Regiment	Tipperary and Kilkenny
Alexandra, Princess of Wales's Own (Yorkshire Regiment)	North Riding of Yorkshire
The Lancashire Fusiliers	Southeast Lancashire
The Royal Scots Fusiliers	Ayrshire
The Cheshire Regiment	Cheshire, Stockport, Wirral
The Royal Welsh Fusiliers	Caernarfon and Denbigh
The South Wales Borderers	Brecknockshire
The King's Own Scottish Borderers	Dumfries, Selkirk and Berwick
The Cameronians (Scottish Rifles)	Glasgow and Lanark
The Royal Inniskilling Fusiliers	Tyrone, Derry, Donegal, Fermanagh
The Gloucestershire Regiment	Gloucestershire
The Worcestershire Regiment	Worcestershire
The East Lancashire Regiment	Preston, Burnley and Blackburn
The East Surrey Regiment	East Surrey

Regular	Reserve	Extra Reserve	Territorial	2nd Line	3rd Line	4th Line	Service	Service Reserve	Home Service
4	1	—	—	—	—	—	—	—	—
4	1	—	—	—	—	—	—	—	—
2	1	—	—	—	—	—	—	—	—
2	1	—	—	—	—	—	—	—	—
1	1	—	—	—	—	—	—	—	—
2	1	—	7	7	6	—	6	2	1
2	1	—	2	2	2	1	5	2	1
2	1	—	2	2	2	—	3	1	1
2	1	—	2	2	2	—	5	1	—
2	1	—	4	4	4	—	19	8	1
2	1	—	4	4	4	—	6	3	—
4	2	1	—	—	—	—	18	10	—
2	1	1	6	6	6	—	8	4	1
2	1	—	3	3	3	—	3	1	—
2	1	—	2	2	2	—	4	2	1
2	1	—	4	4	4	—	3	1	—
2	1	—	3	3	3	—	5	2	—
2	1	—	2	2	2	—	3	1	2
2	1	1	4	4	4	—	9	4	—
2	1	—	1	1	1	—	7	3	1
2	1	—	1	1	1	—	3	2	—
2	1	—	2	2	2	—	6	2	—
2	1	1	—	—	—	—	1	—	—
2	1	—	2	2	2	—	7	3	1
2	1	1	4	4	4	—	11	3	—
2	1	—	2	2	2	—	3	1	1
2	1	—	4	4	4	—	8	2	—
2	1	—	4	4	4	—	11	5	—
2	1	—	1	1	1	—	9	2	—
2	1	—	2	2	2	—	4	2	—
2	1	1	4	4	4	—	5	1	—
2	1	1	—	—	—	—	8	1	—
2	1	—	3	3	3	—	8	3	—
4	1	—	2	2	2	—	5	2	—
2	1	—	2	2	2	—	6	2	—
2	1	1	2	2	2	—	5	3	—

	Recruiting area
The Duke of Cornwall's Light Infantry	Cornwall
The Duke of Wellington's (West Riding Regiment)	West of Yorkshire's West Riding
The Border Regiment	Cumberland
The Royal Sussex Regiment	Sussex
The Hampshire Regiment	Hampshire and Isle of Wight
The South Staffordshire Regiment	South Staffordshire
The Dorsetshire Regiment	Dorset
The Prince of Wales's Volunteers (South Lancashire Regiment)	South Lancashire
The Welsh Regiment	Glamorgan and Carmarthen
The Black Watch (Royal Highlanders)	Perth, Angus and Fife
The Oxfordshire & Buckinghamshire Light Infantry	Oxfordshire and Buckinghamshire
The Essex Regiment	Essex
The Sherwood Foresters (Nottinghamshire and Derbyshire Regiment)	Nottinghamshire and Derbyshire
The Loyal North Lancashire Regiment	Preston and Bolton areas
The Northamptonshire Regiment	Northamptonshire
Princess Charlotte of Wales's (Royal Berkshire Regiment)	Berkshire
The Queen's Own (Royal West Kent Regiment)	Western half of Kent
The King's Own (Yorkshire Light Infantry)	East of Yorkshire's West Riding
The King's (Shropshire Light Infantry)	Shropshire
The Duke of Cambridge's Own (Middlesex Regiment)	Middlesex
The King's Royal Rifle Corps	Based in the Winchester area
The Duke of Edinburgh's (Wiltshire Regiment)	Wiltshire Regiment
The Manchester Regiment	Manchester area
The Prince of Wales's (North Staffordshire Regiment)	North Staffordshire
The York and Lancaster Regiment	Sheffield, Barnsley, Rotherham
The Durham Light Infantry	Newcastle and Durham
The Highland Light Infantry	Glasgow and Lanark
The Seaforth Highlanders (Ross-shire Buffs, the Duke of Albany's)	Sutherland, Caithness, Morayshire, Ross, Cromarty
The Gordon Highlanders	Aberdeen, Banff, Kincardine, Shetland Isles
The Queen's Own Cameron Highlanders	Inverness
The Royal Irish Rifles	Belfast, Counties Antrim and Down
The Princess Victoria's (Royal Irish Fusiliers)	Belfast, Counties Antrim, Armagh and Down
The Connaught Rangers	County Mayo and County Galway
Princess Louise's (Argyll and Sutherland Highlanders)	Stirling, Dumbarton and Renfrew

Regular	Reserve	Extra Reserve	Territorial	2nd Line	3rd Line	4th Line	Service	Service Reserve	Home Service
2	1	—	2	2	2	—	4	2	—
2	1	—	4	4	4	—	5	1	—
2	1	—	2	2	2	—	5	2	—
2	1	—	3	3	3	—	7	2	—
2	1	—	6	6	6	—	5	2	1
2	1	1	2	2	2	—	3	2	—
2	1	—	2	2	2	—	2	1	1
2	1	—	2	2	2	—	6	2	—
2	1	—	4	4	4	—	12	4	—
2	1	—	4	4	4	—	3	1	—
2	1	—	2	2	2	—	4	1	—
2	1	—	5	5	5	—	4	2	1
2	1	1	4	4	4	—	8	3	—
2	1	—	3	3	3	—	6	1	1
2	1	—	1	1	1	—	3	1	—
2	1	—	1	1	1	—	4	1	1
2	1	—	2	2	2	—	5	2	1
2	1	—	2	2	2	—	7	2	1
2	1	—	1	1	1	—	4	1	—
4	2	—	4	4	4	—	12	6	—
4	2	—	—	—	—	—	13	6	—
2	1	—	1	1	1	—	4	1	—
2	1	1	6	6	6	—	12	4	—
2	1	1	2	2	2	—	3	2	—
2	1	—	2	2	2	—	9	2	—
2	1	1	5	5	5	—	11	4	1
2	1	1	5	5	5	—	8	3	—
2	1	—	3	3	3	—	3	1	—
2	1	—	4	4	4	—	5	2	—
2	1	—	1	1	1	—	4	1	1
2	1	2	—	—	—	—	11	4	—
2	1	1	—	—	—	—	6	1	—
2	1	1	—	—	—	—	2	—	—
2	1	1	—	—	—	—	4	2	—

	Recruiting area
The Prince of Wales's Leinster Regiment (Royal Canadians)	Leinster
The Royal Munster Fusiliers	Counties Cork, Kerry and Limerick
The Royal Dublin Fusiliers	Dublin and County Kildare
The Prince Consort's Own (Rifle Brigade)	Based at Winchester
The Honourable Artillery Company	
The Monmouthshire Regiment	Monmouthshire
The Cambridgeshire Regiment	Cambridgeshire
The Herefordshire Regiment	Herefordshire
The Hertfordshire Regiment	Hertfordshire
The London Regiment	London area

Regular	Reserve	Extra Reserve	Territorial	2nd Line	3rd Line	4th Line	Service	Service Reserve	Home Service
2	1	2	—	—	—	—	2	—	—
2	1	2	—	—	—	—	4	—	1
2	1	2	—	—	—	—	5	1	—
4	2	—	—	—	—	—	11	3	—
—	—	—	1	1	1	—	—	—	—
—	—	—	1	1	1	—	—	—	1
—	—	—	1	—	—	—	—	—	—
—	—	—	1	—	—	—	—	—	—
—	—	—	1	—	—	—	—	—	—
—	—	—	26	26	26	4	—	19	6

The Grenadier Guards

The Coldstream Guards

The Scots Guards

The Irish Guards

The Welsh Guards

The Royal Scots
(Lothian Regiment)

The Queen's (Royal West
Surrey) Regiment

The Buffs
(East Kent Regiment)

The King's Own (Royal
Lancaster Regiment)

The Northumberland
Fusiliers

The Royal Warwickshire
Regiment

The Royal Fusiliers
(City of London Regiment)

The King's (Liverpool Regiment)

The Norfolk Regiment

The Lincolnshire Regiment

The Devonshire Regiment

The Suffolk Regiment

Prince Albert's (Somerset Light Infantry)

The Prince of Wales's Own (West Yorkshire Regiment)

The East Yorkshire Regiment

The Bedfordshire Regiment

The Leicestershire Regiment

The Royal Irish Regiment

Alexandra Princess of Wales's Own (Yorkshire Regiment)

The Lancashire Fusiliers

The Royal Scots Fusiliers

The Cheshire Regiment

The Royal Welsh Fusiliers

The South Wales Borderers

The King's Own Scottish
Borderers

The Cameronians
(Scottish Rifles)

The Royal Inniskilling
Fusiliers

The Gloucestershire
Regiment

The Worcestershire
Regiment

The East Lancashire
Regiment

The East Surrey Regiment

The Duke of Cornwall's
Light Infantry

The Duke of Wellington's
(West Riding Regiment)

The Border Regiment

The Royal Sussex Regiment

The Hampshire Regiment

The South Staffordshire
Regiment

The Dorsetshire Regiment

The Prince of Wales's V'teers
(South Lancashire Regiment)

The Welsh Regiment

The Black Watch
(Royal Highlanders)

The Oxfordshire &
Buckinghamshire Light
Infantry

The Essex Regiment

The Sherwood Foresters
(Notts and Derby Regiment)

The Loyal North Lancashire
Regiment

The Northamptonshire
Regiment

Princess Charlotte of Wales's
(Royal Berkshire Regiment)

The Queen's Own
(Royal West Kent Regiment)

The King's Own
(Yorkshire Light Infantry)

The King's
(Shropshire Light Infantry)

The Duke of Cambridge's
Own (Middlesex Regiment)

The King's Royal Rifle Corps

The Duke of Edinburgh's
(Wiltshire Regiment)

The Manchester Regiment

The Prince of Wales's (North
Staffordshire Regiment)

The York and Lancaster
Regiment

The Durham Light Infantry

The Highland Light Infantry

The Seaforth Highlanders

The Gordon Highlanders

The Queen's Own Cameron
Highlanders

The Royal Irish Rifles

The Princess Victoria's
(Royal Irish Fusiliers)

The Connaught Rangers

Princess Louise's (Argyll and
Sutherland Highlanders)

The Prince of Wales's
Leinster Regiment
(Royal Canadians)

The Royal Munster Fusiliers

The Royal Dublin Fusiliers

The Prince Consort's Own
(Rifle Brigade)

The Honourable Artillery
Company

The Monmouthshire
Regiment

The Cambridgeshire
Regiment

The Herefordshire
Regiment

The Hertfordshire Regiment

1st/14th (London Scottish)
Battalion, The London
Regiment

CHAPTER FIVE

THE ARMS

THE INFANTRY

The British Army's principal all-infantry formations were the brigade and battalion.

INFANTRY BRIGADES

Each infantry division had 3 infantry brigades, each commanded by a brigadier-general. Two staff officers, a brigade-major and a staff captain, assisted him; 7 batmen served the officers. Extra officers were added to the headquarters in the course of the war to cope with the multiplying volume of administrative work and the round the clock nature of trench warfare. Three men operated the field post office while the quartermaster sergeant controlled the stores; a sergeant of the

The moment the infantry had trained for, going over the top. With zero hour approaching, men of the 13th Durham Light Infantry anxiously watch the artillery bombardment on Dumbarton Wood prior to 23rd Division's attack along the Menin Road. *(IWM Q5971)*

The ration party was always a welcome sight, although the food was usually cold and congealed. These men are returning from the 6th Queen's front line at St Sauveur on the outskirts of Arras. *(IWM Q4847)*

Military Mounted Police supervised law and order with 4 military policemen.

Five Army Service Corps drivers looked after the transport. One General Service (GS) wagon was loaded with the officers' baggage and 2 were filled with tools; a cart carried supplies. The cook had a cart to carry equipment and food to feed the staff.

An officer from the Royal Veterinary Corps looked after the 13 riding horses and 10 draught horses.

For most of the war a brigade headquarters controlled 4 battalions, totalling 4,055 men and 247 horses; it occupied over 2 miles of road while on the march. Territorial battalions were temporarily attached to brigades in 1914 and 1915, increasing the number of battalions per brigade to 5. At the beginning of 1918 brigades on the Western Front were reduced to 3 battalions. (Canadian infantry brigades remained at 4 battalions).

INFANTRY BATTALIONS

The 1914 establishment of an infantry battalion was 1,007 men and 56 horses, including 13 riding horses for the senior officers.

The battalion was commanded by a lieutenant-colonel with a major as second-in-command. Two captains or lieutenants carried out general HQ duties while the battalion adjutant (usually a captain) dealt with administration; 6 privates acted as officers' batmen. The quartermaster issued stores and organized transport. Like other staffs, battalion staffs also increased in size during the war.

A Royal Army Medical Corps officer ran the regimental aid post with 2 orderlies and 16 stretcher-bearers; supplies and equipment were carried in a cart. A corporal and 4 privates of the Royal Army Medical Corps operated 2 water carts.

The senior NCO, the regimental sergeant-major (RSM), supervised a number of specialist sergeants: quartermaster, signaller, transport, armourer, drummer, pioneer, cook, shoemaker, and orderly room clerk. A corporal and 15 privates comprised the battalion signals section using bicycles for transport. Ten privates were employed as pioneers on engineering duties.

A battalion had 4 companies, each with 227 men at full strength. Guards regiments numbered their companies 1–4; line battalions lettered theirs A–D. A major or captain, assisted by a captain and the company sergeant-major, led the company while 2 privates acted as batmen. The company quartermaster sergeant controlled stores and transport and 3 privates were company drivers.

Companies were divided into 4 platoons, each commanded by a subaltern (a lieutenant or 2nd lieutenant) aided by a batman and drummer. Eight sergeants and 10 corporals led 48 privates, organized into 4 sections each of 12 men.

The 16 battalion bandsmen were supposed to act as stretcher-bearers in the field. (The number of bearers was doubled to 32 in 1915.) The Scots Guards and the Highland regiments had an extra sergeant piper and 5 pipers. Scottish Lowland and Irish regiments drew their pipers from the ranks.

WEAPONRY

Officers and the 5-man team responsible for the battalion's range-finding equipment carried a pistol. Drummers and buglers were unarmed but the rest of the other ranks carried the SMLE rifle and bayonet (the RSM and staff sergeants did not carry a bayonet). Pipers of the Scots Guards and Highland regiments carried a dirk and a pistol.

MACHINE GUNS

By 1914, each battalion had a machine-gun section led by a lieutenant aided by a batman. An NCO ran each of the 2 x 6-man gun-teams, and each team was armed with a Maxim gun or the new Vickers gun.

SNIPERS

Officially each battalion had 8 snipers in the trenches, but the commanding officer could increase the number to 24 in dangerous sections. A few worked alone but most operated in 2-man teams, one observing with a telescope or periscope, while the other waited

American soldiers are schooled in the art of camouflage at the British sniping school at Moulle in May 1918. *(IWM Q10315)*

out of sight ready to fire. The sniping officer kept a plan showing sniping posts and targets.

Most snipers used the SMLE Mark III fitted with special sights. A few obtained American Remington-Enfield P14s or sporting rifles, while captured German Gewehr 98 rifles were treasured items. Rifles were carried in a leather case to keep them clean.

EQUIPMENT AND TRANSPORT

Eleven privates tended to the 43 draught and pack horses pulling the battalion transport. Six ammunition carts carried 32,000 rounds. Stocks at brigade, division and on the lines of communication increased the total available to 550 rounds per man.

Three General Service wagons carried machine guns and tools. Each machine-gun team carried 3,500 rounds with the gun and had another 8,000 rounds in reserve.

BASE DETACHMENT

A subaltern and 2 sergeants ran the battalion's base depot at the regimental headquarters; 91 privates formed the first reinforcement. Four storemen issued equipment, the band sergeant ran the musicians, the sergeant master tailor repaired clothing and the sergeant-instructor of musketry taught new recruits how to fire their weapons.

TYPES OF INFANTRY BATTALION

Between 1914 and 1918 a confusing array of battalions were formed to serve various roles for the expanding Army.

THE REGULAR ARMY

REGULAR BATTALIONS

There were typically 2 battalions of Regulars per regiment in August 1914, with one serving overseas and the other allocated to one of the Expeditionary Force's divisions. Many of the overseas battalions were recalled to Britain to form new divisions in the autumn of 1914. All the Regular battalions sent to France suffered heavy losses, often over 90% during the first three months of fighting; Reservists took the place of the casualties.

RESERVE BATTALIONS

These ran the regiment's administration and barracks, dealing with the soldiers' affairs at home. They also enrolled new recruits and took them through basic training. (This was the 3rd Battalion in most regiments).

EXTRA RESERVE BATTALIONS

Some large English and Scottish regiments had a second Reserve battalion called the Extra Reserve. These essentially carried out the same duties as the Reserve battalions. Irish regiments had an Extra Reserve battalion instead of Territorial battalions.

THE TERRITORIAL FORCE

1ST LINE TERRITORIAL BATTALIONS

These were the pre-war Territorial battalions renumbered when the 2nd Line battalions were formed; in many regiments what was the 4th Battalion until September 1914 was then numbered 1st/4th Battalion.

2ND LINE TERRITORIAL BATTALIONS

Formed in September 1914 to accommodate the home service men from the 1st Line battalions and new recruits. The majority served overseas from the start of 1917.

3RD LINE TERRITORIAL BATTALIONS

When the decision was taken to send 2nd Line Territorial divisions overseas, 3rd Line units were formed for the home service men and new recruits. They posted trained men to 1st and 2nd Line units serving overseas. Home service men were transferred to the Provisional battalions in 1915.

4TH LINE TERRITORIAL BATTALIONS

A few 2nd Line Territorial battalions were sent overseas in the autumn of 1914 and 3rd Line battalions were formed to replace them in the 2nd Line divisions. 4th Line battalions were formed to accommodate the home service men and new recruits.

YEOMANRY BATTALIONS

A number of Yeomanry regiments were reorganized as infantry battalions in Egypt in

A group of soldiers put on a show for the cameraman, displaying a mixture of captured German helmets, caps and weapons while the battalion farrier shoes their horse. *(IWM Q150)*

February 1917. They were grouped together as the 74th (Yeomanry) Division in May 1918 and sailed to France where the formation served as an infantry division until the end of the war.

CYCLIST BATTALIONS

These battalions served on coastal defence duties in south-east England; 2nd and 3rd Line Cyclist battalions were raised in the autumn of 1914.

PROVISIONAL BATTALIONS

These were formed in the summer of 1915 with Territorial home service men and carried out coastal defence duties. Wounded Regular and Territorial soldiers unlikely to recover fully were posted to Provisional battalions.

TERRITORIAL FORCE BATTALIONS

Provisional battalions were renamed Territorial Force battalions in January 1917.

THE NEW ARMY

SERVICE BATTALIONS

Men who responded to Kitchener's call for volunteers were organized into Service battalions (suffixed S) separate from the Regular and Territorial battalions and numbered after them in the regimental organisation. Irish regiments did not have Territorial battalions. Numbering for their Service battalions followed the Reserve and Extra Reserve battalions.

2ND RESERVE (OR SERVICE) BATTALIONS

76 Service battalions were converted into Service Reserve battalions in April 1915 to train new volunteers. They took the men through basic training before sending them overseas to join one of the Service battalions. Wounded Service soldiers unlikely to recover fully were posted to 2nd Reserve battalions to help with training.

TRAINING RESERVE BATTALIONS

The Service Reserve battalions, numbering over 208,000 men, were centralized with the introduction of full conscription in September 1916. They were grouped into brigades and numbered as independent battalions, losing their regimental titles and bringing to an end local recruitment.

GARRISON GUARD BATTALIONS

Formed in France in the spring of 1918, then renamed Garrison battalions, these were used to rebuild divisions reduced to cadre after the German spring offensives and were converted into Service battalions in the summer.

TASK-SPECIFIC BATTALIONS

PIONEER BATTALIONS

In response to the overwhelming amount of engineering work associated with trench warfare, an Army Order was issued in December 1914 to add a Pioneer battalion to each infantry division. The battalion would carry out labouring and construction work, instructed by the Royal Engineers in the divisional area. Battalions were added between late 1915 and mid-1916, by converting surplus infantry battalions.

The basic establishment was 4 officers and 313 other ranks. Extra men could be allotted for particular tasks, however. Where possible, the men had been tradesmen or were experienced labourers in civilian life. They were supplied with a stock of engineering tools and stores. They were also trained as infantry and occasionally fought in the front line during German offensives.

INFANTRY LABOUR BATTALIONS

These battalions were formed in the summer of 1916 to accommodate Category B(ii) men without a trade. They carried out manual labour on the Western Front's lines of communication. Some convalescent men served with these units until they were fit enough to return to the front. The battalions were split into two labour companies and they joined the Labour Corps in the spring of 1917. Some were called Works battalions to begin with.

GARRISON BATTALIONS

Category B men fit for overseas garrison duty served with the battalions at overseas postings.

HOME SERVICE GARRISON BATTALIONS

Category C men fit for garrison duty in Great Britain; the battalions were converted into Royal Defence Corps battalions in the summer of 1917.

TRANSPORT WORKERS BATTALIONS AND DOCK BATTALIONS

These were made up of skilled men and were organized to work at home ports.

ENTRENCHING BATTALIONS

Infantry divisions were reduced to 3-battalion brigades at the beginning of 1918. Many battalions were disbanded or merged in the process and the surplus of men were organized into 25 Entrenching battalions. With German offensives expected in the spring, GHQ allocated the battalions to armies and corps and they set to work on digging trenches in the rear area, allowing the Royal Engineers to concentrate on improving the front-line defensive positions.

YOUNG SOLDIER AND GRADUATED BATTALIONS

The Training Reserve was reorganized in May 1917 to accommodate 18-year-olds into the Army training programme. Fourteen Young Soldier battalions took 18-year-old conscripts through basic training. They were then transferred to one of 28 Graduated battalions to complete their training, while carrying out home defence duties. They were affiliated to 14 regiments in October 1917 with 2 Graduate battalions (numbered 51 and 52) to one Young Soldier (numbered 53) per regiment.

OFFICER CADET BATTALIONS

These battalions trained officers for a temporary commission.

THE ROYAL ARTILLERY

Guns were formed into batteries (all guns in a battery were usually of the same type) and batteries, especially of the lighter calibres of field guns, were formed into brigades (roughly equivalent in manpower to infantry battalions). Brigades could be composed of only one calibre of weapon or of more than one. Some brigades would be part of the various infantry and cavalry divisions; others

Royal Artillery

Royal Engineers

Labour Corps

Army Cyclist Corps

Machine Gun Corps

Guards Machine Gun
Regiment

Motor Machine Gun Corps

Tank Corps

Pioneers of the 16th Royal Irish Rifles fill in a German trench on the opening day of the Battle of
Cambrai to allow guns and ammunition wagons forward on 36th Division's front. *(IWM Q6288)*

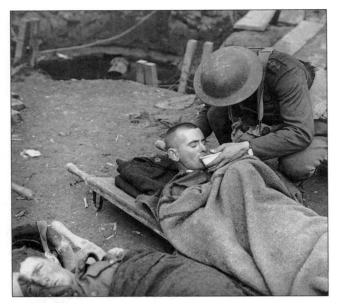

All too often the burden of losses fell on the infantry; this chaplain dishes out warm tea and kind words to wounded men before they are evacuated to the dressing station. *(IWM Q2854)*

and various types of heavy-calibre units, would be controlled by corps, armies or even GHQ.

The Royal Artillery had three divisions controlling different calibres of guns.

ROYAL HORSE ARTILLERY

The fast-moving, all-mounted, gun crews operated the lighter 13-pounder guns supporting the cavalry units.

ROYAL FIELD ARTILLERY

The 18-pounder guns operated by the Field Artillery were the most common type in Royal Artillery service. The teams moved more slowly than the Horse Artillery because the gun crews sat on the limbers and the guns were heavier. The Field Artillery also operated the 4.5-inch howitzer.

ROYAL GARRISON ARTILLERY

The Army's heavy gun in 1914 was the 60-pounder and this cumbersome weapon was operated by the Royal Garrison Artillery. As the need for heavier artillery grew, so did the

number of medium and heavy batteries, and by the end of the war there were around 300, with equipment ranging from the 6-inch howitzer up to the mighty 15-inch railway-mounted howitzer.

ARTILLERY BRIGADES

To begin with divisions had different establishments for their field artillery brigades.

REGULAR INFANTRY DIVISIONS

3 x 18-pounder brigades with 3 x 6-gun batteries – 54 guns.
1 x 4.5-inch howitzer brigade with 3 x 6-gun batteries – 18 howitzers.
1 battery of 60-pounders – 4 guns.

(7th, 8th, 27th and 28th Divisions had different establishments.)

TERRITORIAL INFANTRY DIVISIONS

3 x 15-pounder brigades with 3 x 4-gun batteries – 36 guns.
1 x 5-inch howitzer brigade with 2 x 4-gun batteries – 8 howitzers.

18-pounder guns had replaced the 15-pounder guns by the end of 1915.

NEW ARMY INFANTRY DIVISIONS

New Army field artillery was initially organized into 4 x 3-battery brigades, each battery with 6 pieces, but in January 1915 this was changed as follows:

3 x 18-pounder brigades with 4 x 4-gun batteries – 48 guns.
1 x 4.5-inch howitzer brigade with 4 x 4-gun batteries – 16 howitzers.

CAVALRY DIVISION

2 x 13-pounder horse artillery brigades with 2 x 6-gun batteries – 24 guns.

FIELD ARTILLERY BRIGADE

The Regular field artillery brigade had a headquarters and three batteries, A, B and C. The 18-pounder brigade had 23 officers and 772

The crew of an 18-pounder have stripped to the waist as they work hard in Carnoy Valley, near Montauban on the Somme, to provide a protective barrage for troops attacking High Wood on 30 July 1916. *(IWM Q4065)*

men while the 4.5-inch howitzer brigade had 22 officers and 733 men.

Brigade headquarters was commanded by a lieutenant-colonel assisted by 2 captains or lieutenants, and a trumpeter. The adjutant and clerk carried out administration tasks while the orderly officer organized stores and transport; 8 gunners acted as officers' batmen. The sergeant-major managed the 9 drivers and 7 gunners with the help of 2 corporals and 2 bombardiers. Only 5 men were armed with rifles (no bayonets) for defensive purposes but all NCOs and men wore a bandolier of ammunition. (Note: lance-corporals were called bombardiers and privates were called gunners or drivers in the Royal Artillery.)

An RAMC officer and 3 orderlies cared for the wounded and his equipment was carried in a medical cart. A Veterinary Corps officer cared for the horses, while an RAMC corporal and 3 privates tended to the water cart.

BASE DEPOT

Each brigade had a base depot station at home. A subaltern commanded it while 2 sergeants organized the 40 of more drivers and gunners who would be sent overseas to replace casualties. The sergeant clerk and four storemen maintained the stores.

AMMUNITION

DIVISIONAL ARTILLERY COLUMN (DAC)

The DAC carried ammunition from the divisional refilling points to the brigade dumps. It had 15 officers and 553 other ranks. 709 horses pulled 101 wagons and three carts.

BRIGADE AMMUNITION COLUMN (BAC)

The BAC carried ammunition from the brigade dumps to the field battery horse lines or heavy artillery battery positions. A captain and a subaltern led the 158 officers and men, assisted by 2 batmen and a trumpeter. The column was organized into 2 sections, each led by a subaltern (each with a batman).

The brigade ammunition columns were absorbed into the divisional ammunition column in May 1916.

THE GUN BATTERY

The 6-gun field battery had 5 officers and 193 men led by a major, assisted by a captain and 2 trumpeters. The battery was organized into 2-gun sections, each led by a subaltern and a sergeant-major, assisted by sergeants, corporals and bombardiers; each officer had a batman. Thirty-six gunners and drivers carried rifles without bayonets and all other ranks carried a bandolier of rifle ammunition.

Royal Field Artillery officers and senior NCOs rode on riding horses and 70 men rode on the draught horses, controlling the teams – 6 drivers per gun or ammunition wagon; the rest rode into action on the limbers and ammunition wagons. Field gun teams could move at the canter but the Royal Garrison Artillery's 60-pounders had to be drawn at the walk by 8 heavy draught horses. All Royal

Horse Artillery gunners had riding horses so their batteries could move at the gallop.

A farrier-sergeant and 4 shoeing smiths cared for the horses while 2 saddlers maintained the drivers' equipment. The battery had 6 ammunition wagons for moving the ammunition forward. Three supply wagons carried an array of tools and personal effects; pack-horse drawn carts carried water. Two wheelwrights kept the battery on the move and the quartermaster sergeant issued rations and stores.

FIELD GUN CREW

The officer would either follow instructions from an observer watching the gun's fall of shot, or followed a pre-determined schedule given on a barrage chart. The dial sight would be checked for the angle and the barrel raised or lowered with the elevating gear. The breech was opened and the previous shell-case ejected, and a new shell was pushed into the breech. As the breech closed, the crew made any final adjustments, covered their ears, and fired. Men were trained to change position if

Drenched to the skin, an artillery crew strain to pull a gun into position on the Le Sars road during the German retirement to the Hindenburg Line in March 1917. *(IWM Q4889)*

there were casualties. Typically, during a barrage, a gun fired between 2 and 4 shells a minute; faster rates of fire could only be sustained for short periods.

The buffers compensated for the most of the recoil of the lighter guns but crews anchored the trail with a log and sandbags; loosely-filled sandbags under the wheels also helped to keep the gun in position.

CONTROLLING THE BATTERY

As indirect and map fire took over from direct fire, the reliance on the forward observers increased. They needed to be near the front to adjust the fall of shot while field telephones kept them in contact with the battery. Signallers maintained communications between the forward observers, gun lines and the wagon lines, running out miles of telephone cable using bicycles for transport.

THE GUN LINES

Gun crews and small stocks of ammunition were spaced out in camouflaged gun pits. Field guns were usually roughly 1 mile behind the front line; the heavy artillery was 2 miles or more away. The battery commander and his second-in-command managed the 3 subalterns and their 2-gun sections, usually taking it in turns to control the gun and the horse lines.

THE WAGON OR HORSE LINES

The horse teams, limbers and ammunition wagons were kept at a safe distance. Drivers took the ammunition wagons forward with new supplies for the battery or took the limbers forward when the battery was due to move.

The battery sergeant-major organized the other ranks into 6-horse teams. Drivers controlled the horses while gunners stocked the wagons. Gunners and drivers were armed with rifles (no bayonets) and had ammunition bandoliers; NCOs also carried bandoliers.

Each gun had 2 ammunition wagons, 1 at the gun and 1 at the horse lines; they could be exchanged when fresh stocks were required. The regulation minimum number of shells available to field batteries is shown in the table overleaf.

The gun lines. An 18-pounder battery is deployed at intervals in the open with small stocks of ammunition to limit the chances of a catastrophic explosion. *(IWM Q2107)*

This gun limber has moved up from the horse lines to a battery position near Authuille on the Ancre, bringing ammunition for the attack on Thiepval on 26 September 1916. *(IWM Q1344)*

HEAVY ARTILLERY CREW

Some of the heavy howitzers needed a crew of 70 to keep them operational, taking several minutes to load a single shell. A large howitzer might have 2 men to operate the elevating gear, aligning the barrel according to the instructions of the gunner checking the dial sight. As 2 men opened the breech, another 8 wheeled the shell forward on a trolley; 8 more pushed the shell into the breech with a long ramrod. Four crewmen brought huge slabs of

cordite forward on a trolley ready to be rammed home. Once the breech closed, the whole crew helped to lay (position) the howitzer ready for firing. Typically a 12-inch howitzer would fire 60 rounds a day; 9.2-inch howitzers would fire 6–8 rounds an hour.

REORGANIZATION OF THE FIELD ARTILLERY BRIGADES

By the end of 1915 the 15-pounders serving with the Territorial divisions had been

	18-pounder	4.5-inch howitzer
At the battery position	176	108
With the brigade ammunition column	76	48
With the divisional ammunition column	126	44
At the divisional ammunition park	150	80
Other reserves, on lines of communication	472	520

replaced with 18-pounders. The divisional field artillery was standardized across the Army in April and May 1916 with 4 mixed field artillery brigades, each with 3 x 4-gun 18-pounder batteries and 1 x 4-gun 4.5-inch howitzer battery. The divisional ammunition columns were reorganized and brigade ammunition columns were abolished at the same time.

The 6-gun battery had to be reintroduced during the 1916 Somme campaign due to a shortage of trained brigade and battery commanders; the number of brigades was reduced to 3 per division.

One brigade was withdrawn from each division at the start of 1917 and these became army field artillery brigades; 34 extra army field artillery brigades were sent to the Western Front at the same time.

COMMAND OF THE ARTILLERY

The number of medium and heavy guns increased tremendously during the war, from 36 batteries in January 1915 to 191 in July 1916 and more thereafter, and the organization and command of the batteries changed as the importance of the artillery barrage grew. The first change followed the formation of First and Second Armies in December 1914. The 4.7-inch and 60-pounder heavy batteries were withdrawn from divisional command and grouped together with new 6-inch howitzer batteries into Heavy Artillery Reserves (HAR) by February 1915. A Major-General Royal Artillery (M-GRA) joined each army staff to advise on their deployment.

A reorganization of artillery control was made in time for the Battle of Loos in September 1915. The independent HARs dealt with counter-battery fire while the Brigadier-General Royal Artillery at corps headquarters coordinated the wire cutting and harassment fire carried out by the field and medium guns during the preliminary bombardment. The field artillery reverted to divisional control at zero hour.

A new artillery officer, the Commander of Corps Heavy Artillery, joined each corps headquarters in the spring of 1916 as the HARs were reorganized into Heavy Artillery

A 13-pounder crew of the Royal Horse Artillery gallops into action in June 1918. *(IWM Q6728)*

Groups (HAGs) in time for the battle of the Somme. Each HAG had a mixed complement of 4 or 5 batteries to allow a greater degree of flexibility. Two HAGs were allocated to each army and 2 to each corps. The Brigadier-General Royal Artillery continued to coordinate the divisions' field artillery.

By June 1916 the heavy artillery had to be organized into two categories:

Corps:	Medium artillery	60-pounders, 6-inch, 8-inch and 9.2-inch howitzers, 6-inch guns
Army:	Larger calibres	12-inch howitzers, 15-inch howitzers, railway guns

The heavy artillery was grouped into brigades in January 1918. GHQ had 12 brigades of Royal Garrison and 6 brigades of Royal Field Artillery in reserve; the armies shared the remainder. By November 1918 an M-GRA had around 900 artillery pieces under his command:

3 mobile brigades of heavy and medium artillery.

3 mixed brigades of heavy and medium artillery.

4 brigades of 8-inch howitzers and 3 brigades of 9.2-inch howitzers.

2 Royal Garrison Artillery brigades.

7 batteries of 6-inch guns and 8 batteries of heavier guns.

Up to 16 army brigades of Royal Field Artillery.

IMPROVEMENTS IN ARTILLERY ACCURACY

As the front lines stabilized and men took to digging trenches to protect themselves, it became harder for the artillery to hit targets effectively. The growing number of German heavy guns capable of targeting the Royal Artillery's positions (known as counter-battery fire) had also driven batteries into hiding. Between 1915 and 1918 a number of scientific and mathematical improvements turned artillery bombardments into complicated affairs.

A 60-pounder battery joins in the barrage during III Corps' attack on Contalmaison in July 1916; timber frames have been erected in case camouflage netting has to be used. *(IWM Q831)*

The crew of an 18-pounder make the final adjustments to their gun during 9th (Scottish) Division's attack east of Arras on 9 April 1917. *(IWM Q5171)*

PREDICTED FIRE

As soon as accurate maps began to appear, the artillery were able to fire at unobserved targets using coordinates and trigonometry. After taking a bearing on a fixed object marked on the map, usually a church tower, one gun fired until hits were registered. By marking the centre of the battery and the known point on the map, the zero line could be established with an optical device known as a director. After making adjustments to point all the guns at the same target, the battery was able to switch to any target.

MAP SHOOTING AND ARTILLERY BOARDS

The introduction of 1:20,000-scale maps in 1915 allowed the artillery to start map shooting with confidence. By the summer they had surveyed the heavy batteries and created artillery boards, pre-plotted maps marked with batteries, observers, and targets.

AERIAL OBSERVATION

Experiments with aircraft added a third dimension to artillery observation and the combination of wireless communication, fire control and photography, meant that artillery officers had accurate information to plot new targets.

FLASH-SPOTTING AND THE FLASH AND BUZZER BOARD

Observers watched for gun flashes from coordinated posts and noted the time and

Men of 9th Hodson's Horse practise charging with the lance in September 1916; the few occasions when cavalry were called upon to exploit a breakthrough in the German lines ended in disaster. *(IWM Q4105)*

---

angle; these could be cross-referenced and plotted by intersecting lines on the map to give the location of a battery. The flash-and-buzzer board was introduced to speed up reporting. A series of observers simultaneously buzzed and relayed the angle of a gun flash to a reporting centre, giving instant results.

SOUND-RANGING

The British artillery adopted this French development in October 1915. A number of fixed microphones recorded sound-waves and timings of gunfire; there were 30 sections by 1918. Improved Tucker microphones were introduced in September 1916.

UNREGISTERED SHOOTING

The usual method of registering targets, followed by a preliminary bombardment and wire cutting operations took several days, giving the Germans plenty of warning that an attack was imminent. By the summer of 1917 the Tank Corps had enough tanks to cut through any wire obstacle, relieving the artillery of the difficult task.

The gunners knew that each gun had different properties, either due to manufacturing or wear and tear. Calibrating sections measured the muzzle velocity of each gun on the army range, calculating variations that had to applied. A grid of bearing pickets (survey points) at regular intervals along the front allowed gun batteries to set up quickly, ready to take accurate bearings on targets.

Weather conditions also affected artillery fire and GHQ received daily reports detailing wind, temperature and barometric pressure.

The combination of the above calculations enabled the crews to set up quickly and be confident they would hit a target the first time they fired. Unregistered shooting was tried on a large scale for the first time at Cambrai on 20 November 1917; none of the guns brought into Third Army's area opened fire before zero hour.

THE CAVALRY

The principal cavalry unit of the British Army was the regiment. In August 1914 most of the

BEF's cavalry was deployed in the Cavalry Division. However, each infantry division had a cavalry squadron attached for reconnaissance and similar duties.

THE CAVALRY REGIMENT

The regiment consisted of a regimental headquarters, 3 squadrons (Household Cavalry and Indian regiments had 4) and a machine-gun section. The full strength of a British line regiment was 26 officers and 523 other ranks.

The regimental headquarters was led by a lieutenant-colonel, assisted by a major and regimental sergeant-major; an officer and orderly room clerk sergeant carried out administration. A signals officer and signaller sergeant ran the signals section with a corporal and 4 privates. An officer, aided by a quartermaster sergeant and transport sergeant controlled the squadron stores and transport while 7 privates served as drivers for the horse-drawn transport. A sergeant-trumpeter led the regimental band and the band members (6 trumpeters and 12 drummers) served as stretcher-bearers with the squadrons. Twelve batmen served the officers.

An officer of the Royal Army Medical Corps ran the regimental aid post with 2 orderlies while a corporal and 2 privates of the Royal Army Medical Corps were attached for water duties. The sergeant cook prepared meals.

The three squadrons were lettered A, B and C. Each squadron had had 162 officers and men. The squadron was commanded by a major assisted by a captain, a sergeant-major and 2 batmen. The quartermaster sergeant ran the squadron stores and 2 privates were squadron signallers. The squadron was organized into 4 troops in each of which a subaltern led 38 NCOs and troopers.

WEAPONRY

Officers and sergeants were armed with the Webley pistol while the rest of the men carried the SMLE rifle (with no bayonet); each man carried 120 rounds of ammunition. The officers and men (apart from the drivers and signallers) were also armed with a sword and

The cavalry eventually returned to their role of reconnaissance during the autumn of 1918; these troopers are passing through the village of Chérisy during First Army's advance towards the Canal du Nord at the beginning of September. *(IWM CO3230)*

from the 3 regiments were brigaded together as a squadron with 8 officers, 203 men, 12 Vickers guns and 299 horses.

HORSES AND TRANSPORT

The regiment had 528 riding horses as well as 74 draught horses and 6 pack horses; 7 drivers controlled the regiment's transport. An officer of the Veterinary Corps cared for the animals while a farrier quartermaster sergeant, assisted by 3 farrier sergeants and 12 shoeing smiths kept them well shod. A saddler sergeant and 3 saddlers maintained the saddles.

BASE DETACHMENT

A subaltern and 2 sergeants led the small cadre of 46 privates and 48 riding horses kept at the regimental headquarters. A sergeant master tailor and 3 storemen maintained the stores.

THE ROYAL ENGINEERS

The Royal Engineers were responsible for construction and demolition works, both at the front line and on the lines of communication. Corps and army chief engineers (CE) controlled a variety of works across their area and had a wide range of specialist field companies to fulfil a variety of tasks including:

Installing and maintaining communications equipment.
Building fortifications, accommodation, stores and workshops.
Building and maintaining roads, railways, bridges and tramways.
Operating repair workshops for machinery and vehicles.
Running quarries and forestry operations.
Surveying, mapping and camouflage.
Tunnelling – both offensive mining operations and building underground shelters.
Providing water and improving drainage.
Special companies were added to carry out gas attacks in 1915.

Eleven battalions of labourers, navvies and tradesmen drawn from the New Armies were added in August 1915 to help the engineers.

The cavalry were called upon to man the trenches when manpower was short, particularly during the first winter of the war. These men of the 11th Hussars are cleaning their Maxim machine gun in the trenches at Zillebeke, east of Ypres. *(IWM Q51194)*

some squadrons also carried lances; an armourer sergeant maintained the weapons.

A lieutenant commanded the regiment's machine-gun section, assisted by 2 batmen; a sergeant and a corporal ran the 2 x 6-man Maxim gun teams; Vickers guns replaced the Maxims as soon as possible. Each section carried 3,500 rounds with the gun transport and the regiment had another 16,000 in reserve; 8 drivers looked after the section transport.

The number of machine guns was doubled to 4 in February 1915. A year later the sections

Engineering tasks ranged from the simple: this wiring party of the 11th Canadian Brigade are using head straps, called tump lines, to help them carry their loads into the trenches at Avion, near Lens. *(IWM CO1990)*

30th Labour Battalion, RE, specialized in railways and was eventually split into 3 railway construction companies and a wagon building company.

The Army Ordnance Corps controlled stores at the start of the war but Royal Engineers' parks were soon set up to receive bulk deliveries of tools and materials, distributing them to the front line. Royal Engineer workshops maintained and repaired equipment.

By 1918, the Royal Engineers numbered over 16,000 officers and 340,000 men.

COMMANDER ROYAL ENGINEERS

A Commander Royal Engineers (CRE), usually a lieutenant-colonel, controlled engineering works and communications in the divisional area. Three officers and 10 men ran his HQ; 4 riding horses carried the officers, 4 draft horses pulled 2 carts carrying the HQ equipment and the messenger used a bicycle.

Infantry divisions included 2 Royal Engineer field companies and a signal company in August 1914; a third field company was added at the end of the year, causing a shortage of engineers across the Territorial Force and the New Armies. Infantrymen with appropriate skills were transferred to the Royal Engineers to make up the shortfall. Cavalry divisions had 1 field squadron and 1 signal squadron throughout the war.

Pioneer battalions (infantrymen with labouring skills) were added to divisions to take over semi-skilled work in the front line; they often worked under Royal Engineer guidance. A divisional employment company was added to all divisions in May 1917.

FIELD COMPANIES

A major led 217 officers and men, assisted by a captain, a company sergeant-major, a trumpeter and a bugler. Each company was

To the complex: these engineers have used barges as the piers for a bridge over the Yser Canal in August 1917 at the start of the Third Ypres campaign. *(IWM Q5858)*

organized into 4 sections, each led by a subaltern; 8 batmen assisted the officers. Sergeants, corporals and 2nd corporals controlled the sappers (the Royal Engineer equivalent to private). The majority of men had a trade, including carpentry, bricklaying, stonemasonry, demolition, plumbing and painting; others were blacksmiths, wheelwrights, surveyors or draughtsmen. The company quartermaster sergeant looked after tools, equipment, explosives, ammunition and rations.

The officers and senior NCOs rode 17 riding horses while 37 draught horses and pack horses pulled the company transport. A farrier sergeant and a shoeing smith looked after the horses. An Army Service Corps driver supervised the 37 company drivers while 2 RAMC privates maintained the company water cart.

SIGNALS COMPANIES

Each company comprised 162 officers and men, organized into the company headquarters and 4 sections. A major or captain ran the headquarters, assisted by a company sergeant-major, 2 batmen and a trumpeter. While 1 sergeant ran the headquarters men, a sergeant and corporal worked with the signallers group. A company quartermaster sergeant controlled the company stores.

No. 1 Section organized communications with the corps headquarters; a subaltern and 7 NCOs organized the 28 sappers. Nos. 2, 3 and 4 Sections ran communications with the 3 brigade headquarters. A subaltern led the telephone section and three 2nd corporals organized the 25 sappers. Subalterns led the 2 signaller and despatch rider sections in which 6 NCOs organized 18 sappers; they had 9 motorcycles and 32 bicycles.

The officers and senior NCOs rode 33 riding horses while 47 draught horses and pack horses pulled the company transport; 2 shoeing smiths looked after the horses. An ASC driver assisted the 33 company drivers while 2 RAMC privates maintained the company water cart.

In both types of companies officers were armed with revolvers while the other ranks (apart from the trumpeter and bugler) had the SMLE rifle.

RAILWAYS (STANDARD GAUGE)

French-operated troop trains carried British troops during the opening months of the war. They moved battalions in a single train travelling at 12mph; GHQ preferred loading battalions on 2 trains travelling at twice the speed. Thirty liaison officers worked with the French railway operators to alleviate any problems.

After the BEF moved to Flanders in October 1914 the French handed over control of the railways in the area to British operators. A new Director of Railways was appointed and work began on improving the rail network.

RAILWAY COMPANIES

Railway companies, RE, operated the trains used by the Army Service Corps and the Royal Army Medical Corps. 8th Railway Company sailed to France with the BEF and another 4 companies arrived in the winter of 1914–15.

The Director of Railways had already set up a sub-committee to organize the operation and construction of railways behind the British sector and the New Armies were scoured for men with railway experience. Half of the officers recruited had worked for British railway operators; the rest had overseas experience. After training at Longmoor and Bordon in Hampshire, men joined one of the construction trains; there were 8 operating behind the British lines by the summer of 1915. Each train had 1 or 2 railway companies. Royal Engineer labour companies and Chinese labour carried out the excavation work and prepared the ballast ahead of the track-laying gangs.

Good communications across the battlefield were essential, if difficult and labour-intensive to achieve. These signallers are making their way along a narrow duckboard path between a maze of shell-holes. *(IWM Q5003)*

Many routes were upgraded to double lines, new sidings were added and the existing system had to be maintained. Railway spurs were laid to heavy artillery batteries, casualty clearing stations and tank depots, reducing the strain on the Army Service Corps' wagons and lorries.

Forty-five companies eventually worked on broad-gauge railways in various theatres; the Dominions also formed railway companies. By the summer of 1917 there were 47,000 operating staff and 29,000 construction men working on the railways. Many helped to repair the French and Belgian rail networks after the Armistice.

LIGHT RAILWAYS (NARROW GAUGE)

The first 2-foot gauge light railways were laid in the spring of 1916 relieving the pressure on the divisional trains and ammunition columns. Labour units prepared routes and laid ballast ahead of the track-laying RE railway engineers while the workshops were making pre-fabricated sections.

Some 300 yards of track could be laid by each company every 24 hours. Steel rails and sleepers, welded into pre-fabricated sections, were used to speed up construction, but wider wooden sleepers had to be used to cross poor ground. Wooden trestles carried the tracks across craters and streams.

Light railway operating companies were formed at the start of 1917. The 200 officers and men per company were organized into operating (drivers, guards, brakesmen and traffic controllers) and maintenance (wagon repair shops, track maintenance and stores) teams.

Light railways were a favourite target for enemy artillery and rolling stock had to leave the forward zone before it was light. An engineer officer organized the allotment, loading and despatch of trucks and had to prepare contingency plans if a line was broken. Troops often found it was quicker to unload a truck and carry it around a break in the track, rather than wait for it to be repaired.

PERMANENT ROADS

Existing roads were used where possible but they were obvious targets for artillery. Craters were temporarily repaired by the nearest division. Corps troops made permanent repairs with fascines and half-round logs; tramway sleepers were also used but they were prone to be slippery in wet weather. Craters had to be repaired as quickly as possible as detours were notorious for delaying traffic.

Two-way roads were maintained when possible but on narrow roads Up traffic and Down traffic had to use the section in shifts. Vehicles had to be clear of the artillery zone before daylight.

A light railway train carries men and materials through Elverdinghe up to the Ypres Salient in February 1917. *(IWM Q1699)*

Pioneers lay a duckboard path through the shell craters to 2nd Australian Division's new front line east of Zonnebeke in the Ypres Salient on 5 October 1917. *(IWM E(AUS)837)*

Unpaved tracks (without a stone or timber surface) quickly churned into a quagmire when it rained. Short tracks, known as turn-offs, were built to connect battery positions to the main road.

TEMPORARY TRACKS

Temporary tracks and roads had to be built across the battlefield and maintained to keep the front-line troops supplied. As soon as a new objective had been taken existing roads and tracks had to be extended across the battlefield.

Track-tracing parties followed close behind the assault troops, following predetermined routes plotted from maps and air photographs. They marked the routes with posts or short pickets, erecting notice-boards detailing place names or map references at specific points. Within a short time the ammunition parties could follow the traces while stretcher parties made their way to the rear.

Duck-walks (timber pathways) were built along the traces as quickly as possible –

infantry carrying parties kept the forward dumps stocked with timber. A division could build around 850 yards a day, installing infantry bridges over trenches and craters along the way. A pair of duck-walks (one Up and one Down) was designated the priority route and repair parties worked around the clock to keep it open. A second pair of tracks was installed as soon as possible. Tracks were easy to repair and could be moved to confuse the enemy artillery; they were rarely out of action for long.

Mats were useful for crossing muddy areas ahead of the duck-walks. They were made of canvas and wire netting stretched across wooden slats. They were quick to install but they only had a short lifespan.

THE SIGNAL SERVICE

Pre-war signalling had relied heavily on liaison officers, despatch riders and orderlies for communications. Artillery observers used semaphore to transmit instructions to the

Signallers cling to a telegraph post to check the telephone wires near Hamel on the Somme in October 1916. *(IWM Q1588)*

battery. There was no time to establish permanent communications (either overhead lines or cables laid on or under the ground) during the retreat to the Marne. As soon as the front line stabilized, the Royal Engineer signal companies (the separate Corps of Royal Signals was not formed until after the war) began to install elaborate telegraph systems.

THE SIGNAL SERVICE IN 1914

GHQ: A signal company and wireless section.
Corps: A signal company with 1 air-line and 4 cable sections.
Infantry division: A signal company with 4 sections.
Cavalry division: A signal squadron with 4 troops.

INSPECTOR-GENERAL OF COMMUNICATIONS

An additional signal company operated along the lines of communication.

EXPANSION OF THE SIGNAL SERVICE

During Kitchener's call for volunteers over 17,500 employees of the General Post Office (which was then responsible for the civilian telephone and telegram services) volunteered for the signal service.

First and Second Armies were each allocated a signal company when they formed in December 1914; GHQ expanded its wireless unit to company size a month later. As the BEF expanded, each new army and corps was allocated a signal company. A deputy director of army signals joined each army with an assistant director and a small staff going to each corps. Companies were reorganized into 4 air-line and 3 (ground) cable sections. Divisional signal companies were given a fourth cable detachment and 2 motor despatch riders to serve the artillery brigades.

SIGNAL PRACTICE BEHIND THE LINES

Permanent telephone equipment and cables replaced visual signalling in the trenches whenever possible. A signal system was begun in January 1915 after taking advice from the post office. Exchanges and switchboards appeared at every headquarters while telephones and lines were installed at the dugouts in the front line. A wireless depot and signal school were opened to train operators; corps and divisional signal schools were soon added.

Cables laid on the ground or slung from poles were vulnerable to artillery fire or passing traffic and cable trenches were dug where possible, 18 inches deep to begin with and then deepened to 30 inches. Alternate routes and deeper cable trenches (3 feet was preferred) were added when time permitted.

The signal sections aimed to have buried cables connecting divisions and brigades to the front trenches, but labour and cable were always in short supply. During the Somme campaign of 1916 interconnecting cable systems (known as chessboard layouts) were laid between dugouts in advance of an attack.

RADIOS

Short-range wireless sets were tried for the first time between brigade and divisional headquarters in August 1915 but they failed to impress and it took another two years to produce a viable piece of equipment. The radios were too heavy to be carried into action but some models were used in tanks. Masts and antennae were obvious targets and difficult to camouflage. The only successful portable radios were those used by the Royal Flying Corps' observation planes.

MESSAGE INTERCEPTION

Both sides tried to listen in on telephone messages sent on badly insulated lines. They had limited success but the recorded messages were sent back to be translated and, they hoped, decoded. The introduction of unit code names and pre-planned artillery call-zones helped but it was difficult to limit breaches in security. One lapse led to a German garrison on the Somme overhearing the order to attack on 1 July 1916; British troops found a copy pinned up in a dugout.

Attempts to improve telephone security included using double cable metallic circuits, twisted cables, and extending earths to the rear. During the second half of 1916 buzzers were installed to screen telephone speech and the Fullerphone protected telegraphed messages. At least one corps continued to transmit false information on a poorly insulated earth to try and fool the Germans.

LABOUR UNITS

The British Army did not take any labour units to France and the Engineer-in-Chief initially had to rely on divisions arriving in France and French Territorial battalions to provide unskilled labour. As operations became more sophisticated a dedicated workforce was formed and eventually over 700,000 men were employed on construction and maintenance.

Large quantities of stone were removed from the Marquise quarries near Boulogne while forestry units cut down tons of timber. By November 1918 there were 41,000 men working on roads, 29,000 on railway construction and 11,000 at the ports.

LABOUR BATTALIONS, RE

Labour battalions, RE, were formed to supervise work on defences, roads and water

Labourers toil in the sun to lay ballast for a new light railway near Arras in June 1917. *(IWM Q2475)*

supply. A Regular lieutenant-colonel and his adjutant led qualified civil engineer officers, navvies and tradesmen. By the end of the war each army had 7 labour group headquarters controlling over 50 labour companies.

INFANTRY LABOUR BATTALIONS

Category B(ii) men without a trade were allocated to infantry labour battalions after February 1916. These battalions carried out menial tasks needing the minimum of supervision and only had 2 officers per company. By June 1916 there were 12 labour battalions in France.

NON-COMBATANT COMPANIES

The Military Service Act of March 1916 produced hundreds of conscientious objectors. Some were exempted from combat for recognized religious or moral principles and joined one of the eight companies of the Non-Combatant Corps. Convalescing officers and NCOs supervised them.

FOREIGN LABOUR

The British Army had always employed labour from across the Empire, particularly from Egypt, India and South Africa, but the majority of such workers were employed in the Mediterranean and the Middle East. Eventually the Army followed the French example and signed an agreement with China to supply labour to work on the lines of communication. Overseas labour was based in segregated camps.

The main sources of labour were:

China: 100,000 labourers in France.
Egypt: 100,000 labourers in France and the Middle East.
India: 21,000 labourers in the Middle East and East Africa.
South Africa: 20,000 labourers in East Africa.

Having completed the chamber, tunnellers place sacks full of explosives at the head of the tunnel; the officer on the left is using a geophone to listen for signs of enemy mining activity. *(IWM Q115)*

The South African Native Labour Corps reached France at the start of 1917.

The British and Indian Armies employed over 300,000 foreign workers by November 1918, 193,500 of them on the Western Front.

POW COMPANIES

German prisoners were originally held in prisons across the United Kingdom but from the summer of 1916, they were assessed for fitness and skills at Abbeville before joining a POW labour company. The companies were attached to the Labour Corps and were mainly employed on forestry and in workshops. By the end of the war there were 47 such labour companies, each with 100 men.

TUNNELLING COMPANIES

Royal Engineers received basic training on tunnelling but there were no plans to start operations on the Western Front until the Germans detonated 10 x 100-pound charges under the Indian Corps trenches at Givenchy on 20 December 1914.

A few days earlier General Sir Henry Rawlinson had proposed forming a mining battalion and at the end of the month, Major John Norton Griffiths suggested using civilian tunnellers with experience on the London Underground. The men were used to digging in soft clay, using a wooden crucifix support to lean against as they dug small pilot tunnels, kicking the clay between their feet so it could be removed (they were known as clay-kickers).

There were 500 volunteers and others were transferred from units across the Army. Brigade mining sections were formed in February 1915, expanding into 8 tunnelling companies each with 19 officers and 325 other ranks. During busy times a company could have 550 tunnellers plus over 200 unskilled men helping to remove spoil.

The main mining areas were east of Béthune and on the Messines Ridge. The first mine was blown at Hill 60, south-east of Ypres, on 17 February 1915. Mining was limited to small objectives to begin with, with shallow tunnels started in trenches. Additional mining

Tons of earth are thrown into the air as a mine explodes under Hawthorn Redoubt near Beaumont-Hamel on 1 July 1916. The mine was detonated ten minutes before zero hour, warning the Germans that the attack was imminent. *(IWM Q754)*

areas were added on Vimy Ridge, north of Arras, and on the Somme, but the infantry continued to dictate where the tunnellers worked and cooperation was often poor. Eventually there would be 25 British companies, 3 Canadian, 3 Australian and 1 New Zealand. Mine rescue stations were set up and men were trained at the Mine Rescue School in Armentières from 1915.

Brigadier-General George Fowke, then GHQ's Engineer-in-Chief, formed a mining staff led by an Inspector of Mines in December 1915, looking to plan large-scale mining operations around offensives. For the first time army mining schemes were studied and authorized before companies were distributed. Local corps or divisional chief engineers supervised work while the mining staff monitored progress.

The first mining school opened in June 1916 and tactics, listening techniques and mine rescue work were taught. Over 25,000 men were trained to work underground, digging tunnels, subways, cable trenches and dugouts.

Nineteen mines were fired on 1 July 1916 in support of the Somme offensive but they were too scattered to have an impact on the attack. Local tunnelling continued throughout 1917 but the largest mining operation was carried out on 7 June on Messines Ridge when 19 huge mines shattered the German morale and played a large part in Second Army's success. Mining operations soon went into decline as mobile warfare increased.

The tunnellers were put to work on building large dugouts for headquarters and dressing stations; they were also employed on disarming booby-traps and tank salvage during the advance to victory.

TUNNELLING TACTICS

Underground systems developed into several levels. Shallow tunnels were occupied by

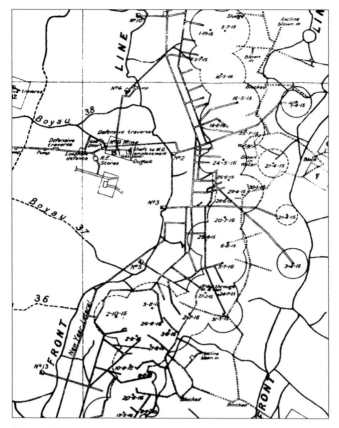

A tunnelling map detailing the underground galleries and craters in no man's land east of Béthune. The craters have linked together to form an impenetrable barrier between the trenches.

listening posts to detect German mining activity and, until the introduction of the geophone, men used stethoscopes or held their ear in a barrel of water to listen for sounds of digging.

The worst sign was when German digging stopped which often meant that the enemy tunnellers were preparing either a full-scale charge, or a small counter-mine (known as a camouflet) to damage the British tunnels without disrupting the trenches above.

Offensive mining involved pushing a deep tunnel forward to dig a large chamber under an enemy trench and then dragging hundreds of sacks loaded with explosives into the detonation chamber. Once the mine had been

blown, the infantry were expected to rush forward and capture the resulting crater up to the lip on the German side, taking cover behind the lip of earth thrown up by the explosion.

Tunnelling was tedious, and miners faced tunnel collapses, gas and underground explosions. On rare occasions opposing tunnellers broke into each other's system, when hand-to-hand fighting with shovels and knives would break out.

THE SPECIAL BRIGADE

The decision to use gas to support the attack at Loos was taken in the summer of 1915. Major Charles Foulkes, RE, recruited men with chemistry qualifications from universities and the New Army divisions, promoting them to chemist corporals of the Royal Engineers. They joined experienced soldiers at Helfaut, near St Omer, in July 1915 and were formed into 186 and 187 Special Companies, RE; 188 and 189 Companies were added a month later. Each company was split into 17 sections of 28 men.

The men were trained in the rudiments of trench warfare, the use of the pistol and compass and identifying weather conditions, as well as how to operate gas cylinders. Gas troops were issued with a red, white and green armband to allow them to head to the rear once they had completed their mission.

The cloud of gas and smoke heralding the Battle of Loos on 25 September 1915 had mixed results, and in some sectors the gas asphyxiated the British troops. The problems were attributed to variable wind speeds, and afterwards General Haig, in his new position of commander-in-chief, asked for the gas companies to be expanded into a brigade, code-named the Special Brigade, in January 1916.

Brigadier-General Henry Thuillier, RE, was made Director of Gas Services and the then Colonel Foulkes became assistant director in command of the brigade. Lieutenant-Colonel S. Cummins, RAMC, took over as assistant director for anti-gas measures.

The Special Brigade's new establishment was completed by May 1918:

A headquarters and depot.

4 special battalions, of 4 companies, to handle gas cylinders and smoke candles.

4 special companies armed with 48 x 4-inch Stokes mortars capable of firing gas shells.

4 special sections of Livens projectors (mortars) with 4 large and 16 portable sets.

The brigade's establishment was 208 officers and 5,306 men.

CAMOUFLAGE

Khaki cloth, coloured earth brown, had been in use by the British Army since the 1880s for uniforms and tents but the arrival of the aeroplane over the battlefield and improvements to heavy artillery made it necessary to camouflage installations some distance behind the front line. After local attempts to conceal look-out posts, machine-gun nests and

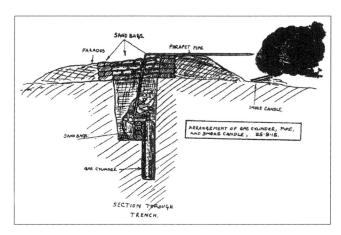

A 1915 drawing showing a cross-section through the dugouts built to protect the Special Brigade soldiers and their gas cylinders; note the smoke candles that were needed to supplement the gas cloud.

trenches proved successful, volunteers with experience in carpentry and theatrical scene painting were organized in January 1916. The

Gas was used during 46th Division's attack on Fosse 8 near Loos. *(IWM Q29001)*

Soldiers weave strips of cloth into netting to make lightweight camouflage. *(IWM Q6748)*

Special Works Park, RE, was sanctioned in March, with 10 officers and 203 other ranks, to begin making camouflage items at a new factory in Wimereux.

They built observation loopholes and painted machine-gun covers while camouflaged suits and dummy heads to attract fire were made to assist snipers. Important buildings were painted to break up their outline, disguising them from the air, while strips of canvas hung from wires concealed roads. Artillery spotters were provided with a range of devices to hide their lookout posts, including dummy trees with steel linings for observers. The infantry were provided with dummy figures painted on boards that could be raised by string and pulleys to draw fire (these were known as Chinese attacks).

Another branch was opened at Amiens in April 1916 to prepare for the Somme offensive and 5 officers and 73 other ranks joined the Special Works Park in June 1916.

As counter-battery fire became more effective, gun batteries and tanks had to be protected by overhead camouflage. Wire netting or old fishnets were woven with painted raffia, canvas or grass. Ammunition dumps and mining spoil heaps were covered by scrim, a loosely woven canvas.

By July 1918 each corps and army headquarters had a camouflage section, with 54 officers and 535 NCOs and sappers. Two new factories at Pont d'Ardres and Rouen had been built and the Special Works Park employed 100 Chinese labourers and 2,000 Frenchmen and women.

SPECIALIST ENGINEER COMPANIES

Each army controlled a wide variety of specialized engineering companies whose work was coordinated by the chief engineer.

MILITARY ENGINEERING WORKS

While field companies and siege companies supervised army troop companies working on the trench systems and strongpoints, field survey companies mapped out both friendly and enemy systems.

INFRASTRUCTURE

The transportation (works) companies supervised labour working on roads while pontoon parks built temporary bridges for fortress companies to install. Artisan companies supervised forestry companies and labour companies worked in the quarries to provide building materials. While drainage companies drained water from low-lying areas to keep the trenches dry, boring sections drilled wells. There were area employment companies, the special works (camouflage) company and an agricultural company.

MAINTENANCE AND REPAIR

Advanced park and base park companies kept the engineers supplied with tools and building materials. The Royal Engineer workshops maintained and repaired equipment while electrical and mechanical companies (the separate Royal Electrical and Mechanical Engineers did not yet exist) and army workshop companies kept the fleet of vehicles on the road.

OTHER UNITS

Flash-spotting and sound-ranging sections coordinated observation of German batteries for the artillery.

THE MACHINE GUN CORPS

It soon became clear that the Vickers and Maxim machine guns were too conspicuous to deploy in the front line and too cumbersome to carry forward during an attack. The introduction of the Lewis gun in the summer of 1915 provided a front-line weapon and a proposal to group the Vickers guns into machine-gun companies for use in a support

Water was a scarce commodity in some areas; these Canadian engineers are boring for a fresh supply near Arras in June 1918. *(IWM CO2810)*

A machine-gun team keep up a steady rate of fire during a gas attack near Ovillers on the Somme in July 1916. *(IWM Q3996)*

role was made to the War Office in September that year.

The Machine Gun Corps was formed a month later with its headquarters at Camiers. The Vickers guns were withdrawn from the infantry battalions and grouped into machine-gun companies (squadrons in cavalry divisions) with 1 per brigade. Each company had 100 men, split into 4 sections (3 in the cavalry divisions), each with 4 Vickers guns. A subaltern, assisted by a sergeant, led each section and a corporal organized the section limbers and belt-filling equipment.

Each infantry battalion (or cavalry regiment) received 8 Lewis or Hotchkiss guns in exchange. Divisions reorganized a brigade at a time when Lewis guns became available and their crews had been trained. It took

several months before all the machine-gun companies had been organized. Twelve New Army divisions received their Lewis guns while training in England and their Machine Gun Corps personnel received instruction at the Grantham Machine Gun Training Centre before leaving for France. As the war progressed the number of Lewis guns per battalion was steadily increased, reaching 32 in 1918.

An extra Vickers machine-gun company was added to each division in the spring of 1917 and a year later the 4 companies were organized into a battalion, which took the number of its parent division. In the autumn of 1915 the corps numbered about 3,000 officers and men and by November 1918 it had grown to over 133,300 officers and men.

GUARDS MACHINE GUN REGIMENT

The 4 machine-gun companies with the Guards Division were amalgamated into the 4th Battalion Machine Gun Guards in March 1918. Two months later the Guards Machine Gun Regiment was formed with 3 Life Guards and Royal Horse Guards machine-gun battalions and the battalion of Machine Gun Guards.

MACHINE GUN CORPS (MOTORS)

A motor machine-gun battery was added to each division in February 1915. Each battery had 18 motorcycle and sidecar combinations, armed with 6 Vickers machine guns; the commanding officer had his own sidecar combination and despatch riders rode 8 motorcycles; 2 or 3 wagons or cars were provided to carry supplies.

Scotts motorcycles were used to begin with but they were too fragile and a variety of Clyno, Enfield, Matchless, Premier and Zenith machines replaced them. Volunteers were motorcycle enthusiasts and riders wore weatherproof garments, gauntlets, leather gaiters and goggles while riding.

The batteries became part of the Machine Gun Corps in October 1915 and they were renamed the Machine Gun Corps (Motors). Six months later, when it became obvious there were no opportunities to deploy them at the front, the batteries were attached to corps headquarters. Many officers and men transferred to the Machine Gun Corps (Heavy Section) in 1916 to work with tanks.

In all 25 batteries were formed but a number were disbanded while others were shipped to the Mediterranean and India. Four were organized into a Motor Machine Gun Brigade in November 1918 and joined Second Army's drive across northern Belgium.

THE TANK CORPS

MACHINE GUN CORPS (HEAVY SECTION)

The development of the tank is covered in Chapter Nine.

A new headquarters was set up at Bisley, England, in March 1916 and men from the Motor Machine Gun Corps were organized into 4 companies (A, B, C and D) of the new Machine Gun Corps (Heavy Section). The companies moved to Elveden near Thetford in June and training began in earnest.

Companies were organized into 4 sections, each with 3 Male and 3 Female tanks. Sections were divided into three sub-sections, with one Male and one Female tank in each; the company also had a reserve machine.

Two companies left for France in August 1916 and assembled at Yvrench, north-east of Abbeville. They were soon heading for the Somme to practise on a realistic training ground called The Loop, north of Bray. Three mobile workshops were set up to service and repair the tanks.

A few days later the 2 companies moved towards the front and, on the morning of 15 September 1916, 42 tanks led Fourth Army's advance through Martinpuich and Flers; another 6 tanks joined Reserve Army's attack on Courcelette. Despite problems with reliability and the difficult terrain the tanks were a success; within days GHQ ordered 1,000 machines.

Mud limited the use of tanks for a time but 16 joined the attack on 25 September, cooperating with aeroplanes for the first time. The next large commitment was on 13 November, when 18 tanks helped to capture Beaumont-Hamel. Meanwhile, 2 new companies had reached France and a fifth was on its way to Egypt.

MACHINE GUN CORPS (HEAVY BRANCH)

The new title was adopted on 18 November 1916 when the companies were expanded into battalions (A Company became A Battalion, etc.) and administrative, engineering and technical personnel were appointed. Originally battalions had 3 companies, each organized into 4 sections of 3 tanks (with another 12 in reserve); a battalion had 32 officers and 374 men.

A central repair shop and store was opened north-west of St Pol at the start of 1917; it repaired 227 machines over the next 12 months.

This Mark I tank, *D17*, came to grief near Flers on 15 September 1916; two days later an infantry company has set up its headquarters inside the wreck. *(IWM Q5577)*

The battalions were grouped into 2 brigades in time for the Battle of Arras and 60 tanks took part in the attack on 9 April. The crews discovered that the Germans had developed anti-tank tactics, digging tank-traps in front of tactical points, while the infantry had been armed with huge anti-tank rifles firing armour-piercing bullets.

A third brigade was added at the end of April when 2 more battalions reached France. The Mark IV tank took to the battlefield for the first time on 7 June at Messines Ridge.

TANK CORPS

The name Tank Corps was adopted on 27 July 1917 and battalions were given numbers (tank names continued to follow the original lettering and numbering – 7th Battalion tanks had names beginning with the letter G, for example *Grumble* and *Grouse*). Four days later

120 tanks joined Fifth Army's attack east of Ypres. Tanks were used on several occasions between August and October but the water-logged ground severely limited movement.

Experiments with supply tanks carrying fuel and ammunition were a success, extending the tanks' fighting range and trials with tank mounted wirelesses proved to be promising. Mounting a 60-pounder or 6-inch gun on a tank chassis was also tried.

The Cambrai offensive beginning on 20 November was the corps' high point of the year. Eight battalions, 324 tanks (with another 54 in reserve), led by Brigadier-General Hugh Elles, smashed through the Hindenburg Line and advanced 6 miles. Wire-cutting tanks dragged sections of wire to one side ahead of the infantry while wireless tanks kept their headquarters updated with progress.

At the end of the year General Elles issued a

training manual, *Instructions for the Training of the Tank Corps in France*, formalizing the physical, moral, technical and tactical lessons learnt by the tank crews. A new training manual, *The Training and Employment of Divisions*, appeared in January 1918 summarizing how the tank crews should cooperate with the infantry and artillery. The corps grew to 4 brigades in January and 5 by March but they were of little use during the German spring offensives; the crews often fought on foot as Lewis gun teams alongside the infantry.

On 26 March the Whippet tank saw action for the first time but, while the British were promoting a lighter and faster tank, the Germans introduced the A7V, a 30-ton machine with an 18-man crew armed with a 57mm gun and 6 machine guns. Only 20 were built and the Germans frequently relied on captured British tanks to support their attacks. The first tank-versus-tank battle took place at Villers-Bretonneux on the Somme in April 1918; it ended in an inconclusive draw.

Tanks were used for the first time at night at Bucquoy on the Somme on 22 June and two weeks later 60 new Mark V tanks appeared on the battlefield at Hamel.

On 8 August 430 tanks supported Fourth Army's attack east of Amiens; it was the largest number of tanks employed in one day. Infantry scouts led the tanks into action and planes flew overhead marking targets with smoke. Some tanks acted as personnel carriers, taking machine-gun teams into action, while others acted as supply carriers.

During the final days of August 3rd Brigade

Repairs complete, a tank leaves the Tank Corps Central Workshops at Teneur. *(IWM Q9880)*

Mark V tanks carry cribs to help them cross the trenches of the Hindenburg Line around Bellicourt on 29 September 1918. *(IWM Q9364)*

joined First Army's drive towards Cambrai while 1st and 2nd Brigades helped Third Army's advance to the Canal du Nord; 4th and 5th Brigades joined Fourth Army's drive to the River Somme. The Mark V*, 6 feet longer than the Mark V, had been introduced to cross wide trenches and on 24 August three covered 40,000 yards (over 22 miles) in 26 hours.

On 27 September First and Third Armies broke through the Hindenburg Line in front of Cambrai with 1st and 2nd Brigades; two days later 3rd, 4th and 5th Brigades led Fourth Army as it stormed the St Quentin Canal defences and the Beaurevoir Line beyond. Armoured cars and Whippet tanks cooperated with the cavalry during the pursuit to the River Selle that followed. 6th Brigade was added on 12 October.

The Tank Corps was virtually exhausted by mid-October. Although 4th Brigade helped Fourth Army across the Selle and 2nd Brigade

joined the pursuit to the Sambre Canal, the rest of the brigades were withdrawn to refit.

On 7 November the decision was taken to organize the 6 tank brigades into 3 groups, nominally with two brigades each:

1st Tank Group – First Army.
2nd Tank Group – Fourth Army.
3rd Tank Group – Third Army.

The Armistice was declared before the groups had assembled.

During the final hundred days of the war the Tank Corps operated 2,245 tanks, in over 2,000 individual actions. Around 1,000 tanks were destroyed in battle and a similar number were temporarily disabled or broke down and later returned to action.

TANK SALVAGE

When a tank was unable to move, the crew removed the Lewis guns and periscopes and then attempted to camouflage the tank. The commander collected his log book and locked up the tank, reporting his position to the company commander. Crews returned to base when ordered, leaving two guards behind with the machine.

Salvage companies, 1 per tank brigade, were trained to carry out battlefield repairs and recover disabled tanks. As soon as the number and condition of ditched tanks was known, the company commander sent out salvage squads, aiming to deal with the straightforward problems first. Labourers carried the squads' tools and gave assistance while repairs were carried out. Sixty tunnellers were attached to the company to dig out ditched machines.

Squads aimed to dig out and repair the tank, escorting badly damaged tanks to the railhead. Tanks beyond repair were stripped and left on the battlefield.

INTELLIGENCE

The Secret Service Bureau had been set up in 1909 to counter spy scares at British ports and shipyards. A new Intelligence Corps was formed on the outbreak of war but its beginnings were chaotic.

During the open warfare in the autumn of 1914 GHQ relied on intelligence from the cavalry and the Royal Flying Corps but the development of the trenches called for new techniques. At the front troops carried out trench raids to seize documents and prisoners for interrogation. French listening sets were introduced in February 1916 to eavesdrop on German messages and skilled linguists

A tank crew uses sheer legs to salvage an engine from a ditched tank as a Chinese labourer looks on. *(IWM Q9864)*

Intelligence officers study sacks full of documents captured during the Austrian retreat in Italy in September 1918. *(IWM Q26733)*

manned the code-breaking unit, MI1b. The number of staff increased from 4 to 84. GHQ also operated its own cipher section compiling the enemy order of battle from an early stage.

While improvements in aerial photography helped to identify new building works behind the front, it was impossible to track German troop movements by train. Networks of agents (mainly Belgian and French refugees smuggled back to their home towns) watched the trains behind the German line, noting their contents and direction of travel. Couriers collected the information and carried it across the Dutch border so it could be assessed and sent back to Britain. Over 5,000 men, women and children from France, Belgium and Luxembourg worked for the British secret service.

German agents smashed one network in the summer of 1916 and in November raided a Dutch passenger ship, finding agents and documents on board. With the overland route blocked, pigeons and wireless sets were tried with some success. Two electrical engineers in Brussels ran the La Dame Blanche system, increasing it to over 900 members by the end of the war; the train spotters provided information which helped GHQ to predict the German spring offensives in 1918.

Strategic intelligence from agents around the world was collected in Whitehall Court, the section in charge of assessing the information being named MI1c in January 1916. Intelligence summaries were issued to government departments, GHQ and the army headquarters every few days.

CHAPTER SIX

THE SERVICES

ARMY SERVICE CORPS (ASC)

Hundreds of tons of equipment, ammunition and food had to be loaded, moved, unloaded and distributed every day to keep the men at the front fed and armed. The Army Service Corps was responsible for keeping the horses and lorries on the road as they carried supplies from bases along the French coast to the front line. It was a vital role recognized by Royal Warrant on 25 November 1918.

In August 1914 the ASC numbered 498 officers and 5,858 other ranks; 13,320 reservists joined during the first weeks of the war. A centralized system of allocating stores and servicing vehicles was difficult to operate and, as soon as the front stabilized, store depots and workshops were set up.

As the months passed, the number of motor vehicles on the Western Front increased dramatically. These lorries are waiting near Contay on the Somme in September 1916. *(IWM Q1084)*

BADGES OF THE SERVICES

Army Service Corps

Labour Corps

Royal Army Medical Corps

Royal Army Ordnance Corps

Army Veterinary Service

Army Chaplain's Department

Military Police

Army Pay Corps

By the end of the war the RASC had grown to 325,000 officers and men organized into 184 British and 32 Dominion ASC companies; they were assisted by tens of thousands of labourers from China, India and Egypt.

THE ARMY SERVICE CORPS COMPANY

A division had 4 companies of 26 officers and 402 other ranks, responsible for supplying the division. Each company had 378 horses, 125 wagons and 17 carts; the messengers used 30 bicycles.

LABOUR COMPANIES AND RAILWAY COMPANIES

Local dockers were used to unload ships at the start of the war; 300 labourers from Britain soon joined them. More followed and 5 labour companies, each with 6 officers and 530 other ranks, were formed in December 1914 to work on the supply lines. New Army volunteers with relevant experience were encouraged to transfer to the labour companies as NCOs; over 21,000 skilled labourers and dock workers joined in 1915, expanding the ASC to 32 labour companies. They were organized into horse transport companies, motor transport companies and depot companies. A railway company was formed in January 1915 and deployed detachments at the main stations to maintain rail lines; a second was added nine months later.

HORSE TRANSPORT COMPANIES

Some 53,000 riding and draught horses sailed to France with the BEF in August 1914. By 1916 the number of animals had risen to over 400,000. Despite the increase in motor transport, thousands of horses continued to pull supply wagons to the front line, in particular from the divisional railheads to the supply dumps. Horse transport companies often had the initials HT in their title.

DIVISIONAL TRAINS

The divisional trains (transport units) carried supplies from the divisional refilling points to the dumps. Each division had 1 divisional and 3 brigade horsed transport companies and a divisional train headquarters. The trains had 26 officers and 402 other ranks looking after 378 horses as they pulled 125 wagons and 17 carts.

RESERVE PARK COMPANIES

Reserve park companies supplied the heavy and medium artillery brigades as well as the corps and army troops. A number were allocated to armies in 1917 and renamed army auxiliary horse transport companies.

HORSE SMALL ARMS AMMUNITION PARK COMPANIES

An increase in air attacks made it necessary to split the large ammunition depots into smaller depots. Three companies carried small arms ammunition between the depots.

BASE DEPOTS AND DEPOT COMPANIES

New recruits joined at one of the four base depots and, after completing their training at the Le Havre base depot, they transferred to the advanced depot at Rouen for posting. A second advanced depot was added in April 1915 and 8 reserve depots were established in London a year later.

A base depot was opened in Egypt to serve the Dardanelles in the spring of 1915 and an advanced depot was set up at Gallipoli once the beachhead had been established. The British Salonika Army and the British Force in Italy had their own base and advanced depots; a mule transport depot was set up in

A queue of converted London omnibuses wait to take troops to the rear. *(IWM Q2690)*

As the howitzers grew in size, auxiliary steam companies were introduced to take over from the horse-drawn limbers. *(IWM Q10415)*

November 1918 to serve the expeditionary force to North Russia.

PACK TRANSPORT

Large numbers of mules were used to carry rations, water and ammunition forward, but they were found to be a hindrance on the narrow duck-walks. They were eventually allowed to make their own way across country, picking a route through the shell craters behind their leader.

MOTORIZED TRANSPORT COMPANIES

The number of vehicles rose from a few hundred cars, lorries and motorcycles to over 120,000. Motor transport units often had the initials MT as part of their title.

Divisional supply columns had companies led by 5 officers with 2 cars for transport; 337 other ranks operated 45 x 3-ton and 16 x 30-cwt lorries. Convoys carried supplies and ammunition from the railheads to the divisional refilling points and, if possible, to the infantry and artillery dumps. Four lorries carried the column's stores and equipment while despatch riders rode on 7 motorcycles.

AMMUNITION PARKS AND AMMUNITION COLUMNS

Motor transport was needed to carry the great quantities of huge shells needed by the heavy artillery. The companies which were stationed at the divisional ammunition dumps were called ammunition parks. The companies working at the corps and army artillery ammunition dumps were called ammunition columns.

MOTOR TRANSPORT MOTOR AMBULANCE CONVOYS

ASC men drove and serviced the ambulances, while RAMC men attended to the wounded (the organization of the ambulance units is covered in the RAMC section).

MOTOR TRANSPORT AUXILIARY (OMNIBUS) COMPANIES

The London General Omnibus Company sent 300 buses to France in October 1914 driven by 330 volunteers. Another 473 buses were eventually sent to France and organized into 4 companies.

AUXILIARY (PETROL) AND (STEAM) COMPANIES

Three auxiliary petrol companies were formed in March 1915. The one at Boulogne maintained the transport at the ports, the others worked out of Etaples and Rouen on the lines of communication; a fourth was formed later. Two auxiliary steam companies operated the traction engines used to pull the heaviest howitzers.

BRIDGING AND PONTOON COMPANIES

Two bridging train companies were formed in May 1915 to build temporary bridges for the engineers to install; they were later known as pontoon parks. One transferred to the Italian front in 1918.

REPAIR AND SUPPLY

Each army had a mobile repair company and workshop to maintain mechanical transport. Major repairs were dealt with at workshops based in St Omer, Boulogne, Paris and Rouen; two depots at Rouen and Calais kept the workshops stocked with spares.

LABOUR CORPS

This organisation was formed in January 1917 to control the workforce labouring behind the lines; ASC companies and a number of infantry battalions transferred to the corps in the spring of 1917, and when the labour companies were broken up in June 1917 the majority of men transferred to the new corps.

Loading shells was back-breaking work. These men are working against the clock to clear a dump near Bapaume during the German offensive in March 1918. *(IWM Q8610)*

Some 175,000 men worked on the roads, railways and bases across Great Britain; 214,900 men were employed behind the lines in theatres across the world. Category B men worked overseas while Category C men remained in Britain.

CHANGES BEHIND THE LINES

As the front line became static, divisional line of communications troop were transferred to higher command. Army corps took over responsibility for distributing ammunition and the divisional ammunition columns, and the divisional ammunition parks were re-formed as GHQ ammunition parks; corps parks and divisional sub-parks were set up to store and distribute ammunition.

An ASC company was formed for each army and corps when they took command of the heavy artillery; they were responsible for supplying the tractor-driven siege batteries.

SPECIALIZED COMPANIES

Each army had a workshop repairing anti-aircraft guns. Water tank companies were attached to GHQ and travelled the front to control the supply of sterilized water.

LINES OF COMMUNICATION

The ASC was responsible for transporting thousands of tons of supplies from the ports on the coast to divisional refilling points a few miles behind the front, sorting them along the way. Some goods were bought locally but the bulk of supplies were brought to the base depots on the French coast by transport ships. As the U-boat menace increased, safe overland routes were negotiated with Spain, Portugal and Italy. Local labour and convicts helped the ASC men unload the ships at the Army Ordnance Corps' base depots and pack the waiting supply trains.

RAIL ROUTES

A division consumed half a train of supplies per day during quiet periods, increasing to 1.5–2.5 trains per day during an offensive.

Each army had designated routes but there was flexibility over the use of rail lines during busy periods.

FIRST ARMY – BÉTHUNE

Supplies were taken from the ports of Le Havre, Rouen and Dieppe and sorted at Abbeville's regulating station. Trains travelled to railheads around Béthune and Hazebrouck. Reinforcements and new divisions were taken straight to Béthune.

SECOND ARMY – YPRES

Supplies were sorted into division-sized loads at Rivière Neuve near Boulogne. The trains travelled through Calais, St Omer and Hazebrouck to railheads around Bailleul and Poperinghe. Reinforcements and new divisions were taken straight to Hazebrouck.

THIRD ARMY – SOMME THEN ARRAS

Third Army took over Abbeville in July 1915. Supply trains ran along single lines through Serqueux and Romescamps, returning via Etaples and St Pol.

FOURTH ARMY – SOMME

Supplies were sorted at Romescamps regulating station, between Le Havre and Amiens. Trains ran through Serqueux, Romescamps and St Roch, west of Amiens. Troops were taken straight to the Amiens area.

ADVANCED SUPPLY DEPOTS

The daily amount of food consumed by a division remained constant and foodstuffs were sorted into mixed loads at the advanced supply depots and then forwarded to the regulating stations. An advanced supply depot was opened at Outreau, near Boulogne, in January 1917, while the depot at Abbeville continued to serve the southern lines of communication.

REGULATING STATIONS

Ammunition and supplies delivered from the bases were sorted into division-sized stacks and loaded onto waiting trains with the foodstuffs at the regulating station. GHQ issued

A queue of lorries waits for shells to be loaded at a railhead ammunition dump. *(IWM Q10451)*

schedules listing divisions' railheads on a daily basis and trucks were loaded and sorted into trains for each railhead. A regulating station was capable of dealing with up to 24 divisions, or one army, at one time.

RAILHEADS

New sidings were built beyond the artillery range of all but the largest guns, usually around 10–15 miles from the front. Train loads were transferred to waiting lorries or light-railway trucks at the railheads. Surplus supplies were stored at the railheads and a supply of rations was always available to feed men on the move.

DIVISIONAL REFILLING POINTS AND BRIGADE DUMPS

Lorries were unloaded and sorted by the divisional and brigade quartermasters in the divisional area. The horse-drawn wagons of the divisional trains carried the supplies to the brigade dumps where the brigade transport officer issued them to the regimental transport. Infantry supplies were stockpiled near the communication trenches ready to be collected while the battery transport took shells and rations straight to the battery wagon lines.

INTO THE TRENCHES

Ration parties carried the supplies by hand into the trenches, usually at night. Surplus stocks, known as trench stores, were handed over to the new arrivals during a relief.

QUANTITIES

Rations, fodder and fuel were bought by the Director of Contracts at the War Office and collected at storehouses at British ports when war broke out. As the months passed the quantities increased enormously and the control of supplies was transferred to the theatres of war.

Horse-drawn limbers took over at the ammunition refilling area. These drivers are waiting to head through Albert during the early stages of the Battle of the Somme in 1916. *(IWM Q4034)*

THE SUPPLY SERVICE

The Expeditionary Force grew from 120,000 men to over 3,000,000 men and the quantity of supplies multiplied in proportion. A Regular officer, aided by a trained staff of accountants and businessmen, managed the Investigation Department and he eventually controlled an annual expenditure of over £80,000,000.

PETROL

The War Office had a lien on petrol stocks in the United Kingdom at the start of the war and small supplies were sent over to France in cans. The daily consumption of petrol had increased to over 67,000 gallons by the start of 1916 and petrol filling plants were set up at Rouen and Calais the following summer to deal with supplies shipped in from America. Ships pumped the petrol directly into storage tanks so it could be piped to can-filling plants. Daily consumption had risen to 435,000 gallons by 1918.

COAL

Deliveries of coal were moved to Cherbourg, Brest and St Malo, relieving congestion at the main ports. From the summer of 1915 coal was obtained from the Bruay coal mines and the French government eventually allowed the Directorate of Forestry to cut wood for fuel.

RATIONS

Field bakeries at the base ports supplied bread during the early days of the war. Daily requirements rose from 67 tons to 1,340 tons so steam ovens and automatic machinery were introduced. Bakeries were established at Le Havre, Boulogne and Calais in 1915 and women took over from the ASC bakers at the 42 British and 6 Dominion field bakeries.

Meat carcasses were cut up in Britain before they were shipped across the Channel. Refrigerated store ships were berthed at each port to accept foreign shipments and cold storage accommodation was eventually found in Boulogne and Le Havre. Butcheries were

Monthly Tonnages	August 1914	November 1918
Meat	1,600 tons	30,100 tons
Bread	2,000 tons	40,200 tons
Forage	2,600 tons	14,400 tons
Petrol	842,000 gallons	13 million gallons

then set up at the French ports. The daily supply of meat rose from 55 tons to 1,000 tons and a stock of preserved meat was kept available to cover temporary shortages.

FORAGE

Between 1914 and the end of the war the amount of forage shipped across the Channel increased from 88 tons to 480 tons a day. An agency of the supplies special purchase department started buying hay and straw from the French after 1915 to conserve forage and the amount of shipping required. Where possible animals were allowed to graze to conserve stocks.

A SUMMARY OF TONNAGES

Approximate monthly shipments of supplies and rations to the Western Front are shown in the table above.

ROYAL ARMY MEDICAL CORPS (RAMC)

The Royal Army Medical Corps staffed the casualty evacuation chain, starting with the stretcher-bearers on the battlefield, through regimental medical officers and a series of dressing stations and collecting points back to the casualty clearing station where surgery could begin. The RAMC's priorities were to collect, sort, treat and evacuate the wounded to a safe area as quickly as possible, in the hope of saving as many men as possible.

The RAMC's casualty load was huge, as is illustrated in the table below, and this necessitated a massive expansion in the corps, shown in the table at bottom.

Disease was a substantial problem in addition to battle injuries. The four greatest causes of illness were: venereal disease (18%), trench foot (13%), nephritis (7%) and dysentery (4%).

REGIMENTAL AID POSTS

The battalion's RAMC officer ran the regimental aid post, aided by 2 orderlies and 16 stretcher-bearers; his supplies and equipment were carried in a cart. The medical officer set up his aid post either in a dugout or the cellars of a ruined building, near the battalion headquarters so he could keep in

NUMBER OF CASUALTIES TREATED IN 1916		
	Wounded	Sick
Admitted	500,000	644,000
Died	37,000 (7%)	10,000 (2%)
Evacuated	292,000 (59%)	247,000 (38%)
Returned to the front	171,000 (34%)	387,000 (60%)

EXPANSION OF THE ROYAL ARMY MEDICAL CORPS:		Officers	Other Ranks	Nurses
BEF	August 1914	200	9,000	516
All theatres	July 1916	10,669	114,939	6,394

close contact with the commanding officer. The facilities were crude and the officer and his orderlies could only administer basic first aid and organize the stretcher-bearers; his priority was to evacuate men to the rear for treatment. The number of stretcher-bearers per battalion was doubled to 32 in 1915.

The aid post could typically deal with 20–30 men at a time, and had basic surgical equipment, dressings and splints to treat wounds, and stretchers and blankets to keep the men comfortable. Blood transfusion equipment was supplied to aid posts towards the end of the war. The post usually had 8 stretchers (increased to 10 in July 1918) but 50 stretchers and 100 blankets might be brought forward before an offensive.

Improvised designs to overcome the problem of moving the regulation stretcher through the trenches were tried and the Rogers trench stretcher was officially recognized; companies each received 4 during the summer of 1915. Hand carriages, wheeled stretchers and trolley lines were also used to evacuate the wounded.

Before an offensive, trenches were designated 'Down' for the evacuation of wounded and 'Up' for men and supplies moving forward. Lightly injured men were encouraged to walk, or crawl, to the aid post, while the stretcher-bearers collected the seriously wounded. Sixteen reserve stretcher-bearers joined the aid post at the start of an offensive. Reserve bearers usually waited at the aid post until the number and location of wounded were known.

Stretcher cases were often gathered in a trench or shell-hole marked by flags, and as

The casualty chain started in the mud and debris of the trenches. Stretcher-bearers attend to two injured Irish Guards officers during the Guards Division's advance across Pilckem Ridge on 31 July 1917. *(IWM Q5732)*

soon as the medical officer knew the map reference a guide took the reserve bearers forward to retrieve them. The optimum time for retrieving wounded was immediately after the objective had been taken, when the infantry could help to locate the wounded and carry them to the rear. Relay bearer posts were set up every thousand yards to speed up the collection of casualties.

While a battalion was in reserve, the medical staff dealt with minor injuries and the sick, and supervised the battalion's sanitation requirements. At the time of mobilization the RAMC provided an NCO and 4 men to maintain the battalion's water carts and attend to the sterilization of water supplies. Men from the battalion were trained to take over the water duties as the number of RAMC personnel available dwindled.

THE FIELD AMBULANCE

Divisions had three field ambulances, each divided into three sections, A, B and C; sections were again split into stretcher-bearer and tented sub-divisions. The bearer divisions were intended to carry the wounded from the regimental aid post to the tent divisions' dressing stations. Each field ambulance had 10 unarmed officers and 224 men. Cavalry field ambulances had only 2 sections, A and B.

Field ambulances came under the orders of the Assistant Director Medical Services, who in turn reported to the divisional commander. The organization had been chosen with colonial campaigns in mind, with sections supporting independent brigades of troops.

On the Western Front the field ambulance sections worked together behind a division's lines. They formed a chain of medical posts between the regimental aid post and the casualty clearing stations, categorizing the wounded into serious and minor injuries, while separating the gassed, the sick and the shell-shocked along the way.

SECTION ORGANIZATION

A lieutenant-colonel commanded the field ambulance as a whole and took direct charge of A Section.

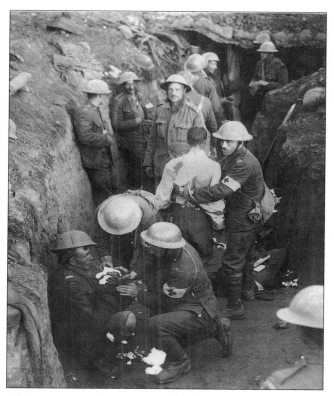

Canadian medics carry out emergency first aid at their regimental aid post during attacks on Courcelette in September 1916. *(IWM CO756)*

Stretcher-Bearer Sub-Division (1 officer and 42 other ranks). A captain or lieutenant, assisted by a sergeant, a corporal and a bugler, led 36 stretcher-bearers and 3 wagon orderlies; Sub-Sections B and C had 2 orderlies.

Tented Sub-Division (1 officer and 21 ORs). Led by a captain or lieutenant and assisted by a quartermaster, a sergeant-major, and 2 orderlies. Two sergeants and 2 corporals commanded 15 privates (Sub-Sections B and C had four sergeants and 13 privates), while the cook and washer man kept the men fed and clean with the help of a water cart and forage cart.

A sergeant, 10 drivers and 4 batmen (all Army Service Corps men) maintained 4 ambulance wagons for the wounded and 2 General Service wagons for the stores.

Orderlies wait outside an advanced dressing station of the 15th (Scottish) Division following the capture of Martinpuich on 15 September 1916. *(IWM Q4353)*

Fourteen riding horses and 52 draught and pack horses pulled the transport. Sections B and C had only 3 ambulance wagons, driven by 9 ASC drivers.

Each field ambulance also had a cook's wagon, driven by an ASC driver. Seven motor vehicles were added to each ambulance at the end of 1914 and each division had a maintenance workshop to service the vehicles; the workshops were absorbed into the supply column in 1916.

DIVISIONAL RESPONSIBILITY

The field ambulances were responsible for sorting the wounded and dealing with the men needing immediate attention. The tent sub-divisions supplied the accommodation for the advanced dressing station (ADS) while the bearer divisions manned the first four stages of the evacuation chain; they could be reinforced by reserve bearers from other units during offensives.

BEARER RELAY POSTS

A chain of relay posts connected the regimental aid post to the divisional collecting post when it was over 1,000 yards away. Around 20 bearers waited at each post in shell-holes, trenches, or bunkers until they were needed. Routes were marked with flags during daylight hours and transparency lamps at night.

DIVISIONAL COLLECTING POSTS

The relay posts converged at the divisional collecting post. An officer and NCO supervised 24 bearers as they loaded the seriously injured onto wheeled stretcher carriers, trolleys or light railways. Walking wounded made their own way to the ADS.

RESERVE BEARER POSTS

Extra men (between 200 and 600) were drafted in to help during offensives. Around half worked at the divisional collecting post while the rest waited near the advanced dressing station ready to help anywhere along the line of evacuation.

ADVANCED DRESSING STATION (ADS)

The field ambulances' tent sub-divisions set up ADSs at the limit of wheeled transport. A large building with good road access was ideal. It had to be protected from shell-fire and gas attacks. An ADS had to be able to deal with at least 100 casualties at a time; larger facilities were built before an offensive. The staff classified casualties and carried out emergency treatment before evacuating them to the main dressing station; serious cases were sent straight to the casualty clearing station. An ADS was often split into two during busy periods. While some of the men loaded stretcher cases into ambulance cars, the rest helped the walking wounded into waiting lorries; empty vehicles waited at a safe distance until they were required.

At the start of an offensive an ADS was stocked with 100 pyjama suits, 60 hot water bottles, 600 blankets, 400 stretchers and a supply of splints; blood transfusion equipment was supplied towards the end of the war.

CORPS RESPONSIBILITY

The seriously wounded were hurried to the rear while the walking wounded, gassed and sick were given the chance to recover. The Deputy Director of Medical Services, the senior doctor of each corps, organized the

Inside the ADS medical officers had to work under difficult conditions as they struggled to improve a man's chances of survival. This Australian dressing station was set up inside a captured German bunker near Polygon Wood during the fighting in the Ypres Salient in September 1917. *(IWM E714)*

Walking wounded collect at a dressing station in Wieltje to have their wounds dressed during the battle for Broodseinde on 4 October 1917; note the pile of salvaged weapons and helmets in the centre. *(IWM Q6042)*

main dressing stations, walking wounded collecting stations, rest stations and sick rooms; tent divisions, or in some cases complete field ambulances, provided the facilities:

MAIN DRESSING STATION (MDS)

MDSs were set up beyond the range of the enemy's medium artillery. Field ambulance tent divisions ran each station, using buildings, huts or tents to accommodate 100 stretcher cases and 25 gassed at a time. Casualties were sorted into three categories:

Wounded able to travel after emergency
  surgery.
Wounded requiring rest before evacuation.
Men beyond assistance.

A convoy of ambulance cars and wagons carried the wounded to the casualty clearing station.

WALKING WOUNDED COLLECTING STATION

Men were given new dressings, room to rest and a place to dry their feet; a collecting post for the sick was often set up alongside. Orderlies recorded individuals' particulars, checked dressings and administered treatment, as the men gathered by the YMCA's refreshment huts. Serious cases were transferred to the MDS; the remainder were moved to rest stations.

REST STATIONS AND LOCAL SICK ROOMS

Tented facilities with dining and recreation areas, baths and ablution rooms could accommodate around 300 men; larger corps rest stations were introduced later in the war. Some were equipped to deal with scabies.

MOTOR AMBULANCE CONVOYS

At the beginning of the war the division relied on 30 horse-drawn ambulances to bring the wounded back. The experience on the Aisne in September 1914 proved that the horse-drawn supply wagons and lorries were uncomfortable and overworked, often leaving the wounded waiting to be evacuated. There was a need for independent convoys of motor transport and the first 50 cars fitted with ambulance bodies arrived in France in September 1914 where they were equipped with straw mattresses.

Each infantry field ambulance received 21 ambulance cars in 1915 while 9 horse-drawn wagons were retained for cross-country routes. Cavalry field ambulances had 6 light and 4 heavy ambulance wagons; motor ambulances replaced the heavy wagons in 1915.

An officer and 120 ASC drivers and mechanics kept the convoy moving while 3 RAMC officers and 120 men looked after the wounded. The officers used 2 motorcars and the despatch rider used a motorcycle, while 3 lorries carried supplies and spares.

Eventually there were 25 convoys, one for each corps, and one in army reserve ready to be deployed during offensives or as back-up if the railway system broke down. Each convoy had three sections, A Section with 20 cars and B and C Sections with 15 cars each, working in groups of 5. A workshop unit was based at the headquarters while a small forward repair workshop was set up near each main dressing station to cover emergency repairs. Individuals or voluntary subscription funded many of the cars.

The convoys operated between the main dressing stations, the casualty clearing stations and the ambulance train sidings using either definite road circuits or working to strict timetables on shared roads. When possible ambulances evacuated the wounded to the dressing stations at night, with spare transport being used to alleviate the pressure on the ambulance convoys.

CASUALTY CLEARING STATIONS (CCS)

Clearing hospitals were mobilized in August 1914 to provide the link between the field ambulances and the lines of communication.

Ambulances wait outside a dressing station in Vermelles following 46th Division's attack against the Hohenzollern Redoubt in October 1915. *(IWM Q29005)*

Motor ambulances delivered the wounded in batches of around 200, returning with new cases when the CCS had evacuated them. Casualty clearing stations, as they became known, had three functions:

To receive and treat the wounded and the seriously ill.
To evacuate men to the bases as soon as they were fit for the journey.
To care for men likely to recover within a few days.

CCSs were set up in municipal buildings or factories beyond the artillery zone and away from military targets. They were placed in built-up areas at the start of the war but, as the motor ambulances increased congestion, they moved into designated camps. Huts and tents were set out alongside railway sidings so the men could be loaded straight onto the waiting ambulance trains. Canal barges were used to evacuate men suffering from serious head and chest wounds.

ACCOMMODATION

Operating theatres and wards for the serious cases were housed in Nissen huts (holding 24 beds or 28 stretchers) or French Adrian huts (40 beds or 60 stretchers). Tents (8 beds or 12 stretchers) and marquees (14 beds or 20 stretchers) protected the rest of the men. CCSs were expanded to 1,000 spaces in 1915 and the number of huts increased as baths, latrines, stores, sterilizing facilities, dental surgeries and X-ray facilities were added.

PERSONNEL

Eight officers, including a quartermaster, and 77 orderlies ran the facilities; nursing sisters, 3 chaplains and a dentist joined later. Personnel from field ambulances, other clearing stations and the base hospitals were drafted in to help during busy periods.

Major surgical operations were transferred to the CCSs when sterile facilities became available at the start of 1915. Two surgeons and a physician made an initial assessment of

A light railway takes wounded of the 9th (Scottish) Division to the rear following the capture of Outtersteene Ridge on 18 August 1918. *(IWM Q6959)*

the men, categorizing their injuries, and advised on treatment. Surgical teams dealt with the wounded in turn, cleaning and closing wounds, carrying out amputations and setting broken bones. By 1917 up to 6 surgical teams could be working at a CCS. Detachments of convalescing men acted as stretcher-bearers and from 1917 venereal disease patients were employed.

TRANSPORT

The CCS started as a mobile unit with 8 lorries but it became practically immobile as its responsibilities grew. Attempts to rationalize the amount of equipment failed but portable operating rooms carried in 2 large trailers were added in September 1916. By the end of 1918 each CCS needed 40 lorries to keep up with an advance.

DISTRIBUTION

There was one CCS per division on the Western Front and they were allotted to armies more or less in that proportion (10 per army, increasing to 15 during an offensive). They were usually grouped in threes, with one around 7 miles behind the front and the other two as far again to the rear; one would often move closer to the front during an offensive.

As the number of CCSs increased, some specialized in types of wounds or illnesses. Some dealt with head wounds, chest wounds or limb injuries; others treated nervous disorders, skin troubles and infectious diseases.

Advanced Operating Centres were also set up close to the front so the seriously injured could be treated quickly.

AMBULANCE TRAINS IN FRANCE

One ambulance train per division was mobilized in 1914 to carry the wounded and sick from the casualty clearing stations to the hospitals along the French coast. Army requirements were reassessed at one train for every 20,000 soldiers at the beginning of 1915; 41 ambulance trains were eventually sent to France.

The Director of Railway Transport and

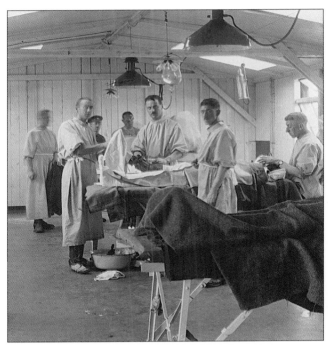

A medical team starts to operate on a casualty in Casualty Clearing Station No. 3. *(IWM CO157)*

Inland Water Transport operated the trains and his staff had to schedule them between the troop and supply trains. Before loading, the operator needed to know the number of patients, types of injuries and the train's destination so he could inform the waiting hospital. The majority of trains operated from the hospitals along the coast, returning to the CCSs with stocks of stretchers and blankets. Six trains worked from bases on the lines of communication, transferring patients between hospitals.

Four ambulance trains were funded by voluntary subscription:

Ambulance Train No. 14 – Lord Michelham's Hospital Train.
Ambulance Train No. 15 – Princess Christian's Hospital Train.
Ambulance Train No. 16 – United Kingdom Flour Millers' Hospital Train.
Ambulance Train No. 17 – United Kingdom Flour Millers' Hospital Train.

The carriage interiors on this train have been converted to accommodate tiered bunks. Nurses and orderlies cared for the patients during the journey to the coast. *(IWM Q8750)*

Dedicated ambulance trains could not cope with the numbers of wounded during offensives so temporary ambulance trains were added to transport sitting patients; they were off-loaded alongside the hospital ships waiting at Boulogne and Rouen after March 1915 to keep the hospitals free for the seriously wounded.

The numbers of sick and wounded moved by ambulance trains during 1916 were:

Ambulance trains: 713,957 at 450 per train.
Temporary ambulance trains: 30,659 at 1,050 per train.

AMBULANCE FLOTILLAS

A flotilla of 6 barges, No. 1 Ambulance Flotilla, joined the Expeditionary Force and operated on the Seine during the retreat to the Marne. Flotillas 2–5 were built in March 1915, each with 6 barges. The barges were fitted with 30 beds; a medical officer, 2 nursing sisters and 9 RAMC orderlies ran each one. Flotillas were controlled by the Director of Railway Transport and Inland Water Transport and operated by engineers. They carried severely wounded men who could not travel by train, usually those with head, chest and thigh wounds. Some worked the Lys and La Bassée Canals, taking the wounded to hospitals in St Omer and Calais, while others carried wounded along the Somme Canal to the hospitals in Amiens and Abbeville.

In 1916 the ambulance flotillas evacuated 16,918 casualties.

GENERAL AND STATIONARY HOSPITALS

The ambulance trains and barges took the wounded to the hospitals along the coast. The original hospitals were around Boulogne, Le Havre and Rouen but many extra ones had been added by the summer of 1915; Dominion hospitals were added when Canadian, Australian, New Zealand and South African troops reached France.

Huge facilities grew around the ports and Rouen was typical with general hospitals housed in municipal buildings and smaller stationary hospitals in huts and tents outside the town. Hospital ships evacuated the wounded to England on a daily basis while nearby camps catered for 2,000 convalescing soldiers.

	General Hospitals	Stationary Hospitals
Abbeville	1	11
Boulogne	5	6
Calais	2	–
Dieppe	1	–
Etaples	10	–
Le Havre	3	1
Le Treport	3	–
Rouen	7	4
St Omer	1	2

The Indian Corps had a stationary hospital at Marseilles and its general hospital was split between Rouen and Marseilles.

Around half the men admitted to a hospital returned to their units after treatment. Some

RAMC men and nurses load stretcher cases onto an ambulance train at Doullens in April 1918.
(IWM Q8752)

were transferred to convalescent depots to complete their recovery, while those requiring further treatment were evacuated by hospital ship to England.

Hospitals started with 32 officers, 206 other ranks and 73 female nurses; the number of staff had more than doubled by 1917. General hospitals were increased to 1,040 beds and stationary hospitals were increased to 400 beds or more. There were 71,651 beds available by the end of 1916.

There were two isolation hospitals for infectious diseases and a detention hospital for prison inmates. The Red Cross operated six small hospitals; the Scottish Red Cross and the St John Ambulance Brigade ran one each.

CONVALESCENT DEPOTS

As soon as they were well enough, men were transferred to a convalescent depot to complete their recovery, releasing hospital

beds for new patients. There was 1 officers' convalescent home and 7 convalescent depots for other ranks; sick nursing sisters were accommodated in 2 convalescent homes. In all 20,786 convalescent beds were eventually provided.

MEDICAL DEPOTS

The base depots at Boulogne, Etaples, Rouen and Le Havre (moved to Calais at the end of 1915) supplied the casualty evacuation chain with medicines and equipment; a depot was opened at Abbeville for Fifth Army in 1916. A boxcar took the supplies to the advanced depots where they were distributed to the CCSs and field ambulances; GHQ had its own advanced depot at St Omer.

HOSPITAL SHIPS

In 1914 the Director of Medical Services (DMS) at GHQ dealt with the disembarkation

Seriously wounded were evacuated on hospital barges. Barge *A458* has just moored at Péronne on the Somme Canal in June 1917. *(IWM Q3102)*

and distribution of the wounded using personnel organized by the War Office and equipment from the Army Ordnance Corps; the Admiralty operated the hospital ships. The cross-Channel operation was quickly central-ized under the DMS Embarkation based in England, and he eventually controlled nearly 100 hospital ships and ambulance transports operated by over 4,500 staff.

Large hospital ships could carry as many as

The stationary hospital on the St Pol–Frevent road lies under the snow in February 1917. *(IWM Q4722)*

4,000 wounded but there was limited berthing and they were only used following offensives. Medium ships, with around 800 beds, were more flexible and they could carry up to another 1,600 sitting cases on deck. The medical staff were split into teams and an officer, 2 nursing sisters and 10 orderlies looked after each 100 beds. They assessed the casualties during the crossing and tagged serious cases with red labels so they could be unloaded first.

To begin with the ships were painted white with a distinctive green band but when it appeared that U-boats were deliberately targeting them, the markings were removed and they were renamed ambulance transports. They sailed under the Red Ensign and were entitled to an armed naval escort. Torpedoes or mines sank 16 hospital ships during the course of the war.

Hospital ships were sent to Gallipoli and surgeries were added to transports so operations could be carried out during the voyage back to Britain.

TREATMENT IN GREAT BRITAIN
THE RECEPTION PORTS

The existing embarkation staff and stores based at Southampton were expanded on the outbreak of war. Dover was opened as a disembarkation port in January 1915 and staff at both facilities were increased to 300.

The wounded were carried ashore by waiting stretcher-bearers, while clerical staff took details and gave directions to the correct ambulance trains. RAMC staff assessed the casualties while local hospital staff and volunteers carried stretchers and distributed food and drink. Between 28 August 1914 and 31 July 1919, 2,655,000 officers and men passed through the ports.

Southampton: 1,317,000 from the Western Front.
Dover: 1,299,000 from the Western Front.
Devonport, Folkestone and Newcastle: 10,000 from the Western Front.
Avonmouth: 22,800 from the Mediterranean and other theatres.

Liverpool and Tilbury Docks, London: 1,700 casualties from the Far East.
Leith: 4,500 casualties from Russia.

DISTRIBUTING THE WOUNDED

The British Army only possessed one ambulance train capable of carrying 100 men when war was declared. Twelve new trains were ordered on 5 August 1914 and they arrived at Southampton Docks at the end of the month, ready to receive the first shiploads of wounded from Mons and Le Cateau; another 8 trains were soon added.

Each train had 10 coaches: 5 coaches each with spaces for 20 patients, an operating coach and a kitchen coach; staff and stores occupied the rest. A sixth patient coach was added later. Four emergency vans, each equipped with 20 stretchers, could be added while standard passenger coaches could be attached to carry sitting cases. An RAMC officer assisted by 2 nursing sisters and 11 orderlies cared for the wounded during the journey.

A number of passenger trains (with 500 seats) and 2 makeshift trains (converted to carry 120 stretcher cases) were kept on stand-by for busy periods. Southampton was often overwhelmed and both University Hospital and Eastleigh Clearing Hospital cared for men waiting for transport and those too ill to travel. Numbers peaked in July 1916 when 47,000 casualties a week were passing through Dover and Southampton.

To begin with there were concerns that patients would not be able to cope with long journeys but the long-term benefits of being cared for in a hospital close to home out-weighed the risks. Ambulance trains carried over 2,600,000 patients across Great Britain and only 6 died en route.

HOSPITALS

Trains were unloaded at city or town centre stations where Voluntary Aid Detachments had rest and refreshment areas to welcome the wounded, meeting the trains at any hour of the day or night. Large canteens were set up at Birmingham and Peterborough to break the journey for men heading north.

Patients were taken to large military and Territorial Force general hospitals, known as central hospitals. Numbers of patients and types of injuries were telegraphed ahead so the hospitals could prepare beds and arrange transport. The St John Ambulance Brigade and the British Red Cross Society worked together with automobile clubs to transfer the wounded to the hospitals. After assessment, men were moved to local affiliated hospitals specializing in the type of treatment they required. The central hospital had to be emptied and prepared for the next ambulance train.

Auxiliary hospitals were manned by voluntary aid organizations, while municipal and private hospitals provided extra bed spaces. Extra central hospitals were opened while smaller hospitals were expanded. Suitable private and municipal hospitals were classified as Class A auxiliary hospitals and could receive patients direct from the ports of disembarkation.

SPECIALIZED HOSPITALS

A small number of hospitals were organized to deal with specific injuries and illnesses:

2nd London General Hospital, Chelsea: Blind patients.
Sobraon Military Hospital, Colchester: Heart cases.
Queen Mary's Hospital, Sidcup: Facial injuries.
Buxton, Harrogate, Bath, and Llandrindod Wells Hospitals: Rheumatism.

Netley Hospital assessed neurological and shell-shock cases before moving them to asylums where they could be treated by trained staff.

Malarial convalescents from Salonika were treated at the University War Hospital, Southampton, before moving to selected hospitals. They completed their malarial treatment at their regimental depot until specialized malaria centres were opened at the end of the war.

Enteric patients had to be kept at isolation

The Queen inspects the South African Hospital in Abbeville on 10 July 1917; the men are wearing the special uniforms issued to convalescing soldiers. *(IWM Q2566)*

Crowds gather at Charing Cross Station in London on 8 July 1916 to cheer the first of thousands of wounded to reach England from the Somme. *(IWM Q56277)*

hospitals until they were free from infection; they were then transferred to Class B auxiliary hospitals to recover. Dysentery patients were treated at special hospitals and then transferred to a convalescent hospital at Barton-on-Sea near Bournemouth.

SPECIAL RULES FOR OFFICERS

Officers were entitled to sick leave and allowed to arrange their own treatment but it sometimes delayed their recovery. After March 1917 officers below the rank of colonel became subject to the same rules as other ranks, though they were cared for in separate officer wards.

DISCHARGING

Recovering men were sent to a convalescent home and eventually given one of the following three classifications:

(i) Soldiers ready to be trained for overseas duty; they were sent to the appropriate regiment's reserve unit.
(ii) Soldiers with overseas experience and likely to be ready for transfer to a reserve unit after convalescence were sent to the appropriate command depot.
(iii) Soldiers who would only be trained for home garrisons or labour companies.

The Army discharged the rest and those too ill to be released were transferred to convalescent or auxiliary hospitals to recover. Amputation cases were cared for in special hospitals until they were ready for artificial limbs.

Discharged Indian and Dominion soldiers were transferred to a port for repatriation when they had completed their hospital treatment.

The medical officer of the 12th East Yorkshires (Hull Sportsmen's Battalion) checks for trench foot in January 1918 when 31st Division was holding the Roclincourt sector near Arras. *(IWM Q10622)*

BELGIANS

Over 9,300 Belgian soldiers were sent to British military hospitals and 48,700 civilians to other hospitals during 1914 and 1915. In February 1915 four King Albert's Hospitals for Belgian soldiers opened, three in London and one in Folkestone; all Belgian soldiers were eventually transferred to them.

PRISONERS OF WAR

To begin with sick and wounded prisoners of war were cared for in military hospitals alongside British soldiers, but before long separate hospitals and wards were set up; over 46,000 enemy prisoners of war were cared for.

COMMAND DEPOTS

When hospitals began to run out of space, four convalescent camps were established at Blackpool, Epsom, Dartford and Eastbourne to accommodate men who needed further rest. Command depots were formed at the beginning of 1916, each capable of holding between 3,000 and 5,000 men fit enough to be hardened and trained.

An officers' command depot was set up in the Great Central Hotel in Marylebone, London; it was renamed the Prince of Wales's Hospital for Officers in August 1917. Infantry other ranks were sent to command depots in home command areas; other arms and the services had their own command depots. The Guards regiments, London Regiment and the Royal Naval Division also had separate depots.

HEALTH

SANITARY SECTIONS

Each unit had a small sanitary detachment responsible for cleanliness at the start of the war. As the front stabilized, sanitary squads were organized to keep the bases, railheads and towns behind the lines clean. Divisional sanitary sections were formed over the winter of 1914–15; a subaltern and his batman led each one, while 2 sergeants and 2 corporals organized the privates. The sections kept trenches and billets clean, maintained water supplies, cleaned latrines, disinfected blankets and clothes, and burned rubbish with the help of portable disinfectors.

The system broke down during the Somme Offensive in 1916 because divisions were rotating quickly, and the disorganization led to an outbreak of dysentery. Sanitary sections were centralized under army command in April 1917; however, the Dominion corps continued to run their own sections while cavalry divisions also had their own sections to clean stabling and dispose of manure.

MOBILE LABORATORIES FOR HYGIENE AND BACTERIOLOGY

A hygiene laboratory and 2 mobile bacteriological laboratories joined each army in 1915 to monitor the troops' health and analyse tissue samples.

MOBILE X-RAY LABORATORIES

Each army was allocated an X-ray laboratory; it usually became attached to one of the casualty clearing stations. X-ray units were eventually attached to each casualty clearing station.

DENTISTRY

A dentist joined each casualty clearing station as the front stabilized and they began to visit divisions to avoid sending men to the rear. Eventually privately funded mobile laboratories were attached to each army to carry out regular inspections. Dental centres, staffed by 3 dentists and 24 technicians, were set up in rear areas to deal with minor problems. Bases usually had their own dental centres while clinics covered the outlying areas on the lines of communication.

Dentistry in the Dominion corps was far more extensive and advanced; Canadian divisions had 10 dentists.

Uniforms and boots are piled high at the ordnance clothing depot near Calais. *(IWM Q29291)*

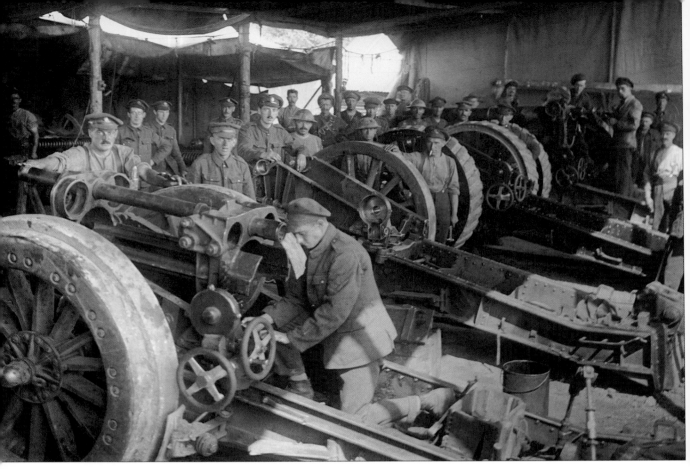

Worn out 60-pounder guns are stripped down and repaired in Lovie ordnance workshop. *(IWM Q2769)*

ARMY ORDNANCE CORPS

Eight Army Ordnance Corps companies left for France in August 1914. They issued every type of stores except for food and fuel (the Director of Transport issued motor vehicles). The following is an excerpt of items issued from the Calais base depot between January and October 1916:

447,000 Lewis-gun magazines and 5,000,000 gas helmets.
3,500,000 yards of flannelette and 1,250,000 yards of canvas.
26,000 tents and 1,500,000 waterproof sheets.
20,000 wheels and 12,800 bicycles.
40,000 electric torches and 40,000 miles of electric cable.
11,000 compasses and 7,000 watches.
4,000,000 pairs of horseshoes and 2,250,000 bars of soap.

An army had 2 ordnance officers and a staff, while each corps had 1 officer and a staff. The Tank Corps provided its own technical equipment but ordnance issued standard clothing and equipment, including tank guns.

ARMAMENTS

Between August 1914 and November 1918 25,430 new artillery pieces were made, rising from 4 pieces per week in 1914 to 227 pieces per week by the end of the war. Nearly 240,000 machine guns were issued.

BASE DEPOTS

The original bases at Boulogne, Le Havre and Rouen were abandoned during the retreat to the Marne but they were reoccupied when the BEF transferred to Flanders in October 1914. Bases grew into large camps, with storage facilities for 22 days' reserve of ammunition and foodstuffs. As new facilities were added, bases specialized in certain types of supplies.

Boulogne: General supplies, medical and veterinary equipment and ordnance.

Le Havre: General supplies, ASC, ordnance.
> **General Base Depot 1** supplied the Royal Garrison Artillery.
> **General Base Depot 2** supplied Field and Horse Artillery.
> **General Base Depot 3** supplied the Canadian Expeditionary Force; the ANZACs took it over in October 1916.

Calais: Opened in April 1915 for Ordnance Corps depots and Veterinary Corps.

Les Attaques: Opened near Calais for First and Second Armies' Royal Engineer stores.

Etaples: Opened near Boulogne to supply British infantry divisions; depots for the Machine Gun Corps and the ANZAC Corps were added later; the Canadians took over the ANZAC facilities in October 1916.

Abancourt: Opened near Le Havre for Third and Fourth Armies' Royal Engineer stores.

Rouen: General supplies, Territorial units, mechanical transport and an ordnance depot.
> **General Base Depot 4** supplied the Royal Engineers.
> **General Base Depot 5** supplied cavalry divisions and the RAMC.

Marseilles: Base for the Indian Corps during its stay in France; Rouen was the advanced depot.

Alexandria: Base for operations in Egypt and Palestine.

AMMUNITION DEPOTS

Ammunition was distributed as quickly as possible to avoid accidents. New ammunition depots were set up prior to the Somme Offensive. Audruicq, near St Omer, stock-piled deliveries made to Boulogne while Grand Quévilly served Rouen, and the daily average delivered had risen from 200 tons to 3,500 tons by 1916.

In July 1916 a German bomb destroyed 9,000 tons of shells at Audruicq, forcing the ASC to distribute ammunition to smaller depots scattered over a wide area. New large dumps were added at Blargies (between Amiens and Rouen), Zeneghem (near Calais), Rouxmesnil (near Dieppe), Saigneville and Dannes (near Etaples). However, the menace from the air continued and in the spring of 1918 air raids destroyed 20,000 tons of ammunition.

NEW EQUIPMENT

The Ordnance Board had three departments involved in designing and testing new weapons and equipment:

Inventions: Designing new items.

Research: Improving existing designs.

Experimental: Testing both its own and private patents, under factory conditions.

Field tests were carried out at the Shoeburyness firing ranges. The Board joined the Ministry of Munitions in November 1915.

ISSUING EQUIPMENT

Each division had an officer and a clerk to order and distribute weapons, equipment and ammunition. Initially it was planned to issue stores on a fortnightly basis, but while the men could wait for clothing and personal equipment, replacement weapons had to be supplied immediately. Sending regular supply lorries with standard loads created surpluses and shortages as requirements changed. The system needed too many lorries and there were no records of what had been issued.

While the echelons continued to carry the ammunition forward, indents were introduced to streamline the supply system for other items. Unit quartermasters put forward specific requests to the Deputy Assistant Director of Ordnance Services so his 14 staff could gather indents and fill lorries with one type of item (uniforms one day, boots the next, etc). The deputy assistant directors aimed to turn requests around in a week using their fleets of 4 lorries. If necessary, stores could be collected from the railheads and taken straight to the divisions.

Spare stores and heavy equipment in the front line were handed over to the relieving unit as 'trench stores' in exchange for a receipt.

AMMUNITION STOCKS AND PRODUCTION CAPACITY 1914		
	Stocks per gun of the original BEF	*Manufacturing capacity*
13-pounder	1,900 rounds (30 guns) = 57,000	10,000 rounds a month
18-pounder	1,500 rounds (324 guns) = 486,000	10,000 rounds a month
4.5-inch howitzer	1,200 rounds (108 guns) = 129,000	10,000 rounds a month
60-pounder	1,000 rounds (24 guns) = 24,000	100 rounds a month

SALVAGE AND REPAIRS

Divisional salvage companies started to collect damaged greatcoats, blankets and horse-rugs for recycling during the first winter of the war, employing a French company to wash and mend clothing. A boot repair factory was opened in Calais in September 1915.

Workshops were set up in Paris to repair personal equipment and two facilities were opened at Abbeville and Calais to repair gas helmets in the summer of 1915; they all employed French women.

Most units had armourers, saddlers, and bootmakers to deal with minor repairs to weapons and kit. Mobile workshops toured the rest areas, carrying out repairs and collecting badly damaged items; ordnance armourers' shops out at Calais and Le Havre undertook major repairs.

Artillery batteries carried out routine maintenance on their guns and crews were able to cannibalize guns to keep others working. Mobile workshops (two light and one medium per corps) visited the gun lines to carry out minor repairs and adjustments. Complicated repairs were dealt with at one of the army's ordnance heavy repair shops.

Major repair work and re-tubing was carried out in Britain. Typically an 18-pounder was able to fire 20,000 rounds before the barrel had to be re-lined; a 6-inch howitzer could fire 10,000 rounds, but the 6-inch gun could only fire 1,500 rounds before it had to be attended to. In all 9,170 guns were repaired between 1914 and 1918. Each army's ordnance gun park maintained a reserve of guns, carriages and machine guns to replace items under repair.

The manufacture of improvised trench stores was mainly carried out in ordnance workshops. However, the Royal Engineer workshops made improvised trench mortars and bombs until the Stokes mortar and the Mills bomb were adopted.

Employment companies absorbed the divisional salvage companies in 1917 and took over salvage work, recovering weapons, clothing and equipment for repair.

THE MUNITIONS INDUSTRY

By October 1914 it was clear that ammunition stocks were woefully inadequate and the Royal Ordnance Factories at Woolwich and the Royal Gunpowder Factory at Waltham Abbey only had a limited capacity as shown in the table above.

Throughout the First Battle of Ypres in November 1914 guns were rationed to an average of 4 rounds per gun per day. Attempts to step up production were limited by a shortage of experienced labour caused by many men joining Kitchener's New Armies; the problem would take months to resolve and ultimately result in a national scandal. Despite Lord Kitchener's attempts to mobilize the private armaments industry to supplement the royal factories, its production was still only 3,000 rounds per month by December 1914, a fraction of what was required.

SUPPORTING SERVICES

ARMY VETERINARY CORPS

Numbers increased from 22 officers and 797 other ranks in 1914 to over 700 officers and 16,500 men in 1918. The chain of command was:

A Director of Veterinary Services at GHQ (other theatres had Deputy Directors).

Male foremen oversee their new female workforce in the shell-case shop at Woolwich Arsenal.
(IWM Q27850)

A Deputy Director of Veterinary Services with
    each army from February 1915.
An Assistant Director of Veterinary Services
    with each infantry corps.
A Deputy Director of Veterinary Services with
    the Cavalry Corps.

Eleven mobile veterinary sections toured
the units, dealing with minor injuries and
referring serious cases to the 6 veterinary
hospitals (each capable of caring for 250
animals); 2 base store depots supplied them
with equipment.

The system of collection, evacuation and
treatment of injured animals was modelled on
the RAMC casualty evacuation chain. After
first aid was administered, horses were
evacuated by road or rail to a veterinary
evacuating station.

There were the following facilities:

Horses were cared for in the same manner as the men. New
arrivals were trained at remount depots while the veterinary
services dealt with injured horses. *(IWM Q8529)*

60 mobile sections (including 11 Dominion) toured the rear areas.

18 evacuating stations (including 2 Dominion) carried out emergency treatment.

20 hospitals (including 2 Dominion hospitals) could each care for 2,000 animals.

4 convalescent depots, each for 200 animals.

2 base depots for stores.

1 bacteriological laboratory.

1 disposal of animals branch.

General health was kept under control and, for example, only 3% of horses had to be isolated with mange. In all, 484,143 horses died from injury, overwork and disease during the war.

THE ARMY CHAPLAINS DEPARTMENT

Chaplains (or padres) represented the various denominations, and they were allowed unrestricted access to the men providing they did not interfere with operations. They often held simple services for the men and comforted the sick and dying as well as overseeing burials. As part of their duties, chaplains became involved in welfare work, organizing entertainments for the men. They often acted as an informal link between the officers and the men. Chaplains kept records of burials before the Graves Registration Commission took over.

Each division of the BEF had 3 Church of England and Roman Catholic chaplains when it left for France. A Presbyterian chaplain accompanied each division with a Scottish battalion while a Wesleyan chaplain travelled between divisions. Two Church of England, one Roman Catholic and one Presbyterian chaplain were stationed at each base; three Wesleyan chaplains were assigned to the bases.

The number of chaplains per division rose to 12 and others were assigned to the hospitals behind the lines. Additional chaplains were appointed to each brigade to cover the needs of Baptists, Congregationalists and Methodists.

Chaplains often set up chapels, complete

A New Zealand chaplain celebrates Holy Communion during a quiet moment behind the lines. *(IWM Q79042)*

A sentry inspects a driver's pass as he enters 20th Division's area near Souchez in June 1918. The steel sentry box protected the guard during bombardments. *(IWM Q6733)*

with quiet areas, behind the lines. One of the most famous of these was Talbot House or Toc H (the signaller's version of the letters T and H) in Poperinghe, founded in December 1915. The Reverend Neville Talbot, senior chaplain of the 6th Division, and the Reverend P.B. 'Tubby' Clayton, the town's garrison chaplain, ran it.

MILITARY POLICE

Military police matters in the United Kingdom came under the office of the Adjutant-General while the Provost Marshal supervised military police duties in the field. Each division had an assistant provost marshal supervising the division's military police (who were known as redcaps due to the red covers worn around their service caps). The police had powers to stop and arrest anyone suspected of breaking military regulations, including potential deserters, men found without passes, and those found plundering or making unlawful requisitions. They could also arrest soldiers suspected of committing offences such as violence against the local population, rape or murder. As well as guarding against spying, they were responsible for collecting and questioning stragglers during offensives and set up posts in the communication trenches behind the front to check men heading to the rear. During emergencies the military police could call upon units in their area to provide extra guards and patrols.

PRISONS

Two ships (three more were added in January 1915) with a capacity for 1,200 prisoners were anchored at Le Havre and Rouen at the start of the war. Prisoners unloaded cargo ships for 12 hours a day under armed guard. Ten camps were later set up near the ports, railheads and depots to replace the ships, and prisoners

New Zealand soldiers queue up to buy luxuries from a field canteen near Albert after receiving their pay in September 1916. *(IWM Q1245)*

---

were put to work on entrenchments, sanitary duties or in quarries. Drill with heavy weights was used when there was no work available.

Rations could be reduced as a punishment. Bread or biscuits replaced part of the meat ration, and luxuries such as jam, cheese, tobacco, rum, tea and coffee were banned.

The demand for cells in the United Kingdom increased as the New Armies and Territorial divisions prepared to go overseas and a number of civil prisons were taken over by the Army.

ARMY PAY DEPARTMENT

Field and base cashiers controlled the Army's flow of cash and cheques. Soldiers were paid in local currency and by November 1918 francs equivalent to £193 million had been issued.

The department began with a clearing house, a command pay office, and a command cash office; auxiliary base offices were added at the ports of disembarkation. The command and base cashiers held reserves of money received from the United Kingdom while the command pay office controlled payments to the civilian population and supervised local purchases, paid civilian labour and dealt with claims for losses or damage.

Officers had advance chequebooks to draw money from a field cashier while other ranks were issued with an active service pay book to allow them to draw money in an emergency. The clearing house recorded each man's pay and forwarded records to his pay office in the United Kingdom. Payments were made in local currency and the pay department dealt with the purchase and exchange of francs.

After starting with a field cashier, divisions soon had cash offices, while corps had two field cashiers to control cash, collecting up to £50,000 from the base cashier every week. One cashier manned the cash office and the other visited divisions in turn. GHQ had its own field cashier to finance the intelligence services and spies.

THE ARMY POSTAL SERVICE

The service had been organized in 1913 with officers and men of the Royal Engineers Army Reserve working for the Post Office. The service had to expand to deal with thousands of letters and parcels as they became the only form of communication between the soldiers and their families. Over 10 million letters and 100,000 parcels were being posted every week by the end of 1916. The vast majority of mail reached its destination a day or two after it had been posted.

WRITING TO THE SOLDIERS

Correspondence was addressed to units and sorted into unit bundles at the General Post Office in London. In France the mail was readdressed at the Base Post Office in Le Havre and loaded onto a train heading towards the unit's location; GHQ gave a daily list of postings to the Advanced Base Post Office at Amiens. Sorting was moved to London during the winter of 1914–15 and postal regulating depots at Rouen and Boulogne began distributing mail; depots were later added at Calais and Le Havre.

Mailbags were sent under guard to the railheads and postal lorries carried them to the supply refilling points. The divisional field post offices collected their mail on a daily basis and handed letters and parcels to unit post orderlies to be delivered as soon as possible to the billets, training areas or trenches. Around 90,000 mailbags a week were being sorted by 1916 with numbers doubling around Christmas.

WRITING HOME

Parcels and letters had to be censored and franked before the brigade sent them to the

The postman was always a welcome sight and these two soldiers are setting off to deliver the mail to a battalion of the 1st Canadian Division at Guémappe in September 1918. *(IWM CO3285)*

branch field post office at the refilling points; supply vehicles forwarded them to the divisional post office at the railhead. Trains took the mail to the Advanced Base Post Office at Amiens (the postal regulating depots when they opened). Field army post offices were established at each army headquarters in December 1914 and stationary offices were added at the bases.

The post offices also registered letters and sold stamps for parcels (letters were delivered free). Postal orders were a safe method of sending money home and by the end of the war 900,000 postal orders a week were being sent home. Telegrams had to be sent from French civil post offices until March 1918 due to censorship.

As well as Army forms and manuals the Printing Service produced humorous items, like this Christmas card celebrating the issue of the daily rum ration.

ranks; it was sent to the post office for return after the relatives had been informed.

The Army Postal Service took over delivery of military mail after August 1915. Sensitive correspondence relating to operations continued to be dealt with by the Director of Signals and the motorcycle Despatch Rider Letter Service.

ARMY PRINTING AND STATIONERY SERVICES

The printing service started with 3 officers producing and distributing a small array of forms, stationery and pamphlets. It took over the distribution of field service postcards in September 1914. An assistant director for stationery services was appointed in December 1914 to run new depots. Hand presses were inadequate and, while local contracts dealt with some orders, confidential material had to be sent to the War Office in London. The first printing press was set up at Le Havre in July 1915 and eventually GHQ and each army had a printing section.

Work varied from operational and training material to Christmas cards and entertainment programmes; training manuals (marked by SS and a number) were issued on a regular basis. By early 1916 paper was in short supply, and the many forms and books were reduced in size while waste paper was sent to Britain for pulping.

The service was reorganized as the Army Printing and Stationery Services in June 1916 with a printing and photographic company and a publications department. The Typewriter Inspection and Repair Service maintained 7,200 machines. A factory produced 57,000 rubber stamps a year.

Four months later the printing service took over the production of trench maps and the presses were soon producing 5,000 a day, adding photographic work to their list of functions at the same time, compiling panoramas, mosaics and stereoscopic photographs.

By November 1918 the printing service was a major concern with over 900 staff. It produced over 36,000 types of forms and over 1,000 army forms and books.

Mail addressed to casualties was redirected to the base post office and forwarded to the hospital, or in the case of the dead, back to the family. Hospitals at first failed to keep up with the volume of post and after December 1914 they filled in redirection cards to update the base post office with patients' movements. The wounded were given simple cards to tick to notify their family about their condition and whereabouts. Correspondence for killed or missing officers was forwarded to the War Office, and to the Record Office for other

CHAPTER SEVEN

DIVISIONAL ORGANIZATION AND HISTORY

Divisions, and particularly infantry divisions, were the principal building blocks of all armies in the First World War. The British Army had 6 regular infantry divisions and 1 cavalry division in August 1914 but by the time of the Armistice in 1918 it had grown tenfold and had over 60 divisions active in theatres across the world. The infantry division was the Army's largest tactical unit and generals and their staffs measured their strength according to the number and efficiency of their divisions. A division usually reported to a corps but occasionally acted as army or GHQ reserve.

A quick cheer for the camera during a roadside halt. *(IWM Q8441)*

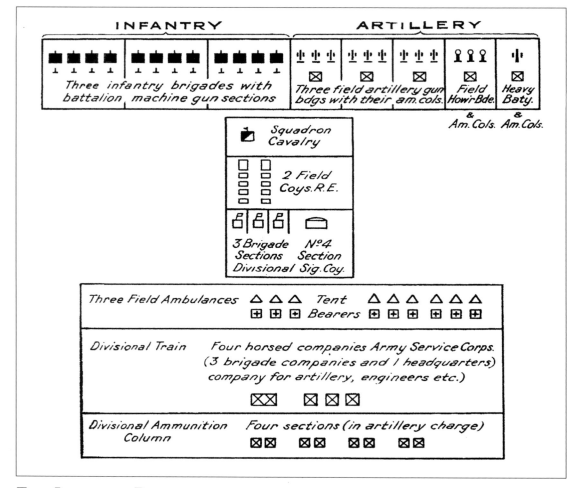

THE INFANTRY DIVISION

The backbone of the division was formed by the 3 infantry brigades (4 battalions each), which were assisted by 4 artillery brigades and support troops so it could operate independently in the field.

Each infantry division was usually commanded by a major-general, assisted in his HQ by 15 officers and 67 other ranks; 54 horses and 5 motorcycles provided transport; a wagon and a cart carried the headquarters equipment.

The division occupied 15 miles on the march (infantry 7½ miles, artillery 5 miles and 3 miles for the support services); it required 40 trains to move it from sector to sector.

The role and the basic structure of the infantry division did not alter throughout the war but the introduction of new weapons and tactics brought about several major changes and many minor changes to its composition.

The 1914 organization is shown in the diagram above and the establishment in the table opposite. Badges of British divisions which saw action and Empire divisions which served in France appear on pages 236–42.

DIVISIONAL STAFF
GENERAL STAFF OFFICER GRADE 1 (GSO 1)

This officer, a lieutenant-colonel, led the staff, composed of GSO 2 and GSO 3 officers. They were responsible for planning operations, collecting intelligence and administrative duties.

INFANTRY DIVISION ESTABLISHMENT 1914	officers and men	horses
Headquarters	82	54
Infantry		
3 x Infantry Brigades each with 4 Battalions	12,165	741
Artillery		
Artillery Headquarters	22	20
3 x Field Artillery Brigades	2,385	2,244
1 x Field Artillery (howitzer) Brigade	755	697
1 x Heavy Battery and Ammunition Column	198	144
1 x Divisional Ammunition Column	568	709
Engineers		
Divisional Engineers Headquarters	13	8
2 x Field Companies, Royal Engineers	434	152
1 x Signal Company	162	80
Other Supporting Units		
1 x Cavalry Squadron	159	167
1 x Divisional Train	428	378
3 x Field Ambulances	702	198
Total Strength	18,073	5,592

BRIGADIER-GENERAL ROYAL ARTILLERY (BGRA)

A brigadier-general organized the artillery brigades.

ASSISTANT ADJUTANT- AND QUARTERMASTER-GENERAL (AA AND QMG)

A lieutenant-colonel. He organized supplies and transport.

COMMANDER ROYAL ENGINEERS (CRE)

A lieutenant-colonel. He supervised all engineering works.

CHANGES BEFORE JULY 1916

HEADQUARTERS

A battalion left a cadre of 108 officers and men, including instructors, signallers and specialists, behind when it went into action so that it would be easier to reconstitute the unit in the event of heavy casualties.

INFANTRY

New Army brigades were exchanged with Regular brigades in some divisions in December 1915 in an attempt to bolster morale and training in New Army divisions.

MACHINE GUNS

The number of machine guns per infantry battalion and cavalry regiment was doubled to 4 in February 1915 and 4 Lewis guns were added in the summer. Battalions handed over their Vickers machine guns to the Machine Gun Corps in October 1915; 4 Lewis or Hotchkiss guns replaced them. The number of Lewis guns was increased to 16 in the spring of 1916.

TRENCH MORTARS

Trench mortars appeared at the start of 1915 with the infantry, artillery and engineers all taking a hand to test experimental weapons. The Stokes mortar was introduced in the summer of 1915, organized into 4-gun batteries.

After December 1915 infantry manned the light mortar units and artillerymen manned the medium (and later the heavy) batteries. In the spring of 1916 each division had a

Infantry help a gun crew manhandle an 18-pounder through the mud near Langemarck during the final stages of the Third Battle of Ypres in October 1917. *(IWM Q3007)*

heavy battery, designated V, 3 medium batteries, designated X, Y and Z, and 3 light Stokes batteries, which were numbered after their parent brigades.

The divisional artillery commander took control of the medium trench mortar batteries, led by the divisional trench mortar officer, and the light batteries came under brigade command. Men were given a badge but a separate trench mortar corps was never formed.

ARTILLERY UNITS

The 60-pounder 'heavy' batteries were transferred to corps heavy artillery in February 1915.

The howitzer brigade was broken up in May 1916 and the 3 batteries were split between the 3 field artillery brigades.

AMMUNITION COLUMNS AND THE DIVISIONAL TRAIN

Brigade ammunition columns were disbanded in May 1916 and the personnel and equipment were reorganized under the divisional ammunition column.

ENGINEERS AND PIONEERS

The number of Royal Engineer field companies increased from 2 to 3 and a pioneer battalion was added to each division to assist with labouring and construction work.

MOUNTED TROOPS

The cavalry squadron and cyclist company were transferred and became corps troops.

MEDICAL SERVICES

The number of stretcher-bearers per battalion

162

was doubled from 16 to 32. A sanitary section was added during the winter of 1914–15.

VETERINARY SERVICES

By late 1914 divisions had a mobile veterinary section, led by a subaltern and run by 26 other ranks of the Army Veterinary Corps.

CHANGES BEFORE JANUARY 1918

MACHINE GUNS

A fourth Machine Gun Corps company was added in April 1917 and came under divisional control.

ARTILLERY

In January 1917 each division's artillery support was reduced by one third when a brigade was transferred to army level. This left 2 brigades, each composed of 2 x 18-pounder batteries and a 4.5-inch howitzer battery, each armed with 6 guns.

TRENCH MORTARS

A heavy trench mortar battery armed with four 9.45-inch mortars was added in July 1916. The heavy batteries were reassigned to corps command in February 1917 and a few weeks later the medium batteries were reorganized into 2 groups of 6 mortars. The 3 brigade trench mortar batteries were increased to 8 Stokes mortars each; one battery was broken up in February 1918.

Welsh Guardsmen make their way along a communications trench heading for the front line at Pilckem, north of Ypres; the following day they would go over the top at the start of the Third Ypres Offensive. *(IWM Q5706)*

MEDICAL SERVICES

Sanitary sections were transferred to corps areas in April 1917.

LABOUR

An Employment company of the Labour Corps, with 1 officer and 106 other ranks was added in May 1917; divisions serving in Mesopotamia continued to use Indian Army units.

FINAL CHANGES

INFANTRY

In January and February 1918, in response to manpower shortages, infantry divisions were reorganized with 9 battalions, 3 to each brigade. Dozens of Territorial and Service battalions were disbanded or merged with sister battalions. Several thousand men were formed into new Entrenching battalions and began work on defensive works behind the front. The rest were distributed across the Army, reinforcing under-strength units.

MACHINE GUNS

The number of Lewis guns per infantry battalion was increased to 32 at the start of 1918. The 4 Machine Gun Corps companies already with each division were grouped together in April 1918 to create a machine gun battalion under divisional control.

DIVISIONS' REPUTATIONS

GHQ rated divisions according to their performance, and although Regular divisions, and the Guards Division when it was formed in August 1915, were given an elite status during the early campaigns, failures reduced some reputations. Territorial and New Army divisions had to develop their own standing based on success. While some became favourites, others failed to impress. However, a change in leadership could often influence the rating of a division. Successful divisions could expect regular action while others spent long periods holding quiet sectors of the line.

CAVALRY DIVISIONS

The BEF's original Cavalry Division went to France with 4 brigades, each with 3 regiments. Other regiments joined the BEF in September 1914 and the cavalry was organized into 2 divisions of 3 brigades, each with 3 regiments.

The 3-brigade division occupied 8½ miles of road on the march, with each brigade requiring 2 miles and the divisional troops taking up the remaining space.

The organization at the start of the war and the establishment of the 3-brigade division are shown in the tables below and opposite.

Badges of the cavalry divisions which served in France are shown on page 242.

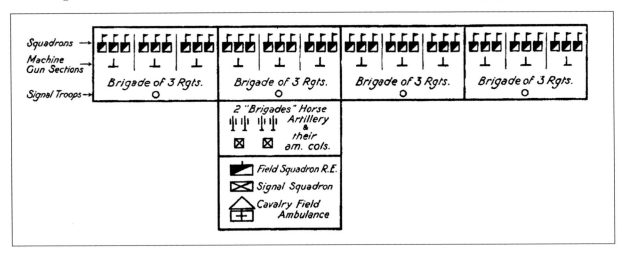

Cavalry Division organization at the start of the war.

ARTILLERY

Each Royal Horse Artillery brigade had 2 batteries armed with 6 x 13-pounders, a total of 24 guns. Two ammunition wagons served each gun.

MACHINE GUNS

There were 24 machine guns, 2 guns per cavalry regiment.

SUPPORTING SERVICES

Three mobile veterinary sections cared for the horses.

The Army Service Corps provided a horse-drawn divisional company (designated HT), two motorized supply column companies (designated MT) and a motorized ammunition park distributed across the division.

A sanitary section served with each division from January 1915 to the Armistice.

MOUNTED AND CYCLIST DIVISIONS

A **Mounted Division** had 4 brigades each with 3 Yeomanry regiments supported by 4 cyclist battalions and 2 artillery batteries with ammunition columns. Four mounted signal troops served the brigades while the divisional signal squadron provided the headquarters with communications. Three Royal Army Medical Corps field ambulances cared for the men while 4 mobile veterinary sections looked after the horses. Transport was provided by 4 Army Service Corps transport and supply columns and a divisional supply column.

2nd Line Territorial mounted brigades took the place of the 1st Line Territorial brigades when they were transferred overseas in 1915, usually to the Mediterranean. The 2nd Line units usually did not have equipment and training was rudimentary. In July 1916 the Yeomanry regiments were dismounted, so the horses could be trained at remount depots and sent overseas. The men were equipped with bicycles and at the end of the month the mounted divisions were reorganized as cyclist divisions.

A **Cyclist Division** had 4 cyclist brigades, each with 4 cyclist battalions. Four cyclist signal troops and a divisional signal company provided communications; 4 cyclist field ambulances dealt with the sick while 4 Army Service Corps cyclist brigades and a divisional transport and supply column were in support.

The Cyclist Divisions were broken up in November 1916.

CAVALRY DIVISION ESTABLISHMENT FROM LATER IN 1914		
	officers and men	*horses*
Headquarters	96	64
Cavalry		
3 Cavalry Brigades	6,872	7,492
Artillery		
Divisional Artillery Headquarters	20	18
2 Horse Artillery Brigades	1,362	1,558
Engineers		
1 Field Squadron, Royal Engineers	191	196
1 Signal Squadron	206	164
Other Supporting Units		
Divisional Army Service Corps HQ	26	11
3 Cavalry Field Ambulances	496	312
Total Strength	9,269	9,815

INFANTRY DIVISION HISTORIES

The divisions of the British and Dominion Armies had varied histories, with some engaged in constant action while others held quiet sectors for long periods. What follows is a brief history for each of the British, Australian, New Zealand and Canadian infantry divisions from the time they reached a theatre of war until the Armistice. Also included are the 2 Indian divisions which served on the Western Front.

To the left is the region the division was serving in (a change in theatre is also given), listing the nearest town if the division was holding a sector or the campaign if the division was in action. The dates appear in the next column. Please note that divisions sometimes rotated in a sector, alternating with another division as it spent time in the line and the rear. Any gaps in the dates indicate that a division spent time behind the lines, resting, training or transferring between armies. The final column gives the limits of the division's sector while holding the line or the ground attacked or captured.

GUARDS DIVISION
1915

France	late August	Assembled in France
Loos	26–27 September	Engaged between Loos and Hulluch
Béthune	October	Engaged at Hohenzollern Redoubt and Hulluch
Béthune	November–February	Held the Neuve Chapelle and Picantin sector

Guards Division. Stretcher-bearers make their way forward prior to the advance from Ginchy towards Lesboeufs on 15 September 1916. *(IWM Q1214)*

1916

Ypres	February–August	Held the Bellewaarde and Wieltje sector
Somme	18–31 August	Held the Serre sector
Somme	10–17 September	Advanced from Ginchy towards Lesboeufs

Somme	21–30 September	Engaged at Lesboeufs, capturing the village on the 25th
Somme	13–30 November	Engaged in the Lesboeufs sector
Somme	from mid-December	Held the Sailly-Saillisel sector

1917

Hindenburg	14–24 March	Advanced across the Canal du Nord to Metz-en-Couture
Ypres	May–July	Held the Boesinghe sector
Ypres	31 July–8 August	Advanced to the Steenbeek stream west of Langemarck
Ypres	September	Engaged north of Langemarck
Ypres	7–14 October	Advanced towards Houthulst Forest
Cambrai	24–28 November	Engaged in the Cantaing and Fontaine sector
Cambrai	30 November	Recaptured Gouzeaucourt

1918

Arras	January–March	Held the River Scarpe and Gavrelle sector
Somme	21–23 March	Engaged between St Léger and Hénin
Somme	25–26 March	Fell back to Moyenneville

The Advance to Victory

Albert	21–23 August	Captured Moyenneville and advanced towards St Léger
Scarpe	26–30 August	Captured St Léger and advanced towards Ecoust St Mein
Canal du Nord	2–4 September	Advanced from Noreuil to Loursies and Moeuvres
Canal du Nord	27 September	Crossed Canal du Nord and advanced past Flesquières
Cambrai	9–11 October	Advanced from Cattenières and Boistrancourt to St Vaast
Selle	20 October	Crossed the River Selle at St Python and Haussy
Sambre	4–11 November	Advanced from Orsival through Audignies and Maubeuge

1ST DIVISION

1914

France	11–22 August	Sailed to France and moved to Mons
Mons	23 August	Held the Peissant and Haulchin sector, east of the attack
The Retreat	24–29 August	Marched via Le Grand Fayet and Etreux to the St Gobain Forest
The Retreat	30 Aug–6 Sept	Across the Aisne and Marne rivers to the Crécy Forest
Marne	9–11 September	Advanced across the Marne to the River Aisne
Aisne	13 September	Crossed the Aisne at Moulins, Vendresse and Paissy
	mid-October	Transferred to Flanders
Ypres	21–25 October	Held the Bixschoote and Langemarck sector
Ypres	31 Oct–11 Nov	Polygon Wood sector, lost Gheluvelt, fought on in Polygon Wood
Béthune	December–February	Held the Givenchy sector

1915

Béthune	February–May	Held the Neuve Chapelle sector; attacked Rue du Bois on 9 May
Béthune	May–September	Held the La Bassée Canal sector

167

| Loos | 25–26 September | Advanced towards Hulluch |
| Béthune | October–July | Held the Hulluch and Loos sector |

1916

Somme	11–26 July	Engaged in the Contalmaison sector
Somme	13 Aug–11 Sept	Engaged west of High Wood
Somme	20–26 September	Engaged north of High Wood
Somme	November–December	Held the sector east of Le Sars

1917

Somme	January–March	Held the Belloy and Barleux sector
Hindenburg	17–20 March	Advanced across the River Somme
Flanders Coast	May–September	Held the Nieuport Bains sector
Ypres	November	Goudberg sector, Ypres
Ypres	December–February	Held the Houthulst Forest sector

1918

| Ypres | February–March | Held the Poelcappelle sector |
| Béthune | April–September | Held the Cambrin sector |

The Advance to Victory

Epéhy	18–26 September	Advanced from Maissemy to Prontruet on the St Quentin Canal
St Quentin	29 Sept–3 Oct	Crossed the canal at Pontruet and captured Thorigny
Selle	18–24 October	Advanced through Andigny Forest and Wassigny sector
Sambre	4–5 November	Advanced through Catillon and crossed the Sambre–Oise Canal

1st Division. Roll call of the 1st Black Watch at Lapugnoy on 10 April 1918 before they move into reserve following the German breakthrough on the Lys. *(IWM Q10880)*

2nd Division. A gun crew strip down and clean their 18-pounder as they prepare to follow up the German withdrawal to the Hindenburg Line in March 1917. *(IWM Q5006)*

2ND DIVISION
1914

France	11–22 August	Reached France and moved via Wassigny to Mons
Mons	23 August	Held a line between Haulchin and Harmignies
The Retreat	25–29 August	Across the Sambre and Oise into St Gobain Forest
The Retreat	30–31 August	Across the Aisne and into Villers-Cotterets Forest
The Retreat	1–5 September	Across the Marne and Grand Morin rivers
Marne	6–13 September	Crossed the Marne and advanced via Oulchy-le-Château
Aisne	13 September	Crossed the Aisne; engaged at Chavonne and Moussy
	mid-October	Transferred to Flanders
Ypres	20–23 October	Engaged at Bixschoote, Zonnebeke and Langemarck
Ypres	24 Oct–11 Nov	Engaged at Polygon Wood and Zonnebeke
Béthune	December–January	Held the Festubert and Richebourg sector

1915

Béthune	February–April	Held the Cuinchy sector
Armentières	May	Held the Richebourg sector
Festubert	15 May	Captured the German line south of Richebourg l'Avoué
Béthune	late May–mid-June	Held the Grenay and Vermelles sector
Béthune	mid-June–January	Held the Cuinchy and Givenchy sector
Loos	25 September	Unsuccessful attack towards Auchy

1916

| Arras | February–May | Angres and Calonne sector |

169

Arras	May–July	Berthonval and Carency sector
Somme	25 July–9 August	Cleared Delville Wood then engaged at Guillemont
Somme	September–November	Held the Serre sector
Somme	13 November	Advanced north of Beaumont-Hamel

1917

Somme	January–March	Held the Pys sector
Hindenburg	14–19 March	Advanced through Grevillers to Ecoust St Mein
Arras	12 April–3 May	Advanced from Willerval towards Arleux and Oppy
Arras	June	Held the Arleux sector
Béthune	July–November	Held the Cambrin and Givenchy sector
Cambrai	27–30 November	Engaged west of Bourlon Wood and withdrew to Havrincourt

1918

Somme	22–23 March	Fell back from Fins and Haplincourt to Grandcourt
Somme	24–26 March	Retired over the Ancre at Beaucourt; engaged at Aveluy
Somme	April–August	Held the Ayette sector

The Advance to Victory

Albert	21–25 August	Advanced via Gomiécourt to Behagnies and Sapignies
	3–4 September	Advanced from Vaulx-Vraucourt to the Canal du Nord
Havrincourt	11 September	Crossed the canal, west of Havrincourt
Canal du Nord	28 Sept–1 Oct	Crossed the Marcoing Canal and took Mont sur l'Oeuvre
Cambrai	8–9 October	Advanced to Forenville
Le Quesnoy	22–25 October	Advanced from Vertain towards Villers-Pol

3RD DIVISION
1914

France	11–22 August	Reached France and moved via Avesnes to Mons
Mons	23 August	Engaged on the Condé Canal at Mons
Le Cateau	26 August	Engaged at Caudry and Inchy
The Retreat	27–31 August	Headed south across the Oise and Aisne, into the Retz Forest
The Retreat	1–5 September	Crossed the Marne and marched south into the Crécy Forest
Marne	6–12 September	Re-crossed the Marne and the Vesle, heading for the Aisne
Aisne	13 September	Crossed the Aisne and engaged north of the river at Vailly
	early October	Transferred to Flanders
La Bassée	19–30 October	Engaged at Richebourg, Neuve Chapelle and Fauquissart
Ypres	5–11 November	Engaged south-west of Gheluvelt
Messines	December–March	Held the Kemmel and Vierstraat sector

1915

Messines	March & April	Held the Vierstaat and St Eloi sector
Ypres	May–November	Hooge sector; captured the hamlet on 16 June

Hooge	25 September	Unsuccessful attack at Hooge
Ypres	November–February	Held the St Eloi and Hill 60 sector

1916

The Bluff	2 March	76th Brigade captured the Bluff under 17th Division
St Eloi	17 March–3 April	In the St Eloi sector, captured St Eloi Craters on 27 March
Messines	April–June	Held the Wytschaete sector
Somme	8–26 July	Engaged at Bazentin-le-Grand, Longueval and Delville Wood
Somme	14–19 August	Engaged south-west of Guillemont
Béthune	September	Held the Loos and Hulluch sector
Somme	October–January	In the Serre sector; attacked on 13 November

1917

Arras	February–April	Held the St Sauveur sector
Arras	9–14 April	Advanced through Tilloy-lez-Mofflaines towards Guémappe
Arras	24 April–14 May	Engaged at Monchy-le-Preux
Arras	June	In the Monchy-le-Preux and River Scarpe sector
Arras	July	In the Hermies and Louverval sector
Arras	August–September	Held the Louverval and Lagnicourt sector
Ypres	22–30 September	Engaged at Zonnebeke, capturing the village
Arras	October–January	Held the Noreuil and Bullecourt sector

1918

Arras	January–March	Held the Croisilles and Guémappe sector
Somme	21–28 March	Forced back to Mercatel and Neuville Vitasse
Lys	12–16 April	Engaged along the Aire Canal at Hinges
Béthune	April–August	Held the Hinges sector

The Advance to Victory

Albert	22–23 August	Advanced from Courcelles through Gomiécourt and Ervillers
Bapaume	1–2 September	Advanced from Ecoust St Mein to Noreuil
Canal du Nord	27 Sept–1 Oct	Advanced from Havrincourt through Flesquières and Rumilly
Cambrai	8–9 October	Captured Seranvillers, Wambaix and Cattenières
Le Quesnoy	23 October	Advanced from Solesmes north-west of Le Quesnoy

4TH DIVISION

1914

France	21–25 August	Sailed to France and joined the BEF at Fontaine-au-Pire
Le Cateau	26 August	Engaged between Esnes and Fontaine-au-Pire
The Retreat	29–31 August	Across the Somme and Oise, through the Compiègne Forest
The Retreat	1–4 September	South through Rozières as far south as Dammartin
Marne	6–12 September	Advanced through the Compiègne Forest and across the River Marne

Aisne	13 September	Crossed the River Aisne; engaged at Bucy-le-Long and Missy
Armentières	19 Oct–2 Nov	Engaged east of Armentières
Messines	November–April	Held the Wulverghem sector

1915

Ypres	25 April–mid-May	Engaged at St Julien; fell back through Wieltje to Pilckem Ridge
Somme	July–January	Held the Beaumont-Hamel sector

1916

Somme	February–May	Held the Foncquevillers and Ransart area
Somme	June	In the sector south-west of Serre
Somme	1 July	Disastrous attack against Redan Ridge
Ypres	from mid-July	In the Boesinghe sector
Ypres	August	Held the Zillebeke and Hooge sector
Somme	19–26 October	Engaged in the Lesboeufs sector

1917

Somme	January & February	Held the Bouchavesnes sector
Arras	9–20 April	Continued the advance to Fampoux
Arras	1–6 & 10–14 May	Engaged at Roeux, capturing the Chemical Works
Arras	mid-June–August	Held the Roeux sector
Ypres	28 September	Engaged at Poelcappelle, advancing north of the village
Arras	November–January	Held the Monchy-le-Preux sector

1918

Arras	February	Held the Roeux and Gavrelle sector
Somme	28 March	Lost Roeux and Gavrelle
Lys	12–16 April	Engaged along the Aire Canal between Hinges and Robecq
Béthune	August	In the Locon sector

The Advance to Victory

Drocourt Line	2 September	Captured the Drocourt–Queant Switch Line at Remy
Canal du Nord	from late September	Held the River Scarpe between Palleul and Sailly-en-Ostrevent
Selle	20 October	Crossed the River Selle at Saulzoir and advanced to Monchaux
Valenciennes	24 October	Crossed the River Ecaillon and advanced to the River Rhonelle
Valenciennes	1 November	Crossed the river and captured Preseau

5TH DIVISION

1914

France	13 August	Sailed to France and moved to the Mons area
Mons	23–24 August	Engaged along the Condé Canal, west of Jemappes
Le Cateau	26 August	Engaged at Troisvilles and Reumont
The Retreat	27–30 August	Through St Quentin and across the Oise and Aisne

5th Division. The support wave moves forward as the assault troops attack Morval on 25 September 1916.
(IWM Q1312)

The Retreat	31 Aug–2 Sept	Through Compiègne Forest and across the River Marne
The Retreat	3–5 September	Across the Grand Morin River and into the Crécy Forest
Marne	6–11 September	Retraced its steps to Nampteuil on the River Aisne
Aisne	13 September	Crossed the river and engaged at Missy and Chivres
	early October	Transferred to Flanders
La Bassée	19–31 October	Engaged at Givenchy and Richebourg l'Avoué, Béthune
Ypres	3–11 November	Part engaged at Ploegsteert Wood, the rest at Hooge
Messines	December–March	Held the Wulverghem and Kemmel sector

1915

Ypres	April	In the St Eloi and Zwarteleen sector
Ypres	17 April–5 May	Engaged at Hill 60 near Zillebeke
Ypres	23–30 April	13th Brigade counter-attacked at Pilckem
Somme	August–March	Held the Mametz sector

1916

Arras	March–July	Held the Beaurains and Roclincourt sector
Somme	20 July–2 August	Engaged at High Wood and Longueval
Somme	28 Aug–7 Sept	Engaged south of Guillemont
Somme	18–26 September	Advanced through Morval
Béthune	October–March	Held the Cuinchy and Richebourg sector

1917

Arras	11–25 April	Followed up the German withdrawal towards La Coulotte
Arras	5–19 May	Engaged in the Fresnoy sector

Arras	mid-June–September	In the Oppy sector; captured Oppy Wood on 28 June
Ypres	1–10 October	Engaged between the Menin Road and Polygon Wood
Ypres	mid-Oct–mid-Nov	Engaged opposite Becelaere
Italy	December–March	Moved to the Italian front; engaged on the River Piave

1918

France	early April	Returned to France
Lys	12–15 April	Held the eastern edge of the Nieppe Forest
Lys	28 June	Advanced to the Plate Becque stream

The Advance to Victory

Albert	22–26 August	Advanced from Achiet-le-Petit north of Bapaume
Bapaume	31 Aug–3 Sept	Advanced through Beugny to the Sambre Canal
Canal du Nord	28–30 September	Advanced through Beaucamp and Villers-Plouich
Selle	20–23 October	Advanced from the River Selle towards Beaurain
Sambre	5–10 November	Advanced across the River Sambre through Fontaine

6TH DIVISION
1914

France	September	Joined the BEF on the River Aisne, Vailly sector
Armentières	15 October	Engaged at Radinghem, Ennetières and Premesques
Armentières	20–23 October	Withdrew towards Bois Grenier and dug in

1915

Ypres	June–March	In the St Julien and Hooge sector
Hooge	9 August	Captured Hooge

1916

Ypres	March–July	Held the Wieltje and Boesinghe sector
Somme	August	In the Beaumont-Hamel sector
Somme	12–18 September	Advanced from Guillemont through Morval
Somme	21–30 September	Advanced from Morval through Lesboeufs
Somme	9–18 October	Engaged in the Gueudecourt sector
Béthune	November–March	Held the La Bassée Canal sector

1917

Béthune	March–November	Held the Loos sector
Cambrai	November	In the Villers-Plouich sector
Cambrai	20 November	Captured Marcoing and Noyelles
Cambrai	4 December	Withdrew towards Flesquières

1918

Cambrai	January	In the Demicourt and Boursies sector
Cambrai	February	In the Lagnicourt sector
Somme	21–22 March	Fell back through Morchies and Vraucourt to Beugnâtre
Ypres	late March	Held the Reutel and Broodseinde sector
Ypres	12–15 April	Withdrew to Zillebeke Lake

The Advance to Victory

St Quentin	12–30 September	Captured Holnon and Gricourt

Cambrai	7–11 October	Advanced from Montbrehain towards Méricourt and Bohain
Selle	17–19 October	Advanced through Ribeauville to Rejet de Beaulieu
Sambre	21–24 October	Advanced from Bazeul to Catillon and Ors on the Sambre Canal

7TH DIVISION
1914

Antwerp	7–8 October	Landed at Zeebrugge and moved to Ostend
Ypres	9–15 October	Withdrew through Ghent towards Ypres
Ypres	19–31 October	Engaged in Polygon Wood and at Gheluvelt
Armentières	November–April	Held the Bois Grenier sector

1915

Festubert	15–19 May	Engaged east of Festubert
Givenchy	15 June	Attacked east of Givenchy
Béthune	September	In the Vermelles sector
Loos	25 September	Advanced towards Hulluch; engaged there until 8 October
Béthune	Nov & Dec	Held the Festubert sector

1916

Somme	February–June	Held the Fricourt sector
Somme	1–5 July	Advanced through Mametz
Somme	12–21 July	Advanced through Bazentin-le-Grand
Somme	23 Aug–7 Sept	Engaged in the Ginchy sector
Messines	September–October	In the Ploegsteert sector
Somme	November–February	Held the Beaumont-Hamel sector

1917

Ancre	17–28 February	Advanced through Puisieux
Hindenburg	15 March–4 April	Advanced to Bucquoy and Croiselles
Bullecourt	4–16 May	Engaged in Bullecourt and again in June and July
Ypres	1–10 October	Engaged north of Polygon Wood
Ypres	24–29 October	Engaged east of Polygon Wood
Italy	November	Transferred to Italy; took over the Piave Front in January

1918

Italy	March–October	On the Asiago Plateau
Vittorio Veneto	27 October	Crossed the Piave front at Papadopoli Island
Italy	3 November	Crossed the River Tagliamento
	4 November	Armistice with Austria-Hungary

8TH DIVISION
1914

| France | November–March | Held the Neuve Chapelle sector |

1915

Neuve Chapelle	10–13 March	Captured Neuve Chapelle
Armentières	April	In the Bois Grenier sector
Armentières	from late April	Holding the Fauquissart sector
Aubers Ridge	9 May	Attacked towards Fromelles on Aubers Ridge
Armentières	June–September	In the sector south of Fleurbaix
Fromelles	25 September	Attacked towards Fromelles

1916

Armentières	January–March	Held the Fleurbaix sector
Somme	March–June	In the sector west of Ovillers
Somme	1 July	Attacked Ovillers
Béthune	July–September	Held the Hohenzollern Redoubt sector
Somme	20–30 October	Engaged east of Gueudecourt
Somme	November	In the Lesboeufs sector
Somme	December–March	Held the Rancourt sector

1917

Somme	March	In the Bouchavesnes sector
Hindenburg	14 March–5 April	Advanced across the Canal du Nord to Villers-Guislain
Ypres	May–July	Held the Hooge sector
Ypres	31 July–3 August	Captured Hooge
Ypres	15–17 August	Engaged north of Westhoek
Armentières	Sept & Oct	Held the Ploegsteert Wood sector
Ypres	November–March	In the Passchendaele sector

1918

Somme	23–24 March	Engaged on the Somme Canal at Cizancourt and Béthencourt
Somme	25–28 March	Fell back through Ablaincourt, Rosières to Aubercourt
Somme	24–25 April	Captured Villers-Bretonneux
Aisne	May	In the Berry and Ville-aux-Bois sector, French sector
Aisne	27–28 May	Fell back across the Aisne Canal and the River Vesle
Arras	June–October	In the Acheville sector

The Advance to Victory

Drocourt–Queant	7–12 October	Advanced to the outskirts of Douai
Douai	17–18 October	Captured Douai, crossing the Scarpe Canal
Schelde	19–23 October	Advanced through the Forest of Raimes to the River Schelde
Mons	11 November	Entered the line north of Mons

9TH (SCOTTISH) DIVISION

1915

France	June–September	Held the Festubert sector, Béthune
Béthune	September	In the Auchy sector
Loos	25–27 September	Captured Fosse 8 and the Dump
Ypres	Oct–Dec	Held the Zillebeke sector

1916

Armentières	January–June	Held the Ploegsteert sector
Somme	3–20 July	Captured Bernafay Wood, Longueval and High Wood
Arras	August	Held the Berthonval and Carency sector
Somme	10–30 October	Engaged east of Le Sars
Arras	November–April	Held the River Scarpe sector

1917

Arras	9–16 April	Advanced through Athies
Arras	28 April–10 May	Engaged at Gavrelle and Roeux
Arras	June	In the Roeux sector
Cambrai	July–September	Held the Beaucamp and Havrincourt sector
Ypres	18–22 September	Engaged east of Frezenburg, capturing Zevenkote
Ypres	10–17 October	Engaged west of Wallemolen
Flanders Coast	November	In the Nieuport Bains sector
Cambrai	December–March	Held the Gouzeaucourt sector

1918

Cambrai	from March	Held the Villers-Guislain and Gonnelieu sector
Somme	21 March	Forced back through Equancourt
Somme	24–26 March	Retired through Montauban to the River Ancre
Ypres	from early April	Held the Hollebeke sector
Lys	10–25 April	Fell back through St Eloi to Voormezeele
Lys	May–July	Held the Meteren sector
Lys	19 July	Captured Meteren
Lys	18 August	Captured Hoegenacker Ridge
Ypres	September	Held the Potijze sector

9th (Scottish) Division. Sergeants of 9th/10th Highland Light Infantry shout out instructions during bayonet practice. *(IWM Q4097)*

The Advance to Victory

Ypres	28 September	Advanced to Dadizeele
Courtrai	14–17 October	Advanced across the River Lys and through Ooteghem
Courtrai	26 October	Reached Berchem on the River Schelde

10TH (IRISH) DIVISION
1915

Gallipoli	6 August	Landed at Suvla and advanced north and east of the bay
Suvla	21–27 August	Failed attacks on Hill 60
	30 September	Left Gallipoli for Macedonia
Macedonia	24 October	Reached Salonika and moved to Bulgarian border
	7–17 December	Withdrew to Salonika

1916

Salonika	September	Advanced to the Strumica Canal sector west of Serres
	3–4 October	Captured Yeniköi

1917

Palestine	September	Sailed to Palestine and concentrated at Rafah
Gaza	1–10 November	Blocked the inland railway near Tell el Sheira
Jerusalem	December	North-west of the city

1918

	Spring	The division was Indianized
Megiddo	19–21 September	Advanced to Nablus
	October	Employed on salvage work
	31 October	Armistice with Turkey

11TH (NORTHERN) DIVISION
1915

Gallipoli	6 August	Landed at Suvla Bay, and took Karakol Dagh and Chocolate Hill
Suvla	21 August	Failed to capture W Hills, east of the bay
	19–20 December	Evacuated the beachhead

1916

Egypt	February–May	Suez Canal defences
France	June–August	Held the Blaireville sector, Arras
Somme	7–26 September	Engaged at Thiepval; captured Zollern and Stuff Redoubts
Somme	December–February	Held the Beaucourt sector

1917

Hindenburg	February	Advanced through Grandcourt
Somme	March–May	Held the Hermies and Lagnicourt sector
Messines	9–14 June	Engaged in the Oosttaverne sector
Ypres	8–26 August	Engaged south of Langemarck

| Ypres | 29 September | Engaged at Poelcappelle; captured the village on 4 October |
| Béthune | November–January | Held the Loos sector |

1918

| Béthune | January–August | Held the Hohenzollern Redoubt sector |

The Advance to Victory

| Scarpe | 30 August | Advanced from the Pelves sector to Hamblain-les-Prés |
| Sambre | 4 November | Switched to the Jenlain sector and advanced to Givry |

12th (Eastern) Division. A sentry stands on guard in the trenches at Beaumont-Hamel during the winter of 1916–17; tall soldiers are warned to Duck their Nut as they pass the gas alarm. *(IWM Q1717)*

12TH (EASTERN) DIVISION

1915

France	June–September	Held the River Lys sector, Armentières
Loos	1–13 October	Hulluch sector then extended to cover Hohenzollern Redoubt
Béthune	December–February	Held the Festubert sector

1916

| Béthune | February–June | Held the Hohenzollern Redoubt sector |
| Somme | 2–9 July | Engaged at Ovillers |

Somme	28 July–13 August	Engaged at Mouquet Farm, west of Pozières
Arras	August	In the Beaurains sector
Somme	1–19 October	Engaged in the Gueudecourt sector
Arras	November–January	Held the Beaurains sector

1917

Arras	January–April	Held the St Sauveur sector
Arras	9 April	Advanced south of Feuchy and captured Monchy-le-Preux
Arras	25 April–13 May	Engaged north-west of Monchy-le-Preux
Arras	June–November	Holding the sector east of Monchy-le-Preux
Cambrai	from November	Holding the Gonnelieu sector
Cambrai	20–21 November	Advanced through la Vacquerie to the St Quentin Canal
Cambrai	4 December	Withdrew towards Villers-Plouich

1918

Armentières	January–March	Held the Bois Grenier sector
Somme	from 26 March	Aveluy sector then the Albert sector along the River Ancre
Somme	from late April	Holding the Beaumont-Hamel sector
Somme	June–August	Held the Aveluy sector
Somme	early August	Holding the Ville-sur-Ancre sector

The Advance to Victory

Amiens	8–9 August	Advanced through Morlancourt
Albert	22–31 August	Advanced through Meaulte, Combles and Maurepas
Bapaume	5 September	Crossed the Canal du Nord at Manacourt
Epéhy	18 September	Captured Epéhy
St Quentin	29–30 September	Captured Vendhuile on the St Quentin Canal
Lens	9–13 October	Advanced through Saullaumines to the Haute Deule Canal
Schelde	17–23 October	Advanced to the River Schelde at Château de l'Abbaye

13TH (WESTERN) DIVISION

1915

Gallipoli	6–31 July	Engaged in the western sector of the Helles beachhead
Anzac Cove	3–28 August	Engaged at Anzac Cove
Suvla	5 September	Landed at Suvla
Helles	19 December	Evacuated the Suvla beachhead and transferred to Helles

1916

	7 January	Evacuated the Helles beachhead and sailed to Egypt
Mesopotamia	March	Landed at Basra and sailed up the Tigris towards Kut
Siege of Kut	5–22 April	Captured Hanna and Fallahiya but failed to take Sanniyat

1917

Battle of Kut	25 Jan–25 Feb	Cleared the Hai Salient and Dahra Bend; the Turks withdrew
Baghdad	7–11 March	Followed the Turks up the Tigris, taking Baghdad

	April–December	Operations north of Baghdad to secure the city

1918

Kirkuk	5–28 May	Advanced to Kirkuk then withdrew to the Kifri area
	June–October	Occupation duties north of Baghdad
	July	39th Brigade headed off to join the North Persia Force
	October	40th Brigade advanced through Kirkuk to the Little Zab River
	31 October	Armistice with Turkey

14TH (LIGHT) DIVISION

1915

France	May & June	Held the St Eloi sector, Ypres
Ypres	June–September	Held the Hooge sector; lost the village on 30 July
Ypres	25 September	An attack at Hooge failed
Ypres	November–February	In the Wieltje sector

1916

Arras	February–July	In the Wailly, Beaurains and Roclincourt sectors
Somme	13–20 August	Engaged in Delville Wood sector
Somme	13–17 September	East of Delville Wood; advanced towards Flers on 15 September
Arras	October–January	Holding the sector east of Arras

1917

Arras	January–April	In the Beaurains sector

14th (Light) Division. Men play cards outside their dugout as they wait for their kettle to boil, oblivious to the shells bursting in the distance. *(IWM Q2259)*

Arras	9 April	Captured the Hindenburg Line north of Neuville Vitasse
Arras	26 April	Engaged west of Chérisy; failed to advance on 3 May
Ypres	18 August	Hooge sector, in Glencorse Wood and Inverness Copse
Messines	September	Held the line east of Messines
Ypres	10–17 October	Engaged in the Broodseinde sector

1918

St Quentin	January–March	Moy and Urvillers sector
Somme	21–23 March	Retired across the Crozat Canal through Jussy and Guiscard
Somme	early April	Bouzencourt sector; fell back north-east of Villers-Bretonneux
	May–July	Reduced to cadre; re-formed in England and returned to France
Ypres	September	In the Vierstraat sector

The Advance to Victory

Ypres	28 September	Captured St Eloi
Courtrai	15 October	Crossed the River Lys and captured Comines
Schelde	9 November	Crossed the River Schelde

15TH (SCOTTISH) DIVISION
1915

France	August & September	Held the Loos sector, Béthune
Loos	25–26 September	Captured Loos and Hill 70
Béthune	October–July 1916	Held the Loos and Hohenzollern Redoubt sectors

1916

Béthune	11 May	Lost the Kink near Hulluch
Somme	8 Aug–17 Sept	West of High Wood; captured Martinpuich on 15 Sept
Somme	9 Oct–5 Nov	Engaged in the Le Sars sector
Somme	December–February	Held the Le Sars sector

1917

Arras	February–April	Held the Blagny sector
Arras	9–12 April	Captured Feuchy and advanced towards Pelves
Arras	19–26 April	Engaged at Guémappe, capturing the village
Ypres	May–July	Held the Wieltje sector
Ypres	31 July–4 August	Captured Frezenberg
Ypres	17–24 August	Engaged in the Frezenberg sector
Arras	September–February	Held the Roeux sector

1918

Arras	February–March	In the Monchy-le-Preux sector
Somme	28 March	Fell back towards Tilloy-les-Mofflaines
Arras	May	In the Feuchy sector
Marne	23 July–3 August	Captured Buzancy and Villemontoire, French sector
Arras	August	In the Neuville Vitasse sector
Béthune	September	Held the Hulluch sector

The Advance to Victory

Lens	4–13 October	Advanced to Pont à Vendin on the Haute Deule Canal
Schelde	15–21 October	Advanced across the canal to Bruyelle on the River Schelde
Antoing	8–11 November	Crossed the river and advanced to the River Dendre

15th (Scottish) Division. A ration party trudges along a muddy track through the ruins of Beaucourt. *(IWM Q2245)*

16TH (IRISH) DIVISION
1916

France	March–August	Held the Hulluch sector, Béthune
Somme	1–10 September	Engaged in the Guillemont sector, capturing Ginchy
Messines	October–March	Held the Messines sector

1917

Messines	March–June	Held the Wytschaete sector
Messines	7 June	Advanced through Wytschaete to Wambeke
Ypres	4–16 August	Engaged in the Frezenberg sector
Arras	August–November	Held the Bullecourt and Fontaine-les-Croisilles sector
St Quentin	December–March	Held the Ronssoy sector

1918

Somme	21–22 March	Forced back through Ste Emilie, Villers-Faucon to Tincourt

Somme	23–25 March	Crossed the Somme at Cléry and fell back to Proyart
Somme	27 March	Retired to Hamel
	April–June	Reduced to cadre and re-formed in England
Béthune	August	Returned to France and took over the Cambrin sector

The Advance to Victory

	20 September	Followed the German withdrawal through Auchy
Lens	2 October	Advanced to Wingles on the Haute Deule Canal
Schelde	15–21 October	Crossed the canal and reached the River Schelde on the 21st
Antoing	8–10 November	Crossed the river and captured Antoing

17TH (NORTHERN) DIVISION

1915

France	August–December	Held the Zillebeke sector, Ypres

1916

Messines	January–March	Held the St Eloi sector; engaged at the Bluff
Armentières	March–June	In the Armentières sector
Somme	1–6 July	Captured Fricourt and advanced towards Mametz Wood
Somme	1 to 13 August	Engaged in Delville Wood
Somme	September–October	Hébuterne sector, Somme
Somme	November	Sector east of Gueudecourt, Somme
Somme	December–February	Held the Morval sector

1917

Arras	12–26 April	Engaged north of Monchy-le-Preux; advanced towards Pelves
Arras	May	In the sector north of Roeux
Arras	June–October	Held the Roeux and Gavrelle sector
Ypres	from 11 October	In the sector south of the Houthulst Forest
Ypres	late October	Held the sector north of Poelcappelle
Cambrai	December–March	In the Flesquières sector

1918

Somme	21–23 March	Forced back through Havrincourt, Hermies and Bertencourt
Somme	24–26 March	Continued through Gueudecourt, Thiepval and across the Ancre
Somme	April	In the Aveluy Wood and Hamel sector

The Advance to Victory

Albert	22–29 August	Advanced from Thiepval to Lesboeufs
Bapaume	2–10 September	Crossed the Canal du Nord and advanced to Gouzeaucourt
St Quentin	18–30 September	Advanced from Gouzeaucourt and engaged at Villers-Guislain
Cambrai	9–12 October	Advanced from Walincourt to the River Selle
Selle	20–23 October	Crossed the river and advanced to Ovillers
Sambre	2–4 November	Advanced from Ghissignies into the Mormal Forest

| Maubeuge | 8–11 November | Advanced from Limont Fontaine, south-east of Maubeuge |

18TH (EASTERN) DIVISION
1915

| France | August–March | Held the Fricourt sector, Somme |

1916

Somme	March & April	Held the Carnoy sector
Somme	May & June	Held the Mametz sector
Somme	1–7 July	Advanced between Mametz and Montauban
Somme	14–18 July	Engaged in Bernafay Wood and Trônes Wood
Somme	25 September	Captured Thiepval and Schwaben Redoubt
Somme	14 Oct–18 Nov	Engaged north-west of Courcelette; captured Regina Trench

18th (Eastern) Division. A fatigue party prepares to carry bombs forward during the attack on Trônes Wood in July 1916. *(IWM Q4052)*

1917

Somme	January & February	In the sector south of Miraumont; captured Boom Ravine
Hindenburg	25 February–10 March	Advanced to Irles
Hindenburg	17–20 March	Advanced through Achiet-le-Grand and Gomiécourt to St Léger

Arras	26 April	Engaged at Fontaine-les-Croisilles
Ypres	4–20 August	In action east of Hooge at Inverness Copse and Glencorse Wood
Ypres	10–24 October	Poelcappelle sector; captured the village on the 22nd
Ypres	from 5 November	In the sector south of the Houthulst Forest

1918

St Quentin	February & March	Held the Travency and Moy sector
Somme	21–23 March	Fell back across the Crozat Canal beyond Quessy and Jussy
Somme	April & May	Hangard and Villers-Bretonneux sector
Somme	June & July	In the sector west of Albert

The Advance to Victory

Amiens	8 August	Advanced from Méricourt south of Morlancourt
Albert	22–30 August	Advanced through Albert, Fricourt and Combles
Bapaume	4 September	Reached Manancourt on the Canal du Nord
Epéhy	18–26 September	Advanced from Ste Emilie through Ronssoy to Lempire
St Quentin	29 September	Advanced south of Vendhuile
Selle	23–24 October	Advanced from Le Cateau through Bousies
Sambre	4–6 November	Advanced through the Mormal Forest to the Sambre

19TH (WESTERN) DIVISION

1915

France	August–September	Held the Festubert sector, Béthune
Béthune	25 September	Attacked at Festubert
Béthune	October–April 1916	In the Richbourg l'Avoué and Neuve Chapelle sector

1916

Somme	2–9 July	Captured La Boisselle
Somme	22–31 July	Engaged at Bazentin-le-Petit
Messines	August	Held the Wytschaete and Ploegsteert sectors
Somme	September	Held the Hébuterne sector
Somme	from 22 October	Engaged at Grandcourt

1917

Somme	January–February	Held the Serre and Puisieux sector
Messines	March–June	In the Wytschaete sector
Messines	7 June	Advanced to Oosttaverne
Messines	September–October	Held the Ypres–Comines Canal sector
Cambrai	November	In the Marcoing sector

1918

Somme	22–23 March	Retreated through Beaumetz, Lebucquerie and Beugny
Somme	24–25 March	Fell back through Bapaume and Puisieux to Hébuterne
Messines	early April	In the sector east of Messines
Lys	10–11 April	Fell back towards Wulverghem
Lys	14–15 April	Fell back south-east of Kemmel
Aisne	May	Transferred to the Aisne, French sector

Aisne	29 May–6 June	Fell back via Faverolles and Fère-en-Tardenois to Bligny
Lys	July	Locon and Hinges sector

The Advance to Victory

Lys	August	Advanced through Locon, Lacoutre and Vielle Chapelle
Béthune	3–7 September	Advanced to Neuve Chapelle
Selle	18–23 October	Advanced from the River Selle to the River Harpies
Sambre	3–6 November	Advanced from Jenlain to the Grand Honnelle River
Maubeuge	7–9 November	Advanced through Houdain and Malplaquet

20TH (LIGHT) DIVISION
1915

France	from August	In the Fauquissart sector, Béthune
Béthune	25 September	Attacked at Fauquissart

1916

Ypres	January–April	Held the Boesinghe sector
Ypres	May–June	In the Wieltje sector
Somme	July–August	Held the Hébuterne sector
Somme	from 21 August	Engaged at Guillemont; captured the village on 3 Sept
Somme	16–23 September	Engaged north-east of Ginchy
Somme	27 Sept–7 Oct	Engaged in the Gueudecourt sector

1917

Somme	January	In the Morval sector
Hindenburg	14 March	Advanced to Metz and Bertincourt
Arras	June	Engaged against the Hindenburg Line north of Lagnicourt
Ypres	from 5 August	Engaged in Langemarck sector; captured the village on the 16th
Ypres	18–28 September	Engaged north-east of Langemarck
Cambrai	October	Held the Gouzeaucourt sector
Cambrai	20 November	Advanced to Masnières on the St Quentin Canal
Cambrai	30 November	Forced back to Gouzeaucourt

1918

Ypres	January–February	Held the Gheluvelt sector
Somme	21–23 March	In reserve then fell back to the Somme Canal
Somme	24–28 March	Fell back through Nesle, Roye, Damery and Aubercourt
Arras	June–October	Held the Avion sector

The Advance to Victory

Lens	6 October	Followed the German withdrawal towards Fresnoy and Méricourt

21ST DIVISION
1915

France	25–26 September	Carried out uncoordinated attacks at Loos
Armentières	November–February	Held the Armentières sector

1916

Somme	March–June	Held the Fricourt sector
Somme	1 July	Made a disastrous attack against Fricourt
Somme	11–17 July	Advanced from Mametz Wood to Bazentin-le-Petit
Arras	August	Held the Roclincourt sector
Somme	17 Sept–1 Oct	Advanced east of Flers
Béthune	October–December	Held the Hohenzollern Redoubt sector

1917

Béthune	January & February	Held the Cuinchy sector
Arras	March	In the Croisilles and Hénin sector
Arras	9–11 April	Advanced east of Hénin
Arras	late April–August	Croisilles sector
Ypres	29 Sept–8 Oct	Advanced from Polygon Wood towards Reutel
Ypres	November	In the Broodseinde Ridge sector
Cambrai	2 December	Reinforced the Epéhy sector

1918

Somme	21–23 March	Fell back across the Canal du Nord
Somme	24–25 March	Fell back along the River Somme at Chipilly
Messines	from early April	Held the Hollebeke sector
Lys	11–17 April	62nd and 64th Brigade engaged at Wytschaete
Lys	14 April	110th Brigade fell back from Hollebeke past Voormezeele
Lys	25–26 April	62nd and 64th Brigades engaged north of Voormezeele
Aisne	May	In line south of the Aisne Canal, French sector
Aisne	27–28 May	Forced back to the River Vesle
Somme	July	Held the Beaumont-Hamel sector
Somme	August	Followed up the German withdrawal to Beaucourt

The Advance to Victory

Albert	21–25 August	Crossed the River Ancre and advanced through Thiepval
Bapaume	30 Aug–2 Sept	Advanced north of Le Transloy
Epéhy	18 September	Advanced from Heudicourt to Villers-Guislain
Cambrai	8 October	Captured part of the Beaurevoir Line and reached Walincourt
Selle	23–24 October	Advanced from Amerval to Englefontaine
Sambre	5–8 November	Moved through Mormal Forest and crossed the Sambre

22ND DIVISION

1915

France	September	Held the Herleville and Dompierre sector, Somme
Macedonia	October	Sailed to Salonika

1916

Macedonia	April	Advanced to the south side of Lake Dojran
	10 August	Attacked Horseshoe Hill
	13 September	Attacked the Grand Melon, north of Machukovo
	Winter	Held sectors west and east of Lake Dojran

1917

Macedonia	April	In line south-west of Dojran
Dojran	24 April & 8 May	Raided Horseshoe Hill and the Sugar Loaf

1918

Dojran	18 September	Raided the Sugar Loaf Hill and the Grand Couronné position
	21–30 September	Advanced to the Bulgarian border
	30 September	Armistice with Bulgaria

23RD DIVISION
1915

France	September–February	Bois Grenier sector, Armentières

1916

Arras	February–June	Held the Angres and Calonne sector
Somme	4–11 July	Engaged at Contalmaison, capturing the village
Somme	26 July–mid-August	Engaged in the Bazentin-le-Petit sector
Armentières	August	In the Ploegsteert sector
Somme	19 Sept–mid-Oct	Engaged in the Martinpuich sector, capturing Le Sars
Ypres	October–June	Held the Zillebeke area

1917

Messines	7 June	Captured Mount Sorrel and Hill 60
Ypres	18–25 September	Engaged south of the Menin Road
Ypres	28 Sept–2 Oct	Engaged in the sector facing Gheluvelt
Ypres	10–23 October	Held the line facing Becelaere
Italy	November	Travelled to the Montello sector on the River Piave

1918

Italy	March–October	Held the Asiago Plateau sector
Vittorio Veneto	26–29 October	Crossed the Piave and Monticano rivers
	4 November	Armistice with Austria-Hungary

24TH DIVISION
1915

France	26 September	Disastrous attack between Hulluch and Loos
Messines	October–January	Held the St Eloi sector

1916

Ypres	January–April	In the Zillebeke sector
Messines	April–July	Held the Wulverghem sector
Somme	11–22 August	Engaged south of Delville Wood
Somme	1–5 September	Engaged north-west of Delville Wood
Arras	September	Held the Berthonval and Carency sector
Béthune	October–March	Held the Loos sector

24th Division. Many of the Royal Fusiliers sleep while the card school flourishes during a rest on the outskirts of Albert; days later they will be in action in Delville Wood. *(IWM Q841)*

1917

Arras	March	In the Souchez sector
Arras	9–14 April	Attacked Givenchy and advanced through Lieven
Messines	7 June	Took over the advance beyond Oosttaverne
Ypres	July	In the Zillebeke sector
Ypres	31 July	Took Shrewsbury Forest and held the sector until August
St Quentin	September–March	Held the Pontruet and Hargicourt sector

1918

Somme	21–22 March	Fell back through Le Verguier to Monchy Lagache
Somme	23–24 March	Retired across the Somme to Pargny and Cizancourt
Somme	26–27 March	Fell back through Chaulnes and Rosières into reserve
Béthune	May	In the sector south-east of Loos
The Advance to Victory		
Cambrai	9–12 October	Advanced east of Cambrai to Haussy on the River Selle
Sambre	4–10 November	Advanced from Jenlain towards Villers Sire Nicole

25TH DIVISION
1915

France	October–April	Held the Ploegsteert sector, Messines

1916

Arras	April–June	In the Neuville St Vaast sector

Somme	7–17 July	Cleared Ovillers
Somme	mid-July–mid-August	Held the Beaumont-Hamel sector
Somme	18 Aug–7 Sept	Engaged south of Thiepval
Somme	1–22 October	North-east of Thiepval; captured Stuff Trench and Regina Trench
Messines	November–March	Held the Ploegsteert sector

25th Division. The 1st Wiltshires advance across no man's land towards Leipzig Salient near Thiepval on 7 August 1916. *(IWM Q1142)*

1917

Messines	March–June	In the Wulverghem sector
Messines	7–14 June	Advanced across the Messines Ridge to Gapaard
Ypres	1–13 August	Engaged at Westhoek; captured the village
Béthune	October & November	Held the La Bassée canal sector
Cambrai	December–March	In the Lagnicourt sector

1918

Somme	21–23 March	Pushed back through Vaulx, Morchies and Beugnâtre
Somme	24–26 March	Fell back through Biefvillers, Achiet-le-Grand and Bucquoy
Messines	from early April	Held the River Lys and Warneton sector
Lys	10–14 April	Driven out of Ploegsteert Wood back to Neuve Chapelle
Lys	10–14 April	74th Brigade fell back through Croix du Bac, Steewerck and Bailleul
Lys	17–19 April	Division reunited and fought at St Jans Cappel
Lys	26–29 April	Engaged at La Clytte
Aisne	28–30 May	Fell back from Muizon to Chambrecy and Sarcy, French sector
	June–September	Reduced to cadre and re-formed in England

The Advance to Victory

Cambrai	8–10 October	Advanced from Beaurevoir to St Souplet on the Selle
Selle	23–24 October	Advanced from Bazeul to Ors on the Sambre–Oise Canal
Sambre	4–7 November	Crossed the canal at Landrecies and moved to Dompierre

26th Division. Officers and men of the divisional train celebrate Christmas Day 1918 with a football match while they wait to return home from Salonika. *(IWM Q31576)*

26TH DIVISION

1915

France	September	Sailed to France but immediately sent to Macedonia
Macedonia	November	Sailed to Salonika

1916

Macedonia	April	Advanced to the south-west of Lake Dojran
`	10 August	Supported the attack on Horseshoe Hill

1917

	April	Moved south of Dojran
Dojran	24 April & 8 May	Raided the trenches on Petit Couronné
	Summer	Held sectors west and east of Lake Dojran
Pursuit	22–30 September	Advanced to Strumica
	30 September	Armistice with Bulgaria

27TH DIVISION

1915

France	January–March	Held the Vierstraat and St Eloi sector, Messines
Ypres	March–April	In the Polygon Wood sector

Ypres	4–13 May	Withdrew to Hooge, then fell back from Bellewaarde
Armentières	June–September	Held the Bois Grenier sector
Somme	September–October	Held the north bank of the River Somme
	November	Sailed from Marseilles to Macedonia

1916

Macedonia	February–August	Held the sector east of Salonika
	August–September	Held sectors either side of Lake Tahinos
	30 September	Attacked and captured Karajaköi Bala and Karajaköi Zir
	17 Nov & 6 Dec	Attacked Tumbitza Farm

1917

| Macedonia | All year | Held sectors either side of Lake Tahinos |

1918

Macedonia	June–August	Held the west bank of the River Vardar
	1 September	Captured the Roche Noire Salient
Strumica	22 September	Crossed the Vardar and headed towards Strumica Valley
	30 September	Armistice with Bulgaria

28TH DIVISION
1915

France	February	In the St Eloi sector, Ypres
Ypres	March–April	Held the Zonnebeke sector
Ypres	4–8 May	Withdrew to Wieltje and then lost Frezenberg
Ypres	from mid-May	Held the Hooge sector; lost Potijze on the 24th
Ypres	June	In the St Eloi sector
Messines	July	Held the Wulverghem and Vierstraat sector
Loos	27 Sept–5 Oct	Engaged at Hohenzollern Redoubt
	November	Sailed via Egypt to Salonika

1916

| Macedonia | August | Advanced north to the River Struma |
| | 2 and 31 October | Occupied Mazirko and then captured Bairakli Jum'a |

1917

Macedonia	April	Extended its line west to Lake Dojran
	15 May	Captured Ferdie and Essex trenches, west of Bairakli Jum'a
	16 October	Captured Bairakli and Kumil

1918

Macedonia	from the summer	Held the sector east of Lake Dojran
Dojran	18 September	84th Brigade joined the Crete Division's attack north of Lake Dojran
	22 September	Pursued the Bulgarians to Trnovo in the Strumica Valley
	30 September	Armistice with Bulgaria

29TH DIVISION
1915

Gallipoli	25 April	Landed on four beaches on Cape Helles and pushed inland
Helles	May–August	Engaged between Gully Ravine and the Krithia road
Suvla	16–21 August	Transferred to Suvla and attacked Scimitar Hill
Helles	December	Returned to Helles

1916

Gallipoli	8 January	Withdrew from Helles and sailed to Eygpt
France	March	Sailed to France
Somme	April–June	Held the Beaumont-Hamel sector
Somme	1 July	Disastrous attack against Beaumont-Hamel
Ypres	August & September	Held the Wieltje sector
Somme	20–30 October	Engaged in the Gueudecourt sector
Somme	December	In the Lesboeufs sector

1917

Somme	January–March	Held the Morval and Sailly-Saillisel sector
Arras	12–23 April	Advanced east of Monchy-Le-Preux
Arras	May	In the Monchy-le-Preux sector
Ypres	8–8 August	Engaged west and north-west of Langemarck
Ypres	21 Sept–14 Oct	Advanced north-east of Langemarck
Cambrai	20–30 November	Continued the advance to Masnières and Marcoing

1918

Ypres	January–10 April	Sector north of Passchendaele
Lys	10–13 April	86th and 87th Brigades fell back from Vieux Berquin
Lys	10–15 April	88th Brigade fell back from Steenwerck
Lys	mid-April–July	Division reunited and held the Vieux Berquin sector

The Advance to Victory

Lys	18 August	Captured Outtersteene Ridge
Messines	4 September	Captured Ploegsteert
Ypres	28 Sept–1 Oct	Advanced through Gheluvelt to Gheluwe
Courtrai	14–19 October	Crossed the River Lys at Ledeghem
Renaix	8–11 November	Crossed the River Schelde and advanced to Lessines

30TH DIVISION
1916

France	January–June	Held the Montauban sector, Somme
Somme	1–13 July	Captured Montauban and fought in Bernafay and Trônes Woods
Somme	22 July	Engaged at Guillemont; unable to capture the village
Béthune	August–September	Held the Givenchy sector
Somme	10–22 October	Engaged east of Eaucourt l'Abbaye
Arras	November–March	Monchy-au-Bois and Blaireville sector

1917

Hindenburg	March	Followed up the withdrawal to Hénin
Arras	9–13 April	Captured Héninel and advanced south of Wancourt
Arras	22–26 April	Advanced towards Fontaine-les-Croisilles and Chérisy
Ypres	May–July	Held the Zillebeke sector
Ypres	31 July–4 August	Advanced through Sanctuary Wood
Ypres	August	Held the Hollebeke sector
Ypres	November	In the Gheluvelt sector

1918

St Quentin	January–February	Held the Barisis and Moy sector
St Quentin	February	In the St Quentin sector
Somme	21–22 March	Driven back to Ham on the Somme Canal
Somme	23–26 March	Fell back across the Canal du Nord and over the River Avre
Ypres	April	In the Poelcapelle sector
Lys	from 25 April	Engaged near Dickebusch and St Eloi

The Advance to Victory

Messines	August	Advanced from Locre to Wulverghem
Ypres	28 September	Advanced to Warneton and Comines
Courtrai	14–21 October	Advanced from Gheluwe through Menin to the River Schelde
Renaix	8–11 November	Crossed the river and advanced towards Ghoy

31ST DIVISION

1915

Egypt	December–March	Suez Canal defences

1916

France	March–April	Beaumont-Hamel sector, Somme
Somme	April–June	Held the Serre sector
Somme	1 July	Attacked Serre then transferred to Neuve Chapelle sector
Béthune	August–September	In the Givenchy sector
Somme	October	Held the Hébuterne sector
Somme	13 November	Another unsuccessful attack on Serre

1917

Somme	January–February	Held the Puisieux sector
Hindenburg	March	Advanced through Gommecourt and Bucquoy
Arras	end of April	Engaged in the Oppy sector; failed to advance on 3 May
Arras	28 June	Captured Oppy Wood
Arras	July–March	Held sectors north-east of Arras

1918

Somme	23–26 March	Forced back from Ervillers to Ablainzevelle
Lys	11–14 April	Brigades engaged at Vieux Berquin, Merris and l'Epinette

| Lys | May–August | Vieux Berquin sector, capturing the village on 13 August |
| Armentières | September | In the Ploegsteert sector |

The Advance to Victory

Ypres	28 September	Advanced to Warneton
Courtrai	15–20 October	Crossed the River Lys and advanced to the Schelde via Tourcoing
Renaix	8–11 November	Crossed and advanced through Renaix to the River Dendre

31st Division. With their feet wrapped in sandbags to stop them slipping on the icy duck-boards, a fatigue party carries supplies up to the 12th East Yorkshires' trenches near Arleux. *(IWM Q10614)*

32ND DIVISION

1916

France	January–June	Thiepval sector, Somme
Somme	1 July	Attacked Thiepval
Somme	9–15 July	Engaged at Ovillers
Béthune	August–October	Held the Cambrin and Cuinchy sectors
Somme	17 November	Beaumont-Hamel sector, advanced onto the Redan Ridge

1917

| Ancre | February | Occupied Puisieux after a German withdrawal |
| Hindenburg | March | Advanced from Chilly sector to Holnon |

| Flanders Coast | May–October | Held the Nieuport sector |
| Ypres | November–March | Held the Wallemolen and Houthulst Forest sectors |

1918

| Somme | April–July | In the Ayette sector |

The Advance to Victory

Amiens	10–11 August	Advanced from Folies and Beaufort to Fouquescourt
Albert	22–29 August	Advanced through Herleville to Brie on the Somme Canal
Bapaume	5–10 September	Crossed the canal and advanced to Vermand and Soyecourt
Beaurevoir	3 October	Advanced from Magny la Fosse to Sequehart
Sambre	4–11 November	Crossed the Sambre Canal at Catillon and advanced to Avesnes

33RD DIVISION

1915

| France | December–July | Cuinchy and Givenchy sector, Béthune |

1916

Somme	15–22 July	Engaged at Bazentin-le-Petit
Somme	7–19 August	Engaged in the High Wood sector
Somme	September	Held the Hébuterne sector
Somme	from 26 October	East of Lesboeufs; captured Dewdrop and Boritska Trenches

33rd Division. A Lewis gun team of the 1st Middlesex keep watch during the German attack against Meteren on 16 April 1918. *(IWM Q6535)*

1917

Somme	January–March	Held the Bouchavesnes sector
Arras	16–25 April	Engaged in the Croisilles sector
Arras	May–July	Held the Croisilles and Fontaine sector
Flanders Coast	August	Held the Nieuport sector
Ypres	24–30 September	Engaged south of Polygon Wood
Messines	October	In the sector east of Messines
Ypres	November	Held the Passchendaele sector

1918

Lys	11–18 April	100th Brigade engaged around Neuve Eglise
Lys	11–14 April	98th Brigade north-east of Bailleul; 19th Brigade south of Meteren
Lys	14–20 April	19th and 98th Brigades lost Meteren
Lys	from 21 April	Engaged east of Dickebusch; captured Ridge Wood on 8 May
Ypres	June–August	Held the Voormezeele and Zillebeke Lake sector

The Advance to Victory

St Quentin	29 September	Advanced from Villers-Guislain to the St Quentin Canal
Beaurevoir	5–7 October	Crossed the canal and advanced to Aubencheul-au-Bois
Selle	9 October	Advanced from Malincourt to the River Selle
Selle	23–27 October	Advanced from Montay to Englefontaine
Sambre	5–8 November	Advanced through Mormal Forest and across the Sambre

34TH DIVISION

1916

Armentières	January–April	Held the Bois Grenier sector
Somme	April–July	In the La Boisselle sector
Somme	1–2 July	Attacked La Boisselle and captured Scots and Sausage Redoubts
Somme	10–17 July	111th and 112th Brigades (from 37th Division) attacked Contalmaison
Somme	1–15 August	The 2 brigades held the Bazentin-le-Petit sector
Armentières	September–February	Bois Grenier sector

1917

Arras	February–April	Held the Roclincourt sector
Arras	9–14 April	Advanced south of Bailleul
Arras	25–30 April	Engaged at Roeux
Arras	May–June	In the sector south of Gavrelle
St Quentin	July–September	River Omignon and Hargicourt sector
Ypres	13–24 October	Engaged north of Poelcappelle
Arras	November–March	Fontaine-les-Croisilles and Guémappe sector

1918

Arras	March	Held the sector east of Croisilles
Somme	21–23 March	Fell back through Croisilles to Boyelles and Boiry Becquerelle

Armentières	late March	Held the Bois Grenier and the River Lys sector
Lys	10–13 April	Fell back through Nieppe towards Bailleul
Lys	15–21 April	Evacuated Bailleul and fell back towards St Jans Cappel
	May & July	Reduced to cadre then reassembled
Marne	30 July	Advanced through Droizy to the River Crise, French sector
Ypres	August	In the sector east of Ypres
Messines	September	Held the Wytschaete sector

The Advance to Victory

Ypres	28–29 September	Advanced to Houthem on the Ypres–Comines Canal
Menin	14–16 October	Cleared Gheluwe and advanced through Menin
Courtrai	17–25 October	Crossed the River Lys and advanced to Bossuyt on the Schelde
Schelde	26–31 October	Advanced from Klienberg and Heinweg east of Anseghem

A sentry and Lewis gunner of 34th Division keep watch over no man's land in the Guémappe sector east of Arras in January 1918. *(IWM Q10609)*

35TH DIVISION
1916

France	January–June	Neuve Chapelle sector, Béthune
Somme	15–29 July	Trônes Wood sector, attacking towards Guillemont
Somme	19–26 August	Engaged south of Guillemont

Arras	September–February winter	Held the Roclincourt sector Many Bantams rejected as unfit and replaced

1917

Somme	February	In the Chaulnes sector
Hindenburg	March	Advanced to Pertian
St Quentin	April	In the Prontruet sector
Cambrai	May–October	Held the Villers-Guislain sector
Ypres	October	Engaged south of Houthulst Forest
Ypres	November	In the Poelcappelle sector

1918

Somme	24–26 March	Fell back from Montauban across the Ancre to Dernacourt
Lys	July–September	Locre sector
Ypres	September	Voormezeele sector

The Advance to Victory

Ypres	28 September	Advanced to Wervicq
Courtrai	14–16 October	Advanced from Gheluwe to the River Lys
Courtrai	17–21 October	Crossed the river and advanced to Knokke
Schelde	27 Oct–2 Nov	Captured Tieghem
Renaix	9–11 November	Crossed the Schelde at Berchem, advanced to the River Dendre

36th Division. RAMC personnel use a light railway trolley to ferry wounded to the rear from the Messines sector in May 1917; the man on the left is carrying a Yukon pack. *(IWM Q5839)*

36TH (ULSTER) DIVISION
1916

France	February–June	River Ancre sector, Somme
Somme	1 July	Penetrated the German line astride the Ancre
Messines	mid-July–June 1917	Held the Wytschaete sector

1917

Messines	7 June	Advanced over the Messines Ridge to Wambeke
Ypres	4–17 August	Engaged in the St Julien sector
Somme	from late August	Held the Trescault and Hermies sectors
Cambrai	20 November	Advanced astride the Canal du Nord towards Moeuvres
Cambrai	from 3 December	Held the Trescault and Hermies sector

1918

Cambrai	January–March	Held the Villers-Guislain sector
Somme	21–23 March	Forced back across the St Quentin and Somme Canals
Somme	24–26 March	Fell back through Cantigny and Roye
Ypres	from end March	Held the Poelcappelle sector
Lys	12–15 April	108th Brigade engaged at Wulverghem
Lys	16 April	Withdrew to Wieltje then the Yser Canal
Lys	July & August	In the Bailleul sector

The Advance to Victory

Messines	30 August	Advanced onto the Messines Ridge
Ypres	29–30 September	Advanced from Becelaere to Dadizeele
Courtrai	14–16 October	Advanced towards Courtrai
Anseghem	27–28 October	Crossed the Lys at Harlebeke and advanced to Anseghem

37TH DIVISION
1915

France	August–May	Foncquevillers and Ransart sector, Somme

1916

Somme	10–17 July	111th and 112th Brigades attacked Contalmaison under 34th Division
Somme	1–15 August	111th and 112th Brigades engaged in the Bazentin-le-Petit sector
Arras	August (Division)	Held the Berthonval and Carency sector (with 102nd and 103rd Brigades of 34th Division)
Béthune	September & October	Held the Souchez and Loos sector
Somme	14 November	111th Brigade attacked Beaucourt under 63rd (Royal Naval) Division
Béthune	December–February	Held the Neuve Chapelle sector

1917

Béthune	February	In the Loos and Hulluch sector
Arras	9–11 April	Captured Monchy-le-Preux
Arras	20–30 April	Captured Gavrelle

Ypres	June & July	Held the Hollebeke sector
Ypres	31 July	Attacked south of Hollebeke; held the sector until September
Ypres	October	Engaged in the Menin Road sector
Ypres	November–January	Held the Hollebeke sector

1918

Ypres	February	Returned to the Menin Road sector
Somme	end of March	Engaged in the Hébuterne and Bucquoy sector

The Advance to Victory

Albert	21–26 August	Advanced to Bapaume
Havrincourt	3–20 September	Cleared Havrincourt Wood and Trescault
Cambrai	4–10 October	Crossed the River Schelde and advanced to Briastre
Selle	12 October	Crossed the River Selle at Briastre
Selle	22–24 October	Advanced from Beaurain through Ghissignies
Sambre	4 November	Entered the Mormal Forest

38TH (WELSH) DIVISION
1916

France	January–June	Held the Givenchy and Neuve Chapelle sectors, Béthune
Somme	5–12 July	Engaged in Mametz Wood
Somme	late July	In the Serre sector
Ypres	August–July	Held the Boesinghe sector

1917

Ypres	31 July–4 August	Advanced across the Pilckem Ridge to the Steenbeek stream
Ypres	19 August	Returned to the Langemarck sector
Armentières	September–April	Held the Fleurbaix and Armentières sectors

1918

Somme	April–August	In the Albert and Aveluy sector

The Advance to Victory

Bapaume	1–4 September	Advanced through Pozières to the Canal du Nord
	5 September	Crossed the canal at Etricourt
Havrincourt	from 10 September	Held the Gouzeaucourt sector
Cambrai	5–9 October	Crossed the River Schelde and captured Villers-Outreaux
Selle	20–25 October	Crossed the River Selle and advanced towards Mormal Forest
Sambre	4–8 November	Advanced through Mormal Forest to Dimechaux

39TH DIVISION
1916

France	March–August	Givenchy and Festubert sector, Béthune
Somme	August–September	Held the Beaumont-Hamel sector
Somme	October	Thiepval sector, capturing Schwaben Redoubt and Stuff Trench

Somme	13 November	Captured St Pierre Divion
Ypres	December–July	Held the Wieltje sector

1917

Ypres	31 July	Advanced to the Steenbeek stream near St Julien
Ypres	early September	Advanced from Shrewsbury Forest to Tower Hamlets
Ypres	October–December	Held the Gheluvelt sector
Ypres	December–January	In the Wallemolen sector

1918

Cambrai	January–March	Held the Villers-Guislain sector
Somme	22–29 March	Retired from Longavesnes across the Somme to Proyart
Lys	from 16 April	Engaged in the Voormezeele sector
	May–November	Reduced to cadre and trained American and British troops

40TH DIVISION
1916

France	July–October	Held the Loos sector, Béthune
Somme	November–March	Held the Bouchavesnes sector

1917

Cambrai	April	In the Villers-Plouich and Beaucamp sector
Cambrai	21 April-5 May	Captured the two villages and Fifteen Ravine
Cambrai	22–25 November	Engaged in Bourlon Wood
Arras	December–March	Held the Noreuil and Croisilles sector

1918

Somme	22–24 March	Fell back from St Léger and Vraucourt through Gomiécourt
Armentières	late March	Held the sector south of Armentières
Lys	9–12 April	Driven back through Bac St Maur and Steenwerck
	May & June	Reduced to cadre then re-formed
Lys	June	In the Neuf Berquin sector

The Advance to Victory

Lys	August	Advanced to the River Lys at Erquinghem-Lys
Ypres	28 September	Advanced and captured Armentières and Houplines on 3 October
Roubaix	16–19 October	Crossed the River La Bassée Deule, capturing Roubaix
Schelde	8–9 November	Crossed the River Schelde at Warcoing

41ST DIVISION
1916

France	May–August	Held the Ploegsteert sector, Armentières
Somme	10–17 September	Delville Wood sector; advanced through Flers on the 15th

41st Division. This 18-pounder battery is supporting the division's advance beyond Mont Kemmel on 2 September 1918. *(IWM MH30165)*

| Somme | 4–7 October | Engaged north of Flers |
| Messines | October–June | In the Vierstraat sector |

1917

Messines	7 June	Advanced north of Oosttaverne
Ypres	July–August	Held the Hollebeke sector
Ypres	early–22 September	Engaged in Shrewsbury Forest
Flanders Coast	October	In the Nieuport Bains sector
Italy	November–January	Held the Montello sector, River Piave

1918

Italy	February–March	Held the Ciano sector, River Piave, then returned to France
Somme	22–26 March	Forced back from north-east of Bapaume to Achiet-le-Grand
Ypres	April–May	Held the Passchendaele sector and withdrew to Wieltje
Lys	July–August	In the Kemmel sector

The Advance to Victory

Lys	September	Advanced to Wytschaete
Ypres	29 September	Advanced from Kortewilde to Comines
Courtrai	14–18 October	Advanced from Gheluwe through Courtrai
Courtrai	19–20 October	Crossed the River Lys and advanced to Knokke
Schelde	25–26 October	Captured Avelghem
Renaix	10–11 November	Advanced towards the River Dendre

42ND (EAST LANCASHIRE) DIVISION

1914

Egypt	October–April	Suez Canal defences, Egypt

1915

Gallipoli	May	Engaged at Gully Ravine and Krithia Road, Helles
Helles	4 June & 6 August	Two unsuccessful attacks astride the Krithia Road
	27 December	Evacuated Helles and sailed to Egypt

42nd (East Lancashire) Division. A sergeant of the 1st/4th East Lancashires keeps watch on no man's land at Nieuport Bains using a mirror fixed to his bayonet. *(IWM Q2876)*

1916

Egypt	All year	Held part of the Suez Canal defences

1917

France	February–May	Sailed to France and took over Epéhy sector, Somme
St Quentin	June	In the Trescault and Canal du Nord sector
Ypres	mid-Aug–mid-Sept	Engaged in the Frezenberg sector
Flanders Coast	October–November	Held the Nieuport sector
Béthune	December–March	Held the Cuinchy and Festubert sector

1918

Somme	24–25 March	Fell back from Ervillers to Bucquoy and Ablainzevelle

| Somme | April–June | In the Hébuterne sector |
| Somme | June–August | Held the Beaumont-Hamel sector |

The Advance to Victory

Albert	24–26 August	Advanced through Miraumont, Warlencourt and Le Barque
Bapaume	29 Aug–3 Sept	Advanced from Bapaume to the Canal du Nord tunnel at Ytres
Canal du Nord	26–30 September	Advanced from Trescault past Beaucamp and Ribecourt
Selle	18–24 October	Crossed the Selle at Briastre and advanced to Beaurain
	6–10 November	Entered Mormal Forest and moved to Ferrière-le-Grand

43RD (1ST WESSEX) DIVISION

Sailed for India in October 1914 and replaced the Regular battalions stationed at Peshawar, Delhi, Allahabad, Dinapore, Barrackpore, Lucknow, Bombay, Ferozopore, Multan, Lahore, Bareilly, Jullundur, Ambala, Rawalpindi, Agra, Mhow and Meerut. Remained in India for the duration of the war.

44TH (HOME COUNTIES) DIVISION

Sailed to Bombay, India, in November 1914 and replaced the Regular battalions stationed at Lucknow, Cawnpore, Fyzabad, Mhow, Kamptee, Jubbulpore, Jhansi, Dinapore and Fort William; 2 battalions were stationed in Burma at Rangoon and Maymyo. Remained in India and Burma for the duration of the war.

45TH (2ND WESSEX) DIVISION

Sailed to India in December 1914 and replaced the Regular battalions stationed at Kirkee, Secunderabad, Bangalore, Bombay, Poona, Ahmednagar, Karachi, Quetta, Wellington and Meiktikia. Remained in India for the duration of the war.

46TH (NORTH MIDLAND) DIVISION

1915

France	March–May	Held the Wytschaete sector, Ypres
Ypres	June–September	In the Zillebeke sector
Loos	13 October	Engaged at Hohenzollern Redoubt
Armentières	October–December	Held the Neuve Chapelle sector
	December	Started to sail for Egypt but the order was cancelled

1916

Arras	March–April	Held the Neuville St Vaast sector
Somme	May–June	In the Gommecourt sector
Somme	1 July	Engaged at Gommecourt
Somme	July–March	Held the Monchy-au-Bois and Gommecourt sector

1917

| Hindenburg | 14–22 March | Advanced through Gommecourt and Bucquoy |
| Béthune | March–April | In the River Souchez and Loos sector |

Arras	23 April	Attacked La Coulotte
Arras	28 June	Advanced towards Lens
Béthune	July–March	Held the Loos and Hohenzollern Redoubt sector

46th (North Midland) Division. A guard of the 1st/7th Sherwood Foresters mans a barbed wire gate in the Cambrin sector. *(IWM Q6020)*

1918

| Béthune | March–April | In the River Souchez and Loos sector |
| Béthune | April–August | Held the Festubert and Locon sectors |

The Advance to Victory

Béthune	late August	Advanced towards Neuve Chapelle
St Quentin	19–28 September	In the Pontruet sector
St Quentin	29 September	Crossed the St Quentin Canal north of Bellenglise
Beaurevoir	3 October	Advanced from Joncourt to Montbrehain
Cambrai	10 October	Advanced from Sequehart towards the Andigny Forest
Selle	17–19 October	Advanced through Wassigny Forest to Sambre Canal
Sambre	6–11 November	Advanced from Barzy to Avesnelles

47TH (1ST/2ND LONDON) DIVISION
1915

France	April–June	Festubert and Cuinchy sector, Béthune
Béthune	June–September	In the Loos sector
Loos	25 September	Advanced south of Loos

1916

Arras	March–August	Held the Carency and Souchez sector
Somme	10–18 September	High Wood sector; captured the wood on the 15th
Somme	1–21 October	Engaged in the Le Sars sector
Ypres	November–June	In the Zillebeke sector

1917

Messines	7 June	Advanced towards Hollebeke
Ypres	mid-August	Engaged in the Westhoek sector
Ypres	mid-September	Again engaged in the Westhoek sector
Arras	October–November	Held the Oppy sector
Cambrai	28 November	Held Bourlon Wood; withdrew to Havrincourt on 4 December

1918

Cambrai	February–March	In the Villers-Plouich sector
Somme	21–23 March	Fell back through Beaucamp and Metz-en-Couture
Somme	24–25 March	Continued through Contalmaison and across the Ancre at Aveluy
Somme	May–August	Held the Albert sector
Somme	August	In the Morlancourt sector

The Advance to Victory

Albert	22 August	Captured Happy Valley
Bapaume	1–5 September	Advanced through St Pierre Vaast Wood towards Villers-Faucon
Lys	late September	Hazebrouck and the Laventie sector
	2–4 October	Advanced to Erquinghem
Lille	15 October	Advance to the Haute Deule Canal opposite Lille
Schelde	9–11 November	Crossed the River Schelde north of Tournai

48TH (SOUTH MIDLAND) DIVISION
1915

France	April–May 1916	Ploegsteert sector, Armentières

1916

Somme	May–July	In the Foncquevillers sector
Somme	1 July	Held the Foncquevillers sector
Somme	15–28 July	Cleared Ovillers
Somme	August & September	Held the Beaumont-Hamel sector
Somme	October	In the Hébuterne sector
Somme	November–February	Held the Le Sars sector

1917

Somme	February	In the Péronne sector
Hindenburg	17 March–5 April	Crossed the Somme; moved through Péronne to Lempire
Arras	May–July	In the Lagnicourt sector
Ypres	6–22 August	Engaged in the St Julien sector
Ypres	28 Sept–10 Oct	Engaged south of Poelcappelle
Arras	November	Held the Méricourt sector
Italy	December–March	Move to the Montello sector on the Piave Front

1918

Italy	April–October	Cesuna sector, Asiago Plateau
Vittorio Veneto	1–4 November	Advanced through the Val d'Assa Pass and Caldonazzo
	4 November	Armistice with Austria-Hungary

49TH (WEST RIDING) DIVISION
1915

France	April–June	Held the Bois Grenier sector, Armentières
Ypres	July–December	In the Pilckem sector

1916

Somme	February–June	Held the Thiepval sector
Somme	2 July–September	Engaged at Thiepval
Arras	October–December	In the Monchy sector

49th (West Riding) Division. A working party make their way along a duckboard track through the flooded wasteland of the Ypres Salient in January 1918. *(IWM Q8428)*

1917

Béthune	January–June	Held the Neuve Chapelle sector
Flanders Coast	July–September	Held the Nieuport and Dunkirk sector
Ypres	9 October	Attacked at Wallemolen
Ypres	October	Engaged on Broodseinde Ridge

1918

Lys	10–16 April	147th Brigade engaged at Nieppe
Lys	10–16 April	148th Brigade engaged at Neuve Eglise and Bailleul
Lys	from 26 April	The division assembled and was engaged at La Clytte
Ypres	June–August	Held the Zillebeke sector
Arras	September	In the Gavrelle sector

The Advance to Victory

Selle	11–12 October	Advanced from Iwuy to the River Selle
Valenciennes	1–3 November	Advanced from Famars beyond Aulnoy

50TH (NORTHUMBRIAN) DIVISION
1915

France	24–29 April	Engaged at St Julien, Ypres
Messines	June	In the Wulverghem sector
Armentières	July–November	Held the Armentières sector
Ypres	November–May	In the Zillebeke sector

1916

Messines	May–August	Held the Wytschaete sector
Somme	9–15 September	Martinpuich area; advanced east of the village on the 15th
Somme	26 Sept–2 Oct	Advanced towards Le Sars
Somme	late Oct–12 Nov	Engaged east of Le Sars
Somme	December–February	Held the Le Sars sector

1917

Somme	February	In the line west of Péronne
Arras	12–24 April	Engaged on Wancourt Ridge
Arras	June–October	Held the Guémappe sector
Ypres	late Oct–9 Nov	Engaged south of Houthulst Forest
Ypres	December–March	In the Passchendaele sector

1918

Somme	21–23 March	Fell back from Bourcy, across the River Somme at Brie
Somme	24–27 March	Continued through Foucaucourt and Rosières to Aubercourt
Lys	9–13 April	Driven back from Lestrem and Sailly to Nieppe Forest
Aisne	May	Held the Ville-aux-Bois and Craonne area, French sector
Aisne	27–29 May	Retired across the Aisne and the Vesle east of Fismes
	July	Working on lines of communication in the British zone

The Advance to Victory

Beaurevoir	4–9 October	Advanced across the Canal du Nord tunnel through Vendhuile

Selle	17–22 October	Crossed the River Selle south of Le Cateau
Sambre	4–5 November	Advanced through the Mormal Forest
Sambre	6–11 November	Crossed the River Sambre and advanced to Solre-le-Château

51st (Highland) Division. Sentries guard prisoners taken during the tank attack on Flesquières on 20 November 1917. *(IWM Q6276)*

51ST (HIGHLAND) DIVISION

1915

France	May & June	Sector south of Richebourg l'Avoué, Béthune
Somme	July–February	Held the La Boisselle and River Ancre sector

1916

Arras	March–July	In the Roclincourt and Neuville St Vaast sector
Somme	21 July–6 August	Engaged at Longueval and Bazentin-le-Petit
Armentières	August–September	Held the Armentières sector
Somme	October	In the Hébuterne and Beaumont-Hamel sectors
Somme	13 November	Captured Beaumont-Hamel
Somme	December–January	Held the Courcelette sector

1917

Arras	February	In the Roclincourt sector
Arras	9–12 April	Advanced towards Bailleul

Arras	17–25 April	Engaged at Fampoux and Roeux
Arras	May	Engaged in the Rouex sector, capturing the village
Ypres	July	Held the Pilckem sector
Ypres	31 July–8 August	Advanced over Pilckem Ridge towards Langemarck
Ypres	20–24 September	Engaged south of Langemarck
Arras	October	In the Fontaine-les-Croisilles and Guémappe sector
Cambrai	November	Held the Beaucamp and Trescault sector
Cambrai	20–24 November	Advanced through Flesquières to Cantaing and Fontaine
Cambrai	1–4 December	Engaged at Moeuvres, withdrew to Boursies and Demicourt

1918

Somme	21–23 March	Fell back through Beaumetz to Velu and Lebuquerie
Somme	24–26 March	Fell back across the Ancre through Puisieux and Hébuterne
Lys	10–13 April	Fell back from Locon and Lestrem to Hinges and Calonne
Arras	May–June	Held the Bailleul and Willerval sector
Aisne	20–27 July	Advanced from Nanteuil and Pourcy to Chambrecy
Arras	August	Returned to the British zone and took over Fampoux sector

The Advance to Victory

Scarpe	26–30 August	Advanced through Roeux and Gavrelle to Plouvain
Schelde	11–12 September	Crossed the Schelde Canal and advanced to Avesnes-le-Sec
Selle	19–28 October	Advanced from Noyelles and Neuville sur l'Escaut to Famars

52ND (LOWLAND) DIVISION
1915

Gallipoli	6 June	Landed at Helles and attacked Gully Ravine on the 28th
Helles	July–December	In line east of the Krithia Road

1916

Gallipoli	8 January	Evacuated Helles and sailed to Egypt
Egypt	March–April 1917	Suez Canal defences

1917

Gaza	19 April	Attempted to reach the southern outskirts of Gaza
Gaza	28 October	Engaged Turkish positions south-west of Gaza
	7–10 November	Cleared Wadi el Hesi and headed north to Burqa
	13–21 November	Pushed inland capturing Junction Station
	December	Established a line north of Jaffa on the coast

1918

France	April–August	Held the Fresnoy and Méricourt sector, Arras

The Advance to Victory

Scarpe	23–24 August	Advanced from Mercatel to Hénin
Drocourt	1–3 September	Advanced from Bullecourt to Inchy on the Canal du Nord
Canal du Nord	11–12 September	Captured Moeuvres
Canal du Nord	27 September	Crossed the canal south of Moeuvres
Cambrai	1–5 October	Advanced south of Cambrai and captured Proville
Mons	8–11 November	Crossed the Canal du Jard and advanced to Jurbise

53RD (WELSH) DIVISION
1915

Gallipoli	9 August	Landed at Suvla Bay
	12 December	Withdrew from the peninsula and sailed to Egypt

1916

Egypt	All year	Suez Canal defences

1917

Gaza	26 March	Unable to advance towards the town
Gaza	17–19 April	Advanced up the coast towards Gaza
	1–6 November	Advanced north of Beersheba
Jerusalem	7–10 November	Attacked through Bethlehem and north of Jerusalem

1918

Megiddo	19–21 September	Held positions north-west of Jericho
	31 October	Armistice with Turkey

54TH (EAST ANGLIAN) DIVISION
1915

Gallipoli	10 August	Landed at Suvla Bay
	3 December	Left the peninsula and headed to Egypt
Egypt	December–March	161st Brigade engaged the Senussi in the Western Desert

1916

Egypt	April–March 1917	Suez Canal defences

1917

Gaza	26 March	Failed to secure the high ground east of the city
Gaza	19 April	Unable to advance south-east of Gaza
	28 October	Held Burbaye Ridge
	2–8 November	Held the coastal sector
	late November	Held positions at Lydda, astride the Haifa Railway
	late December	Moved north along the railway

1918

Megiddo	19 September	Attacked positions east of the railway
	October	Worked on lines of communication

55TH (WEST LANCASHIRE) DIVISION

1916

France	January–July	Re-formed and took over the Ransart sector, south of Arras
Somme	1–15 August	Engaged in the Guillemont sector
Somme	7–11 September	Engaged in Delville Wood
Somme	17 September	In action north of Flers and captured Gueudecourt on the 26th
Ypres	October–July	Hooge and Wieltje sector

1917

Ypres	31 July–4 August	Advanced to St Julien
Ypres	18–24 September	Engaged in the St Julien sector
Cambrai	October & November	Held the Ronssoy and Villers-Guislain sector
Cambrai	30 November	Driven out of Villers-Guislain and Banteux Ravine by German counter-attacks

1918

Béthune	January–April	Held the Givenchy sector
Lys	9–15 April	Held off German attacks against Givenchy
The Advance to Victory		
Béthune	24 August	Followed up the German withdrawal towards La Bassée

55th (West Lancashire) Division. A wiring party of the King's Liverpool Regiment carry materials up to the Ransart sector, east of Arras, in April 1916. *(IWM Q525)*

56th (1st London) Division. A piper of the London Scottish leads the men to Durham Camp near Mont St Eloi on 30 March 1918. *(IWM Q10582)*

The Final Advance in Artois

Lens	2 October	Followed up German withdrawal to Haute Deule Canal
Tournai	16 October	Crossed the canal at Don and advanced to Tournai
Schelde	8–11 November	Crossed the River Schelde and advanced to Ath

56TH (1ST LONDON) DIVISION

1916

France	May–July	Held the Hébuterne sector, Somme
Somme	1 July	Attacked Gommecourt
Somme	early September	Engaged in Leuze Wood, east of Guillemont
Somme	26 Sept–8 Oct	Captured Combles
Lys	November–March	In the Neuve Chapelle sector

1917

Arras	March–April	Held the Beaurains sector
Arras	9–12 April	Advanced through Neuville Vitasse and Wancourt
Arras	28 April–5 May	Engaged at Guémappe
Arras	June	In the Guémappe sector
Ypres	13–17 August	Engaged east of Hooge
Cambrai	September	Held the Boursies and Lagnicourt sector
Cambrai	21 November	Advanced to Tadpole Copse south of Moeuvres

| Cambrai | 4 December | Pulled back to Boursies and Lagnicourt |
| Arras | December–March | Held the Gavrelle and Oppy sector |

1918

Somme	28 March	Forced out of Gavrelle
Arras	April–July	Held the Tilloy-les-Mofflaines sector
Arras	from early August	In the Neuville Vitasse sector

The Advance to Victory

Scarpe	23–30 August	Advanced from Boyelles through Croisilles to Bullecourt
Arras	September	In the Palleul sector
Canal du Nord	27 September	Crossed the Canal du Nord, capturing Sauchy Lestrée
Cambrai	1–17 October	Sensée Canal sector between Aubencheul and Palleul
Sambre	3–10 November	Advanced south of Valenciennes to Harveng

57TH (2ND WEST LANCASHIRE) DIVISION
1917

France	February–October	Picantin and Bois Grenier sector, Armentières
Ypres	from 26 October	Engaged north of Poelcappelle
Ypres	December	In the sector south of Houthulst Forest

1918

Armentières	January–April	Held the Armentières sector
Somme	April–June	In the Hébuterne sector
Arras	July–August	Held the Fampoux sector

The Advance to Victory

Drocourt	30 Aug–2 Sept	Advanced from Hendecourt towards Inchy
Canal du Nord	28–30 September	Advanced from Graincourt and Anneux to Canal du Nord
Cambrai	9 October	Cambrai sector; captured the town
Lille	17 October	Crossed the Haute Deule Canal and occupied Lille

58TH (2ND/1ST LONDON) DIVISION
1917

France	February–March	Berles and Wailly sector, Arras
Hindenburg	17–19 March	Advanced to Croisilles and Hénin
Bullecourt	May & June	Engaged east of Bullecourt
Ypres	18–27 September	Engaged north-east of St Julien
Ypres	24 Oct–13 Nov	Engaged south of Poelcappelle
Ypres	December	Poelcappelle sector

1918

St Quentin	January	Barisis and Travecy sector
Somme	21 March	Withdrew across the River Oise
Somme	22–27 March	Held a line between Condren and Barisis
Somme	April	Held the Hangard sector
Somme	24 April	Advanced south of Villers-Bretonneux
Somme	June & July	Held the Dernacourt and Albert sector
Somme	August	In the Sailly-le-Sec sector

During 58th Division's advance across Chipilly Ridge on 9 August 1918, signallers report progress to a contact plane; while the soldier on the left keeps a look-out for messages from the front line, the man on the right uses a heliograph to signal. *(IWM Q9191)*

The Advance to Victory

Amiens	8–10 August	Captured Sailly Lorette, Chipilly and Etinhem
Bapaume	22 Aug–5 Sept	Advanced from Bray to the Canal du Nord at Moislains
Epéhy	18 September	Cleared Epéhy and Peizière
	2 October	Occupied Lens
Lens	9–12 October	Advanced to Haute Deule Canal east of Pont à Vendin
Schelde	16–21 October	Advanced to the River Schelde south of Antoing
Ath	8–11 November	Crossed the Schelde and advanced beyond Blaton Canal

59TH (2ND NORTH MIDLAND) DIVISION
1917

France	early March	Into line west of Péronne
Hindenburg	17 March–5 April	Advanced to Le Verguier and Hargicourt
Ypres	23–30 September	Engaged south-west of Gravenstafel
Arras	October	In the Avion–Lens sector
Cambrai	from 28 November	Engaged east of Bourlon Wood
Cambrai	4 December	Withdrew west of Flesquières

1918

Arras	February–March	Held the Noreuil and Croisilles sector
Somme	21–22 March	Fell back through Noreuil and Ecoust to St Léger and Mory
Somme	23–24 March	Retired through Gomiécourt to Ablainzeville
Ypres	from early April	Held the Passchendaele sector
Lys	14–18 April	Engaged at Bailleul; fell back to Dranoutre
	May & June	Reduced to cadre then re-formed
Somme	from 25 July	In the Mercatel sector

The Advance to Victory

Albert	21–22 August	Advanced towards Hénin
	September	Advanced from Lestrem towards Mauquissart and Picantin
Lens	4 October	Advanced from Fleurbaix to the Haute Deule Canal
Lille	18–21 October	Crossed the canal north of Lille and advanced to the River Schelde
Ath	9–11 November	Crossed Schelde at Havron and advanced to Dendre Canal

60TH (2ND/2ND LONDON) DIVISION

1916

France	July–October	Roclincourt and Neuville St Vaast sector, Arras
	November	Ordered to Salonika

1917

Macedonia	February–May	Sector east of the River Vardar
	June	Embarked for Egypt and Palestine
Gaza	30–31 October	Acted as a blocking force during the capture of Beersheba
	2–6 November	Advanced north along the railway towards Tell es Sheria
Jerusalem	8 December	Captured the high ground west of the city
	26–30 December	Held positions north of Jerusalem during Turkish attacks

1918

	13–20 February	Cleared the hills west of Jericho
	21–27 March	Trans-Jordan raid against Amman
	30 April	Second Trans-Jordan raid
	May	Indian units replaced British units
Megiddo	19–21 September	In reserve
	October	Employed on salvage work
	31 October	Armistice with Turkey

61ST (2ND SOUTH MIDLAND) DIVISION

1916

France	June–July	Held the Neuve Chapelle sector, Béthune
Fromelles	19 July	Attacked towards Fromelles
Somme	November–February	Held the Grandcourt sector

61st (2nd South Midland) Division. Lewis gunners man the bridge over the Aire Canal near Robecq at the height of the German attack on the Lys in April 1918. *(IWM Q6612)*

1917

Hindenburg	26 February	Advanced through Chaulnes
Hindenburg	20 March–7 April	Crossed the Somme Canal and reached Holnon and Maissemy
St Quentin	April	In the Savy and Holnon sectors
Arras	May & June	Held the Guémappe sector
Ypres	17 Aug–12 Sept	Engaged in the St Julien sector
Arras	September & October	Held the Gavrelle sector
Cambrai	1–4 December	In the Crèvecoeur sector; forced back to Welch Ridge

1918

St Quentin	January	Held the Fayet and Gricourt sector
Somme	21–23 March	Fell back across the Somme Canal to Nesle
Somme	24 March	Fell back from Moyencourt to Roye
Lys	12–16 April	Engaged at Robecq and Calonne; fell back to the Nieppe Forest

The Advance to Victory

Lys	August	Advanced across the River Lys
Selle	24–25 October	Advanced from Bermerain towards Sepmeries
Valenciennes	1–2 November	Advanced towards Jenlain

62ND (2ND WEST RIDING) DIVISION
1917

France	February–March	Held the Grandcourt sector, Somme
Hindenburg	March	Advanced through Achiet-le-Petit to Gomiécourt
Bullecourt	April–November	Bullecourt sector; attacked the village on 3 May
Cambrai	November	Held the Havrincourt Wood sector
Cambrai	20–28 November	Took Havrincourt and Graincourt, engaged in Bourlon Wood

1918

Arras	January	In the Gavrelle sector
Arras	February–March	Held the Arleux sector
Somme	24–26 March	Engaged in the Gommecourt sector
Aisne	20–29 July	Advanced from Pourcy to Bligny, French sector
St Quentin	August	In the Mory sector

The Advance to Victory

Drocourt	2 September	Captured Vraucourt and Vaux Vraucourt
Havrincourt	12 September	Advanced from Hermies to Havrincourt
Canal du Nord	28–30 September	Advanced from Flesquières to Masnières
	October	Held the Solesmes sector on the River Schelde
Selle	20–24 October	Crossed the river and captured Solesmes
Sambre	4–6 November	Advanced from Le Quesnoy across the River Sambre
Maubeuge	9–11 November	Entered Maubeuge and advanced beyond Colleret

ROYAL NAVAL DIVISION – 63RD (ROYAL NAVAL) DIVISION FROM JULY 1916
1914

Belgium	27–31 August	Royal Marine Brigade briefly visited Ostend
Antwerp	19 September	Division sailed to Antwerp
	9 October	1,500 men were cut off; the rest escaped to Ostend

1915

Belgium	February	Sailed to Egypt en route for Gallipoli
Gallipoli	25 April	Staged a diversionary landing in the Gulf of Xeros
Helles	25 April	Several battalions on beach duties
Helles	28 April–6 May	Several battalions engaged under 29th Division
Anzac Cove	28 April–12 May	Several battalions engaged at Anzac Cove
Helles	4 June	Attacked east of the Krithia Road

1916

Gallipoli	8 January	Evacuated Helles; eventually returned to England
France	July	Renamed 63rd (Royal Naval) Division
Arras	July–September	Held the Souchez sector
Somme	from 8 October	In Beaucourt sector, capturing village on 13 November

1917

Hindenburg	March	Advanced through Miraumont
Arras	20 April–2 May	Engaged at Gavrelle and Oppy

Arras	May–October	Held the Gavrelle and Oppy sector
Ypres	26 Oct–5 Nov	Engaged at Wallemolen
Cambrai	December	In the Villers-Plouich sector

63rd (Royal Naval) Division. The 7th Royal Fusiliers move to the rear after heavy fighting near Mesnil on the River Ancre in May 1918. *(IWM Q10592)*

1918

Cambrai	February	Held the Ribecourt sector
Somme	21–23 March	Fell back through Havrincourt and Bertincourt
Somme	24–25 March	Fell back through Le Transloy and Thiepval to Aveluy
The Advance to Victory		
Albert	26–29 August	Engaged at Thilloy
Bapaume	3 September	Advanced from Hendecourt to Inchy on Canal du Nord
Canal du Nord	28–30 September	Advanced from Graincourt across the Marcoing Canal
Cambrai	8–9 October	Engaged at Niergnies
Mons	8–11 November	Advanced from Audregnies to Villers St Ghislain

66TH (2ND EAST LANCASHIRE) DIVISION
1917

| France | March–June | In the Hohenzollern Redoubt and Festubert sector, Béthune |

Flanders Coast	June–September	Held the Nieuport Bains sector
Ypres	early October	Engaged in the Passchendaele sector
Ypres	mid-November	Engaged in the Broodseinde sector

1918

Somme	February & March	Held the Villeret and Hargicourt sector
Somme	21–24 March	Fell back to the River Somme south of Péronne
Somme	25–29 March	Fell back through Dompierre and Harbonnières to Aubercourt
	April–September	Reduced to cadre and trained conscripts; then re-formed

The Advance to Victory

Cambrai	8–10 October	Advanced from Beaurevoir to the River Selle
Selle	17–20 October	Crossed the river at Le Cateau
Avesnes	8–11 November	Advanced from St Hilaire towards Sivry

74TH (YEOMANRY) DIVISION
1917

Egypt	April	Formed from Yeomanry regiments in Egypt
Gaza	1–10 November	Advanced towards Tell esh Sheria
Jerusalem	8 December	Attacked from north-west of the city

1918

| Lys | April–July | Sailed to France, re-trained and then held the St Venant sector |

The Advance to Victory

Lys	August	Advanced to Lestrum
Canal du Nord	3–7 September	Crossed the Canal du Nord and advanced to Villers-Faucon
Epéhy	18 September	Advanced towards Le Catelet on the St Quentin Canal

The Final Advance in Artois

	3–4 October	Advanced from Neuve Chapelle to Haute Deule Canal
	15–21 October	Crossed the canal and advanced to Tournai
	8–11 November	Entered the city and crossed the River Schelde

75TH DIVISION
1917

Palestine	April–August	Formed in Palestine
Gaza	28 October	Held positions south of the town
	6–14 November	Advanced north, moving inland to capture Junction Station
	19–21 November	Attacked Nabi Samweil west of Jerusalem
	December	Covered the inland railway at Lydda

1918

Megiddo	19 September	In reserve
	October	Employed on salvage work
	31 October	Armistice with Turkey

1ST AUSTRALIAN DIVISION
1915

Gallipoli	25 April	Landed at Anzac Cove and advanced inland
Anzac Cove	May–July	Engaged on the hills overlooking the beachhead
Anzac Cove	6–10 August	1st Australian Brigade captured Lone Pine
Anzac Cove	20 December	Withdrew from Anzac and headed to Egypt

Inside the cramped dugout of an Australian artillery brigade headquarters. *(IWM E(AUS)690)*

1916

France	March–July	Sailed to France; held the Bois Grenier sector, Armentières
Somme	20–26 July	Engaged in the Pozières sector
Somme	16–23 August	Fighting for Mouquet Farm, north of Pozières
Ypres	September & October	Held the Comines Canal sector
Somme	November–February	In the Gueudecourt sector

1917

Ancre	24–27 February	Followed up the German withdrawal through Thilloy
Cambrai	April	In the Hermies and Lagnicourt sector
Bullecourt	3–12 May	Engaged east of Bullecourt
Ypres	16–22 September	Advanced through Nonne Boschen into Polygon Wood

Ypres	3–10 October	Engaged north of Polygon Wood
Ypres	27 Oct–10 Nov	Held the sector south-east of Broodseinde
Messines	November–March	Held sectors around Hollebeke

1918

Lys	12–15 April	Engaged along the eastern edge of the Nieppe Forest
Lys	May–July	Held the Meteren and Strazeele sector

The Advance to Victory

Amiens	9–11 August	From reserve advanced into Lihons
Albert	22–23 August	Advanced from Proyart to Chuignes
Albert	25–26 August	Advanced along the River Somme to Cappy
Epéhy	18 September	Advanced from Roisel to the Hindenburg Line at Bellicourt
	until November	In reserve

2ND AUSTRALIAN DIVISION

1915

Gallipoli	August–20 December	Engaged at the Anzac Cove beachhead

1916

France	January–March	Sailed to France; sector south of Armentières
Somme	25 July–7 August	Engaged in the Pozières sector
Somme	23–29 August	Engaged at Mouquet Farm, north of Pozières
Ypres	September	Held the Sanctuary Wood and Hooge sector
Somme	November	In the sector north of Flers
Somme	December–January	Held the sector north-east of Lesboeufs

1917

Hindenburg	25 Feb–17 March	Advanced through Bapaume to Vaulx-Vraucourt
Bullecourt	mid-April–July	In line north of Noreuil; engaged east of Bullecourt 3–7 May
Ypres	16–22 September	Advanced north of Polygon Wood
Ypres	3–10 October	Advanced from Zonnebeke through Broodseinde
Ypres	24 Oct–14 Nov	Held the sector east of Broodseinde
Armentières	December–March	Held the Ploegsteert Wood sector

1918

Somme	early April	Engaged south of Albert
Somme	July	In the Villers-Bretonneux sector; captured Hamel on the 4th

The Advance to Victory

Amiens	8 August	Captured Warfusée Abancourt and Lamotte-en-Santerre
Amiens	9–11 August	Captured Framerville and La Flaque
Albert	26–30 August	Advanced from Cappy to the River Somme
Péronne	31 August	Crossed the River Somme, taking Mont St Quentin
Beaurevoir	3–6 October	Advanced across the Torrens Canal and captured Beaurevoir
	until November	In reserve

An Australian battalion assembles near Fricourt before heading up the line to Pozières in September 1916. *(IWM Q1559)*

3RD AUSTRALIAN DIVISION
1916

France	December–April	In the sector east of Armentières

1917

Messines	May	In the sector north of Ploegsteert Wood
Messines	7 June	Advanced towards Warneton
Messines	August & September	Held the sector east of Messines
Ypres	1–8 October	Advanced north of Zonnebeke
Ypres	11–18 October	Engaged in the Gravenstafel sector
Messines	from mid-November	Held the Ploegsteert Wood sector
Armentières	December	In the sector east of Armentières

1918

Somme	early April	Engaged south of Dernacourt
Somme	May–August	In the Villers-Bretonneux sector; captured Hamel on 4 July

The Advance to Victory

Amiens	8 August	Advanced towards Morecourt
Amiens	10–11 August	Captured Méricourt
Albert	23–24 August	Captured Bray-sur-Somme and Neuville

Somme	25–31 August	Advanced through Suzanne and Curlu to Bouchavesnes
Bapaume	1–10 September	Advanced from Mont St Quentin to Jeancourt
	until November	In reserve

Wounded Australian soldiers wait their turn to be attended to at Kandahar Farm Dressing Station following the attack on Messines Ridge on 7 June 1917. *(IWM E(AUS)482)*

4TH AUSTRALIAN DIVISION

1916

France	June	Held the sector east of Armentières
Somme	29 July–16 August	Fighting for Mouquet Farm, north of Pozières
Somme	27 Aug–4 Sept	Again engaged at Mouquet Farm
Messines	September	Held the Vierstraat and Comines Canal sector
Somme	November	In the sector north of Flers

1917

Bullecourt	April	In the sector north of Noreuil; engaged east of Bullecourt
Messines	7–14 June	Advanced south-east of Messines towards Warneton
Messines	August	Held the sector east of Messines

Ypres	23–30 September	Advanced north of Polygon Wood
Ypres	11–24 October	Engaged east of Broodseinde

1918

Ypres	January	In the Hollebeke sector
Somme	28 March–5 April	4th Australian Brigade engaged at Hébuterne
Somme	mid-June–mid-July	Astride the River Somme; captured Hamel on 4 July

The Advance to Victory

Amiens	8–10 August	Advanced through Morecourt to Méricourt and Proyart
Albert	16–24 August	Held the sector east of Lihons
Somme	10–17 September	In the Jeancourt and Vadencourt sector
Epéhy	18 September	Advanced through Le Verguier towards the St Quentin Canal
	until November	In reserve

5TH AUSTRALIAN DIVISION
1916

France	July–October	In the sector opposite Fromelles; attacked on 19–20 July
Somme	22 Oct–4 Nov	Engaged in the Flers sector
Somme	December–February	Held the Lesboeufs sector

1917

Hindenburg	24 Feb–21 March	Advanced through Thilloy and Bapaume to Louverval
Bullecourt	April–July	In line east of Bullecourt; attacked 9–17 May
Ypres	23–30 September	Advanced through Polygon Wood
Ypres	11–27 October	Engaged south of Broodseinde
Messines	November–March	In the sector east of Messines

1918

Somme	April	Held the line north of Villers-Bretonneux
Somme	24–25 April	Advanced north of Villers-Bretonneux
Somme	May–July	Held the line astride the River Somme, south of Albert

The Advance to Victory

Amiens	8–9 August	Advanced through Bayonvillers, Harbonières and Vauvillers
Albert	18–22 August	Engaged east of Proyart
	26–29 August	Advanced from Chuignes to Eterpigny on the Somme
Bapaume	1–10 September	Crossed the river and captured Péronne
St Quentin	30 September	Cleared Bellicourt tunnel and captured Estrées and Joncourt
	until November	In reserve

NEW ZEALAND AND AUSTRALIAN DIVISION – LATER THE NEW ZEALAND DIVISION
1915

Gallipoli	25–26 April	Landed at Anzac and advanced inland
Anzac Cove	2 May	Engaged on Baby 700 Hill
Helles	6–8 May	New Zealand Brigade engaged at Helles

After taking their objective, Australians of the 8th (Victoria) Battalion sleep by the roadside on the outskirts of Bapaume. (*IWM E(AUS)346*)

| Anzac Cove | 6 August | Engaged on Sari Bair |
| | 19 December | Withdrew from Anzac and headed for Egypt |

1916

Egypt	March	Reformed as the New Zealand Division
France	May–August	In the Armentières sector
Somme	10 Sept–3 Oct	Advanced from Longueval to the north of Flers
Armentières	October–February	Held the Bois Grenier sector

1917

Armentières	February & March	In the Armentières sector
Messines	March & June	Held the line north of Ploegsteert Wood
Messines	7 June	Captured Messines
Messines	July–September	Held the Ploegsteert sector
Ypres	1–12 October	Advanced through Gravenstafel
Ypres	from mid-November	In line east of Polygon Wood

1918

Somme	early April	Engaged at Beaumont-Hamel and Hébuterne
Somme	July & August	Held the Puisieux sector
The Advance to Victory		
Albert	21–26 August	Advanced to Bapaume

Bapaume	30 Aug–4 Sept	Advanced to Ytres on the Canal du Nord tunnel
Havrincourt	5–10 September	Cleared Havrincourt Wood
Canal du Nord	29 September	Advanced to Crèvecour on the Canal du Nord
Cambrai	8–10 October	Advanced through Beauvois to Briastre on the Selle
Le Quesnoy	22–24 October	Took over the advance towards Le Quesnoy
Sambre	4–6 November	Cleared Le Quesnoy; advanced into Mormal Forest

1ST CANADIAN DIVISION

1915

France	March	Held the Fleurbaix sector, Armentières
Ypres	April	In the Poelcapelle and Gravenstafel sector
Ypres	22–25 April	A gas attack forced the division back beyond St Julien
Festubert	19–26 May	Engaged east of Festubert
Givenchy	June	In the Givenchy sector; unsuccessful attack on the 15th
Messines	July–October	Held the Ploegsteert and Wulverghem sector
Messines	November–March	Messines sector

1916

Ypres	from March	In the Ypres–Comines Canal sector
Ypres	2–13 June	Engaged at Mount Sorrel
Somme	1–12 September	Engaged in the Pozières sector
Somme	18–28 September	Advanced west of Courcelette
Somme	5–17 October	Engaged west of Le Sars
Arras	November–January	Held the Neuville St Vaast and Souchez sector

1917

Béthune	January–March	Held the River Souchez and Loos sector
Arras	April	In the Neuville St Vaast and Ecurie sector
Arras	9–13 April	Advanced across Vimy Ridge to Arleux
Arras	28 April	Captured Arleux followed by Fresnoy on 3 May
Hill 70	July–September	Held the sector east of Loos, captured Hill 70 on 15 August
Arras	October	In the Avion and Lens sector
Ypres	4–12 November	Engaged north-west of Passchendaele
Arras	December	Returned to the Avion and Lens sector

1918

Lens	January–March	Held the St Emile and Hill 70 sector
Arras	April–June	In the Beaurains sector
Arras	July	Held the Neuville Vitasse and River Scarpe sector
Somme	early August	In the Gentelles and Canchy sector

The Advance to Victory

Amiens	8–9 August	Advanced through Aubercourt, Cayeux and Rouvroy
Scarpe	29 August	Advanced from Vis-en-Artois north of Hendecourt
Drocourt	2–3 September	Advanced to Sains-lez-Marquion on the Canal du Nord
Canal du Nord	27 September	Crossed the Canal du Nord and advanced to Abancourt
Cambrai	11–12 October	Crossed the River Sensée and advanced to Sensée Canal
Valenciennes	17–24 October	Crossed the canal and advanced to the Canal du Jard

2ND CANADIAN DIVISION
1915

France	September–March	Held the Vierstraat sector, Messines

1916

St Eloi	April	Engaged at St Eloi
Ypres	May–September	Held the Comines Canal sector
Somme	11–30 September	Captured Courcelette
Béthune	October–January	Held the Loos sector

1917

Arras	February	In the Roclincourt sector
Arras	March	In the Neuville St Vaast sector
Arras	9–14 April	Advanced over Vimy Ridge towards Lens
Arras	23 April–3 May	Attacked at La Coulotte, Arleux and Fresnoy
Béthune	July & August	Held the Cité St Laurent sector
Hill 70	15 August	Advanced to Cité Ste Elisabeth
Arras	September	In the Avion and Méricourt sector
Ypres	3–11 November	Cleared Passchendaele
Arras	December–February	Returned to the Acheville and Méricourt sector

1918

Béthune	February–March	In the Lens sector
Arras	April–July	Held the Neuville Vitasse and Boisleux St Marc sector

The Advance to Victory

Amiens	8–10 August	Advanced through Marcelcave and Rosières
Scarpe	26–28 August	Advanced from Neuville Vitasse to Chérisy
	September	Held the Canal du Nord sector, north of Inchy
Canal du Nord	1–2 October	Advanced north of Cambrai
Cambrai	8–11 October	Advanced across the Schelde Canal to Iwuy
	17–19 October	Crossed the Sensée Canal at Estrun
Mons	5–11 November	Crossed the Grand Honelle; advanced east of Mons

3RD CANADIAN DIVISION
1916

France	March–September	In Hooge sector, Ypres; engaged at Mount Sorrel in June
Somme	13–22 September	Engaged at Mouquet Farm, north of Pozières
Somme	27 Sept–14 Oct	Engaged north-west of Courcelette
Arras	November–April	Held the Neuville St Vaast and Roclincourt sector

1917

Arras	June	Held the River Souchez sector; captured Avion on the 26th
Arras	September & October	In the sector west of Acheville
Ypres	23 Oct–4 Nov	Engaged north-west of Passchendaele
Béthune	December–February	Held the sector east of Loos

Canadian soldiers swap stories and news over a cup of coffee near Arras; many of the men are wearing trench waders. *(IWM CO1030)*

1918

Arras	February–April	In the Avion and Méricourt sector
Béthune	April–June	Held the Loos sector
Arras	July	In the Neuville Vitasse sector

The Advance to Victory

Amiens	8–9 August	Advanced from Domart to Beaucourt and from Folies to Bouchoir
	15–17 August	Engaged at Damery
Scarpe	26–30 August	Advanced from Feuchy through Monchy-le-Preux and Haucourt
Canal du Nord	28–29 September	Advanced from the Canal du Nord to the St Quentin Canal
Cambrai	8–9 October	Cleared the northern part of Cambrai
Valenciennes	1–3 November	Captured Valenciennes and advanced to the Schelde
Mons	4–11 November	Advanced through Bossu to Mons

4TH CANADIAN DIVISION
1916

France	August & September	Held the Messines sector
Somme	10 Oct–28 Nov	Engaged in Courcelette sector, capturing Regina Trench
Arras	December–April	Held the Neuville St Vaast and Souchez sector

4th Canadian Division's reserves move forward during the advance to the Canal du Nord in September 1918. *(IWM Q9326)*

1917

| Arras | 9–14 April | Advanced though Givenchy towards Lens |
| Béthune | late June | Captured Avion |

Béthune	August & September	In the Méricourt and Lens sector; attacked Lens on 21 August
Ypres	22 Oct–4 Nov	Advanced east of Gravenstafel to Passchendaele
Arras	December	Held the Méricourt and Avion sector

1918

Arras	January–March	Held the Lens and St Emile sector
Arras	April–June	In the Oppy and Gavrelle sector
Arras	July	Moved to the Arleux and the River Scarpe sector

The Advance to Victory

Amiens	8–9 August	Advanced through Beaucourt and Le Quesnel
	15–17 August	Engaged at Damery
Drocourt	1–3 September	Advanced from Hancourt to the Canal du Nord
Canal du Nord	27–29 September	Crossed the Canal du Nord and advanced to the St Quentin Canal
Schelde	17–22 October	Crossed the Sensée Canal and advanced to the Schelde Canal
Sambre	1–6 November	Advanced to Queivrain

3RD (LAHORE) DIVISION
1914

France	October	Reached France and moved to Flanders
La Bassée	November	Engaged at Neuve Chapelle

1915

Béthune	mid-March–May	In line north of Neuve Chapelle
Aubers Ridge	9 May	Held its positions north of Neuve Chapelle
Festubert	15–18 May	Held its positions north of Neuve Chapelle
Béthune	mid-May–mid-August	Held the Neuve Chapelle sector
Armentières	August & September	In the Richebourg l'Avoué sector
Béthune	October & November	Held the Neuve Chapelle sector
Mesopotamia	December	Left France and sailed to Mesopotamia

7TH (MEERUT) DIVISION
1914

France	mid-October	Reached France and moved to Flanders
La Bassée	November	Engaged at Neuve Chapelle

1915

Neuve Chapelle	10–13 March	Engaged south of Neuve Chapelle
Béthune	mid-March–May	In line north of Neuve Chapelle
Aubers Ridge	9 May	Unsuccessful attack south of Neuve Chapelle
Festubert	15–18 May	Unsuccessful attack south of Neuve Chapelle
Armentières	mid-May–September	Held the Richebourg l'Avoué and Fauquissart sector
	25 September	Attacked Fauquissart
Armentières	October & November	Richebourg l'Avoué sector
Mesopotamia	December	Left France and sailed to Mesopotamia

The usual position for the cavalry was in reserve, waiting for news that a breakthrough had been made; it rarely happened. On 26 May 1917, these troopers were waiting to hear if they would be advancing east of Arras. *(IWM Q2213)*

CAVALRY AND MOUNTED DIVISION HISTORIES

Cavalry acted as mounted infantry during the retreat from Mons, screening the infantry as they fell back to the Marne and then provided reconnaissance during the advance to the Aisne. After the BEF transferred to Messines in October, the cavalrymen fought dismounted alongside the infantry until the end of the First Battle of Ypres.

The trenches gave few opportunities to deploy cavalry and, although the troopers occasionally held the line, the divisions were kept in reserve. Attempts to deploy mounted troops, for example at High Wood on the Somme in July 1916, and at Monchy-le-Preux east of Arras in April 1917, ended in disaster. Cavalry cooperated with the Tank Corps during the Battle of Cambrai on 20 November 1917 but they were soon withdrawn.

Opportunities for the cavalry came during the Advance to Victory and the cavalry carried out reconnaissance duties alongside armoured units; they led the advance to the German frontier after the Armistice.

The open terrain of Egypt, Palestine and Mesopotamia presented ideal opportunities for mounted troops and they took part in several successful campaigns against the Turks.

CAVALRY ON THE WESTERN FRONT

The **Cavalry Division** (**1st Cavalry Division** after September 1914) accompanied the BEF to France in 1914. **2nd Cavalry Division** was formed in September 1914 and **3rd Cavalry Division** reached Belgium the following month. All three served on the Western Front until the end of the war.

1st Indian Cavalry Division reached France in October 1914 and **2nd Indian Cavalry Division** followed a month later. They were renamed the **4th** and **5th Cavalry Divisions** in November 1916 and finally disbanded in

March 1918. The Indian units were transferred to Egypt and joined the new 1st and 2nd Mounted Divisions.

MOUNTED AND CYCLIST DIVISIONS

1st Mounted Division assembled for home defence duties in Suffolk. 2nd Line brigades were formed as individual brigades and went overseas, the last one leaving in March 1916. The division moved to Norfolk in November 1915. The horses were sent to remount depots in July 1916 and the division was renamed the **1st Cyclist Division**. The division was disbanded in November 1916.

2nd Mounted Division formed in Suffolk in September 1914 and was employed on home defence, moving to the Norfolk coast in November. It sailed to the Mediterranean in August 1915 and was engaged on the Gallipoli Peninsula. The division was broken up when the campaign came to an end.

2nd/2nd Mounted Division was formed in March 1915 to form depots for 2nd Mounted Division and it assembled in Norfolk. Constantly called on to provide drafts, the division was renamed the **3rd Mounted Division** in March 1916 and then the **1st Mounted Division** in July 1916. After moving to Kent, the trained men were transferred to Reserve cavalry regiments and the division was reorganized as the **Cyclist Division**.

4th Mounted Division was formed in March 1916 for home defence in south-east England, however, it was reorganized as **2nd Cyclist Division** in July. It moved to Essex in September and was disbanded in November.

CAVALRY IN EGYPT AND PALESTINE

The **ANZAC Mounted Division** was formed in Egypt in March 1916 with 3 Australian Light Horse brigades and the New Zealand Mounted Rifles brigade; all had fought dismounted at Gallipoli.

The **Imperial Mounted Division** was formed in January 1917 with 2 Australian Light Horse brigades and 2 mounted brigades; it was renamed the **Australian Mounted Division** in June 1917.

The mounted troops of the Desert Column were formed into 3 mounted divisions in July 1917. The **Yeomanry Mounted Division** was formed with brigades from the Imperial Mounted Division, the ANZAC Mounted Division and one from Salonika.

74th Yeomanry Division was formed from three dismounted brigades and took part in the battles for Gaza in 1917. It transferred to France in May 1918 and served on the Western Front until the end of the war. It is listed in the infantry division histories section above.

Mounted troops were reorganized in April 1918 when Indian units arrived from France. **1st** and **2nd Mounted Divisions** were formed from the Yeomanry Mounted Division and the Indian elements of the 4th and 5th Cavalry Divisions; they were renamed the **4th** and **5th Cavalry Divisions** on 22 July prior to the final offensive in Palestine, in which the mounted troops played a notable part.

CAVALRY IN MESOPOTAMIA

6th Indian Cavalry Brigade formed in February 1915 and was joined by **7th Indian Cavalry Brigade** in August 1916; the two were formed into a division in December 1916 for the Battle of Kut al Amara. **11th Brigade** reached Mesopotamia in November 1917 but it did not join the division. The division dispersed in April 1918 and the three brigades served independently until the end of the war.

Guards Division

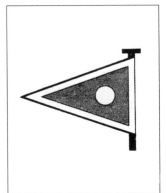

1st Division

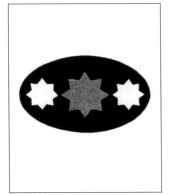

2nd Division

3rd Division

4th Division

5th Division

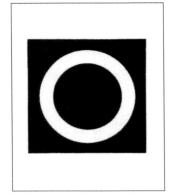

6th Division

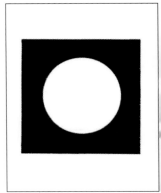

7th Division

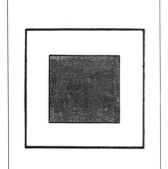

8th Division

9th (Scottish) Division

10th (Irish) Division

11th (Northern) Division

12th (Eastern) Division

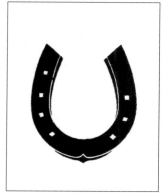

13th (Western) Division

14th (Light) Division

15th (Scottish) Division

16th (Irish) Division

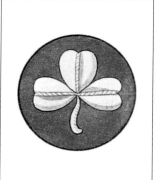

16th (Irish) Division
(variant)

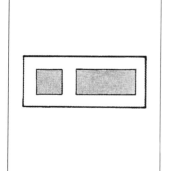

17th (Northern) Division

18th (Eastern) Division

19th (Western) Division

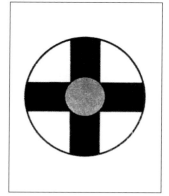

20th (Light) Division

21st Division

22nd Division

23rd Division

24th Division

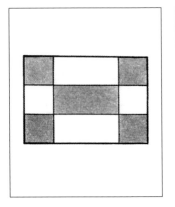

25th Division

26th Division

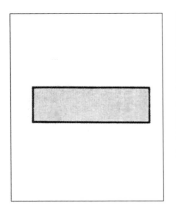

27th Division

28th Division

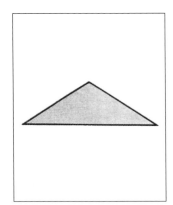

29th Division

30th Division

31st Division

31st Division
(variant)

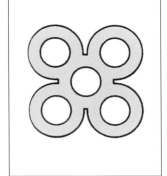

32nd Division

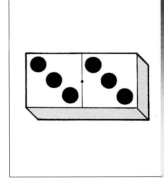

33rd Division

34th Division

35th Division

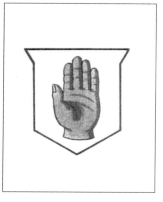

36th (Ulster) Division

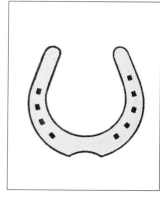

37th Division

38th (Welsh) Division

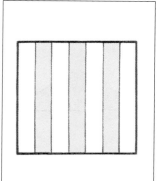

39th Division

40th Division

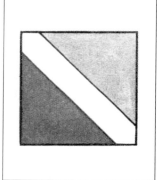

41st Division

42nd (East Lancashire)
Division

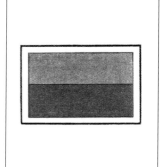

46th (North Midland)
Division

47th (1st/2nd London)
Division

48th (South Midland)
Division

49th (West Riding) Division

50th (Northumbrian) Division

51st (Highland) Division

52nd (Lowland) Division

53rd (Welsh) Division

54th (East Anglian) Division

55th (West Lancashire) Division

56th (1st/1st London) Division

57th (2nd West Lancashire) Division

58th (2nd/1st London) Division

59th (2nd North Midland) Division

60th (2nd/2nd London) Division

61st (2nd South Midland)
Division

62nd (2nd West Riding)
Division

63rd (Royal Naval) Division

65th Division

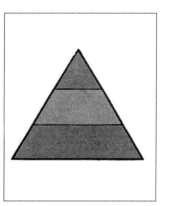

66th (2nd East Lancashire)
Division

74th (Yeomanry) Division

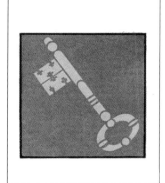

75th Division

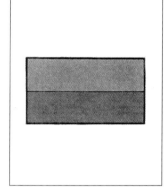

1st Australian Division

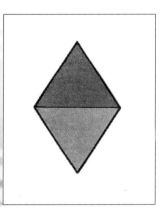

2nd Australian Division

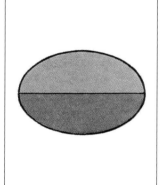

3rd Australian Division

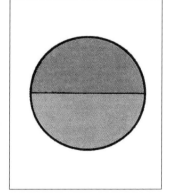

4th Australian Division

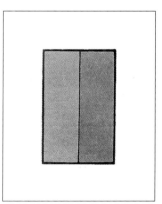

5th Australian Division

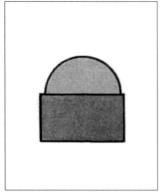

1st Canadian Division

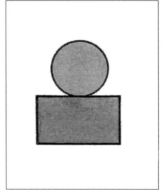

2nd Canadian Division

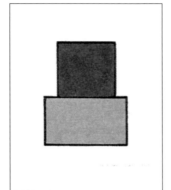

3rd Canadian Division

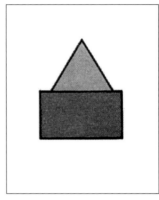

4th Canadian Division

Australian and New Zealand
Division – later the New
Zealand Division

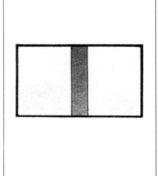

1st Cavalry Division

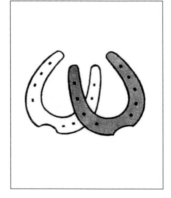

2nd Cavalry Division

3rd Cavalry Division

CHAPTER EIGHT

THE SOLDIER

1914 UNIFORM AND EQUIPMENT

The standard service dress (SD) was coloured khaki, a light earth-brown colour chosen to blend in with the landscape. Officers and men had three types of dress worn for different duties:

No. 1 Dress	Ceremonial or walking out
No. 2 Dress	On the march
No. 3 Dress	Drill

Officers had two extra styles:

No. 4 Dress	Mess Dress
No. 5 Dress	Undress; a frock coat

The King inspects a Guardsman in July 1917 as he trains for the attack on Pilckem Ridge at the end of the month. *(IWM Q5600)*

A sentry of the 2nd/9th Gurkhas wears the colonial uniform issued for warmer climates such as Mesopotamia. *(IWM Q24361)*

Fur waistcoats help to keep out the cold as these Canadian soldiers inspect German helmets captured at Courcelette in October 1916. *(IWM CO1013)*

Officers had tailored jackets with an open front showing the shirt collar and the tie; other ranks' jackets were buttoned to the neck. The jackets had large pockets. Officers displayed their badges of rank on their cuffs; NCOs wore stripes on their sleeves; and all other ranks had metal regimental badges on the shoulder straps.

Mounted infantry officers wore cord breeches with leggings while dismounted officers wore knicker-bocker breeches with puttees (strips of khaki cloth wound around the calf). Other ranks had serge trousers and puttees. Highland regiments wore a kilt of the appropriate tartan covered by a khaki apron and gaiters on the lower leg. All infantrymen wore brown ankle boots.

Cavalry officers also had breeches but wore brown boots with spurs; the other ranks wore trousers with puttees and ankle boots complete with spurs.

Colonial dress replaced the trousers with shorts and dispensed with the heavier items of clothing.

CAPS

English, Irish and Welsh regiments wore a peaked cap with a prominent regimental badge on the front. The wire inside the cap could be removed to make the cap more comfortable. Scottish regiments wore a Glengarry with a decorative chequer-pattern band. Troops serving in warmer climates were issued with a domed pith helmet.

BELTS AND WEBBING

The officer's pistol holster and sword scabbard hung from a leather Sam Browne belt comprising a waist belt and shoulder strap. He carried a small haversack containing a water bottle, mess tin, compass and binoculars as well as wire cutters. A leather valise, for paperwork, personal effects, spare clothing, washing and shaving equipment, was carried by the unit transport. The sword was quickly disposed of in the trenches.

Other ranks carried everything they needed on the march with the help of the 1908 Pattern webbing, a set of belt and braces. The straps and belt were connected together with self-locking fastenings so the wearer could take it off in one piece. A bayonet scabbard, entrenching tool and water bottle were slung from the belt while 150 rounds of ammunition were carried in two leather pouches attached to the front of the webbing.

Rations and personal possessions were stored in a small haversack so they were readily available on the march. A greatcoat, woollen cap, spare clothing, underwear, mess tins and toiletries were stored in a pack. Each man carried a ground sheet and two could be fastened together to form a small tent; a spare pair of boots was strapped to the sides of the pack.

A fully equipped soldier carried around 60lb (30kg) in weight but the pack could be removed without upsetting the balance of the load. Packs were left with the company quartermaster sergeant before going into action.

Cavalrymen attached their groundsheet, greatcoat, water bucket and corn sack to the saddle.

WARTIME MODIFICATIONS

During the first winter of the war, stocks of comforters and leather or goatskin jerkins were issued to combat the cold. Relief agencies collected gloves, scarves and balaclavas while families posted clothing to the front to keep their loved ones warm. Gumboots and waders were always in short supply.

Officers began to move their rank badges to their shoulder straps and wear other ranks' uniforms to avoid being conspicuous to snipers. The men ditched surplus equipment, filling their haversacks with ammunition, rations and personal effects. Bombers and Lewis gun teams used a variety of sacks and pouches to carry the large amounts of ammunition they needed. Rifles were often wrapped in sacking to keep them clean.

Snipers sometimes operated in no man's land dressed in home-made canvas suits, complete with hood and a camouflaged rifle cover. Two official designs were introduced later: the Boiler Suit with detached hood, and

As the months passed, the soldiers adapted their uniforms to deal with the harsh trench conditions and the weather extremes. These two soldiers share a cigarette before heading into the trenches at Beaumont-Hamel in December 1916. *(IWM Q1713)*

the Symien Sniper Suit made of painted scrim. They came with matching rifle covers and gloves, and foliage or straw could be added to improve the effect.

HELMETS

The French Army started to use steel helmets in the spring of 1915 to reduce the number of head wounds and GHQ soon asked for a new, heavier design. One had been approved by September and a month later, 3,500 had been issued, 50 per battalion, initially for the machine-gun teams.

The helmet was made of hardened manganese steel and weighed 2lb; it could stop shrapnel travelling at 750 feet per second and reduced the number of head wounds by a

This man had a lucky escape when a piece of shrapnel pierced his helmet; note the sacking wrapped around his rifle to keep it clean. *(IWM Q1778)*

soon issued. Cotton wool pads, used by the Admiralty during smoke-screen experiments, proved to be useless.

Lieutenant Leslie Barley of the 1st Cameronians devised the Barley Respirator in May 1915. A cotton waste pad, soaked in sodium carbonate and sodium hyposulphate, was tied across the mouth and nose while goggles protected the eyes. Chemist Herbert Baker produced the Black Veiling Respirator, a copy of a German gas mask; it only gave short-term protection and was prone to leak.

H OR HYPO HELMET

Captain Cluny MacPherson of the Newfoundland Regiment developed a cloth helmet that was pulled over the head and tucked under the jacket collar. The flannel bag had talc eyepieces and a rubber breathing tube to hold between the teeth. The flannel was dipped in a neutralizing solution. The helmets were greasy and the men struggled to breathe through the tubes, making the design unpopular.

The first batch of gas helmets was issued in June 1915 but large-scale use in the Battle of Loos exposed many problems. The single thickness of flannel sometimes failed to give protection and the eyepieces were liable to break. Celluloid eyepieces and flannelette were used in later models. Over 2.5 million were issued.

P OR PHENATE HELMET

A double flannelette bag with glass eyepieces was sprayed with a compound of thio-sulphate, sodium carbonate and glycerine. It reached the front line in November 1915 and improved versions protected against phosgene and prussic acid. Over 9 million were made.

PH OR PHENATE-HEXAMINE HELMET

The PH helmet appeared in January 1916 with hexamine added to the neutralizing compound to combat phosgene gas. Over 14 million were issued.

PHG HELMET

A variant with rubber sponge around the

quarter. Manufacturing increased so that men overseas could be issued with one, and starting in September 1917 troops serving at home also received them. Over 7.25 million were made during the war, including 1.5 million for American troops.

EARLY GAS MASKS

After the Germans used chlorine gas in the Ypres Salient in April 1915, crude gas masks made of a handkerchief soaked with an alkaline solution were used (many troops used urine).

Masks made of lint strips secured by tapes and 60,000 pads soaked with lime-water were

A gas sentry stands by his alarm near Fleurbaix; he is equipped with the PH gas helmet. *(IWM Q669)*

eyepieces gave protection against tear gas; 1.7 million were issued, usually to key troops.

LARGE BOX RESPIRATOR

The Large Box Respirator (known as Harrison's Tower) was issued to the artillery, engineers and the Special Brigade in the spring of 1916. It used a box of solid absorbents to neutralize gases; it was large and cumbersome and was quickly superseded by the smaller version.

SMALL BOX RESPIRATOR (SBR)

The SBR had a loose-fitting mask made from a pleated piece of treated material. It gripped tightly across the forehead, down the sides of the cheeks and under the chin, and it was held in place by elastic straps and tapes to create a tight seal. Goggles protected the eyes against tear gas and finger pockets in the temple allowed them to be wiped clear. A nose-clip forced the user to breathe through

An Australian chaplain demonstrates an early version of the Small Box Respirator. *(IWM Q670)*

the mouthpiece, regulated by valves, and a tube led to the absorbents' box. Charcoal made from coconut husk was mixed with soda lime manganate granules to absorb and neutralize the gas.

The SBR became the standard gas mask after August 1916. The celluloid eyepieces were replaced by shatterproof glass and a pad of dry cotton wool in an extension box was added at the start of 1917 to protect against toxic smoke. Over 13.5 million respirators were issued. At the front line men carried their gas mask everywhere and practised putting them on daily.

OTHER GAS PROTECTION

Treated blankets were used to stop gas seeping into dugouts while sprays and decontamination chemicals would be used to neutralize gas in trenches and shell-holes. Horses and mules were provided with specially designed gas masks while pigeon baskets could be covered with treated material.

BODY ARMOUR

Men started wearing padded vests as a protection against shrapnel and at the end of 1915 GHQ asked for a bomber's shield that was light enough to be carried. Experimental designs by Chemico and Dayfield were ordered the following June but they proved to be unpopular with the men. A lighter version was issued in 1917.

THE DAILY RATION

$1\frac{1}{4}$lb of fresh or frozen meat and 1lb of preserved meat.
$1\frac{1}{4}$lb of bread, or 1lb of biscuit or flour in hot climates.
8oz of fresh vegetables or 2oz of dried vegetables.
4oz of bacon and 3oz of cheese.
$\frac{5}{8}$oz of tea, $\frac{1}{16}$ of a tin of condensed milk and 3oz of sugar.

The men in most units received a daily ration of rum, usually issued during stand to at first

A travelling field kitchen dishes out food to men gathered at Aveluy on the Somme in November 1916. *(IWM Q4472)*

light, though some commanders did not allow rum to be issued.

Every week men received 4oz jam, 1oz of pickles and small amounts of salt, pepper and mustard. Oatmeal could be provided as an extra three times a week and butter was an extra until July 1917.

In October 1915 the meat ration was

RESPONSIBILITIES AND BADGES OF RANK

Field Marshal	Crossed batons surrounded by a wreath, surmounted by a crown	Commanded the BEF
General	Crown and star with crossed sabre and baton below	Commanded an army of 3–5 corps and around 200,000 men
Lieutenant-General	Crown with crossed sabre and baton below	Commanded a corps of 2–5 divisions and between 30,000 and 75,000 men
Major-General	Star with crossed sabre and baton below	Commanded a division of around 15,000 infantry or 9,200 cavalry
Brigadier-General	Crown with three stars below	Commanded an infantry brigade of around 4,000 infantry
Colonel	Crown with two stars below	A regiment's senior battalion commander before 1914, commanding around 2,000 men or an artillery brigade of 18 guns
Lieutenant-Colonel	Crown with one star below	Commanded an infantry battalion of around 1,000 men
Major	Crown	Usually a battalion's second-in command or senior company commander or commander of an artillery battery of 6 guns
Captain	Three stars (known as pips)	Commanded a company of around 250 men
1st Lieutenant	Two stars	Commanded a platoon of around 60 men or a 2-gun artillery section
2nd Lieutenant	One star	Similar responsibilities to a 1st Lt

Other Ranks

Regimental sergeant-major	Single large crown on the lower arm
After 1915 also known as	
Warrant Officer Class I	Small Royal Arms insignia on the lower arm
Regimental Quartermaster Sergeant	Four chevrons on the sleeve with a star above
After 1915 also known as	
Warrant Officer Class II	Large crown and wreath on the forearm
Company Sergeant-Major	Three chevrons and a crown on the sleeve
After 1915 also known as	
Warrant Officer Class II	Single large crown on the forearm
Sergeant	Three chevrons (known as stripes) on the upper sleeve
Corporal	Two chevrons on the upper sleeve
Lance-corporal	One chevron on the upper sleeve
Private	No badge of rank but proficiency badges were awarded and worn on the sleeve; e.g. bomber's badge

Captain Bruce Bairnsfather's character 'Old Bill' sums up the soldiers' frustration at the Army diet with the words 'When the 'ell is it goin' to be strawberry?'

reduced to 1lb, while preserved meat was reduced to ¾lb. Jam was reduced to 3oz in April 1916 and condensed milk was increased to 1/12 of a tin to compensate. The daily ration of bread was cut to 1lb in January 1917 and cheese was reduced to 2oz a day at the same time; troops working on the lines of communication had further cuts.

CAMPAIGN MEDALS

Virtually every soldier who served in the British Army qualified for a campaign medal. These were awarded according to each man's period of service overseas.

The **1914 Star** (also known as the **Mons Star**) was awarded to all who served in France and Belgium between 5 August and 22 November 1914, covering the retreat from Mons, the advance to the Aisne and the First Battle for Ypres. A bar inscribed '5 Aug to 22 Nov 1914' was given to all those who served under fire. Over 350,000 were issued. Men serving in other theatres during this period did not qualify.

The medal is a 4-pointed bronze star with the upper point cast as an imperial crown with a circular clasp. A pair of crossed swords is overlaid with a circular oak laurel wreath on the obverse, with the royal cipher at the bottom. Scrolls inscribed 'Aug – 1914 – Nov' are in the centre. The recipient's name was engraved on the reverse. It was worn with a red, white and blue ribbon.

The **1914–15 Star** was the same as the 1914 Star with a scroll in the centre inscribed 1914–15. It was awarded to servicemen and women who served in a theatre before 31 December 1915 and who did not qualify for the 1914 Star; over 2 million were issued.

The **British War Medal** was issued to anyone who served outside the United Kingdom, even if they did not serve in a theatre of war. Over 6 million were issued, including 110,000 to Chinese, Indian and Maltese labourers.

The silver, circular medal has a straight clasp with a bust of King George V on the obverse and St George on horseback, trampling on the eagle and shield of the Central Powers on the reverse. The ribbon has a yellow and white central band and black and blue stripes.

The **Victory Medal** was awarded to all servicemen and women who entered a theatre of war; around 6 million were issued.

The bronze medal has the figure of Victory on the obverse, and the inscription 'The Great War for Civilisation 1914–1919' and a laurel wreath on the reverse. The ribbon is a double rainbow and an oak-leaf emblem was added for those who were mentioned in despatches.

Over 2.5 million trios of the 1914–15 Star, Victory Medal and British War Medal were issued and they were sometimes referred to as 'Pip, Squeak and Wilfred', after popular

Mons Star

1914–15 Star

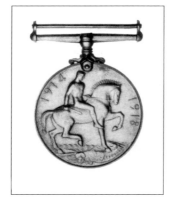

British War Medal

Victory Medal

Memorial Plaque

Victoria Cross

Distinguished Service Order

Military Cross

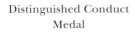

Distinguished Conduct
Medal

Military Medal

Silver War Badge

cartoon characters in the *Daily Mirror*. Over 3.2 million pairs of Victory Medal and British War Medal were issued and they were given the nickname 'Mutt and Jeff', again named after cartoon characters, this time in the *San Francisco Chronicle*.

The **Territorial Force Medal** was issued to members of the Territorial Force who had completed 4 years' service before 30 September 1914 and also served overseas. However, recipients of the 1914 or 1914–15 Stars were excluded and only 34,000 were issued.

There is a bust of George V on the obverse; the words 'For Voluntary Service Overseas 1914–1919' surrounded by a wreath and the words 'Territorial War Medal' on the reverse. It was accompanied by a watered gold silk ribbon with dark green stripes at the edges.

THE MEMORIAL PLAQUE

Approximately 1 million men and women of the British Empire lost their lives during the Great War and every bereaved family received a memorial plaque. The 4.75-inch plaque depicts the figure of Britannia and a lion with the words 'He [or she] died for freedom and honour [and the name of the deceased]'. The next of kin also received a parchment scroll listing the deceased's name and unit.

GALLANTRY MEDALS

Awards for gallantry were announced in the *London Gazette* and citations (a short summary of the act of bravery or good conduct) were published for the higher awards.

The **Victoria Cross** (VC) was introduced as the highest award for gallantry in 1856 and 633 were awarded between 1914 and 1918. A lion and a cross are engraved on the obverse, above the words 'For Valour'; the date of the act of bravery is engraved on the reverse of the medal while the recipient's name and unit appear on the rear of the suspension bar. Army recipients wore the VC with a crimson ribbon (Royal Navy recipients had a blue ribbon up to 1918).

Three officers had to give independent eyewitness statements before a regimental-level recommendation was made and both the King and the Secretary of State approved the final submission. Many awards were made posthumously.

The **Distinguished Service Order** (DSO) is a white enamelled cross mounted with a green laurel wreath and crown. The medal was unnamed and had a royal monogram and wreath on the reverse; it was worn with a blue edged crimson ribbon. It was awarded to officers (usually of the rank of major and above) for meritorious or distinguished service, or for gallantry (where the award of the Victoria Cross would not be appropriate).

The **Military Cross** (MC) was instituted on 31 December 1914 to award gallantry or meritorious service of captains, lieutenants and warrant officers. It is an ornamental cross with the royal cipher engraved in the centre and straight arms tipped with crowns. It was worn with a white and purple striped ribbon. Over 40,000 were awarded and after August 1916 bars were awarded for further acts of gallantry.

The **Distinguished Conduct Medal** (DCM) is a circular medal awarded to other ranks for distinguished service or gallantry; after 1916 it ranked higher than the Military Medal. An arrangement of drums, helmets and flags appears on the obverse and the words 'For Distinguished Conduct in the Field' appear on the reverse. The soldier's name, rank, number and the date of the act appear on the rim of the medal and it was worn with a crimson and dark blue ribbon.

The **Military Medal** (MM) was instituted in March 1916 to award other ranks for acts of bravery that did not merit the DCM. The circular medal has the King's effigy on the obverse and the words 'For Bravery in the Field' on the reverse. The ribbon has dark blue edges and thin white and red stripes in the centre. Over 115,000 were conferred in the Great War.

The **Silver War Badge** was issued to men and women who had been invalided out of the Army after September 1916 to prove that they had done their bit.

Gunners lay out their saddlery ready for a kit inspection. Damaged or missing items would result in deductions from the men's pay. *(IWM Q2709)*

MENTIONED IN DESPATCHES

Acts of gallantry worthy of note were originally mentioned in the commander-in-chief's despatch. Eventually men were allowed to wear a bronze oak-leaf on the Victory Medal ribbon. The man also received a certificate with his service details and a reference to the despatch.

CRIME AND PUNISHMENT

MINOR OFFENCES

The powers of sentencing under the Army Act were wide-ranging and punishments varied from fines and periods of hard labour for minor misdemeanours, through to imprisonment and the death penalty for more serious crimes. The Army had a long list of regulations and it was easy for the errant or absent-minded soldier to fall foul of the strict rules. Life in barracks was often boring and young soldiers were exposed to a wide range of temptations when they went overseas. The Army Act ruled that a number of offences could be dealt with more severely on active service.

Officers and NCOs dealt with minor infringements, such as damaged or missing equipment, failing to salute, arriving late on parade or breaching a curfew, and they could issue reprimands, cautions or fines. Serious misdemeanours or repeat offences were punished with extra fatigues, guard duty, exercise or by confinement to camp.

The unit's commanding officer tried and sentenced men for major misdemeanours and possible sentences ranged from up to 28 days' detention in the unit prison to stoppages in pay for up to 28 days. The CO was also able to sentence a soldier to Field Punishment No. 1 or No. 2. The Provost Marshal's office administered field punishments unless the unit was on the move.

FIELD PUNISHMENT NO. 1

A soldier was fettered or handcuffed and placed on labouring duties for up to 21 days. He could be tied to a post or a wagon wheel for two hours a day, three days out of four (a practice known as crucifixion).

FIELD PUNISHMENT NO. 2

A similar sentence to Field Punishment No. 1 without the crucifixion; it carried a maximum sentence of 28 days.

SERIOUS OFFENCES

The majority of offences related to military conduct but penalties were also set out for offences normally punishable in civilian law such as murder or rape. Men were tried and sentenced by one of the four types of courts martial:

REGIMENTAL COURT MARTIAL

A 3-man panel chaired by a captain dealt with minor offences committed by corporals and privates; the maximum sentence was 42 days' detention.

DISTRICT COURT MARTIAL

A 3-man panel chaired by a major (or higher rank) was able to sentence men to up to 2 years' hard labour or imprisonment. It could also reduce NCOs to the ranks and discharge soldiers. Sergeants were always tried by a district court martial or higher.

GENERAL COURT MARTIAL

A 5-man panel chaired by a colonel dealt with serious crimes and had the power to impose all sentences up to the death penalty. These were formal affairs and simplified field general courts martial were usually convened on active service. Officers were always tried by a general court martial or field general court martial.

FIELD GENERAL COURT MARTIAL

A 3-man panel chaired by a major or higher and again the maximum sentence was the death penalty if all three members agreed. Two-member panels could be called but they had limited powers.

COURT MARTIAL PROCEDURE

Courts martial were designed to be well-documented, thorough investigations. After the charge had been read, the accused gave his plea; from 1915 not guilty was automatically given to a crime carrying the death sentence. The unit adjutant cross-examined as prosecutor while the accused theoretically had access to an officer, or prisoner's friend, as his defending counsel. Few 'friends' had legal experience and some soldiers had to represent themselves. Courts martial were often hurried affairs and many failed to follow the regulations.

Those found innocent were acquitted immediately; the guilty had to wait for their punishment to be announced. In all 5,952 officers and 298,310 other ranks were court-martialled; 89% were convicted and 8% acquitted.

Some offences and their sentences are given below.

PENAL SERVITUDE

Pretending to take a wounded man to the rear.

Destroying property without orders or stealing.

Attacking or threatening a superior officer.

Refusing to obey an arresting officer or striking a custodian (officers could be cashiered).

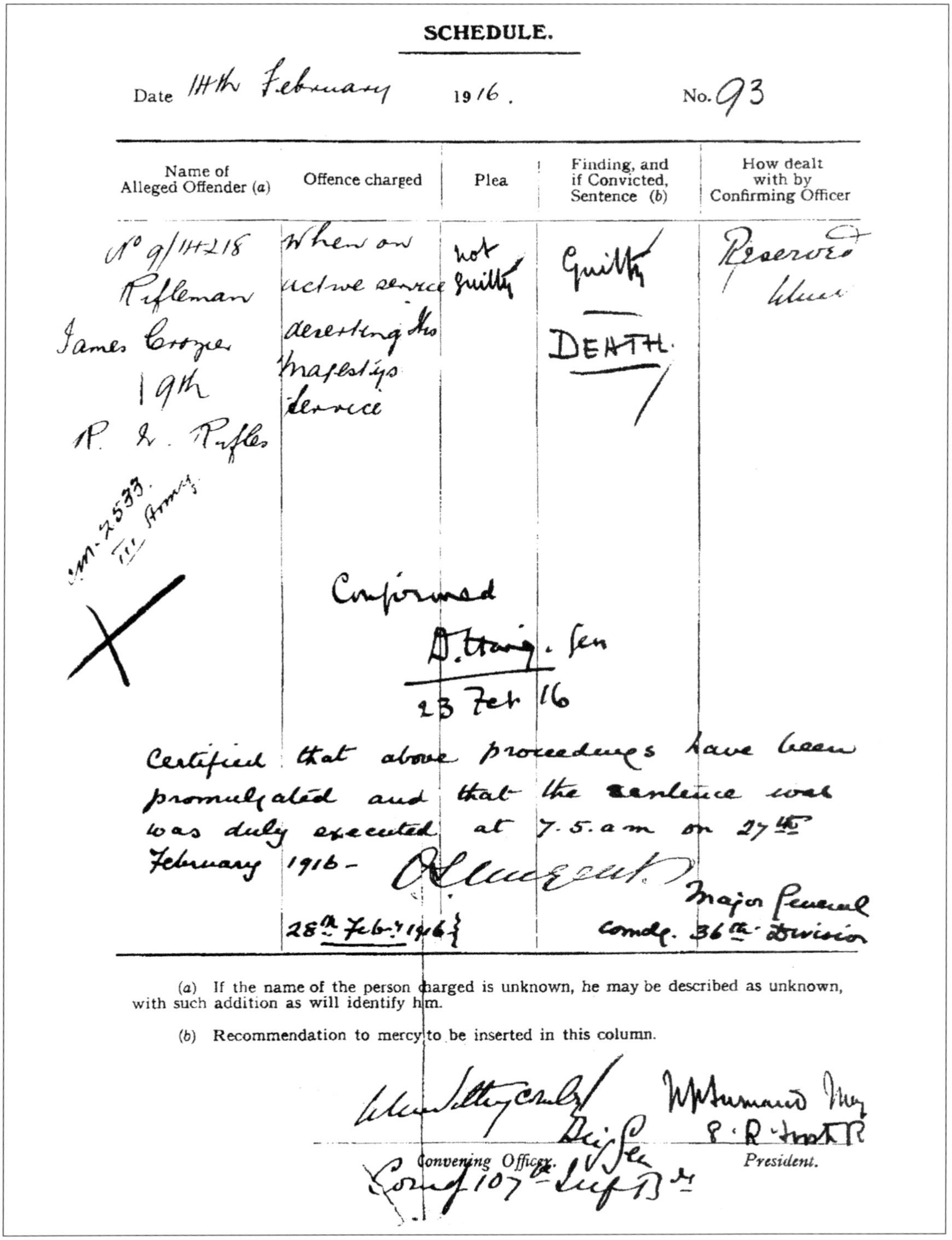

SCHEDULE.

Date 14th February 1916. No. 93

Name of Alleged Offender (a)	Offence charged	Plea	Finding, and if Convicted, Sentence (b)	How dealt with by Confirming Officer
N° 9/14218 Rifleman James Crozier 19th R. I. Rifles	When on active service deserting His Majesty's service	not guilty	Guilty DEATH.	Reserved

M.2533. 1st Army

X

Confirmed

D. Haig. Gen

23 Feb 16

Certified that above proceedings have been promulgated and that the sentence was was duly executed at 7.5. a m on 27th February 1916 –

28th Feb 1916

Major General Comdg. 36th Division

(a) If the name of the person charged is unknown, he may be described as unknown, with such addition as will identify him.

(b) Recommendation to mercy to be inserted in this column.

Convening Officer.

Comd 107th Inf Bde

President.

The Army form recording the accusation, the charge, and the implementation of the death penalty on Rifleman James Crozier of the 36th (Ulster) Division in February 1916.

Discharging firearms in camp, causing a false
alarm (officers could be cashiered).
Drunkenness (officers could be cashiered or
imprisoned).

DEATH PENALTY

Committing rape or murder.
Desertion, cowardice, casting away one's arms
or sleeping at a post.
Disobeying or striking an officer.
Starting or inciting a mutiny.

If the death sentence was pronounced, the
panel could put forward a recommendation
for mercy to the next level of command. All
cases were ultimately passed to the
commander-in-chief who would study a
summary of the condemned man's value as a
fighting soldier.

In all 3,080 men were sentenced to death;
312 men were executed (the majority for
desertion) while the rest of the sentences were
commuted. A firing party shot the condemned
man at dawn and soldiers were sometimes
drawn from the condemned man's unit. The
next of kin was rarely told the circumstances
of their relative's death.

British, Canadian and New Zealand soldiers
were executed but despite strong represen-
tations to the Australian government, it
refused to sanction the use of the death
penalty.

COURT OF INQUIRY

A Court of Inquiry investigated general
failures of discipline. Subjects could vary from
studying the outcome of a failed attack to
investigating the loss of equipment. The
results of the inquiry and its recommendations
would be forwarded to the convening officer
and individuals suspected of breaching the
Army Act could be called before a court
martial.

Inquiries could also be convened to
investigate an absentee soldier, starting three
weeks after his last known movements. The
evidence was studied and witnesses would be
interviewed before a man was declared a
deserter. If the man was caught, he would be
returned to his unit and held either under
open or close arrest until the court of inquiry
had forwarded its findings to the officer
charged with convening a court martial for the
offence.

Deserters arrested in Great Britain were
taken before a court of summary jurisdiction
(magistrates' court) before they were sent
back to their unit; the practice ceased in 1917
to prevent unfavourable reporting in the
newspapers.

CHAPTER NINE

WEAPONS

REVOLVERS

.455-INCH WEBLEY REVOLVER, MARK IV

The British Army had used revolvers made by Webley & Scott Revolver and Arms Company Ltd since 1887. The Mark IV had been in use since 1899.

Length: 9.25in (235mm) with a 4.0in (102mm) barrel
Weight: 2.25lb (1.02kg)
Muzzle velocity: 705ft/sec (215m/sec)
Loading system: loose rounds, or a quick-loader
Chambering: .455in (11.6mm), rimmed
Rifling: 7-groove, concentric, right-hand
Magazine: 6-chambered rotating cylinder
Sights: open barleycorn front sight and fixed notch rear sight

.455-INCH WEBLEY REVOLVER, MARK V

An improved version for cordite ammunition was adopted in 1913. Over 20,000 were made and many Mark IV revolvers were upgraded to Mark V standard. Officers were issued with the Webley Mark V but they were allowed to buy their own .455-inch revolver of any design. Commercial gun dealers soon ran out of revolvers in the autumn of 1914 and the Webley became the officers' standard firearm.

.455-INCH WEBLEY REVOLVER, MARK VI

Adopted on 24 May 1915. It had a 6-inch barrel and an adjustable front sight; over 300,000 were issued.

Length: 11.25in (286mm) with 6in (152mm) barrel
Weight: 2.4lb (1.09kg)
Muzzle velocity: reduced to 650ft/sec (199m/sec)
Sights: adjustable blade front sight and fixed U-notch rear sight

EMERGENCY REVOLVERS

A number of foreign models were imported to make up the shortfall. Over 13,000 .455-inch M1911 Colts and Smith and Wesson New Century revolvers were bought from the USA, while Colt New Service revolvers were chambered to accept .455-inch ammunition. .45-inch Colts were standard in the Canadian Army but they suffered in muddy conditions; they were usually issued to rear area officers and aircrew. Two types of .455-inch, Ordnance Pattern Revolver, Mark I, were bought from Spain.

The officer's standard firearm, the Webley revolver.

257

AUTOMATIC PISTOLS

Attempts to design an approved automatic pistol were unsuccessful and many patents were fragile, heavy or low-powered, including a self-loading Webley revolver.

RIFLES

SUPPLYING RIFLES AND AMMUNITION

The Royal Small Arms Factory at Enfield was the only factory producing rifles in 1914, with a weekly output of 1,000. The Army's reserve of 600,000 rifles soon ran low and the London Small Arms (LSA) Company and the Birmingham Small Arms (BSA) Company were contracted to supply rifles, but by Christmas 1914 only 240,000 rifles had been delivered.

American companies were contracted to make Lee-Enfield rifles and Canadian Ross rifles were ordered but the first shipment did not arrive until the late autumn of 1914. Japanese Arisaka rifles were also imported for training purposes and the Royal Navy handed over its Lee-Enfields in exchange for Arisaka and Ross rifles. A range of training and sporting rifles was collected from gun shops across the country and obsolete weapons were brought out of storage for the New Armies to practise with. Some of the first Territorial units sent to France were armed with the Charger-Loading Lee-Enfield Rifle.

The 600,000 volunteers of Kitchener's New Armies had to share 200,000 live weapons and 200,000 training rifles for many months. Men often trained with an assortment of British Snider, French Gras, single-shot Remington, Russian Berdan, Belgian Albini-Braendlin, American .44-40 Winchester and even German Mauser weapons.

Output had risen to 15,000 rifles a week by the summer of 1915, peaking at 24,000 rifles a week by November 1918; 3,954,200 rifles were issued during the war.

Mark VII .303-inch ammunition was capable of penetrating 9 inches of brick or 18 sandbags at short ranges. The Army's reserve of 400 million rounds had fallen to 2 million by the spring of 1915 even though firing practice in the United Kingdom had been severely restricted. Monthly output rose from 26 million to over 100 million rounds during the first six months of 1915. American contractors supplied 150 million rounds in 1915 and by 1916 British monthly output had increased to 300 million rounds.

.303-INCH, LONG, MAGAZINE, LEE-ENFIELD RIFLE, MARK I

This rifle was adopted in 1895 with a new design of rifling to accommodate smokeless cartridges; it was known as the Long Magazine when the short version appeared in 1902.

The secret of the Lee-Enfield's success was a rear-locking bolt that was faster to reload than a front-locking version enabling a trained soldier to fire 15 aimed rounds a minute, and up to double that number if he used rapid fire. The British soldier became renowned for his ability to fire rapid short bursts of aimed fire, effective up to 800 yards and deadly at short ranges.

Length: 49.5in (1,257mm) with a 30.25in (770mm) barrel
Weight: 9lb 4oz (4.2kg) without the sling
Muzzle velocity: 2,060ft/sec (628m/sec)
Chambering: .303in (7.7 x 56mm), rimmed
Rifling: 5-groove, concentric and left-hand
Magazine: detachable staggered-row box with 10 loose rounds
Sights: open barleycorn front sight and leaf-and-slider rear sight
Sight settings: minimum 200 yards and maximum 2,000 yards; long-range sights increased maximum range to 2,800 yards

A Mark I* Lee-Enfield was issued without a clearing rod and the Navy used a Charger-Loading Version, stamped with the letter N.

.303-INCH, MAGAZINE, LEE-ENFIELD, CAVALRY CARBINE, MARK I

A shorter version with 6-round magazine was adopted in 1896 to fit cavalry scabbards; artillery crews also used them with a larger bayonet. The differences are given below:

Length: 39.94in (1,014mm) with a 20.75in (527mm) barrel

Top: The Short Magazine Lee-Enfield Mark I; many were brought back into service for the New Army volunteers to practise with. *Second top:* The British Army's standard firearm during the Great War, the SMLE Mark III. *Second bottom:* Territorial and New Army soldiers were often issued with Japanese Arisaka rifles until the SMLE III was available. *Above:* The Ross Rifle.

Weight: 7lb 7oz (3.37kg) empty, without sling
Muzzle velocity: 1,940ft/sec (591m/sec)

The Short Magazine Lee-Enfield replaced this weapon but the Territorial Yeomanry cavalry were still using it in 1914.

.303-INCH, SHORT, MAGAZINE, LEE-ENFIELD RIFLE, MARK I

An improved Lee-Enfield rifle (5 inches shorter than the Long version) suitable for all arms of service, whether foot or mounted, was officially adopted by the Army on 23 December 1902:

Length: 44.5in (1,132mm) with a 25.25in (640mm) barrel
Weight: 8lb 2oz (3.69kg)
Muzzle velocity: 2,060ft/sec (628m/sec)
Sights: protected blade front sight and tangent leaf-and-slider rear sight

Over 363,000 SMLE Mark I rifles were made. In addition 60,000 Mark 1* rifles were made with a modified magazine. This design had storage for the oil bottle and pull-through cord in the butt plate; the sling had a swivel. An improved version, the Mark II, was made available a few weeks after the Mark I was approved and thousands of Lee-Metfords and Mark Is were upgraded. A charger-loading version was also made.

303-INCH, SHORT, MAGAZINE, LEE-ENFIELD RIFLE, MARK III

The standard rifle during the war, the SMLE Mark III, was introduced in January 1907 with a number of minor improvements. Charger guides and improved sights were added while the nose-cap and rear sight protectors were improved. The changes are given below:

Weight: increased to 8lb 10oz (3.93kg)
Muzzle velocity: increased to 2,230ft/sec (680m/sec)
Magazine: protruding detachable box with 10 charger or loose rounds

The magazine and receiver body were modified in 1910 to fire the new Mark VII bullet with its high-velocity cartridge. After 1916 long-range sights were abandoned and the finishing process was speeded up; the wartime model was known as the Mark III*. Mark II rifles upgraded to Mark III standard were known as Converted Mark IV rifles.

.303-INCH, ENFIELD MAGAZINE RIFLE, PATTERN 1914, MARK 1

The War Office had been developing a .276-inch Pattern 1913 rifle but work was halted in August 1914. The new pattern was designed for mass production and it was modified to fire the .303-inch cartridge and offered to American companies. Both Winchester and Remington Arms made 200,000, known as Mark I (W) and Mark (I) R; Mark I (E) rifles were made at the Eddystone factory.

Length: 46.25in (1,172mm) with a 26-inch (660mm) barrel
Weight: 8lb 10oz (3.94kg) without sling
Muzzle velocity: 2,525ft/sec (770m/sec)
Chambering: .303in (7.7 x 56mm), rimmed
Rifling: 5-groove, left-hand concentric rifling
Magazine: integral box with 5 charger or loose rounds
Sights: protected blade front sight and leaf-and-slider aperture rear sight

Sight settings: minimum 200 yards and maximum 1,650 yards; maximum range increased to 2,600 yards with long-range sights

JAPANESE .256-INCH ARISAKA RIFLE

Over 150,000 1900 and 1907 Pattern Arisaka rifles were bought from Japan for training purposes. As supplies of SMLE rifles became available the Arisakas were handed in and many were sent to Russia.

1907 PATTERN

Length: 50.25in (1,274mm) with a 31.5in (799mm) barrel
Weight: 9.12lb (4.12kg)
Muzzle velocity: 2,493ft/sec (760m/sec)
Chambering: 6.5 x 50mm semi-rimmed
Rifling: 6-groove, right-hand concentric rifling
Magazine: internal box with 5 charger or loose rounds
Sights: open blade front sight and tangent-leaf rear sight
Sight settings: 200 yards minimum and 2,400 yards maximum

CANADIAN ROSS RIFLE MARK IIIB

The Ross was the standard rifle in the Canadian Expeditionary Force at the start of the war but it was inclined to jam in muddy conditions and hence was far from ideal in the trenches; it was quickly replaced by the SMLE. The British Army used the Ross for training purposes and donated 45,000 to the Royal Navy in 1917.

Length: 50.5in (1,282mm) with a 30.5in (775mm) barrel
Weight: 9.88lb (4.48kg), without sling
Muzzle velocity: 2,600ft/sec (792m/sec)
Chambering: .303in (7.7 x 56mm), rimmed
Rifling: 4-groove, left-hand, concentric rifling
Magazine: internal box with 5 charger or loose rounds
Sights: adjustable blade front sight and tangent aperture rear sight
Sight settings: minimum 200 yards and maximum 2,000 yards

OBSOLESCENT RIFLES

Large quantities of obsolescent Martini-pattern rifles and .303-inch carbines had been withdrawn and placed into storage as soon as the SMLE rifles became available. They were reissued to the New Armies and Territorial units in 1914 for drill purposes.

SNIPER RIFLES

Telescopic sights were in short supply and early sniper rifles were often full-length Lee-Enfields fitted with two lenses; only a few sporting rifles had German-made sights. Mass production of telescopic sights for the SMLE rifle did not start until the spring of 1916. The Periscopic Prism Company's sight was graduated from 100 to 600 yards. They were mounted to the left so the rifle could be reloaded and the aim had to be compensated. The first top-mounted periscope with adjustable fittings appeared in April 1918. Telescopic sighted rifles were marked with a 'T' and nearly 10,000 were issued.

PERISCOPES

Soldiers used periscopes to look across no man's land without exposing themselves. Mirrors were often attached to sticks or bayonets and lifted above the parapet. Box periscopes, with mirrors mounted inside a metal or wooden tube, gave a better view but they were easily spotted.

The artillery tried various types of periscope to aid observation and the Ross periscope was in widespread use by the end of the war. At ten feet high it had to be hidden inside chimneys or behind buildings.

BAYONETS

The Pattern 1903 sword bayonet had a 12-inch non-fullered (non-grooved) blade. It was carried in a leather scabbard with metal fittings at both ends and it was slung from the belt by a leather loop, known as a frog. The Pattern 1907 was introduced for the Short

New Zealand troops rest in a fire trench near Fleurbaix while a sniper team pick out a target. The man on the right is using a box periscope to scan no man's land while the man on the left has mounted his rifle on a cradle and aims through a smaller periscope. *(IWM Q666)*

Magazine Lee-Enfield and it was 5 inches longer to compensate for the shorter rifle; the scabbard was increased to 18 inches in length. The bayonet weighed 1lb 1oz (0.48kg). A hook was added to the hilt, or quillion, so the soldier could hook his blade around an enemy's bayonet to pull him off balance. The blade had a groove, or fuller, on both sides. The Pattern 1907 was still in service in 1914 but the hooked hilt had been removed and many early models had their hooks ground off. It was fitted to the end of the rifle by clipping lugs in the centre of the pommel onto the end of the rifle. A hole was added to the pommel in 1916 to make it easier to clean out the lug track.

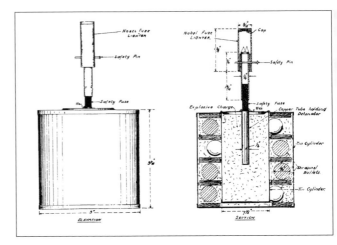

GRENADES

The British Army had no reserve of grenades at the start of the war and by November 1914 only 70 hand and 630 rifle grenades were being issued every week. Field Marshal French wanted 4,000 hand and 2,000 rifle grenades per month, a target reached in March 1915.

In the meantime, the men at the front made their own bombs; the Indian Corps' Chief Engineer, Brigadier-General Herbert Nanton, was instrumental in promoting new designs.

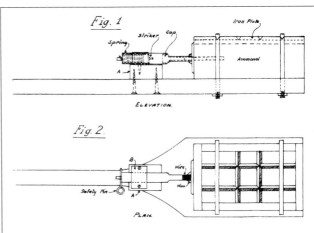

JAM POT BOMB

An empty tin was filled with a mixture of shredded gun cotton and nails. A No. 8 detonator and a short length of Bickford's fuse were sealed into the tin with clay. A French cardboard friction lighter was useless in wet weather and the bomber usually kept a pipe or cigarette burning. The bomb was nicknamed Tickler's Artillery, after the jam manufacturer.

BATTYE BOMB

Designed by Major Basil Battye, RE. A small, perforated cast-iron cylinder was filled with ammonal, armed with a fuse and detonator and sealed with a wooden plug. A Nobel fuse lighter (a coal mining device) was then added; a light tap ignited the fuse.

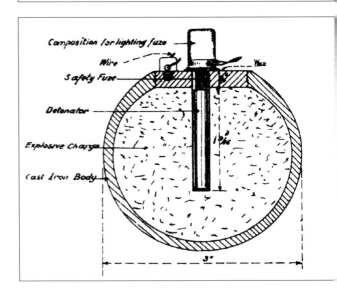

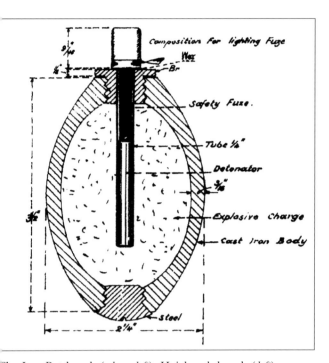

The Jam Pot bomb (*above left*), Hairbrush bomb (*left*), Ball bomb (*below left*) and Lemon bomb (*above*).

HAIRBRUSH OR RACKET BOMB

A paddle-shaped piece of wood with a slab of gun cotton strapped to one side; it was ignited in the same way as the Jam Pot bomb.

EXPERIMENTAL TYPES

Many different designs were sent to France; all failed to impress:

No. 1 Grenade: A cylindrical brass head mounted on a cane handle. The cap was switched from travel to fire and the safety pin was pulled before throwing; a webbing streamer unwound as the bomb flew through the air to make it land nose first.

No. 2 Grenade: A percussion grenade.

No. 3 and No. 4: Hale's grenade, a rifle grenade with a small rod attached.

Newton's Pippin: A pear-shaped device, also used as a rifle grenade.

Grenades 6 and 7: Christened 'lemons' from their shape.

Bombs 8 and 9: Double cylinder bombs, official light and heavy versions of the jam tin.

No. 12 Grenade: A factory version of the hairbrush bomb armed with a spring lighter.

Nos. 13 and 14: Pitcher grenades armed with friction lighters.

No. 15: A cricket-ball-shaped grenade.

PATTERN NO. 5: THE MILLS BOMB

The bomb had a segmented barrel-shaped cast-iron casing, 3.75 inches long and 2.3 inches in diameter. A base plate was screwed

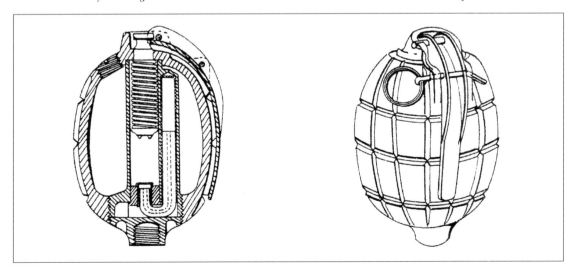

The internal workings and exterior view of the Mills bomb.

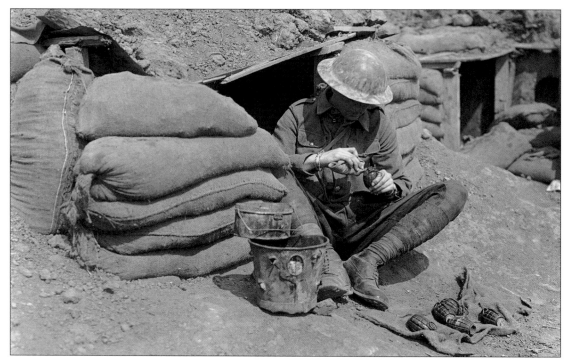

A soldier sits alone outside his dugout while he cleans and arms his stock of Mills bombs. *(IWM Q4115)*

to the bottom, leaving two tubes for the detonator inside the casing. A brass screw was cemented into the filling hole at the top to secure the explosive; a primed grenade weighed 1lb 7oz.

The operator removed the safety pin and the lever flipped off, allowing the striker to hit the cap, igniting the 5-second fuse.

The first batch of 48 Service Pattern No. 5 grenades were tested in March 1915 and by July 1915 16,000 Mills hand grenades had been delivered to the front. They were immediately accepted and weekly output had risen to 800,000 a week by July 1916. The Mark 23 Mills Bomb, with a safer internal design, was introduced in 1917.

RIFLE GRENADES

The Hale's Grenade, adopted as Grenade, Rifle, No. 1, had an explosive-filled serrated cast-iron tube fitted with an impact fuse. A protruding steel rod fitted into the barrel of a Lee-Enfield rifle and a blank cartridge fired

A soldier of the 113th Infantry (Jats) demonstrates the firing position for aiming rifle grenades. *(IWM Q24791)*

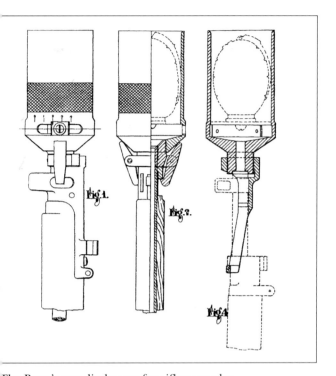

The Burn's cup discharger for rifle grenades.

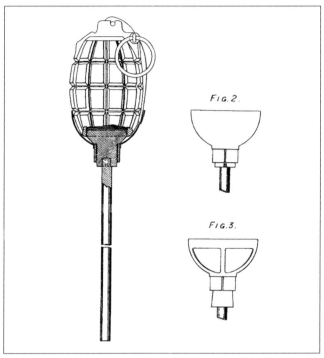

No. 23 rifle grenade.

the grenade up to 100 yards. Prolonged use damaged the rifle barrel and reduced accuracy.

The No. 23 Hand & Rifle Grenade appeared in 1915. It was a No. 5 Mills Bomb with a short rod drilled into the base-cap. Again the grenade damaged the rifle barrel after prolonged use.

The SMLE Mark III EY and SMLE Mark III* EY employed a cup discharger clamped to the end of the barrel. A No. 36 Mills grenade (with a 2-inch diameter plate screwed to its base) was inserted into the cup and could then be fired up to 125 yards. Copper wire had to be wound around the rifle stock and soldered to stop the barrel bursting.

By 1918 the Army had a store of over 7 million grenades.

TRENCH WEAPONS

The rifle, bayonet and grenade were the soldier's standard weapons for hand-to-hand fighting. When the men became confined to the trenches, many decided to make or buy additional non-regulation weapons which they could use in close-quarter fighting, in particular during raids on enemy trenches aimed at securing prisoners. The emphasis was on stunning the enemy in silence, so he could be bundled back across no man's land for interrogation. Home-made batons were fashioned out of wood, many with nails embedded to increase their effectiveness. Companies across Great Britain produced a range of weapons including knives, knuckle-dusters and coshes. None were ever accepted by the Army and the decision to purchase was down to the individual.

SWORDS

INFANTRY OFFICER'S SWORD

The 1897 Pattern sword had a 32-inch-long blade and a three-quarter pierced steel basket hilt. It was sheathed in a two-ringed steel scabbard and slung from the Sam Browne belt with a sword frog.

CAVALRY OFFICER'S SWORD

The 1912 Pattern sword was redesigned after the introduction of the 1908 Pattern Trooper's sword. The hilt had a large nickel-plated steel bowl decorated with scroll etching and a wire-wrapped leather grip. The 35.5-inch-long blade was sheathed in a steel-tipped brown scabbard.

CAVALRY TROOPER'S SWORD

The lightweight 1908 Pattern sword had a steel bowl-guard hilt complete with a simulated rubber grip and a steel pommel. The 35.5-inch-long carbon-steel blade was sheathed in a steel scabbard and slung from the belt by two rings.

ROYAL ARTILLERY OFFICER'S SWORD

The sword was based on the 1822 Light Cavalry Sword complete with a chequered back strap. The etched blade was 34 inches long and sheathed in a Sam Browne pattern scabbard, tipped with a leather drag.

MACHINE GUNS

The machine gun became a dominant weapon on the First World War battlefield and the numbers of guns per infantry division increased from 24 heavy machine guns at the start of the war to 288 light and 64 heavy machine guns in the later stages, as detailed in Chapter Seven.

SUPPLYING MACHINE GUNS

In 1914 each infantry battalion and cavalry regiment was armed with 2 machine guns. The lighter Vickers had been introduced in 1912 but many units still had the older Maxim gun. The British Army ordered 192 weapons on 11 August 1914, adding another 100 a month later. Another 1,500 machine guns were soon requested, becoming an open order for 200 a week in February 1915; contracts were also placed with America suppliers.

The first order for 250 of the new Lewis light machine gun, was placed in August 1914 but the Birmingham Small Arms Company could not start mass production until November; the first batch reached the trenches in July 1915.

The Mark I Vickers gun complete with ammunition box and condenser tank.

Demand exceeded supply until July 1916 and French-designed Hotchkiss guns were used in the interim. Weekly output rose to 2,500 guns and by November 1918 nearly 240,000 had been made.

MAXIM GUN

Introduced in 1890, the weapon was sturdy and reliable with a heavy phosphor-bronze water jacket. A new .303-inch model was introduced and older versions were re-chambered and designated .303-inch Converted Mark 1.

Length: 42.5in (1,076mm) with a 28in (711mm) barrel
Weight of gun: 60lb (27.21kg) empty
Rate of fire: 400rds/min fired at 1,800ft/sec (549m/sec)
Muzzle velocity: 1,800ft/sec (549m/sec)
Ammunition supply: 250 rounds held in a fabric belt and fed through the side receiver
Chambering: .303in (7.7 x 56mm), rimmed
Rifling: 5-groove, right-hand concentric rifling
Sights: open barleycorn front sight and leaf-and-slider rear sight

Vickers gun team of the Machine Gun Corps use their weapon to engage a German plane during the Battle for Arras in April 1917. *(IWM Q5173)*

VICKERS MACHINE GUN MARK I

This tripod-mounted weapon was introduced in November 1912 with a lighter sheet-steel water jacket. Firing 1,000 rounds evaporated a pint of water and the steam condensed into a can; the jacket held 7 pints. A barrel had to be changed after 10,000 rounds by lifting the gun and pulling the barrel backwards, inserting a large cork into the opening at the front of the barrel jacket. After the gun was lowered the barrel could be withdrawn and replaced.

To set up the gun, No. 1 held the tripod while No. 2 attached the barrel. No. 2 inserted a brass tag at the end of the ammunition belt into the feed block as No. 1 pulled the belt through with a crank handle. After flicking the sights up and flipping the safety catch off, the gun was ready to fire.

No. 3 and No. 4 brought up ammunition and water as No. 2 fed ammunition belts into the gun. No. 5 was the runner while No. 6 usually acted as range-taker. Each man was trained to change roles if there were casualties.

Crews were trained to fire in short observed bursts of around 200 rounds per minute and the gun had an effective range of 2,000 yards. Some 20% of shots were expected to hit their target at 800 yards doubling to 40% at 400 yards.

Length: 45.5in (1,155mm) with a 28.5-inch (723mm) barrel
Weight of gun: 40lb (18.1kg) with a filled water jacket
Weight of tripod: 50lb (22.68kg)

Indian cavalrymen practise with their Hotchkiss machine gun in the summer of 1916; note the cartridge strip magazine. *(IWM Q4070)*

Rate of fire: 450rds/min
Muzzle velocity: 2,450ft/sec (745m/sec)
Ammunition supply: 250 rounds held in a fabric belt and fed through the side receiver
Chambering: .303in (7.7 x 56mm), rimmed
Rifling: 4-groove, right-hand concentric rifling
Sights: open blade front sight and leaf-and-slider rear sight

HOTCHKISS .303-INCH MACHINE GUN, MARK I

Mark 1, No. 1 was supplied to the infantry. No. 2 was used in tank sponsons and it had new sights and a shoulder extension piece on the butt. There was an ammunition pan to carry a folded cartridge belt and a bag for spent cases. A Mark I*, capable of firing three strips joined together, was introduced in June 1916 to reduce loading time.

Length: 46.75in (1,187mm) with a 23.5in (597mm) barrel

Weight: 27lb (12.24kg); it could be mounted on a small bipod or tripod
Rate of fire: 500rds/min
Muzzle velocity: 2,450ft/sec (747m/sec)
Ammunition supply: side-loaded 30-round metal strip
Chambering: .303in (7.7 x 56mm) rimmed
Rifling: 5-groove, right-hand concentric rifling
Sights: open barleycorn front sight and leaf-and-slider rear sight
Maximum range: 2,000 yards

Mud often jammed the cartridge strips and an new inverted version intended to avoid this was difficult to load. A Benet-Mercié pattern selector allowed single shot or sustained firing

LEWIS .303-INCH MACHINE GUN, MARK 1

Designed by Isaac Newton Lewis, a retired US Army officer, this gun had failed to win orders in America but Birmingham Small Arms had shown interest and tested experimental

A soldier of the 1st/7th King's cleans his Lewis gun in the trenches at Givenchy. A few days later the gun would be in action when the Germans tried to take the village from 55th Division on 9 April 1918. *(IWM Q10738)*

models during the winter of 1914. It was cheap to manufacture and proved popular with the troops.

A gas-operated, air-cooled weapon, it could fire at a cyclic rate of 600 rounds per minute but was best used in short bursts. A full magazine could be fired in 5 seconds. One man carried the weapon using a sling to give protection from the hot barrel; it could also be fired from the hip. Three men carried ammunition, using 4-pouch carriers after July 1916.

Length: 50in (1,270mm) with a 26in (660mm) barrel
Weight: 26lb 5oz (11.9kg) without magazine
Ammunition supply: 47-round top loading circular magazine
Chambering: .303in with 4-groove rifling

G MAXIMS

Captured German Maxims were converted from 7.92mm to .303-inch ammunition and reissued.

TRENCH MORTARS

EARLY EXPERIMENTAL MODELS

As early as October 1914 Field Marshal French was appealing for 'some special form of artillery which can be used with effect at close range in the trenches'.

The Germans had the Minnenwerfer and many British designs were direct copies of this fearsome weapon. Twelve experimental 3.7-inch mortars were sent to France at the end of 1914 but they proved to be dangerous. The Vickers 1.57-inch trench howitzer was approved in January 1915 and the first six examples reached the front line two months later.

Improved 4-inch mortars were made from 6-inch shell casings; First Army workshops converted iron water pipes to throw jam tin

A Stokes mortar team of the 28th (Western Australia) Battalion set up their weapon in a captured trench near Villers-Bretonneux in July 1918. *(IWM E(AUS)2677)*

bombs; Second Army tried fixing a 3.7-inch brass tube to a flat base. All were unreliable and rejected. Experiments with a 5-inch mortar and a rifled 4-inch version with adjustable legs were also abandoned as dangerous. Lieutenant-Colonel A. Rawlinson acquired 40

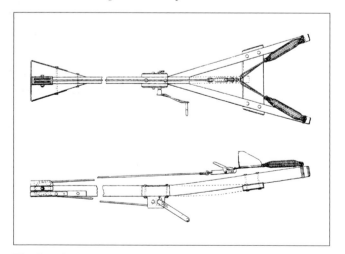

The Leach catapult.

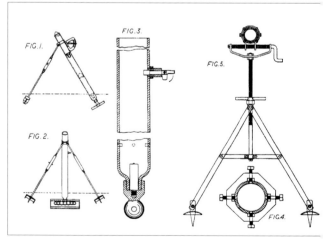

The Stokes mortar.

obsolete Coehorn mortars (called Toby mortars, Rawlinson's nickname) from the French Army and they were used in action at Neuve Chapelle and Aubers in the spring of 1915.

CATAPULTS

Improvised catapults were used to throw bombs in 1915 but the practice was dangerous. Two designs were officially adopted.

The **Leach Catapult** had a sling tied with rubber springs to a Y-shaped wooden frame. The operator wound back the springs with a crank and loaded a bomb into the sling, depressing a trigger plate to fire. It had a range of 200 yards and 3,000 were issued.

The **West Spring Gun** used a rigid shooting arm and the wooden base was loaded with sandbags. A lever tensioned the springs while a second lever released the cocked arm, hurling the bomb 300 yards.

STOKES MORTAR

The Army accepted Wilfred Stokes's bipod-mounted mortar in the summer of 1915. It was light, robust and simple to use. Bombs were dropped into a 3-inch tube and a striker at the bottom activated the firing cartridge. It had a high rate of fire and had a range of 50–430 yards, using different charges for different ranges. Improved propellants increased the range to 2,500 yards. The first batch of 1,000 weapons was issued in August 1915; 200 x 4-inch versions were made to fire gas and smoke ammunition.

2-INCH MEDIUM MORTAR

The nicknames 'toffee apple' and 'tadpole' describe the peculiar shape of the bomb fired by this weapon. The guide pole was pushed into the 2-inch diameter tube, leaving the charge protruding. The first batch arrived at the end of 1915; it had been superseded by June 1917.

6-INCH NEWTON MORTAR

The Stokes mortar formed the basis for this medium model, introduced in the summer of 1917.

Troops arm a 2-inch mortar in Mesopotamia. *(IWM Q24286)*

The crew of a 9.45-inch mortar prepare to fire their weapon at the German trenches around Gommecourt in March 1917. *(IWM Q4923)*

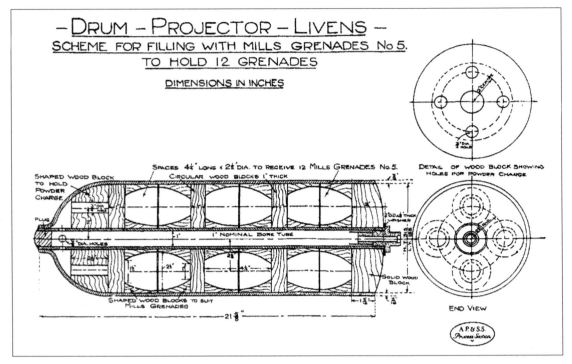

The Livens projector could fire a variety of projectiles; this particular design incorporates twelve Mills bombs as its payload.

9.45-INCH (HEAVY) MORTAR

Introduced at the end of 1916, this weapon fired a 150-pound bomb, nicknamed the 'flying pig'.

LIVENS PROJECTOR

Captain William Livens designed a simple mortar drum in the summer of 1915. They were arranged in groups of about 25, and could fire oil canisters up to a range of 200 yards using a remote electrical firing system. Improvised projectors were made from steel drums planted in the ground at an angle and they were used for the first time in July 1916. Mills bomb charges were used to fire gas projectiles.

They were simple to set up and could saturate an area with burning oil or gas. Light, medium and heavy versions were tried and the largest projector had a range of 1,300 yards. Some 140,000 were made between January 1917 and the end of 1918.

FLAMETHROWERS

The Germans used a heavy backpack flame-thrower at Hooge, in the Ypres Salient, in July 1915 and the British Army was soon looking to inventors for a model suitable for the trenches. Captain Livens invented a heavy flamethrower capable of squirting a mixture of light and heavy flaming oil 100 yards with the help of deoxygenated compressed air at a rate of 1 ton of fuel in a 10-second squirt. The weapon weighed 2 tons and the crew had to assemble it in the trenches; it was also expensive and only five were delivered.

Livens had more success with a semi-portable flamethrower, consisting of a 4ft 6in long galvanized steel cylinder carrying 10 gallons of oil and an equal amount of pressur-ized nitrogen. Weighing in at 150 pounds, it was capable of squirting flaming oil 40 yards, but two men had to hold the nozzle while it was lit; no one ever got close enough to the

An 18-pounder gun crew deploys in the open near Albert during the German offensive in March 1918. *(IWM Q8648)*

enemy and survived and the weapon was discontinued in the autumn of 1916.

FIELD ARTILLERY

The Ordnance Factory, Armstrong, Vickers, Beardmore and Coventry Ordnance began manufacturing quick-firing artillery pieces in 1904. The Royal Field Artillery received an 18-pounder while the Royal Horse Artillery had the lighter 13-pounder. Hydrostatic buffers absorbed the recoil during firing while recuperators returned the barrel to its firing position without disturbing the gun carriage; a screw-threaded breechblock speeded up loading. Fixed-charge ammunition, with its encased propellant and shell, could be fired with greater accuracy than before.

18-POUNDER FIELD GUN
Weight: 2,821lb (1.28 tonnes)
Shell: 3.3in (84mm) calibre, weighing 18.5lb (8.4kg)
Maximum elevation: 16 degrees
Maximum range: 6,525 yards

The Mark II with improved recuperators was introduced in 1916. There was no Mark III but the Mark IV, with a faster loading mechanism and a maximum elevation of 30 degrees, came into service towards the end of the war.

13-POUNDER FIELD GUN
A lighter weapon to support the cavalry:

Shell: 3-inch (76mm) calibre, weighing 12.5lb (5.7kg)
Maximum range: 5,900 yards

4.5-INCH HOWITZER
Introduced in 1909 to give divisions their own heavy artillery.

Weight: 3,010lb (1.36 tonnes)
Shell: 4.5-inch (114mm) calibre, weighing 35lb (15.9kg)
Maximum elevation: 45 degrees
Maximum range: 7,300 yards

A Mark II was introduced in 1917 with an improved sliding-block breech.

5-INCH HOWITZER
These howitzers were obsolescent in 1914 and had to be brought out of storage; they were quickly replaced by new 4.5-inch howitzers and then used at home for training.

The crew of a 4.5-inch howitzer uses a shell crater for shelter during the fighting near Flers on 16 September 1916. *(IWM Q4413)*

MEDIUM AND HEAVY ARTILLERY

The Royal Garrison Artillery manned the Army's medium and heavy artillery. Heavy artillery was in short supply at the start of the

Although larger weapons began to arrive on the Western Front, the 60-pounder gun saw service throughout the war. *(IWM Q8651)*

war and by July 1915 the BEF only had 3 x 15-inch howitzers; 14 x 9.2-inch howitzers; 4 x 8-inch howitzers; 40 x 6-inch (obsolescent) howitzers; 8 x 6-inch guns and 36 of the lighter 60-pounders. By the end of the war the number of heavy and medium guns had risen to 2,200.

MARK II 60-POUNDER GUN

Introduced in 1904, a 4-gun battery was allocated to each division.

Weight: 9,856lb (4.4 tonnes)
Shell: 5-inch (127mm) calibre, weighing 60lb (27.3kg)
Maximum range: 10,300 yards

Modifications added an extra ton in weight and caterpillar steam tractors had to take over from the horse-drawn limbers. The Mark III appeared at the end of 1915 with a modified gun carriage. Improvements to the firing mechanism increased the maximum range to 12,300 yards.

6-INCH (BL) HOWITZER

Six medium siege batteries, each armed with 4 breech-loading 6-inch howitzers, joined the Expeditionary Force in September 1914.

Weight: 8,142lb (3.7 tonnes)
Shell: 118.5lb (53.8kg)
Maximum range: 5,200 yards
Maximum elevation: 35 degrees

The 30cwt barrel was replaced by a 26cwt version in 1915. It could be raised to 45 degrees, increasing the range to 11,400 yards; over 3,600 saw service.

9.2-INCH HOWITZER

Four new Mark I 9.2-inch howitzers, nick-named *Mother*, were used at Neuve Chapelle in March 1915.

Weight: 15.5 tons plus a 9-ton counterweight bolted to the platform
Shell: 290lb (132kg)
Maximum range: 10,050 yards

The Mark II increased the range to 13,935 yards; it needed an 11-ton counterweight.

A 9.2-inch howitzer fires from its hidden position on 1 July 1916. *(IWM Q98)*

12-INCH HOWITZER

The Mark I 12-inch railway howitzer could fire a 750-pound (340.5kg) shell to a range of 11,340 yards (10.36km) and the barrel could be elevated to 70 degrees. The Mark II, a carriage-mounted version, was introduced in the summer of 1916; it weighed 37.5 tons and required an additional 20-ton counterweight. It needed a crew of 70 and was extremely slow to load. The Mark III railway weapon and the Mark IV carriage-mounted version increased the range to 14,350 yards (13.12km).

OBSOLESCENT GUNS

There was a lack of modern artillery pieces during the early months of the war and the Territorial divisions used obsolescent 15-pounders and 5-inch howitzers to begin with in France. Only a third of the New Army's artillery pieces had been delivered by July 1915 and they were forced to train with obsolescent guns. A variety of out-of-date medium and heavy guns were pressed into action during the early moths of the war.

15-POUNDER BLC GUNS AND 15-POUNDER QUICK FIRER GUNS

Both models could fire a 14-pound (6.3kg) shell 6,400 yards (5.85km); the Quick Firer was an obsolescent German model.

4.7-INCH QUICK FIRER GUN

The predecessor to the 60-pounder, weighing 3.8 tons, was difficult to operate and un-reliable. It could fire a 46-pound shell up to 10,000 yards but it was only accurate at short ranges. Those used in France were quickly replaced and sent to Salonika.

Territorials of the 2nd/2nd London Brigade (Woolwich) train with an obsolete 15-pounder gun in a London park. *(IWM Q54287)*

8-INCH HOWITZER

A number of obsolescent 6-inch guns were given 8-inch barrels capable of firing a 200-pound (90.8kg) shell 12,300 yards (11.24km).

15-INCH HOWITZER

A single naval howitzer, nicknamed *Grandmother*, was used at Neuve Chapelle; it fired a 1.4-ton shell 10,795 yards.

ARTILLERY AMMUNITION

SHRAPNEL

Shrapnel shells could be set to explode on contact or in the air using a timing device. They showered a target with steel balls and metal fragments. Shrapnel was effective against troops in the open but useless against trenches. Shrapnel could be used to cut wire but the timing of the air burst needed to be very precise for this to be effective.

HIGH EXPLOSIVE

High explosive (HE) shells showered the target with jagged pieces of steel if the shell exploded in the air. Usually they exploded on contact, creating a huge shock wave and a crater. HE was the only type of ammunition effective against fortified positions and was initially supplied solely for howitzers; HE ammunition for the 18-pounder field guns first reached the front in October 1914.

A new French-made No. 106 percussion fuse was introduced at the beginning of 1917, detonating a shell the instant it grazed the ground. For the first time high explosive could be used to destroy barbed wire without leaving a crater. Delay fuses, that allowed the shell to bury itself into the ground, were used against strongpoints and batteries.

GAS SHELLS

Discussed under Gas, below.

AMMUNITION STATISTICS

Production of 18-pounder ammunition
    peaked at 1,400,000 shells a week.
Production of 6-inch howitzer ammunition
    peaked at 330,000 shells a week.

148,000 tons of shells were fired on the Somme between 24 June and 23 July 1916.

Over 1.7 million shells were fired prior to the Somme offensive on 1 July 1916.

3,258,000 shells were fired during the Battle of Messines in June 1917.

The cost of the preliminary bombardment for Third Ypres in July 1917 was £22 million.

Two armies consumed 943,837 shells (40,000 tons) on 27 September 1918; more than the total quantity consumed during the three-year-long Boer War.

ANTI-AIRCRAFT GUNS

The first batch of 1-pounder Pom-Pom guns reached France in September 1914; a 2-pounder gun on a mobile mounting arrived a few weeks later. They were useless. Machine guns mounted on improvised carriages were used until converted 13-pounder and 18-pounder field guns arrived on the Western Front. An improved 13-pounder and a relined 18-pounder reached France in the spring of 1916, superseding the variety of weapons in use; they had a maximum ceiling of 19,000 feet.

Shrapnel was ineffective and high explosive was dangerous to use; a dedicated anti-aircraft shell appeared in April 1916. A handbook for anti-aircraft gunners introduced in September 1917 coordinated the work of pilots, gun crews and searchlights. Corps allocated specially mounted machine guns to protect their troops from low-level attack.

New weapons continued to appear and by November 1918 3-inch and 12-pounder guns had been introduced, and improved light and heavy models of the 13-pounder were in operation.

14th Battery, Australian Field Artillery, has a large stock of shells to hand during the bombardment of Polygon Wood on 28 September 1917. (*IWM E920*)

The crew of a Canadian anti-aircraft battery scramble to man their lorry-mounted weapons during an air attack on Angres in April 1918. *(IWM CO2671)*

TANKS

DEVELOPMENT

The war correspondent Colonel Ernest Swinton suggested using Holt caterpillar tractors to cut gaps in belts of barbed wire but tests at Shoeburyness in February 1915 were disappointing. Winston Churchill, First Lord of the Admiralty, formed the Land Ship Committee to see if track-laying vehicles and steamrollers could be used to smash wire and cross trenches. Early prototypes, including a Pedrail Landship, a converted tractor called the Tritton Trench Crosser, and a huge tricycle driven by three track-laying units all failed to impress.

William Tritton of William Foster and Company in Lincolnshire and Lieutenant Walter Wilson, a Royal Naval Volunteer Reserve officer, eventually produced No. 1 Lincoln Machine, a large steel box mounted on two tracks. Plans to install a rotating turret

were abandoned and, after modified tracks and new track rollers had been fitted, the machine (christened *Little Willie*) completed the War Office's obstacle course on 30 November 1915.

The War Office made the tests more difficult, forcing the two men to redesign the tank as a rhomboid to increase the length of the tracks; gun mountings (called sponsons) were also bolted to the sides. *Mother*, as it was known, passed the new tests and an order for 100 tanks was placed in December 1915.

TANK MARK I

The tank weighed 28 tons and measured over 26 feet long and 13 feet wide. The 105hp Daimler engine gave it a top speed of 4mph on flat ground, but it slowed to a crawl on the battlefield. It could cross trenches up to 10 feet wide, mount obstacles up to 5 feet high, climb a 1:11 gradient and crush wire entanglements. Fuel capacity was 50 gallons which limited the tank to a 10-mile circuit.

Two models were produced. The Male was armed with 2 x 6-pounder Hotchkiss guns and 4 Hotchkiss machine guns. Female tanks were armed with 6 machine guns, 5 Vickers and 1 Hotchkiss. The two types were designed to work together in pairs.

A subaltern led each tank's 8-man crew. The driver directed the two gearsmen, as they manoeuvred the tank. Brakes were applied to a track to make a gentle turn. Severe turns involved stopping the tank and disengaging one of the gearboxes so that the tank turned on the other track. Trail wheels to aid steering and improve balance were tried but they were soon abandoned. Four gunners clambered around the cramped interior to operate the weapons.

Early tanks were mechanically unreliable and liable to become bogged down but they proved to be invaluable during their first battle on 15 September 1916. GHQ responded to the success by requesting 1,000 machines.

They were vulnerable to artillery fire and when bullets or shrapnel struck the tank molten metal splashes sprayed the inside. The crews wore chain-mail visors, leather skullcaps and overalls but these gave little protection, and the heat, noise and exhaust fumes from the engine were debilitating.

TANKS MARK II AND MARK III

Mark II and Mark III training tanks, with thin armour, were built at the end of 1916 and used at Bovington training area in Dorset. A small number took part in the Battle of Arras in April 1917.

TANK MARK IV

A larger fuel tank increased the range and the armour thickness increased to 15mm. The smaller Lewis machine guns were used and the 6-pounder gun was shortened. Narrower sponsons meant that these did not have to be removed when the tank was transported by rail. An un-ditching beam, a huge timber baulk chained to the roof of the tank, was also added. It could be dragged underneath the

The prototype tank, known as *Mother*, negotiates an obstacle course in front of War Office observers. *(IWM Q70941)*

German prisoners carry a wounded soldier to the rear as a Mark IV tank heads up to the front line. The crew would drop the timber beam under the tracks to gain traction if the tank became stuck. (IWM CO2973)

tracks and provide extra traction if the tank was stuck. Fascines, huge bundles of wood, were also often tied on top of tanks ready to be dropped into wide trenches to form a bridge.

The first Mark IV tanks reached the front in May 1917 and went into action for the first time on 7 June on Messines Ridge.

TANK MARK V

A new engine increased the operating range to 45 miles and the improved steering and control mechanism allowed the driver to steer the tank single-handed. The Mark V was used for the first time on 4 July 1918 at Hamel. Variants were used as supply carriers and gun carriers to transport machine-gun teams into battle.

TANK MARK V*

The Mark V* was 6 feet longer that the Mark V and was able cross wide trenches without using a fascine. It was particularly useful for crossing the extensive trench systems during the Battles of the Hindenburg Line in September 1918.

WHIPPET TANK

William Tritton of Fosters designed this light tank (also known as the Medium A or Tritton Chaser), which was operated by a crew of three or four men and weighed only 14 tons. It still only had an average speed of 6mph (top speed 8mph) but it did have a large operating radius. It was armed with three Hotchkiss machine guns and a spare.

Whippet tanks were used in action for the first time on 26 March 1918, during the

German attack on the Somme. They were used extensively during the Advance to Victory.

ARMOURED CARS

The Eastchurch Squadron of the Royal Naval Air Service operated a number of unarmoured cars in support of the Royal Navy Marine Brigade's operations in Belgium in September and October 1914. While operating in the reconnaissance role for the Belgian Army, several cars were armoured by adding boiler plates to their sides.

Early armoured models were Rolls-Royce Silver Ghost and Lanchester tourers built for the Admiralty and the first batch of 50 cars reached the BEF at the end of 1914; Seabrook made armoured cars for the Royal Naval Air Service.

The Royal Navy expanded the squadrons into an Armoured Car Division of 15 squadrons, each with 3 sections of 4 cars. An armoured lorry and two General Service wagons carried spares and ammunition; 8 despatch riders rode motorcycles.

The division was disbanded in the summer of 1915 and 13 of the squadrons transferred to the Army. Two squadrons went to the Mediterranean intended for Gallipoli; they had to be directed to Egypt when the campaign bogged down. Several squadrons served in East Africa.

No. 20 Squadron was converted into an experimental unit working with the Land Ship Committee on the development of the tank. No. 15 Squadron served for a time with the expeditionary force in north Russia.

GAS

Poison gas affected thousands of men and, while the majority of casualties were soon back on duty, many would suffer with breathing difficulties for the rest of their lives (only 3% of gas casualties died).

The Mark V had changed little from the original model; this Male version is armed with 6-pounder guns. *(IWM Q14485)*

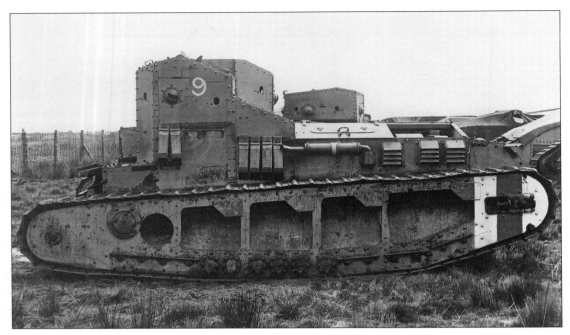

The lighter, and marginally faster, Whippet tank was armed with machine guns. *(IWM STT229)*

CHLORINE GAS

The Germans used chlorine gas for the first time against French troops north of Ypres, on 22 April 1915, creating havoc across the Salient. Despite widespread condemnation of this type of weapon, experiments were started in Britain and the first test took place on 13 May. Pressurized iron cylinders with a siphon and stopcock were used to spray the gas into no man's land, and batteries of cylinders formed gas clouds. GHQ's meteorological section had to monitor the weather and predict favourable wind conditions so that the clouds would be blown over the German lines.

The first consignment was known as Accessory Number One (later code-named Red Star) and the first gas attack was launched at Loos on 25 September 1915 using over 5,000 cylinders. Despite the disappointing results, General Haig expanded the gas troops into the Special Brigade when he took command of the BEF at the end of 1915.

PHOSGENE GAS

On 19 December 1915 the Germans released phosgene (carbonyl chloride) near Ypres. The gas had no distinctive smell and a man could inhale small amounts before he noticed the effects. It attacked the body in a similar way to chlorine, slowly dissolving the lungs. When used from cylinders the phosgene was mixed with chlorine. Phosgene was used under the code name White Star; 98 British gas attacks consumed 1,120 tons of gas during the 1916 Somme campaign.

OTHER COMPOUNDS

Three other mixtures were tried in an attempt to improve on White Star. They were unsuitable and were only used in small quantities:

Two Red Star: a mixture of hydrogen sulphide and carbon bisulphide.
Green Star: a mixture of hydrogen sulphide and chloropicrin.
Yellow Star: a mixture of chlorine and chloropicrin.
Chloropicrin was known as **PS gas**, from the factory at Port Sunlight.

The crew of an armoured car has stopped alongside a dressing station on the road to Guillemont as medics of the Guards Division load wounded onto a waiting ambulance. *(IWM Q1222)*

LACHRYMATORY OR TEAR GAS

The Germans first used lachrymatory shell in March 1915 to blind men temporarily during an attack on the Western Front. Gas masks were improved to counter the effects and GHQ requested its own version in June 1915. Lachrymatory shell for the 4.5-inch howitzer, filled with ethyl idoacetate (code-named SK as it was produced at South Kensington) arrived in September 1915.

MUSTARD GAS

Mustard gas (dichloroethyl sulphide) was used by the Germans for the first time in July 1917; it permanently damaged major organs and acted as a blistering agent on the skin. The official code name was Yellow Cross, but the soldiers sometimes referred to it as HS gas, or 'Hun Stuff'. Mustard gas would linger for days in shell-holes and dugouts and it accounted for 80% of British gas casualties during 1918.

A field demonstration of a gas cylinder. *(IWM Q113282)*

GAS SHELLS

Distributing gas cylinders along the front line took time and labour and favourable weather for this type of attack could not be guaranteed or reliably predicted. General Haig therefore requested lethal gas shell in January 1916, particularly so the artillery could gas German billets and artillery batteries some distance behind the front line. Trials with Jellite (JL), a prussic acid mixture, proved successful and 160,000 lethal gas shells had been fired by the end of the year. Phosgene gas shells were perfected in 1917 and used in great quantities. Mustard gas shells were introduced too. Gas shells were also made for the 4-inch Stokes mortar.

EXPERIMENTAL SECTION

An Inventions Committee with General Staff, Royal Artillery and Royal Engineer officers, was set up at GHQ in June 1915 to examine new inventions and modifications to existing weapons. An Experimental Section replaced the Committee and tested items under field conditions, reporting the results to the Chief Engineer.

Experiments with grenades, catapults, mortars and land mines were carried out while armour-piercing bullets, body armour and mobile shields were tested on firing ranges. Many aids, including wire cutters, flares, smoke producers, anti-tank defences, and optical instruments were also tried.

Many strange inventions, including bows to fire arrows tipped with high explosive, chain shot, a boomerang hand grenade to throw around corners, a kite to drop explosives and even a death ray (which proved to be a fake), were offered. Fire hoses to flood enemy trenches, grappling hooks to pull wire aside and fans to repel gas were all tried but most were impractical and failed to pass the section's rigorous tests.

CHAPTER TEN

TACTICS

OPEN WARFARE IN 1914

THE INFANTRY

The main infantry weapon was the rifle and great emphasis was placed on fire and movement. Part of a company or platoon advanced in extended order, moving forward in short rushes to establish a firing line 200 yards from the enemy position. The rest of the men gave covering fire joined by the machine guns and the artillery. More men moved forward until the unit had fire superiority and it was time to push home the attack. Supports were supposed to reinforce the line where the advance had stalled but it soon became clear

Troops deploy in a roadside ditch during the early days of the fighting around Ypres; before long they would be digging their own trenches. *(IWM Q53320)*

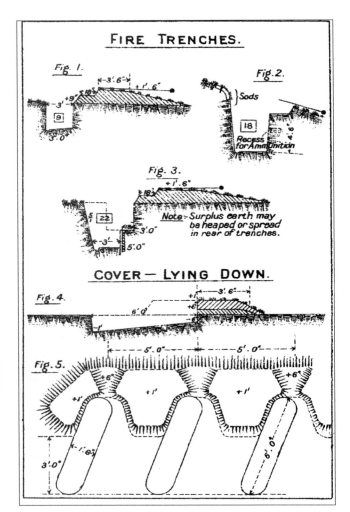

The textbook methods for creating prone cover and fire trenches.

that success depended on outflanking the enemy position.

The infantry used natural terrain features for concealment and only dug in when they expected to stay in the same place for some time. They would dig a shallow scrape and heap the earth to form head cover to begin with, digging deeper when the opportunity offered.

A machine gun was estimated to be equivalent to 40 rifles and they were placed at strategic points, preferably with extensive fields of fire.

THE CAVALRY

Despite setbacks for the cavalry during the Boer War, many senior commanders persisted in focussing training on large-scale shock charges. Others believed that the cavalry's primary role would be as mounted infantry, performing reconnaissance during an advance or acting as a rearguard during a retreat.

According to the regulations in force in 1910, cavalrymen only spent a fraction of their time practising reconnaissance and marksmanship but the balance was restored two years later and by the summer of 1914 the troopers could fire aimed shots as rapidly as the infantry.

Apart from a handful of isolated (usually impromptu) charges against formed troops, the cavalry worked tirelessly to cover the infantry during the retreat from Mons and the advance to the Aisne, providing vital intelligence on the German dispositions.

THE ARTILLERY

Pre-war training placed the emphasis on direct fire support for the infantry. Crews would deploy near the firing line, shooting over open sights at visible targets. Indirect fire (shooting at hidden targets) and predicted fire (firing at map references) were considered to be a waste of ammunition. However, direct fire meant that gun crews were vulnerable to the enemy, and the shields on the gun carriages gave little protection.

The guns could be set up out of sight of the enemy to protect the crews from enemy fire, while an observer positioned himself on high ground ahead of the battery. Targets and range adjustments would be signalled with semaphore flags and the observer would direct ranging shots by one gun until it scored a direct hit. The officer then calculated the adjustments required by each gun before the battery fired for effect.

TRENCH WARFARE
EARLY TRENCHES

The first trenches were dug where the advancing forces came to a halt but in many

An 18-pounder keeps up a rapid rate of fire in Mesopotamia. The officer gives instructions while No. 1 makes alterations with the trail. No. 2 and No. 3 sit either side of the barrel, setting the range and opening the breech respectively. No. 4 loads the shell into the breech while No. 5 and No. 6 (not pictured) pass shells to the crew. *(IWM Q24267A)*

areas the Germans withdrew to high ground so they could overlook the battlefield. British troops dug their first crude trench systems on the Aisne Heights in September 1914. After the move to Flanders, the BEF was forced to dig in around Ypres as its numbers dwindled in the face of fierce attacks. Trenches conserved manpower and protected the men from machine-gun and artillery fire. The short sections of trench were gradually joined into one continuous line during the winter of 1914–15 and then expanded into extensive systems as the troops prepared for a long war.

Under ideal conditions a platoon of soldiers could dig a 3 feet deep fire trench, piling the spoil to form a parapet, in less than 2 hours; it took far longer when men were under fire. Tools and materials were always in short supply and the small stock of sandbags was quickly exhausted (each battalion only had 32 in 1914). The men foraged for timber and used gabions or sacks filled with earth to support the trench. Barbed wire was usually a single strand festooned with tin cans to serve as an alarm. Caltrops or planks studded with nails would be scattered in front of the wire.

The style and condition of trenches varied considerably. The heavy clay and high water table across Flanders resulted in shallow, flooded trenches. Pumps and sump holes were used to drain the water but some trenches were permanently flooded. Duckboards (timber walkways) allowed the water to drain away, leaving a dry path. Water turned the clay into a slurry, leaving clothes and weapons coated in mud. In some areas sandbag walls, known as breastworks, increased the protection. Chalk subsoil and a low water table on the Somme allowed the men to dig deep trenches and dugouts. Timber shoring, known as revetting, stopped the sides caving in.

THE LAYOUT OF THE TRENCHES

NO MAN'S LAND

A wasteland of abandoned crops, shell-holes and corpses separated the two front-line trenches. It could be half a mile wide in flat areas, narrowing to a few yards apart on important terrain features.

BARBED WIRE

Wire entanglements were erected in no man's land to disorganize attacking troops, keeping them out of bomb-throwing range of the fire trench. At night wiring parties crawled out through prearranged gaps to mend damaged sections or add new obstacles. From single fences, the wire grew into large entanglements interspersed with rolls of concertina wire. Trench lines were eventually protected by several belts connected by single strands, known as spider wire, set to trip up the careless soldier. Belts of wire would be hidden in ditches and dead ground while deliberate gaps were left to funnel the enemy towards hidden machine guns.

THE FIRE TRENCH

The front trench was made up of a series of traverses and bays (creating a zig-zag line) to minimize the damage from artillery fire; it also made the trench easier to defend if the enemy entered it. There was usually a small step at the front of the trench (called a fire step) so men could step up and peer over the parapet (often a wall of sandbags); observation posts and loopholes were built into the sandbags. A low wall of sandbags or earth, called the parados, was built behind the trench so that

A perfect example of a communications trench in the Ypres Salient. While duckboards keep the bottom dry, revetting and sandbags keep the sides stable. *(IWM CO277)*

men did not present a clear silhouette. Wooden frames wrapped in barbed wire, known as knife-rests, were placed at regular intervals along the trench, ready to be dragged into place to form a barrier.

SUPPORT LINE

The second trench, or support line, had many dugouts for headquarters, first aid posts, signal stations, stores and water points. To begin with men dug shallow holes into the side of the trench for shelter but funk holes ('funk' was slang for 'fear'), as they were known, undermined the sides of the trench and were discouraged.

When materials became available, dugouts were built from corrugated iron and timber frames, and covered with earth and sandbags. They protected the men against bullets, grenades and shrapnel but a direct hit by a high explosive shell would collapse the shelter, burying the men inside. Most dugouts were only large enough for a couple of men but elaborate shelters housed company head-quarters and battalion aid posts. In areas with a high water table, entire shelters would be constructed above ground.

Each battalion appointed a bombing officer to organize supplies and training. Detonators were inserted in the bombs in shelters to the rear and they were then brought forward in boxes to dumps at the heads of the communication trenches. Bomb stores were installed at the end of short T-shaped trenches in case of an explosion.

Machine-gun and trench mortar teams and rifle grenadiers were often stationed in the support trench. Their posts usually had a crew dugout and an ammunition shelter. Latrines, usually a hole covered by a plank seat, could also be found in the support line.

COMMUNICATION TRENCHES

Connecting trenches ran perpendicular to the front lines. They were the only way into and out of the trench for men and supplies.

STRONGPOINTS

Strongpoints were built at regular intervals

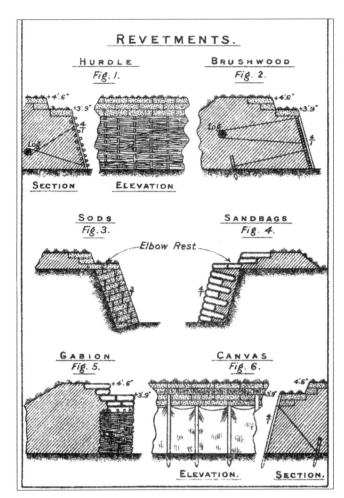

Different methods for supporting the sides of a trench.

behind the front line in case of an enemy breakthrough. They protected men during the enemy's artillery barrage, enabling them to emerge unscathed to engage the enemy infantry. Engineers fortified ruins, or built large dugouts with firing slits with an all-round view; it was desirable to have more than one entrance. Inside there would be room for weapons, ammunition and sleeping space for the men; a telephone kept the strongpoint in contact with its headquarters. In many cases trenches were dug around the strongpoint so that the men could cover every angle with fire.

As the months passed, strongpoints became more elaborate and they were often linked together into defended localities, protecting villages and hills. A company-sized strongpoint would have machine-gun posts and dugouts for the men on the perimeter with a head-quarters dugout and accommodation for a reserve platoon in the centre.

PILLBOXES

The British Army did not build concrete structures in great numbers until 1918. However, the Royal Engineers built numerous observation posts for the Royal Artillery, constructing towers and strengthening the roofs of buildings with concrete.

The Germans invested heavily in reinforced positions, strengthening buildings and building machine-gun posts, pillboxes and shelters along the front line; command posts, field hospitals and communication centres were built in the rear areas. British troops often used captured concrete shelters but they were prone to attract artillery fire.

By the end of 1917 the Royal Engineers had started to study the German structures and work started on prefabricated concrete pill-boxes. First Army experimented with a reinforced blocks and beams system while Second Army developed wall blocks with channels and holes for reinforcing bars. Trials at the artillery grounds at Shoeburyness in

Hands and feet numbed by the cold, a sentry of the 12th East Yorkshires keeps a watch over no man's land near Roclincourt. *(IWM Q10620)*

This was the usual state of a trench following a bombardment: collapsed sides, torn sandbags, shattered debris and corpses. In some cases the trench could be reduced to nothing more than a shallow ditch. *(IWM Q28972)*

Essex in August 1918 proved that both patterns could withstand a direct hit from a German 5.9-inch shell. GHQ adopted First Army's reinforced blocks and Second Army's design.

Sir Ernest Moir of the Ministry of Munitions invented the Moir Pillbox, capable of withstanding a direct hit from a field gun and a near miss by a 5.9-inch shell. Interlocking curved concrete blocks were built into a cylinder, six feet in diameter. A steel dome, with a revolving Vickers machine-gun mounting hung inside, was placed on top of the wall. It was usually dug into the ground, with the entrance at trench level, leaving the dome protruding. They could be built above ground in marshy areas and surrounded with reinforced concrete. About 1,500 were made and erected in the summer of 1918.

Major-General J. Talbot Hobbs, commander of 5th Australian Division, designed the Hobbs Pillbox, a revolving steel cupola for a two-man machine-gun team. It was bolted onto steel sheeting, cast into a concrete floor, and the entire structure was encased with concrete; 210 were delivered to France.

Captain Webb, an Australian engineer, designed the Webb Observation Post, a small look-out post made of curved sections of corrugated iron (known as elephant shelters) on their sides; the mould was then filled with concrete.

SNIPING

Enemy sniping took its toll on the men, restricting movement and lowering morale, but British Army sniping took some time to gain official recognition and individual

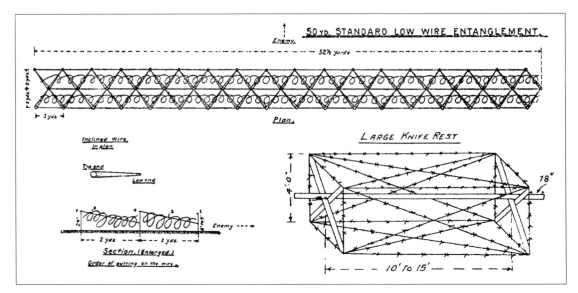

Low wire entanglements kept the enemy at bay while knife rests were kept on stand-by in the trenches in case they broke through.

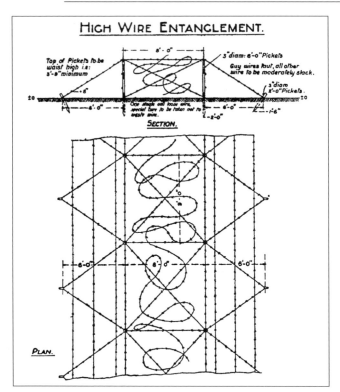

Pickets, wooden or steel posts, kept the entanglements stable.

regiments formed private schools. Army schools eventually took over training.

Apart from making life difficult for the men across no man's land, snipers were continually trying to outwit their opposite number in a deadly game of cat and mouse. One team would work as a decoy, encouraging snipers to shoot while other teams watched for muzzle flashes. On the rare occasions that a battalion found itself under attack in daylight, snipers were instructed to fire at key members of the enemy unit, targeting officers and machine gunners.

LIFE IN THE TRENCHES

Conditions varied considerably along the front and, while many sectors were quiet for long periods, snipers and the occasional artillery shell kept the men on their guard. Tactical positions were constantly fought over and the men in such areas were shelled and shot day and night while underground mines could explode without warning.

Each season brought its problems. The spring and autumn rains turned the trenches into drains. The wet conditions numbed feet and men were crippled by trench foot, a condition where the flesh died and rotted away. Summer heat encouraged lice, flies and maggots to breed while rats fed on discarded waste and corpses. Snow and ice in winter caused exposure or frostbite.

DAYTIME ROUTINE

Trench life was a mixture of boredom, physical work and sheer terror. Dawn was a likely time for an enemy attack so 'stand to' was called shortly before and the men in the front trench climbed onto the fire step ready to meet an enemy assault. It rarely came and the men returned to their daily routine. During daylight hours the men were kept busy according to a timetable of ration parties, repair works and sentry duty. Men in the front trench carried their weapons at all times and bayonets would be fitted at night or in poor visibility.

Sentries, usually one man in ten during the day, kept a close eye on no man's land at lookout posts or with the aid of a box type periscope. Working parties collected ammunition, equipment and rations requested by the battalion quartermaster sergeant and carried them by hand down the communication trenches to shelters in the trenches. Many men were kept busy digging new trenches and repairing damaged ones with sandbags.

There was an officer on duty at all times in each company sector. He moved along the line, visiting sentries and working parties, while checking weapons and equipment were in good order. Sergeants and corporals kept their men busy, reporting to the duty officer every hour; they inspected the men's rifles twice a day. A man needed his NCO's permission to leave a post while officers granted permission to leave the trenches.

As most activity took place at night the remainder of the men were allowed to rest, writing, reading or sleeping where they could.

ROUTINE AT NIGHT

After stand to at dusk, the number of sentries increased to one man in four as no man's land

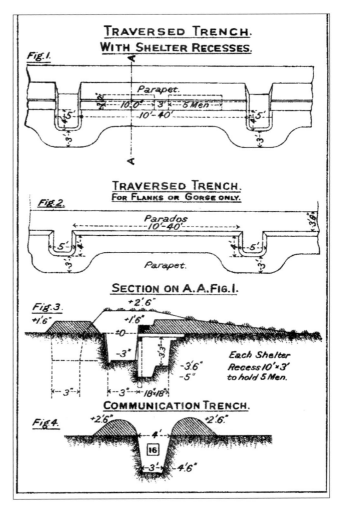

The standard dimensions for trenches and dugouts, but in reality the trenches were anything but standard.

came alive. Boredom, fatigue and the cold or wet weather conspired to distract the sentry as he struggled to remain vigilant for signs of activity. Once alerted he could call for illumination flares to light up the area and put the rest of his unit on alert; coded flare signals could call down artillery SOS bombardments on predetermined points.

Sentries were often posted in camouflaged outposts known as saps. Towards the end of the war the number of saps manned by Lewis gun teams increased, so that fewer men were needed to hold the fire trench.

Two Highlanders pay little attention to the jumble of weapons, tools and equipment scattered around their dugout near Mametz Wood, as they eat their rations. *(IWM Q4445)*

When it was dark, wiring parties crept out from their trenches into no man's land to mend damaged wire and put up new entanglements while sentries kept a look-out. The men worked as silently as possible, knocking in posts with muffled mallets (pickets with corkscrews at the base which did not need to be hammered in were introduced before long) and hanging wire. It was nerve-racking work and the smallest sound could alert a German sentry.

TRENCH RAIDS

One night-time activity the men detested was the trench raid. Before setting off the men taking part would remove excess equipment, strap down anything likely to make a noise and blacken their faces and hands. Bombing parties were useful for leading trench raids, and the men armed themselves with an array of revolvers, bayonets, knives or improvised weapons like knobkerries (nail-studded batons) rather than rifles.

A raiding party, ranging in size from a platoon to several companies, would attempt to crawl across no man's land without being seen. The artillery shelled the surrounding area while other units tried to draw attention away from the raiders. Once in the enemy trenches, the raiders caused mayhem, silencing sentries, throwing bombs into dugouts and attacking anyone who came to investigate. The objective of the raid was usually to discover the identity of the enemy unit, taking papers or shoulder patches off the dead; the real prize was to take a prisoner back across no man's land alive.

ROTATION AND RELIEFS

During the early months of the war, battalions could spend weeks in the line without a rest. By the spring of 1915 a system of rotation had been introduced and a brigade would usually hold its trenches with two battalions. A support battalion would be sheltering in dugouts or ruined buildings close by, while the remaining battalion was billeted in villages, farms or camps at a safe distance. Both the support and reserve battalions were kept busy with training or manual work and each night parties would carry rations and supplies into the trenches.

Usually battalions spent eight days in the line, four days in support and four days in reserve, continually rotating to give the men time to rest. Handing over a sector (called the relief) was a dangerous time and had to be carried out in complete silence. Officers went first to make arrangements with their opposite numbers and review the section of trench. One by one platoons and sentries would exchange positions until the relief was complete; the operation could take all night.

THE ARTILLERY

The batteries used ruined buildings and copses to hide their guns to begin with but these soon became recognized targets for the enemy artillery. When labour became available purpose-built emplacements were established and the corps artillery staff sequenced the construction work as follows:

Surveyors marked out gun pits so artillery boards could be prepared.

Splinter- and weather-proof observation posts were built.

Brigade headquarters were fixed and work started on underground telephone cables.

Command posts and communication centres were built.

Weather-proof covers were erected to camouflage the gun pits.

Labourers dug the gun pits, ammunition recesses and crew shelters.

Battery positions within 3,000 yards of the front line were surrounded with wire.

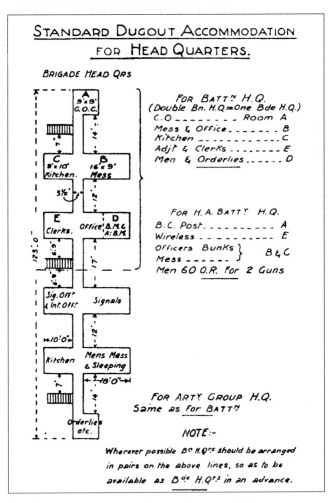

Headquarters dugouts could be elaborate affairs dug by tunnellers.

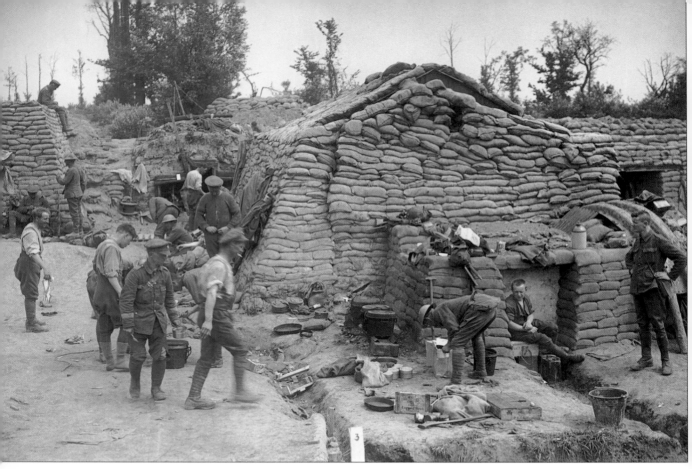

Thousands of sandbags were used to turn isolated positions into fortified emplacements like this example near Kemmel. *(IWM Q5477)*

Ideally observation posts could overlook an area 1,000 yards beyond the front line and special posts for long-distance observation were built and long-range periscopes installed. A flexible communications system allowed the batteries to talk to different observation posts and connections to kite balloons, sound-ranging sections and observation groups allowed a brigade commander to call down a rapid concentration of fire on pre-determined targets. A large number of alternative gun pits would be built so guns could be moved if the German artillery discovered a battery position.

PREPARING FOR BATTLE

There was plenty of work for the infantry, engineers, pioneers and artillery to do when an offensive was imminent. By 1915 large-scale models of the objectives, made of sand, wood and bricks, were being used and while the assault troops rehearsed behind the lines, their officers visited the front trenches to view the battlefield.

The influx of assault troops into an area required extra dugouts and trenches; new assembly trenches would be dug in no man's land where it was wide. Dummy trenches, dug a few inches deep with turf piled alongside and extra breastworks were often built to distract the Germans' attention from the real trenches. Extra communication trenches were added. Some were labelled Up trenches for men and ammunition moving forward, and others were designated Down trenches for evacuating the wounded.

It was essential that the men were able to form up and move quickly into no man's land. Ladders were placed in the trenches and bridges were laid over the top the night before an attack to improve access and hidden openings were made in breastworks so the men did not have to climb over the top. Out in no man's land working parties opened gaps in the British wire, usually making oblique passageways that were difficult to spot.

All along the front extra supplies, including water, rations, tools and stores, were stockpiled in new shelters while ammunition and grenades were stored in shellproof magazines. Behind the lines new roads and tracks were built and hidden by camouflage netting; one-way systems had to be used to prevent traffic jams. Light railways were also built to within a few hundred yards of the front line to carry supplies forward.

The artillery needed new gun positions and, while some were dug into the ground and camouflaged, in other places platforms of bricks and planks had to be built on soft ground to stop the guns sinking into the mud. Observation for the preliminary and supporting bombardments was also important. The Royal Flying Corps hunted for targets and engineers built new observation posts in houses, churches, chimneys and even haystacks.

THE PRELIMINARY BOMBARDMENT

Neuve Chapelle in March 1915 was the first time that timetables and set targets were issued to batteries, dictating rates of fire and boundaries of the bombardment. The divisional heavy batteries and the siege artillery had also been organized into three heavy artillery groups and were controlled by GHQ during the battle. From September 1915 the various corps headquarters took control of the bombardment, coordinating observation and target allocation, while arranging communications and ammunition supply. Batteries reverted to divisional control at zero hour.

By 1916 the practice of intensifying the barrage in the countdown to zero was abandoned and the artillery rehearsed the barrage on a daily basis to lull the enemy into a false sense of security.

WIRE CUTTING

The field artillery started attempting to cut the barbed wire early in the bombardment.

Batteries used direct fire in daylight hours, firing in short, sharp bursts from hidden positions close to the front line. The same areas were targeted at night to harass working parties. A corps could consume 17,000 rounds a day on wire cutting. Larger trench mortars were used to cut barbed wire when observation was difficult.

FIRE TRENCHES AND STRONGPOINTS

The howitzers were positioned around 2 miles from the German front line. Heavy howitzers shelled the front-line trenches with random barrages, aiming to isolate the men there from the rear. Small sections of trench, in particular junctions, were targeted with short bursts until the guns were registered; the trench could then be shelled by the whole battery. Howitzers doubled their rate of fire at night when the enemy were likely to be supplying the front line.

When gas shells were introduced, batteries would fire high explosives to drive men underground. Gas shell would then be mixed in with the HE in the hope of catching the enemy as they emerged from their dugouts.

Heavy howitzers aimed to destroy strongpoints completely, firing successive barrages at random intervals. These small targets were difficult to hit and rarely targeted at night. Delayed-action fuses improved the chances of knocking out a strongpoint.

COMMUNICATION TRENCHES

Medium 4.5-inch howitzers tried to destroy short sections of trench and then targeted the same area at random intervals to disrupt working parties. A corps could consume 3,700 rounds a day on cutting communication trenches.

COUNTER-BATTERY FIRE

Heavy artillery reserve groups concentrated on counter-battery work, relying on information gathered by the Royal Flying Corps. It was estimated that over 100 rounds of 6-inch howitzer shell were needed to destroy a gun position so the heavy howitzers hit the ammunition dumps and ammunition wagons

Engineers concrete the roof of a strongpoint near Wieltje in the Ypres Salient. *(IWM Q10264)*

instead, aiming to isolate the guns from their supplies. They concentrated on the battery positions during the final hours of the bombardment. Gas shells were frequently used to discomfort the crews.

BILLETS AND ROADS

The 60-pounders and 6-inch guns targeted tracks, headquarters or observation posts and batteries would randomly switch targets, using different types of bombardment to confuse the enemy. The batteries would use map fire at night to target roads and billets where there would probably be a considerable amount of movement.

MACHINE GUNS

Machine-gun teams set up their weapons on portable platforms, ideally with a good view over the enemy trenches. They fired random barrages to disrupt working parties and ammunition parties, paying particular attention to the enemy's barbed wire at night, hoping to disrupt repairs.

RANDOM CREEPING BARRAGES

The heavy and medium artillery would occasionally fire creeping barrages, starting at the front line and walking the fire forwards over a mile beyond the final objective, while the field artillery and machine guns swept the enemy front line.

DIVISIONAL ORDERS

While the artillery went ahead with the pre-liminary bombardment, the staff officers at corps headquarters were putting their final touches to the divisional orders. Divisions often only moved into the front line a few days (or even hours) before the attack and the staff had to be fully briefed on what to expect. Orders were complex and they varied enormously to suit individual objectives. The following is a list of items covered:

GENERAL CONSIDERATIONS

The times for assembly and assembly areas were listed.

Brigade dumps and allocated communications trenches were referenced.

Objectives and the boundaries were given with map references, trench names and locations.

Maps were issued showing the layout of the enemy trenches and the objective lines coloured.

The deployment of the German forces in the front line was outlined.

Details of German reserves in the area were given as well as their expected time of arrival.

THE ARTILLERY PLAN

The artillery and machine-gun timetables were detailed.

Arrangements for liaison between the artillery and the infantry were noted.

Timetables for the redeployment of the artillery and machine guns were listed.

THE INFANTRY PLAN OF ATTACK

The division's boundaries and deployment were given, detailing battalion dispositions.

Each stage of the attack was outlined, detailing objectives and timings.

The locations of battalion and brigade head-quarters were given.

Arrangements for tank deployment and coordination with the infantry were set out.

The positions of machine guns giving direct support to the infantry were given.

CONSOLIDATION

Orders for consolidating the objective, detailing the use of reserves, were listed.

COMMUNICATIONS

Methods of communicating with headquarters were given.

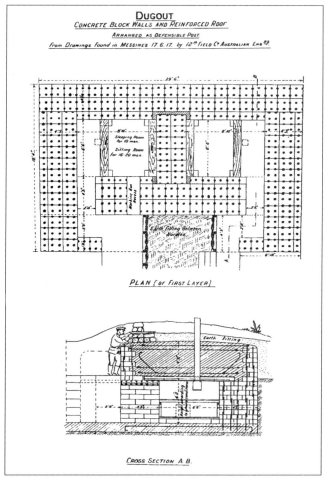

Bunkers were built using concrete block walls, reinforced by steel bars; the structure was then covered by earth. The men could shelter inside until the enemy bombardment ended.

Timings for communicating by messenger and the times of contact planes were timetabled.

OTHER CONSIDERATIONS

Transport arrangements for supplies and the wounded were scheduled.

Any methods of deception to be employed, for example fake attacks, were detailed.

The arrangements for mining operations (when available) were outlined.

Collection points for prisoners and the location of transfer camps were referenced.

THE FINAL HOURS

As soon as it was dark, units moved to their designated assembly points, aiming to be in position before the early hours. En route the men would drop off their packs at the brigade dump, picking up ammunition, tools, equipment and rations; several platoons (often four per battalion) would be left at the dump to act as carrying parties.

Men took their gas masks, rations for the day, water bottle and an iron ration into battle as well as their rifle with 120 rounds of ammunition, bayonet and entrenching tool. Each man had to pick up a signalling flare and four empty sandbags and every second man carried a pick or a shovel strapped to his back while others carried wire cutters. Everybody carried two Mills bombs in their pockets and

The infantry were kept busy maintaining their trenches while the enemy artillery did their best to destroy them. As these men of the 15th Royal Welsh Fusiliers (London Welsh) fill sandbags in the Fleurbaix sector, others bring curved corrugated iron sheets to complete a dugout. *(IWM Q8372)*

A wiring party carry a new supply of screw picquets up to the front line at Feuchy, east of Arras, in May 1917. *(IWM Q5258)*

had to drop them off in the captured trench for the bombing squads; each company also took phosphorous bombs for clearing out dugouts.

At brigade headquarters, a staff officer from corps headquarters paid a visit to synchronize watches and a couple of hours before zero guides led the assault troops into the trenches. In some cases white tapes and boards covered in luminous paint marked the start line (jumping off line) for the first wave in no man's land. The aim was to get the men into position an hour or two before zero. If tanks were being used, guides would lead them forward to their assembly areas, as planes flew overhead to drown out the engine noise.

Battalions often deployed on a company, or 4-platoon front, with waves following at 75-yard intervals; it would take around 6 minutes for a battalion to leave the trenches. The support waves waited in the assembly trenches, moving forward as each wave climbed out into no man's land. Parties of engineers and pioneers mingled among the infantry, ready to advance to tactical points to begin building strongpoints.

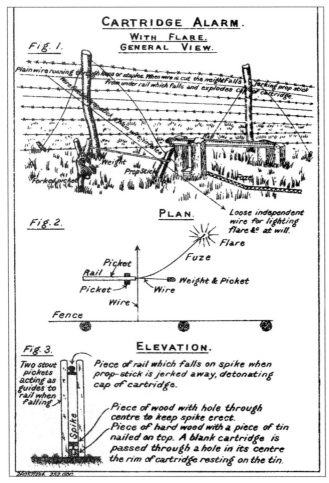

Troops used a variety of methods to lay traps to stop enemy patrols breaking through the wire; this example uses a trip wire and a blank cartridge to ignite a fuse that would light a flare over the wire entanglement.

Behind the lines, field ambulances cleared their dressing stations ready to accept the wounded while artillery crews fired their final phase of the preparatory bombardment.

With everyone in place, the assault troops had to wait as the minutes ticked by, hoping that the preliminary barrage had been successful; for many their last few minutes alive would be spent waiting for zero. As the officers blew their whistles, men wished each other good luck and climbed out of the trench into the unknown.

THE INFANTRY ASSAULT
DEPLOYMENT

Typically a division deployed 2 brigades in the trenches with the third in reserve; the divisional commander needed clearance from corps headquarters to deploy his reserve. Deployments varied but each brigade usually placed 2 battalions in front and 2 behind; each battalion either deployed its 4 companies one behind the other, or 2 in front and 2 behind. As zero hour approached the leading wave would climb out of their trench and form up beyond the wire in no man's land close to their barrage.

CROSSING NO MAN'S LAND

During the battles of 1915 and the early stages of the Somme in 1916, the men filed through gaps in their wire, dressed their ranks, and advanced at the walk at 5-yard intervals. One battalion followed a compass bearing across no man's land and the rest of the division was supposed to conform.

As each wave moved forward, the next one assembled in no man's land and advanced at the prescribed time. Platoons moved off at 20-yard intervals and a company typically occupied an area 300 yards wide and 60 yards deep. Companies sometimes advanced on a 2-platoon frontage, halving the width and doubling the depth. The next company would leave a gap of around 75 yards before moving off. The 2 remaining companies would deploy in small columns of men spaced at wide intervals (known as artillery formation) to avoid unnecessary casualties from shell-fire.

Typical timings for an advance to the first objective were as follows:

0–20 minutes	The infantry leave their trenches and advance close behind the barrage, as it moves forward at 50 yards per minute.
20–30 minutes	As the infantry approach the first objective, the barrage moves forward to cover the area in front.

A patrol prepares to raid the German trenches. Moments later a shell killed or injured several of these men. *(IWM Q5098)*

30–60 minutes Infantry clear and consolidate the first objective while the second wave moves up.

The artillery and infantry usually moved at a slower pace to subsequent objectives.

TAKING THE OBJECTIVES

The advance would be broken down into a series of objectives, marked by coloured lines on the infantry's map: for example the Green Line, Brown Line, Blue Line and finally the Red Line. On some occasions the leading company would be tasked to advance to the battalion's final objective while those following cleared the trenches behind in succession. If there was sufficient space for a covering barrage between objectives, the leading wave would consolidate the first objective and give covering fire as the next wave passed through, or leapfrogged, to the next objective.

The support waves had the problem of avoiding the German counter-barrage that inevitably started to hit no man's land a short time after zero hour. If possible the men kept close to the assault wave, crossing before the barrage began; there was, however, a danger that they would overcrowd the assembly trenches. Alternatively subsequent waves could cross no man's land in artillery formation, with the men spread out in small columns.

Following the same procedure as the first wave, the advance continued until the second objective had been taken; the remaining two waves could capture and consolidate the third objective. The support battalion would move through to attack the final objective, leaving a strong force covering the new front line, as the assault battalion regrouped.

Advances rarely went to plan and machine-gun fire could decimate companies, splitting the survivors into small groups as they bypassed craters. Casualties mounted as the men queued up to pass through narrow gaps in the wire and by the time the first wave reached the first enemy trench it would have been broken into disorganized groups.

CLEARING THE TRENCH

Tactics were soon developed to take an objective. While riflemen kept a watch from above, bombing teams systematically cleared the trench. Two bayonet men led each team as two grenadiers (called bombers from 1916) threw grenades into the next bay of the trench. Bombers sometimes worked in pairs, one for short throws and one for long throws. After the bombs exploded, the bayonet men entered the bay to deal with any survivors. Two men followed carrying a supply of bombs in

Filthy and exhausted after a spell in the Gueudecourt sector, the 4th Worcestershires assemble near Fricourt before moving to the rear in September 1916. *(IWM Q1455)*

A framework of timber and tree trunks holds together the sandbags on this field gun emplacement in the Ypres Salient; branches and foliage have been used to try and camouflage the position. *(IWM Q29072)*

buckets or boxes; pocketed vests were introduced later. The process was repeated until the bombers had cleared their section of trench. Two men followed with sandbags ready to build a barricade if the enemy counterattacked and they could also step in if there were casualties in the team. Two bombs were thrown into dugouts before the bayonet men checked for survivors. The use of phosphorus bombs (P bombs) to destroy dugouts was soon discouraged so the shelters could be reused. On the crater fields of the Somme and Flanders battlefields, a sniper and two rifle bombers sometimes accompanied the team, to keep the Germans at bay.

CONSOLIDATING THE OBJECTIVE

Once an enemy trench had been taken, the men started to put it into a state of defence while parties kept a look-out for the enemy.

Lewis gun teams, advancing with the second wave, occupied tactical points at the first opportunity, ready to give covering fire. Support weapon teams were easy to spot as they moved across the battlefield and they usually waited until the objective had been secured. Stokes mortars were set up in the trench while a number of Vickers gun teams occupied shell-holes to the rear, ready to give indirect fire support. Carrying parties followed, ferrying ammunition and stores to the assault troops.

Meanwhile, the infantry began reversing the trench to face the other way: making new fire steps, digging entrances and clearing obstacles. Royal Engineer field sections supervised work on strongpoints at preselected sites while the signals section started to bury their cables. The division's pioneer battalion was kept busy digging communication trenches and forming tracks for wheeled traffic across no man's land.

PLATOON TACTICS

By the autumn of 1916, the platoon had evolved into a small combined-arms unit with 4 sections each of about 9 men and their tactics were designed to make full use of the Lewis gun and the rifle grenade. *Instructions for the Training of Platoons for Offensive Action* was issued in February 1917, covering tactics for bombing parties and attacking pillboxes. It was the first time that the Lewis gun had been designated as the platoon's light support weapon.

Platoon officers and section NCOs were trained to use their own initiative, using the 4 sections to cover each other as they advanced, while looking to give covering fire

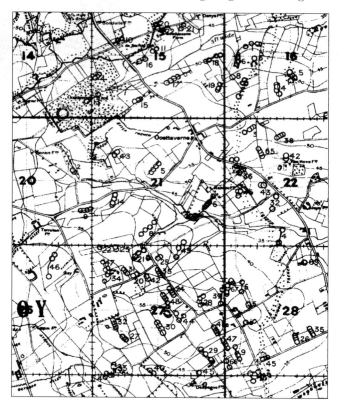

German batteries on Messines ridge are numbered so that observers could quickly call down artillery fire without referring to complicated map references.

to platoons on the flanks. The blob (where sections advanced as a small group) and the worm (where they moved forward in single file) were both tried. Scouts led the way and section commanders moved the men forward in short rushes, moving from shell-hole to shell-hole. The platoon diamond formation was also developed, with the 4 sections giving each other covering fire as they moved forward.

THE RIFLE SECTION

Riflemen were responsible for sniping and scouting, allowing the platoon leader to deploy the rest of the platoon in front of an enemy position. During the final assault some riflemen gave covering fire for the bombing team while the rest continued to snipe, making enemy officers and machine-gun teams a priority.

THE LEWIS GUN SECTION

The Lewis gun section often advanced in the centre of the platoon, the gun team moving separately to avoid attracting attention. Once close to an enemy position, the team usually moved out to one flank to give covering fire while the rest of the section brought up ammunition and set up a firing line on either side of the gun. The gun gave covering fire while the riflemen and bombers moved in for the final assault.

THE RIFLE BOMBER SECTION

This section was added to the platoon in 1916. The men fired smoke grenades to cover the platoon's advance, concentrating on blinding the enemy while the bombers crept forward. They switched to explosive grenades moments before the assault, hoping to stun the enemy.

BOMBING SECTION

The bombing party evolved into the bombing section. As the rest of the platoon gave covering fire, the team worked their way forward, one by one, until they were close enough to assault the enemy position. When they were in position, the Lewis gun team and riflemen gave covering fire and the rifle

A 12-inch railway gun targets German batteries on the Somme from its siding near Albert. *(IWM Q1372)*

bombers fired their grenades. During the final assault the bombers hurled bombs into the machine-gun post or bunker. Bombers reverted to the role of riflemen during the mobile warfare of 1918.

The Engineers

During the early stages of the war, engineers went forward with the assault waves to supervise the infantry as they consolidated the captured trench. The practice ceased during the 1916 Somme campaign due to heavy casualties and instead engineering teams crossed no man's land with the support waves. Their work on fortifications often went unnoticed due to poor coordination with the infantry and the engineers were eventually kept in the rear. They maintained lines of communications during the early stages of an attack, moving forward when objectives had been taken to supervise consolidation.

Support Weapons

Commanders were reluctant to take Stokes mortars into action because of the number of men required to carry the ammunition forward. Crews were trained to operate captured machine guns and would use them if ammunition was available; alternatively they would take them to the rear.

A Typical Supporting Barrage

Before the 1916 Somme campaign, the artillery barrage had moved forward in steps after zero hour, jumping large distances from objective to objective. Communications between infantry and the artillery were extremely limited and, until air-reporting improved in the summer of 1916, ground observers had to watch for the infantry raising coloured cloth screens once they reached their objective.

The disastrous outcome of 1 July proved

307

As zero hour approaches a Canadian officer explains the plan for an advance north of Courcelette to his men in October 1916. *(IWM CO957)*

that the infantry had to reach the enemy trenches before their machine-gun teams could emerge from their shelters. The answer was to use a creeping barrage where the guns extended their range in small steps just ahead of the assault troops; around 50 yards was typical. The speed of the infantry advance dictated the planning of the artillery bombardment for the first time; over poor ground it could be as slow as 25 yards per minute.

Close liaison between the artillery and infantry was essential and a heavy artillery officer was posted to each infantry division's headquarters; he was connected to the corps bombardment group by a direct telephone link. Another heavy artillery officer joined the corps Royal Flying Corps squadron headquarters ready to act on information provided by their contact planes.

Before zero hour artillery liaison officers joined the infantry brigade headquarters ready to advise on situations as they arose. A liaison officer also joined the assault battalions and moved his observation post forward as the infantry advanced, aiming to keep a close eye on each objective.

The following is a summary of a typical barrage carried out during the Somme campaign in 1916. Guns had to fire to a strict timetable to provide cover for the infantry. The plan worked as long as the men kept moving according to their schedule but problems soon arose if they were held up at any point. Until instant communication between the infantry and their supporting guns was introduced, there was no way of readjusting an artillery bombardment at short notice.

FIELD ARTILLERY

The 18-pounders reverted to divisional control at zero hour and worked as sub-groups allocated to infantry brigades, simplifying artillery and infantry cooperation. The division usually split its field artillery into three groups to execute creeping, stationary and long-range barrages:

The Creeping Barrage: One battery fired shrapnel immediately ahead of the infantry with the shell-bursts creeping forward in small bounds of 50 yards a minute as the men followed 50 yards away. The barrage would creep 300 yards forward as the infantry approached the objective, forming a protective screen while they consolidated the position.

Guns fired as many as 3 rounds per minute during the advance across no man's land, reducing to as little as 1 round every 3 or 4 minutes during the final phases. A gun fired around 300 shells during a 6-hour advance. After the final objective was reached the creeping barrage ceased and the guns prepared to deal with counter-attacks; the stationary barrage took over covering the infantry.

These men of the King's Own Yorkshire Light Infantry are setting the fuses on Stokes mortar bombs. *(IWM Q6025)*

As the minutes tick by the Germans shell the assembly trenches near the Menin Road as 13th Durham Light Infantry wait for zero hour on 20 September 1917. *(IWM Q5968)*

The Stationary Barrage: Three batteries shelled the enemy trenches ahead of the infantry, jumping from objective to objective. They would join the creeping barrage's protective screen while the infantry consolidated an objective. The rate of fire and consumption of shells was similar to the guns carrying out the creeping barrage.

The Long-Range Barrage: Two batteries shelled communication trenches, approach roads and headquarters with shrapnel.

MEDIUM AND HEAVY HOWITZERS

Starting 30 minutes before zero hour, every spare howitzer opened fire. Some medium batteries added their firepower to the stationary barrage, others targeted enemy gun emplacements. The heavy howitzers shelled strongpoints or villages throughout the attack. The rate of fire was heaviest during the first hour, with crews firing 30 to 40 rounds an hour.

MACHINE-GUN BARRAGE

Several Vickers machine guns were placed in the front line to sweep the first German line, paying particular attention to areas of high ground. The remainder were set up 1,000 yards behind the front line and split into two groups. The first fired at specific targets while the rest formed a creeping barrage, ahead of the artillery; Vickers guns could be used up to a range of 3,000 yards. The timing of the lifts during the barrage was synchronized with semaphore signalling boards, known as flappers. Depression stops made sure that the crews fired over the advancing infantry.

Machine guns consumed an enormous amount of ammunition and belt-filling machines were placed near the guns. Men fed loose rounds into the machines' hoppers while the mechanism fed them into belts. The machines made it possible to provide the standard stockpile of 24,500 rounds for each gun:

3,500 rounds in belts at the gun, stacked on sandbags to keep the belts clean.

8,000 rounds in boxes at the belt-filling machine.

8,500 rounds in boxes at reserve dumps.

4,500 rounds in boxes in the ammunition limbers.

Pack trains usually carried the ammunition forward but Yukon carriers (rucksacks with a headband to take the burden off the back) were also used.

FURTHER IMPROVEMENTS

By 1917 the bombardment had evolved into a complex sequence of barrages, up to 1,000 yards deep, with each phase designed to anticipate the German reaction. While the creeping phase of the barrage moved constantly to the objective, other parts moved backwards and forwards, aiming to catch infantry reserves in the open, disorganizing them as they moved forward. Typically the phases of the bombardment advanced together, forming curtains of shrapnel and high explosive at 200-yard intervals. However, batteries could change the elevation of their guns so their barrages either combined or spread out. The overall objective was to confuse and disrupt the enemy infantry.

Around one-third of the batteries had pre-set plans to deal with counter-attacks and observers watched for SOS flares fired by the infantry when they needed artillery support. Planes circled overhead looking for targets and batteries had pre-planned barrages (known as zone calls) calculated to fire on roads and communication trenches.

COMMUNICATIONS

Commanders expected an hourly telegraphed

A bombing party of 1st Scots Guards get ready to advance along Big Willie Trench towards Hohenzollern Redoubt during the Battle of Loos in October 1915. *(IWM Q17390)*

report from the front line while important events had to be reported immediately. The divisional observation officer received messages at one of the artillery forward observer officer's dugouts and after 1916 a wireless station kept him in contact with the corps set.

It took time to establish communications and the commanders were in the dark for some time. Brigades ran cable lines across no man's land as soon as possible but they were vulnerable to shell-fire and battlefield noise made it difficult to hear messages. Signallers often relied on visual signalling and a signals officer was added to each battalion in the

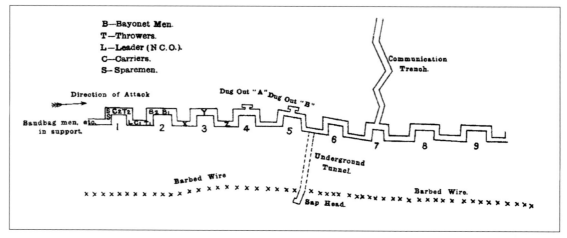

The diagram used to train bombing parties, indicating the positions of the bayonet men, the bombers and the bomb carriers.

summer of 1916. Semaphore signalling was dangerous so a variety of instruments were used to transmit Morse code signals:

Coloured discs, dark on one side and white on the other, were flipped back and forth.
Coloured shutters were operated in the same manner as Venetian blinds.
The electric Lucas lamp replaced the oil signal lamp for night signalling.

Observers at visual stations along the front watched through trench periscopes and messages were repeated three times to avoid mistakes. Messages were later transmitted to the artillery by coloured rockets, using pre-arranged codes.

A pigeon service was organized in April 1915 but, although birds could deliver messages to the corps headquarters, they were obviously unable to take messages back to the front line. Battalions received two pigeons a day; advanced brigades were provided with extra birds. (*See* Air and Ground Cooperation, pages 324–6, for aerial communications).

The front line unit's last resort was the despatch runner, a man carrying a hand-written note back along the network of communication trenches. Relays would often be placed at 300-yard intervals and flags would mark the route across no man's land (they were replaced by lamps at night). Many runners were killed or injured en route and officers often sent several men at intervals with the same message.

A RETHINK IN STRATEGY

During the Third Ypres campaign in the summer of 1917, the Germans started to man the front line with smaller numbers, concentrating on counter-attacking the British at the first opportunity. This defensive strategy often resulted in spectacular advances, disorganized the assault troops and isolated them from their artillery. A swift counter-attack often resulted in a chaotic retreat. The experience called for a rethink in the offensive strategy.

A short advance, of around 2,000 yards every two or three days, resulted in fewer casualties and allowed the troops to meet the counter-attacks in consolidated positions; the artillery and logistics chain could also keep pace with the advance.

ARTILLERY

As well as following the planned barrage schedule, observers kept a look-out for SOS signal flares fired by the infantry, indicating a threat or a tempting target. The artillery plan had prepared SOS barrages designed to saturate possible avenues of attack with a heavy concentration of shells. Signals were given by firing a rifle grenade that burst into three coloured lights, a combination of red, white and green. The infantry could fire an arranged combination of colours if, for example, their artillery support was falling short, warning the batteries to lengthen their range.

Once the objectives had been taken, guns had to move forward to a schedule. A number of batteries moved immediately, looking to deploy at pre-determined locations so they could respond to SOS calls from the infantry straight away. The rest of the batteries moved forward gradually, to keep as many guns as possible in action at any one time. The plan was usually to have all the artillery in place by nightfall, allowing the gun crews time to carry out practice barrages ready for the following day. The heavy artillery continued counter-battery fire as long as possible. Where possible howitzers had been placed close to the front line so that they could cover the objectives and targets beyond for as long as possible.

OPENING UP COMMUNICATIONS ACROSS THE BATTLEFIELD

Trace parties followed the assault troops across

The crew of a 6-inch gun targets German batteries during the countdown to the first tank attack on 15 September 1916. *(Q7235)*

Machine-gun teams in action near Mouquet Farm, north of Pozières, in September 1916; the crew on the right are using a captured German weapon. *(IWM Q1419)*

no man's land, marking out tracks for working parties to follow. The priority was to clear a way through for gun teams and ammunition wagons before improving the road for general traffic.

Each division prepared a road plan and a traffic timetable before the attack. However, local conditions often changed the layout and the engineers had to send in regular reports to the divisional headquarters to keep the traffic moving. Traffic control had to be enforced at trench crossings and parties of men were on stand-by to pull out stranded wagons.

BEHIND THE LINES

As the reserves moved forward along the Up communication trenches, aiming to reach their assembly positions before nightfall, the wounded headed along the Down trenches to the rear. The walking wounded were met at the divisional collecting post where RAMC orderlies took over, sending helpers back to the front; stretcher-bearers carried the seriously wounded to the advanced dressing station.

Regimental police posts (known as battle stop posts) were set up at the end of the communication trenches and military police took the names and numbers of stragglers before ordering them to rejoin their units. Men without their weapons were escorted to the brigade headquarters for questioning.

Prisoners were gathered up and taken to the nearest brigade headquarters for interrogation before they were transferred to the corps prisoner cage; an escort of one man to ten prisoners was considered sufficient.

ON THE DEFENSIVE

The Allied superiority in numbers dwindled during the winter of 1917–18 as German divisions were being transferred from the Eastern Front following the Russian collapse. With offensives imminent in the spring and the US Army still assembling and far from ready to fight in force, it was time to dig in. Three zones of defence, the forward zone, the battle zone and the rear zone, were organized. Each one had successive lines of continuous trenches and defensive positions around tactical points, such as villages and high ground. They were fortified with machine-gun posts and strongpoints, while switch trenches ran between the zones to form interlocking fields of fire.

THE FORWARD ZONE

The existing front system was strengthened where possible and the emphasis was on guarding against surprise attacks. The front-line troops were expected to hold their positions for as long as they could, breaking up attacks or stalling an advance while the local reserves deployed ready to counter-attack.

THE BATTLE ZONE

This zone had several lines of trenches around 2,500 yards deep on favourable ground around one or two miles behind the forward zone (the distance could vary from 600 to 5,000 yards). Commanders rarely expected to hold the forward zone, but the troops holding it were meant to disrupt and delay the German assault so that the divisional and corps reserves would be able to man the battle zone. They in turn gave time for the corps or army reserve to reach the rear zone.

The crew of a Stokes mortar shell the enemy trenches near Ploegsteert during a raid by 18th (New South Wales) Battalion. *(IWM E(AUS)1448)*

THE REAR ZONE

The rear zone was supposed to be a place for troops to fall back on, between 4 and 8 miles behind the battle zone. Due to the lack of labour it had only been surveyed and wired in many sectors while shallow trenches were few and far between.

DEFENSIVE SCHEMES

Army commanders planned defensive schemes to guard against local attacks or full-scale offensives. The plans included orders for the front-line troops and the artillery, while the reserves needed contingency plans so they could cover attacks along the whole front or against the flanks. Corps supervised the defensive works and prepared maps and plans for the divisions rotating through their sector.

Divisions were expected to hold a sector 4,000–5,000 yards wide for 48 hours to allow reserves to deploy. Valleys and dead ground were blocked with wire covered by Lewis gun teams, to stop the Germans infiltrating. Villages were considered to be key positions and many were protected by all-round defensive positions; the garrisons were expected to hold on until they were overrun.

Lewis guns formed the backbone of a successful defence and teams were often hidden out in no man's land, ready to catch

Artillery signallers use a daylight lamp to relay a message to their battery near Fricourt Wood on the Somme. *(IWM Q4131)*

advancing infantry off their guard. Vickers guns would fire over the front trenches, covering no man's land and the enemy assembly trenches. Some guns were formed into SOS groups, and would fire pre-determined patterns on danger areas. Trench mortars were deployed ready to bombard the German front line and the crews had plans to shell the British front line if it was lost.

It was recognized that prompt action by the artillery could stop an enemy attack breaking through and brigade and battery commanders had to study plans laid down by the corps' counter-attack schemes. However, it was impossible to cater for every type of emergency and they were allowed to react to developing situations, moving their guns if necessary. Brigade and battery commanders had an observation post attached to their headquarters so they could engage the enemy at close range if they broke through.

Field batteries were positioned well back, ready to fire on and behind their own front line if necessary. The main positions remained silent in camouflaged gun pits until they were needed, to reduce the effects of counter-battery fire. Single guns and detached sections were continuously on the move, firing from different positions to mislead the German observers.

A small number of camouflaged field guns (preferably captured German 77mm guns) were positioned to cover likely avenues of approach. They would hold their fire until after the Germans broke through, firing over open sights at the advancing infantry.

If the Germans started a prolonged bom-bardment, the medium guns would target roads to disperse troops and ammunition parties to isolate the front-line troops. The heavy howitzers concentrated on counter-battery work, often using gas to disrupt the crews, and they were deployed as far forward as possible so they could engage a large number of targets.

UNDER ATTACK

The Germans remained on the defensive in France until the spring of 1918. However,

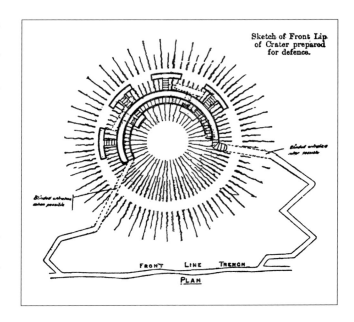

A diagram showing how to turn a mine crater into a defensive position. However, in reality the British infantry usually ended up holding one lip while the Germans held the other.

raiding parties continually probed the front-line trenches looking to take prisoners while counter-attacks were launched to drive the British back after an advance.

When an attack was imminent or under way, sentries fired coloured flares to request an SOS barrage and the artillery responded with pre-arranged barrages on the German lines. While the field artillery and trench mortars shelled the German trenches and no man's land, the medium howitzers targeted head-quarters and roads; the heavy howitzers engaged in counter-battery fire.

All along the line formation headquarters accumulated reports and as soon as the limits and size of the attack were known, the field artillery and trench mortars switched to firing a creeping barrage across the German trenches and supply routes; gas shells would be used to force the assault troops to wear their masks.

While the artillery did its best to break up the assault waves in no man's land, the infantry manned their parapets and prepared for the onslaught. Brutal hand-to-hand fighting could follow when the Germans reached the trench as the men grappled with bayonets, rifle butts and bombs. Knife-rests (hurdles wrapped in barbed wire) were pulled across trenches to stop infiltration

During the last year of the war, German assault teams were trained to bypass strongpoints, aiming to penetrate as far as possible in the chaos of the first hours of battle; the follow-up troops would surround and engage the strongpoints.

Of course, the above plans did not account for the problems caused by the German preliminary bombardment and by the time an attack was under way the British front line could be a shambles. The wire and the parapet might be smashed, dugouts and machine-gun posts destroyed and communications cut. The men at the front might have to be left to fend for themselves while the divisional headquarters tried to reestablish contact and send reserves forward.

GAS ATTACKS

Empty shell-cases or vehicle horns were sounded to warn the troops of a gas attack until the Strombos Horn, a megaphone alarm, was introduced. As soon as the gas alarms rang out, men pulled on their masks and sealed their dugouts with gas curtains.

Corps headquarters would notify the army's chemical adviser of the extent of the attack so he could check the weather conditions and calculate the danger area. He warned camps and headquarters in the affected area and in some cases units up to 20 miles from the front

Following the capture of Vimy Ridge on 9 April 1917, these Canadian machine-gun teams dig in ready to meet the German counter-attacks. *(IWM CO1146)*

An 18-pounder horse team strains to pull their gun and limber through the mud to a new battery position. *(IWM Q5011)*

line had to be alerted. The French mission at the army headquarters warned the local population while the provost marshal notified traffic control posts so they could alert troops entering the affected area.

ANTI-TANK DEFENCE

On the few occasions that tanks (usually captured British machines) were used by the Germans, the infantry relied on the Royal Flying Corps to spot them while the artillery covered the approach route with a dense barrage.

Camouflaged field guns waited until the tanks came close and then opened fire over open sights, using a mixture of smoke, to blind the crew, and high explosive. Each forward gun battery kept a crew on stand-by ready to engage tanks. Infantry were encouraged to fire their machine guns on a tank to distract the crew but it took a brave man to move in close enough to use grenades.

Rifle grenadiers were armed with the No. 44 anti-tank grenade.

Earth embankments, tree stumps and craters were used as barricades and ditches were dug across roads; light bridges were built so that infantry and horses could cross.

REINFORCING A FRONT

As reports of the attacks flooded in to the headquarters (and many were much exaggerated), corps and army staff tried to make sense out of the chaos. While the various headquarters ascertained the limits and extent of the attack, each corps prepared to deploy its reserve divisions while the army and GHQ reserves were alerted.

While the local reserves marched to the front line, tactical trains moved army reserves (1 division or equivalent artillery per 24 hours) to the railheads behind the front. Strategic trains prepared to move reserves (one division or equivalent artillery per 24

It was important to dig trenches across no man's land as soon as possible. These men are struggling to cut a communication trench through the tangle of tree roots in what remains of Delville Wood on the Somme. *(IWM Q4417)*

hours) from other parts of the front while the adjacent armies prepared to send 1 division to the danger area on foot.

Typically, each corps could expect to receive 2 field and 6 heavy artillery brigades within 48 hours, with a similar number arriving over the next 48 hours. The artillery would move into prepared camouflaged battery positions, complete with observation points, headquarters dugouts and com-

munications. Additional prepared positions would be available to accommodate the corps' own artillery units when it was time for them to withdraw.

WITHDRAWING REAR AREA TROOPS

As reserves began to flood into a corps area, the thousands of men working behind the lines had to be withdrawn to safety without blocking roads or mixing with the men

RESERVES AVAILABLE		
Corps reserve	immediately available	1 or 2 infantry divisions
Army reserve	ready to move at 6 hours' notice	1 infantry division and 1 heavy artillery brigade
GHQ reserve	ready to move at 24 hours' notice, but it could be reduced to 12 hours	1 infantry division and 1 brigade of tanks, 3 heavy and 2 field artillery brigades

moving forward. Engineers and Army Service Corps personnel continued to work at the dumps and railheads until new orders arrived or it became too dangerous to carry on. Foreign labour units close to the front line assembled at a pre-determined rendezvous point so they could be directed to dig new trenches and improve defences behind the lines. The rest of the units working behind the lines, including prisoners of war, were withdrawn as soon as possible.

INFANTRY AND TANK COOPERATION

When tanks were introduced in September 1916, cooperation between tanks and infantry was crude. The artillery would leave gaps in the barrage while the tanks advanced a short distance ahead of the infantry, targeting machine guns and strongpoints. Beyond the first trench system, ten men escorted each tank to keep the German infantry at bay and remove wounded from the path of the tank. The infantry were instructed not to wait for a ditched or disabled machine and tanks withdrew to refuel and rearm as soon as the final objective had been consolidated.

Closer cooperation had been developed by the time of the Cambrai offensive in November 1917. After breaking through the wire the tanks would engage strongpoints as the infantry cleared the trenches.

THE ASSEMBLY

Tank commanders reconnoitred the routes to the assembly area, checking the route was clear and white guide tapes had been laid.

Prisoners were usually treated with compassion. This Tommy is giving a wounded German soldier a sip of water before escorting him to the rear. *(IWM Q13255)*

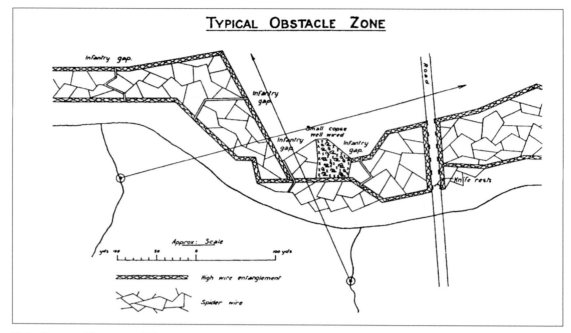

TYPICAL OBSTACLE ZONE

Infantry gap.

Infantry gap

Small copse well wired

Infantry gap

Infantry gap

Road

Knife rest

Approx: Scale

yds 100   50   0   100 yds

High wire entanglement

Spider wire

This diagram illustrates different methods for wiring a section of trench. Two thick entanglements are linked by spider wire while small gaps are left for friendly raiding parties. The alignment of the wire is designed to lead enemy infantry into the path of two machine guns.

They also familiarized themselves with the objective while their crews practised the advance with the infantry. Telephone cables had to be buried or lifted out of the way and trenches had to be bridged.

The tanks waited under cover until the night before the attack, heading off at dusk while planes flew overhead to drown out the noise of their engines. By the early hours the tanks were in position alongside the infantry. Zero hour was usually at dawn, so the drivers could see, but a smoke screen would be used to cover no man's land as the tanks and infantry moved off together.

TANK TACTICS

Tank companies were usually given two objectives, divided into tank section attack areas. The emphasis was on taking tactical points rather than sending forward an evenly spaced line of tanks. There was, on average, one tank every 100–200 yards. The tank commanders headed towards tactical points,

ideally following a direct route to the objective. Sections or pairs of tanks worked together and the male tanks used their 6-pounder guns to engage strongpoints while the female tanks gave the infantry covering fire with their machine guns.

Four advanced guard tanks led the company, aiming to draw fire from the objective, while the main body headed towards the objective in four pairs (an advanced guard tank took the place of any disabled main body tanks). The advanced guard tank crossed the wire and turned left to crawl along the front of the German trench. The main body tanks crossed the wire at the same point (or over 100 yards away to prevent the crushed wire springing up). The first main body tank dropped its fascine into the fire trench, crossed it and turned left. The next tank crossed the support trench, again using a fascine, and turned left so that the three tanks moved parallel between the trenches. Tanks dropped red and yellow flags at the fascines so

The crew of an 18-pounder prepare to fire from an exposed position during the German breakthrough on the Lys in April 1918. *(IWM Q8712)*

---

the infantry could mark the trench crossings. By the time the infantry had crossed the wire, all three tanks were moving parallel alongside the German trenches.

INFANTRY TACTICS

The first wave of infantry platoons (each 16–40 men) followed close behind in section files or in small platoon columns of four single files abreast. They were ordered not to bunch behind the tanks and instead kept their distance to avoid the tangled wire as the tanks crawled through the entanglement. After marking the gaps in the wire, the platoons fanned out and began clearing the trenches. Three waves of infantry were allocated for each trench and numbers following each tank company were as follows:

Trench cleaners: The leading wave of 8 platoons sent its bombers into the trench while the rest of the men remained in the open to cover the tank.

Trench stops: Another 8 platoons followed and consolidated the trench, building barriers, placing ladders and making exits; they also widened the gaps in the wire, marking them with flags.

Supports: Finally 16 platoons in two waves followed. They formed a firing line in shell-holes beyond the trenches and prepared to give covering fire. Tanks left them supplies of ammunition or bombs before moving forward.

THE SECOND OBJECTIVE

A second echelon of tanks and infantry followed the cleared routes and headed

A fresh battalion moves up along a planked road to relieve the assault troops. *(IWM Q2217)*

towards the next objective while the first echelon cleared the front line. The tanks and infantry used the same method to capture the German second line and the tanks from the first echelon joined as soon as they had cleared their own area. However, tanks soon had to return to their depots so the crews could rest while their machines were refuelled and repaired ready for the next day.

COMMUNICATIONS AND SIGNALLING

The tank crews used the following signals to communicate with the infantry and contact aircraft:

FLAG SIGNALS
Red flag: out of action.
Green flag: on the objective.

Other flags were used for communicating between tanks.

LAMP SIGNALS
A series of T's: out of action.
A series of H's: on the objective.

COLOURED DISCS
Green disc: wire crushed down.
Red disc: wire uncut.
Red/Green or Green/Red: have reached objective.

Infantry signalled to tanks with their rifles:

Rifle waved above head: enemy in sight.
Helmet on rifle held above the head: tank assistance required.

Each tank carried two pigeons to send messages.

AIR AND GROUND COOPERATION

Early attempts at air-to-ground observation were crude – the main problem for the air observers was how to distinguish between the British and German troops moving across the battlefield.

Wireless telegraphy was first used in the spring of 1915 but squadrons were restricted to three planes reporting at any one time to prevent their signals jamming each other. Results were inconsistent as planes flew aimlessly over the battlefield looking for targets. During the first half of 1916 training and improvements in organization led to a closer cooperation between the air observers and the battery commanders as they discussed and practised artillery programmes. Improvements in wireless technology and the introduction of the clapper break (a device to transmit identifiable tones from the aircraft's radio) allowed ground operators to monitor individual machines' reports.

Contact patrols were sent over the battlefield to report on the infantry's progress. A major difficulty was how to transmit information from the ground without also revealing a position to the enemy. Large white strips were tried in 1915 and lines of linen were laid out on the objective while arrows were pegged out to point to enemy strongpoints. They proved to be difficult to spot. Experiments with smoke signals, Very lights, rockets and lamps proved that they drew the attentions of the German artillery. Attempts to observe metal tags attached to the men's uniforms (to catch the sun) failed on the dusty battlefield.

A French technique was adopted in May 1916 and used for the first time on the Somme. Contact planes flew overhead at predetermined times and either fired a white flare or sounded a Klaxon horn to draw the infantry's attention. Each company lit flares at 20-yard intervals in the objective trench where they could be seen from the air but not from the ground. The observer marked the line of red flares (solid if the objective had been

Canadian troops hitch a ride on a Mark IV tank during a training exercise in the summer of 1918. *(IWM CO3082)*

Infantry and Mark V tanks move forward into Grevillers on 25 August 1918. *(IWM Q11262)*

Men of the Australian Signal Service pose with short-wave wireless sets. *(IWM Q29369)*

taken, broken if not in places) on a trench map. The pilot then flew back over the local corps reporting centre and dropped the maps, and written messages, onto a target in loaded bags. For the first time corps had regular and up to date information from the front line.

Zone (or area) calls were introduced as pre-arranged signals for artillery support. The grids on the 1:40,000 trench maps were quartered into four lettered squares (50 yards by 50 yards) with two-letter map references suitable for transmitting by Morse code. The Morse code signal to the artillery included the type of target so that the battery could decide what type of barrage and ammunition to use. Battery commanders prepared charts with angles and distances to all the zones in their range and they could open fire immediately. The air observers reported results with a pre-arranged Morse code signal.

CHAPTER ELEVEN

MAPPING

TRENCH MAPS

On the outbreak of war the Royal Field Artillery intended to use direct fire, deploying near the infantry lines and shooting at visible targets. Indirect fire, where the battery stayed hidden and relied on observers to correct the aim of the guns, was considered to be a waste of ammunition. However, the gun crews soon discovered that it was suicidal to deploy in the open and moved into cover. This meant that accurate maps were needed so that batteries could plot their positions and calculate angles and distances to their target. Throughout the First World War the artillery constantly demanded, and received, improved maps with greater accuracy and detail.

1914

GHQ planned to use the existing French maps of the area of operations and the Army's three survey sections were left behind when the Expeditionary Force left for France; it was to prove to be a costly oversight. As the BEF moved to Mons it became clear that the available maps were outdated and at too large a scale; they were useful for general orders and the RFC could map troop movements on squared grids, but they were useless for plotting artillery targets.

As the front stabilized on the Aisne in September 1914, the first series of trench maps was issued, plotted on a new gridded French 1:50,000 map. However, the scale was still too large and attempts to enlarge the

maps resulted in unacceptable distortions. 1:40,000 and 1:20,000 maps of Belgium were distributed when the BEF transferred to Flanders in October (copied from plates evacuated from Antwerp) but, while the infantry were satisfied, the artillery discovered that the grids had large errors. It was time to survey the BEF's area.

1915

Pre-war handbooks put mapping in the hands of Intelligence but the topographical sub-section of GHQ's general staff (known as 1c, Mapping) only had three trained officers and it took until the end of the year to complete the survey; it proved that the existing maps were wildly inaccurate.

The Ranging Section, RE, started a plane-table survey of the British area in January 1915, producing the first accurate maps for the artillery and they extended their survey as the British sector extended south to Loos. The area behind the German lines was plotted from aerial photographs, relating trenches to known landmarks, and by the spring a new series of 22.5 x 17.5-inch maps covering the BEF's area had been issued.

Divisional field companies, RE, were supposed to plot new trenches but they were fully engaged, and results were sporadic. However, new air cameras had arrived by February 1915 and the RFC systematically photographed the whole British area to bring the maps up to date. The first copies reached

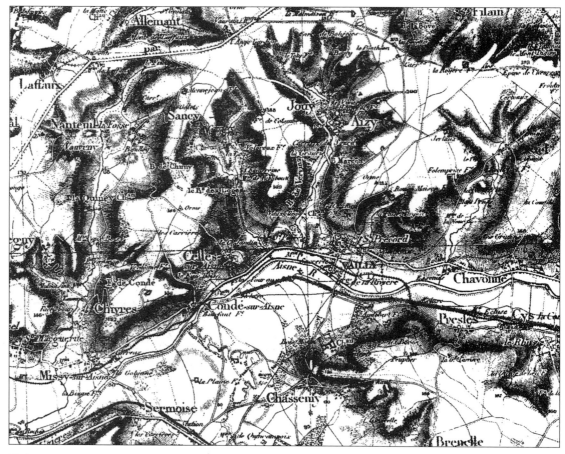

To begin with the BEF had to cope with schematic maps provided by the French. The infantry were able to use this map during the crossing of the Aisne but it was useless for plotting accurate artillery fire.

First Army in March and the artillery used them to plot the first structured preliminary barrage for the Battle of Neuve Chapelle.

Work on mapping continued throughout the summer of 1915 and after the battles of Aubers Ridge and Festubert First Army started work on a new series of comprehensive maps. The maps issued for the Battle of Loos detailed new assembly trenches, supply dumps, headquarters and medical facilities, while the German area showed trenches, strongpoints, and artillery batteries. However, maps were still inaccurate (by over 300 metres in places) and battery commanders still had to rely on old French maps to pinpoint fixed points. Printers struggled to keep up with demand and update slips, showing new trenches and objectives, were issued and pasted onto maps.

During the winter of 1915–16 Third Army started work on a 1:10,000-scale series of maps of the Somme. The French supplied co-ordinates of the canals and railways behind the German lines and aerial photographs provided the details. The new maps started to appear in December 1915; they would set the standard for all future mapping.

1916

Surveying was reorganized in February 1916 with the introduction of new field survey companies attached to each army headquarters. The companies were responsible for coordinating surveying, mapping and sound-ranging. The demand for maps outstripped supply during the Somme offensive and, as the daily situation changed, the front-line head-quarters resorted to issuing tracings and crude hand-drawn tactical maps to keep the troops informed. Civilian firms worked around the clock to print backgrounds while mapping personnel at GHQ added new detail by hand, a time-consuming task. At the end of the year photography equipment capable of repro-ducing information solved the problem.

The amount of tactical detail on maps increased throughout the autumn of 1916 and units were issued with tracings setting out defence schemes for consolidating captured trenches. Details on cuttings, embankments, weak culverts and broken or marshy ground were also added for the benefit of the Tank Corps crews.

The artillery had also introduced a new range of specialized maps to cover different types of barrages. The heavy artillery used position maps, marking enemy gun batteries with large dots for counter-battery fire (solid dots for occupied gun pits, small circles for unoccupied positions, partially coloured if the observer was unsure). The introduction of the creeping barrage meant that the field artillery needed 1:10,000-scale barrage maps with the timings and lifts of the bombardment phases over-printed. Corps headquarters staff preferred 1:20,000-scale maps, because they could plot all their schemes on one map. Zone call maps over-printed with predetermined SOS barrages allowed the infantry to call for artillery support at short notice.

1917

During the winter of 1916–17 corps topo-graphical sections took over the copying and distribution of maps while the Ordnance Survey set up a branch in France to speed up production. Observation techniques improved, giving the map makers plenty of information to mark up and by April 1917 Third Army knew where over 90% of the German batteries were on the Arras front.

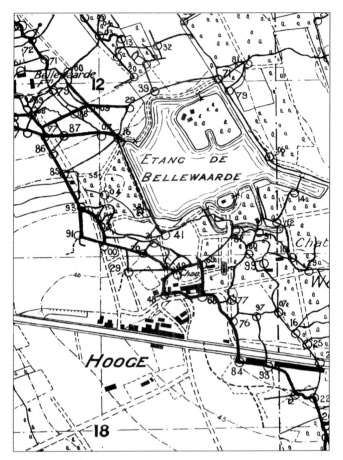

By the spring of 1915 crude trench maps had started to appear; this example covers the German trenches (British trenches were only shown on Secret copies) around Hooge, in the Ypres Salient.

The introduction of process cameras in the spring allowed the survey staff to use photographic negatives to produce different scale maps with ease and within a few weeks all army fronts were covered by new 1:20,000 and 1:10,000 sheets. A message form (a list of prompts and questions) was also printed on the back of the map, helping officers to prepare marked-up maps and accurate situation reports.

The number of mapping staff involved in the Ypres Offensive in 1917 rose to over 1,000 and a dedicated survey staff was organized at GHQ in August (the survey companies were

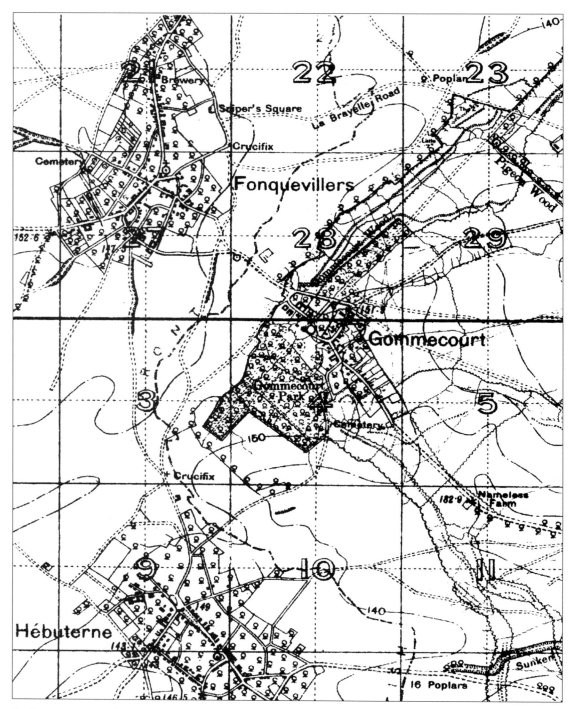

By the summer of 1916 maps had become accurate depictions of the battlefield and this section covers the Gommecourt Salient attacked by Third Army on 1 July 1916. Square 4a covers the northern part of Gommecourt Park.

eventually organized into battalions in June 1918). Third Army set up new corps topographical sections at the same time to catch up with outstanding work and the rest of the armies followed suit a few months later.

By the end of 1917 maps were so accurate that the artillery was ready to use predicted fire on a large scale. Accurate surveys of the British and German batteries meant that the preliminary bombardment could be dispensed with and the batteries could hit their targets with confidence without having to range their guns in. The technique was used for the first time during the attack at Cambrai on 20 November; it was a success and set the pattern for the offensives of 1918.

1918

Early in the year, printing equipment reached each company and before long the supply of maps finally met demand. Field Marshal Foch called for uniformity between French and British mapping systems when he became generalissimo of the Allied forces in April. However, the fast-moving advance during the summer and autumn meant that there was no time to start redrawing maps.

By the Armistice over 34 million maps had been produced on the Western Front. From humble beginnings, the trench mapping service had developed into an exact science providing the infantry and artillery with accurate and up-to-date information.

MAP REFERENCES

The map sheets were sub-divided into lettered rectangles which were in turn divided into numbered squares and positions within these could be specified by eastings and northings in the usual way so that positions could be identified precisely.

NAMING THE TRENCHES

Brigadier-General A. Hunter-Weston, GOC 11th Brigade, started to name 4th Division's trenches during the battles on the Aisne and the system quickly became universal. It was far easier to quote trench names in orders rather than give a long list of map references; many

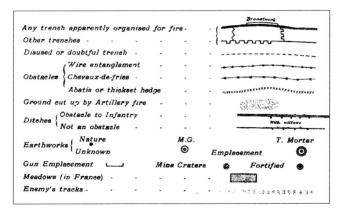

Typical symbols used on trench maps from 1916 onwards.

typographical errors were also eliminated.

The trenches in the Ypres Salient were named during the first winter of the war and many were called after the nearest village or wood while battalions adopted farms. The Hampshires, the Argylls and the Warwicks all named farms while Birr Crossroads and Mount Sorrel were named after unit training camps in Great Britain. Units often named places after their commanding officers, for example Prowse Point and Hull's Farm near Plogsteert Wood. Terrain features were usually given English titles, replacing the unfamiliar French names, and although Polygon Wood, Kitchener's Wood, Shrewsbury Forest, Inverness Copse and Sanctuary Wood were devastated in the battles for Ypres, they still appeared on trench maps. Hills were often named after their spot heights on the map; Hill 60 south of Ypres and Hill 70 east of Loos are two well-known examples.

As new trenches were added, divisions turned to their home towns for inspiration and 49th Division named the trenches north of Ypres after the towns and streets of the West Riding of Yorkshire; similarly the trench map covering Cuinchy and Givenchy is littered with London street names.

The Western Front was a dangerous place and some notorious locations were given descriptive titles; three corners near Ypres, Hellfire, Hellblast and Shrapnel, were favourite targets for the German artillery.

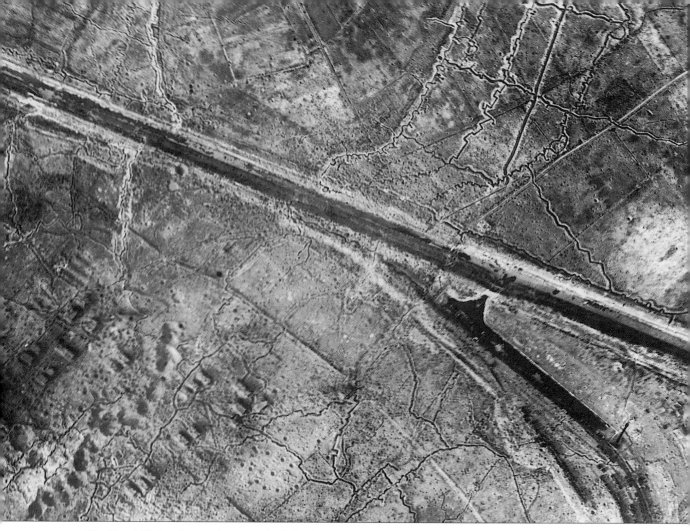

The Royal Flying Corps photographed the German trenches so draughtsmen could trace them onto maps. This photograph covers no man's land south of the La Bassée Canal. The line of circles in the bottom left-hand corner shows the mine craters in the Brickstacks area. *(IWM Q44785)*

Unlucky names were avoided, and Shell-Trap Farm in the Salient was quickly renamed Mouse-Trap Farm.

Enemy trenches were sometimes given German names; Hohenzollern Redoubt was connected to Little Willie and Big Willie Trenches, the nicknames of the Kaiser and the Crown Prince, while names such as Tirpitz, Fokker, Potsdam and Pommern could be found in the Ypres Salient. In some sectors the German trenches were named in alphabetical order, taking the initial letter from the trench map area; the trenches opposite Bois Grenier were named Index, Increase, Inconsistent, Incomplete, Income, Incline and Incision; Index Trench was the front line and Index Support was the second line while Index Avenue, Drive and Row were the various communication trenches running to the rear area.

As more trenches were added, new terms had to be used and a network of Streets, Roads, Avenues and Ways could all have the same name; the French term *Boyau* was often used for communication trenches. Fire trenches connecting a front line and a support system became common towards the end of the war and they were known as switches.

CHAPTER TWELVE

BEHIND THE LINES

TRAINING FACILITIES

OFFICER TRAINING

Although there was a serious lack of trained officers for the growing Army, formal training did not start until July 1916. The new army schools could not cope with the numbers of students and training centres had to be opened at home and abroad three months later.

Senior officers were withdrawn from their units and put through a ten-week course at the Senior Officers School at Aldershot, while lieutenant-colonels and majors attended classes at Auxi le Château near Doullens.

After February 1916 a prospective officer had to pass the 20-week-long Officer Cadet Course before he was awarded a temporary commission. Candidates graduated from the

NCOs learn how to spot and identify targets at one of the many training schools. *(IWM Q33343)*

Having learnt how to put on a gas mask, troops were led into a chamber to experience the full horror of a gas attack. *(IWM Q33345)*

of 100 and it was teaching 1,000 candidates per month by June 1915.

Education became an important part of life in the Army, particularly for officers and NCOs who were expected to pass on their knowledge when they returned to their unit. The table at the bottom of the page gives an idea of the range of schools established on the Western Front and the level of HQ running them.

Huge encampments were built along the coast (the Bull Ring at Etaples was notorious for its tough regime) to put new recruits through their final training.

TRAINING EXAMPLES

GAS
Schools opened at the start of 1916 and men practised putting on gas masks before entering a sealed hut filled with gas.

SNIPING
Army schools were established in 1916 but teaching methods differed until the training pamphlet SS 195 *Scouting and Patrolling* appeared the following year. Courses lasted two weeks. Following lessons on observation, maps and telescopes in the classroom, candidates took part in practical exercises covering shooting, observation and unarmed combat. Men also practised trying to spot a camouflaged instructor as he crawled forward and then tried to do the same in front of their fellow students; they also learnt how to locate the sources of shots and find enemy snipers. At the end of the course snipers were allowed

Officers' Training Corps and the number of veteran NCOs who were commissioned increased as the months passed. At the start of 1917 a new Training Directorate started to coordinate training across the Army.

TRAINING SCHOOLS IN THE FIELD

Schools of instruction started to open in France at the end of November 1914 and one of the earliest was the Machine Gun School at Wisques, near St Omer. It started with a class

TRAINING SCHOOLS	
GHQ	Machine Guns, Lewis Guns, Trench Mortars, Wireless, Royal Engineer, Cadet Course, Staff College Course
Army	Artillery, Infantry, Signal, Scouting, Observation, Sniping, Mining, Anti-Gas
Corps	Infantry, Bombing, Trench Mortars, Lewis Guns, Anti-Gas
Engineers	Officer Training, Bridging, Light Railways, Mechanical Transport, Transportation
Miscellaneous	Machine Gun Corps, Labour Corps, Anti-Aircraft, Ammunition Handling, Cookery, Intelligence, Young Officers' Training, Royal Army Medical Corps, Tank Tactics, Chaplains

to wear a brass or cloth fleur-de-lys badge on their right sleeves.

BOMBING

Schools relayed the lessons learnt in the trenches to new bombing teams. Officers and 12 NCOs from each infantry battalion were taught and they passed on the techniques to their men; 1 NCO and 8 men per infantry platoon were given extra training.

After lessons on the mechanism of the bomb and the fuse, men practised making and firing small charges. Finally they practised with live bombs. *The Training and Employment of Grenadiers* manual was published in October 1915 and the three-day basic course was supplemented with an advanced course for bombers. Successful candidates were allowed to sew a badge with a red grenade and white flames onto their upper right arms.

LEWIS GUNS

The introduction of the Lewis gun during the autumn of 1915 called for a rapid programme of instruction and by the summer of the following year, each battalion had a trained Lewis gun officer. Candidates studied the gun's mechanism, stripping and cleaning the weapon, clearing stoppages, and maintenance. Practical tests included high-speed set-ups, firing, changing and filling the magazine. The officer was expected to pass on his knowledge to the Lewis gun sections in his battalion, using the training manual *Method of Instruction in the Lewis Gun.*

TANK CORPS

The Tank Corps split training into five schools:
Gunnery School: Men practised with air rifles fixed to a Lewis or Hotchkiss gun.
Mechanical and Driving School: Manoeuvring and emergency repairs.
Anti-Gas School: How to operate the tank during a gas attack.
Wireless Signalling School: The use of the wireless set and communications.
Battle Practice Range: Tank crews worked together to practise tactics.

After enduring the mud of the Ypres Salient, Australian soldiers wait their turn outside a bathhouse. *(IWM E(AUS)1066)*

SOLDIERS AT REST
BILLETING

Soldiers marched out of the front line tired, dirty and with frayed nerves but a few days in the rear area revived them ready for their next tour. Billeting officers bargained with the locals for accommodation, offering five francs for an officer and one franc for other ranks.

Typically a company would occupy a small farm. While the officers billeted in the house, the men found shelter in the barns and out-buildings. The families made additional money by offering food and there was a lot of bartering as the soldiers used pidgin French and sign language to agree a price. In isolated areas soldiers were billeted in bell tents, 12 to a tent, while Nissen huts capable of sleeping 24 were introduced later in the war.

WASH HOUSES, FOOD AND PAY

Bathhouses (often sited in breweries or factories) were capable of cleaning several thousand men a day. After stripping off and

A field bakery keeps the men supplied with a fresh batch of bread. *(IWM Q31662)*

handing in their uniforms, the soldiers soaked in huge vats or showered with hosepipes, hoping that the warm water lasted until they were clean. Jackets, trousers and greatcoats were ironed to kill lice and the men received a new set of underwear.

The men then looked forward to a hot drink and a meal. The company cooker, a huge range on wheels, served up simple high-calorie meals that would be washed down with morning coffee or afternoon tea.

A mixed group of soldiers listen to the latest gossip over a cup of cocoa. *(IWM Q1594)*

The men lined up and stood at ease while the officer called them forward one by one to receive their pay; the quartermaster and his sergeant kept an eye on proceedings. Pay was in local currency, in France usually issued in 5-franc notes.

EXPEDITIONARY FORCE CANTEENS

Early arrangements to purchase luxuries in Paris came to an end when the BEF moved to Flanders. Although local outlets sold watered-down beer or home-made wine and cigarettes, they were unpopular and prices were high.

The Canteen and Mess Co-operative Society was invited to manage Expeditionary Force canteens in January 1915 and the canteens started supplying small luxuries. Before long alcohol, tobacco, underclothing, boots and even footballs were sold; they also supplied non-regulation clothing and equipment. The canteens also supplied the divisional canteens after the autumn of 1915, although alcohol was banned from brigade and battalion canteens. As the number of canteens increased, the society also expanded to run cinemas, theatres, officers' clubs, rest houses, bakeries and piggeries. It was absorbed into the Army Service Corps in September 1916.

Prices were kept to a minimum and profits were used to improve facilities. By 1918 300 canteens employed 3,000 staff (including 700 women of the Queen Mary's Army Auxiliary Corps) and the monthly turnover was 37 million francs (£1.5 million).

ENTERTAINMENT

During the long hours of boredom behind the lines men looked for sources of amusement to pass the time. Gambling with cards or dice robbed many soldiers of their pay, and games like pitch and toss, under and over or crown and anchor, where the men bet on the outcome of coin tosses or dice rolls, were particular favourites; house (now called bingo) was also played. Others read books or newspapers at one of the canteens or rest centres. Some units produced their own newspapers and these were filled with black

Men of the London Scottish gather round to cheer on their favourite during a boxing tournament; no doubt many will have had a wager on one of the contestants. *(IWM Q321)*

humour, parodying life in the trenches. Satirical comments on the running of the war were interspersed amongst poems, funny stories and spoof adverts for ridiculous inventions, tonics and absurd items of clothing. Famous examples include the *Wipers Times*, *Somme Times*, and *BEF Times*.

ESTAMINETS

Soldiers could visit one of the small bars (called *estaminets*) run by French families in their houses. They sold a limited range of hot food – egg and chips being a favourite – and drinks – including coffee, weak beer and wine; only officers could buy spirits. A number were houses of ill repute and the high rate of venereal disease among soldiers was a constant drain on medical resources.

CONCERT AND THEATRICAL PARTIES

During the winter of 1914–15 the troops began to improvise concert parties. Before long most divisions were running shows by groups with such names as The Whizz-Bangs and The Follies. Over 600 professional artistes gave their services and, while the YMCA organized lodgings and venues, the organizers raised funding. The artistes staged concert parties at the bases and hospitals along the French coast while some groups toured the rear areas. Corps also set up and ran privately funded cinemas.

AUXILIARY SOCIAL SERVICES

Religious bodies, associations and individuals provided centres for recreation, entertainment or spiritual comfort behind the lines. In 1918 privately run facilities were absorbed into the larger organizations.

YOUNG MEN'S CHRISTIAN ASSOCIATION (YMCA)

Over 250 recreation centres were opened across Great Britain when war broke out to serve the thousands of Regular and Territorial

Men of the 8th KOYLI gamble their pay on a card game while they wait for orders to move up to the front line. *(IWM Q6034)*

soldiers moving to their war stations. By November 1914 the Army had granted permission for YMCA centres to operate with the BEF in France. Eventually over 40 large YMCA (or Red Triangle) centres served base camps and hospitals, while 300 smaller centres were set up along the lines of communication. The larger facilities were equipped with a games room, a quiet room and a chapel; some had music rooms or theatres for visiting concert parties, but the main part of the centre was the canteen serving food and tobacco at low prices. A reading room equipped with old books and newspapers provided a place to relax and many used the supply of writing paper to write home.

Smaller buffets were set up at the military depots, hospitals, convalescent areas, training camps and schools. Buffets at railway stations and major road intersections were sometimes open around the clock, serving free hot drinks to the troops. After June 1915 YMCA centres were permitted in army rear areas and they could be found in most towns and villages by the end of 1916. In 1917 YMCA centres were set up alongside casualty clearing and dressing stations where the staff dispensed drinks and comfort to the wounded and helped them to fill in postcards with information for relatives.

The YMCA also set up hostels for relatives visiting the seriously injured. A car met the relatives at the port and accompanied them during their visit; the service cared for over 100 visitors a day.

SALVATION ARMY

The Salvation Army organized hostels and huts across the United Kingdom, and thousands of soldiers were billeted in its citadels when accommodation was short; it also housed and cared for thousands of refugees forced out of Belgium.

Forty hostels and huts had been set up at the base depots and hospitals along the

French coast by the end of the war while donations had paid for 30 motor ambulances. The Salvation Army also ran a Relatives War Graves Visitation Department to accommodate and accompany visitors to war graves; photographs were sent to those who were unable to visit. Members visited the wounded and the bereaved across Great Britain, financially supporting widows until their pensions were settled.

Church Army and Church of Scotland

The Church Army held church services at camps and training centres across the United Kingdom and it opened a voluntary hospital in Caen in September 1914. Church Army centres started to appear on the Western Front in March 1915 and eventually 2,000 volunteers ran over 1,100 centres in all theatres.

The Church of Scotland's Women's Guild organized welfare tents at the New Army camps across Scotland during the first winter of the war and the first overseas centres were opened in 1916. The Scottish Churches Huts Joint Committee was formed to pool the two organizations' funds and eventually opened 34 centres manned by 350 volunteers.

Catholic Club and Catholic Women's League

These two organizations started work at the base depots in 1915 and eventually opened 26 recreation clubs. A camp chaplain took Mass in the morning and led prayers in the evening; he would hold extra services for men moving up to the front at unsociable hours. The two organizations amalgamated in 1918.

Women's Voluntary Organizations

Thousands of women volunteered to work in hospitals and canteens, while others raised funds for the war effort. As the months passed, industries recognized that women could replace the men who had volunteered to go to war but it was some time before the government organized women's labour.

The *Wipers Times* kept the soldiers amused with ridiculous stories lampooning events at the front.

Performers from the Royal Flying Corps Kite and Balloon Section rehearse for *Cinderella* in the ruins of Bapaume. *(IWM Q8380)*

Australian troops gather around a YMCA hut near Curlu in September 1918, while a guard watches over prisoners captured at Mont St Quentin. The sign makes it clear that there are no luxuries for sale. *(IWM E(AUS)3208)*

QUEEN ALEXANDRA'S IMPERIAL MILITARY NURSING SERVICE

Some 3,000 nurses were mobilized in August 1914 and the service had grown to 23,000 members by the end of the war

TERRITORIAL FORCE NURSING SERVICE

A nursing service administered by the county associations.

WOMEN'S VOLUNTEER RESERVE AND THE WOMEN'S LEGION

A group of high society women and feminists started the Women's Emergency Corps, a fund-raising organization, in August 1914; it was soon renamed the Women's Volunteer Reserve. However, it was expensive to join and the Marchioness of Londonderry organized the Women's Legion in July 1915 to cater for the working classes. The legion's canteens were run along military lines and members wore uniforms; it became the largest voluntary body in Britain.

VOLUNTARY AID DETACHMENTS

Over 47,000 members of the Red Cross and the St John Ambulance Brigade offered their services in August 1914. Red Cross members supported the Territorial Forces while St John Ambulance Brigade members trained nurses and provided first aid. Many members assisted the wounded at the railway stations and hospitals across Great Britain. Numbers nearly doubled over the next four years.

FIRST AID NURSING YEOMANRY

Several thousand members worked in hospitals and canteens while over 100 volunteered to serve as ambulance drivers with the Red Cross in France.

WOMEN'S AUXILIARY FORCE

Launched in 1915 for part-time workers. Uniformed members ran canteens and social clubs while others worked on the land and in hospitals.

WOMEN'S HOSPITAL CORPS AND THE SCOTTISH WOMEN'S HOSPITALS

The British Army rejected offers of assistance from the Women's Hospital Corps so the members organized two hospitals for French troops in September 1914. The authorities soon changed their mind and allowed the corps to run a military hospital in London. The Scottish version organized the Scottish Suffrage Societies to fund and staff a hospital. Again the British Army rejected offers of help and 14 units served with other Allied armies.

ORGANIZING WOMEN'S LABOUR

After the Derby Scheme and the Military Service Act removed many men from industry, thousands of women were drafted in to replace them. Eventually some 750,000 women were employed on munitions work; others found work in businesses, banks, railways, in manual work or as drivers. At the end of 1916 the government introduced the following women's military services to organize women's contribution to the war effort:

WOMEN'S AUXILIARY ARMY CORPS

Known as Queen Mary's Army Auxiliary Corps after April 1918, this body was organized along military lines with controllers, administrators and forewomen being the senior ranks. Workers volunteered for the duration of the war and the first contingent went to France in March 1917. Over 57,000 women carried out clerical work, storekeeping, telephony, catering and vehicle maintenance.

WOMEN'S LAND ARMY

Formed in February 1917 to support the agricultural industry; over 113,000 women were employed on the land, one-third of the agricultural work force.

WOMEN'S FORAGE CORPS

Formed in 1915; it was eventually taken over by the Army Service Corps.

WOMEN'S FORESTRY CORPS

Organized by the Board of Trade to supply timber.

ALMERIC PAGET MILITARY MASSAGE CORPS

A voluntary organization of 50 masseuses was adopted by the War Office and started work in France in 1917. It grew to over 2,000 staff.

Hundreds of thousands of women directly or indirectly played a parted in supporting the war effort, while running a family home and worrying about their loved ones serving overseas. Their contribution during the Great War laid the foundation for women's emancipation.

HOME LEAVE

Leave was issued to officers and men on a random basis to begin with but they could expect one or two leave passes a year, ranging from four to ten days depending on the

The two women of Pervyse ferried hundreds of wounded to the rear with their ambulance. *(IWM Q2660)*

distance they had to travel. After travelling from the trenches to the ports, over the Channel, and across Great Britain, it left little time at home. Arranging transport for men on leave was a huge task (an average of one week of leave per man per year involved 40,000 men on the move at any one time) and it took until 1916 to organize leave rotas.

Usually men were only told on the day their leave started, and they quickly headed for the nearest railway station to catch one of the special leave trains. They were issued with a new uniform and underwear at the port, and after crossing the Channel to Folkestone travelled to Victoria Station in London where they were fed by volunteer canteens and given luxuries by the waiting crowds.

While some men caught up with their sleep once they got home, others found it difficult to adjust to their domestic surroundings. Married men headed home as quickly as possible to see their families while single men often stayed in London and spent their time in the pubs and clubs. Drunkenness was a problem and sexual dalliances increased. The men found that civilians knew little about life at the front and many of them had a romantic vision of the trenches, far removed from the squalid reality.

Leave passed quickly and ended abruptly with a race against time to return to Victoria Station. Depression would set in on the leave train as the men compared stories and tried not to think of what lay ahead.

Queues of troops on leave wait for their train at a London station. *(IWM Q30517)*

CHAPTER THIRTEEN

LEGACY

THE ARMISTICE

The Great War came to abrupt end at 11:00 a.m. on 11 November 1918 as the guns all along the Western Front fell silent. Although there were celebrations at home, there was an overwhelming feeling of apathy at the front as the reality of the Armistice took time to sink in. The men were tired and unconvinced; the news was just too good to be true.

The terms of the Armistice called for the occupation of the Rhineland by the Allied armies and British Fourth and Second Armies, each with 16 divisions, started their advance towards Germany on 17 November with 3 cavalry divisions leading. Second Army took over the British sector at the German border on 1 December, reaching Cologne on the 6th, where guards were put on the bridges across the Rhine; the east bank was occupied on 12 December. Second Army was renamed the British Army of the Rhine on 2 April 1919 and on the 21st General Sir William Robertson took over command from General Sir Herbert Plumer.

DEMOBILIZATION

The rest of the armies waited in France and Belgium to demobilize and officers were kept busy keeping the restless soldiers occupied, organising sports and concerts to break up the monotony of route marches and fatigues. Attempts to prepare the men for civilian life in

Field Marshal Haig and his army commanders in Cambrai on 11 November 1918. *Front from left to right* – General Plumer (Second Army), General Byng (Third Army), Haig, General Birdwood (Fifth Army), General Rawlinson (Fourth Army) and General Horne (First Army); their chiefs of staff stand on the steps behind. *(IWM Q9689)*

training schools did little to alleviate the tension.

Plans for demobilization had been drawn up three years earlier, and the clerical arrangements were in place by the end of November, but it would take many months to transfer everyone home. The priority was to get Britain back to work and men with vital trades (miners, agricultural and transport

343

After sailing up the Rhine, these demobilized men look forward to the final journey back to Britain and home. *(IWM Q7665)*

workers) left first, with little regard for a man's length of service or his family needs.

When the time came to leave the Army, men made their way to one of the 26 dispersal stations along the French coast. They were paid any arrears, given a demob suit (or a 52s 6d allowance), a free travel pass home and free unemployment insurance – men without a job to return to were promised 24s unemployment allowance a week for 12 months, with extra payments if they had children. Men also handed in their equipment and weapons but they were allowed to keep their uniforms and helmet.

By August 1919 nearly 2,750,000 officers and men had been demobilized but the process took until 1922 to complete. Protests over the length of time it took were quickly replaced by protests at the high rates of unemployment and shortages of food and coal in Great Britain.

The initial euphoria that followed the Armistice in Great Britain had faded away by the time the demobbed soldiers reached their homes and they found that they were civilians once again, left only with the memories that set them apart from the rest of society. It took many years to adjust to their new life and, while most tried to forget, nightmares plagued the shell-shocked for years to follow and the gassed struggled for breath for the rest of their lives.

In all 2,414,000 were entitled to an invalidity pension (awarded in relation to their disability) and thousands of men had to come to terms with their injuries as they struggled to survive on their meagre settlement. Full disability pay was only 25s per week, the equivalent of an unskilled labourer's wage, while an amputee had to survive on 16s as he struggled to find work and become accepted into society.

CEMETERIES AND MEMORIALS

The nature of trench warfare meant that different types of cemeteries were formed behind the front line, ranging from tiny unit graveyards to huge cemeteries built alongside hospitals. After the war many small cemeteries were closed and the remains in them were taken for re-burial in more accessible concentration cemeteries to reduce maintenance costs.

Men often buried their comrades in small battlefield cemeteries just behind the front line. While every attempt was made to identify a body by identity tags, pay books or personal items, some bodies had been disfigured beyond recognition. The graveyards were often split into scattered unit plots and there were often separate areas for the officers' graves during the early days; this practice virtually ceased with the arrival of the New Armies on the Western Front. Later fighting damaged many of these cemeteries and headstones engraved with the words 'Buried Near This Spot' remember lost graves. The casualty clearing stations and base hospitals were able to form large orderly plots that grew into large well-tended cemeteries. Working parties often had to dig mass graves in the cemeteries when an offensive was imminent, ready to cope with the influx of casualties.

POSTWAR CLEARANCE OF THE BATTLEFIELDS

After the war, the battlefield was systematically searched several times, with exhumation companies searching for signs of a burial. Likely locations were marked and the teams followed, exhuming and identifying bodies before they were re-interred in a nearby cemetery. Unidentified remains were buried beneath individual headstones carved with

Hundreds of thousands never went home. The Commonwealth War Graves Commission maintains their graves and memorials in perpetuity. *(IWM Q5875)*

The ranks of graves in Tyne Cot Cemetery in the Ypres Salient (the largest cemetery on the Western Front) stand silently, a lasting memorial to the men killed in the Great War.

Rudyard Kipling's words 'A Soldier of the Great War – Known unto God'. Partial identification of rank or regiment, using badges or buttons, was noted on the headstone.

Larger cemeteries have a Cross of Sacrifice and a Stone of Remembrance, an altar-shaped stone that forms the focal point of remembrance ceremonies. Kipling's words 'Their Name Liveth for Evermore' are carved on the stone.

The names of the missing were carved on huge memorials and every man and woman who died in service either has a marked grave or their name on a memorial. The Menin Gate and a Memorial Screen at Tyne Cot Cemetery remember those killed in the Ypres Salient; a huge memorial at Thiepval lists the names of the missing on the Somme. Smaller examples, which sometimes take the form of a memorial screen surrounding one of the larger cemeteries, can be found along the Western Front and in other theatres.

Remains continue to be found to this day; they are taken to a nearby military cemetery and buried with full military honours.

MAINTAINING THE CEMETERIES AND MEMORIALS

Although the Royal Engineers were supposed to bury the dead, they were usually too busy and soldiers were often left to inter their own comrades, either where they died or in civilian cemeteries. A chaplain, or the unit adjutant, recorded the details of front-line deaths while the Royal Army Medical Corps kept account of men who died in its charge.

In October 1914 Commissioner of the British Red Cross Society, Mr (later Sir) Fabian Ware, volunteered his ambulance unit and began to mark and record military burials. His unit was named the Graves Registration Commission in February 1915 and the Red Cross Society provided personnel and transport until the commission was given military status in October 1915. The commission split the BEF's zone into seven areas and systematically recorded graves, marking them with a simple wooden cross or memorial. The Joint Committee of the Red Cross Society and St John's Ambulance sent photographs of the graves to the next of kin.

During the winter of 1915–16 a committee was appointed to acquire land from the French government and make provision for permanent care of the graves; it also took on the responsibility for answering enquiries from relatives.

The commission was renamed the Commission of Graves Registration and Enquiries in March 1916 with Lieutenant-Colonel Ware as Director. It was later called the Imperial War Graves Commission and after the war it took charge of building and maintaining the hundreds of permanent

The Thiepval Memorial, where thousands of the men killed on the Somme who have no known grave are remembered.

cemeteries and memorials across the world. The name Commonwealth War Graves Commission was adopted in later years.

THE BRITISH LEGION

The Legion was founded in 1921 as a charitable organization to support ex-soldiers who had fallen on hard times. In 1922 Major George Howson formed the Disabled Society to help the thousands of men who were struggling to live on their meagre pensions.

The first fund-raising day was held in Britain on 11 November 1921 and the poppy was used as a recognizable symbol of Remembrance; it had been the only flower to thrive on the devastated battlefields. The poppy connection was immortalized in a poem by John McCrae, a Canadian medical officer who died of his wounds.

> In Flanders' fields the poppies blow
> Between the crosses, row on row

Howson organized a factory in Richmond where disabled workers could produce poppies to offer for contributions. The factory still makes poppies for the Poppy Appeal held every year, culminating with Remembrance Sunday on the Sunday nearest 11 November. The Legion has grown into the United Kingdom's largest charity, with over 500,000 members, and provides financial and social support for thousands of soldiers both serving and retired.

WAR MEMORIALS IN THE UNITED KINGDOM

THE UNKNOWN SOLDIER

Over one-third of the men killed in action were listed as missing with no known grave and the decision was taken to bury an unknown soldier in Westminster Abbey as a symbol of national mourning and as a focus for ceremonies. A body was randomly selected and brought to Dover before it was taken to London by train with the full military honours afforded to a field marshal.

On the morning of 11 November 1920 the funeral procession headed through the streets of London to Whitehall to attend the unveiling of the Cenotaph; it then continued to Westminster Abbey, followed by King George V, other members of the royal family and the prime minister. Twelve pallbearers, including Lord Haig, Lord French and Lord Beatty (former commander of the Royal Navy's Grand Fleet), carried the coffin past a 100-strong guard of honour of Victoria Cross holders.

No one knew if the man (or woman) had been a sailor, a soldier or an airman, or whether they were from England, Scotland, Wales, Ireland, India or from one of the other Dominions; only one thing was sure, they had given their life serving the British Empire during the Great War.

THE CENOTAPH

A temporary plaster and wood Cenotaph was built on Whitehall for the Victory Parade in London on 19 July 1919. Following public demand for a permanent Cenotaph Sir Edwin Lutyens was asked to produce a design and offered a simple unadorned memorial in Portland stone. King George V unveiled the Cenotaph at 11.00 a.m. on Armistice Day, 11 November 1920 in front of the Unknown Soldier's funeral procession. After two minutes of silence and the sounding of the Last Post, the procession moved on to Westminster Abbey.

Wales, Northern Ireland and Scotland each erected their own national memorials.

The Cenotaph has been the focal point for the nation's annual remembrance ceremony.

MILITARY MEMORIALS

The arms and services have large memorials and the majority can be found in central London. Divisions erected their memorials overseas, close to the site of a memorable action. Regiments erected a memorial in their garrison town and deposited a roll of honour in the local cathedral or church; many cathedrals have regimental chapels. The pals battalions of Kitchener's New Armies had strong local connections and many towns erected special memorials to remember their battalions.

WAR MEMORIALS

The First World War devastated local communities and, for the first time, large numbers of memorials were erected in communities, both large and small, across the Empire. In the United Kingdom the Royal

Academy arranged a War Memorial Exhibition in 1919 displaying models and photographs; designs by Sir Edwin Lutyens and Sir Reginald Blomfield proved to be popular. The type of memorial chosen by a community depended on the amount of money raised by public and private donations.

Large towns and cities had extensive financial support; however, prolonged discussions about the type of memorial and its location often delayed construction. Names were usually omitted on the ground of cost but books of remembrance containing the roll of honour were usually deposited in a local municipal building or church. Some communities spent their money on a hospital, an art gallery or museum, accompanied by a small memorial.

Small towns often chose to erect a simple cross or sculpted figure in a prominent position. Church halls, memorial halls and hospital wings would sometimes be built, while several communities opted to set up a funding scheme for the bereaved.

The village memorial, usually a small monument on the green, portrays the sense of loss felt by small communities. They were often quite detailed and the lists of fathers, sons and brothers records individual family bereavements.

Places of work, study and leisure usually chose to remember their members with a small memorial, a plaque or a book of remembrance. Schools and universities sometimes built memorial rooms or chapels to remember their old boys, while churches had memorial windows to honour members of the congregation. Wealthy families often made an individual effort to remember their loved ones and plaques and church memorial windows were common. These small memorials were a comfort to families who lived some distance from the large city memorials.

THE COST

In all 704,803 men and women from Great Britain lost their lives in action, or died from wounds or disease or in accidents. Over a third of those were missing presumed dead. Another 251,900 men and women from Canada, Australia, India and other parts of the Empire also died. The Western Front accounted for 564,715, or 60%, while 26,213 were killed on the tiny Gallipoli Peninsula. The remainder lost their lives in other theatres across the world.

Some 2,272,998 British soldiers were injured, either in action or accident (though the total is misleading because men wounded several times appear more than once). While nearly 1.5 million returned to active duty, over 400,000 were only fit enough to be employed on the lines of communication or in garrisons. In all 159,000 died of their wounds or illness and the remainder, over 181,000, were invalided out of the Army. After the war 580,000 young men and women had been seriously disabled by their war service.

POETRY AND LITERATURE

Some of the lasting impressions of the Great War are expressed in poetry, and the verse written by the war poets is highly regarded in the world of literature. Early patriotic poetry was quickly replaced by a more sombre and reflective style of writing, expressing the anguish and hopelessness felt by the men in the trenches. The short list below gives some of the best-known poets.

RUPERT BROOKE

Brooke joined the Royal Naval Division on the outbreak of war and took part in the Antwerp expedition in October 1914, recording his experiences in several poems including *Peace, Safety* and *The Soldier*. He sailed for the Dardanelles in February 1915 but died of acute blood poisoning on 23 April; he was buried on the Greek island of Skyros.

JOHN McCRAE

McCrae was a medical officer with the Canadian Expeditionary Force and following the Second Battle of Ypres in April 1915 he wrote his celebrated poem, *In Flanders Fields*. He died of pneumonia in 1918. *Flanders Fields and Other Poems* was published posthumously in 1919.

WILFRED OWEN

Owen joined the Artists' Rifles in October 1915 and was commissioned as a 2nd lieutenant. He transferred to the Manchester Regiment in January 1917 and began writing poetry to express his thoughts on his experiences. Owen was concussed by a shell on the Somme in the summer of 1917 and was only rescued after spending several days in a bomb crater with the corpse of a fellow officer. He was diagnosed as suffering from shell-shock. While recovering at Craiglockhart War Hospital he met Siegfried Sassoon. Sassoon encouraged Owen and over the months that followed Owen wrote many poems including *Anthem for Doomed Youth, Disabled, Dulce et Decorum Est* and *Strange Meeting*. He returned

Town war memorials usually occupy prominent positions presenting a lasting reminder of the sacrifice made by previous generations. This is Harrogate in North Yorkshire.

to the front in August 1918 and was awarded the Military Cross during the fighting for the Beaurevoir Line. Owen was killed leading his men across the Sambre Canal on 4 November 1918, a week before the Armistice. Sassoon arranged for the publication of his *Collected Poems* after his death.

ISAAC ROSENBERG

Rosenberg had emigrated to South Africa to recover from poor health but he returned to England in February 1915 and enlisted in a bantam battalion the following October. He was killed on 1 April 1918 and his body was never recovered. Friends arranged for his poems, *Collected Works*, to be published.

CHARLES HAMILTON SORLEY

Sorley returned from Germany when war broke out and enlisted in the Suffolk Regiment. Lieutenant Sorley arrived in France in May 1915 and was quickly promoted to the rank of captain. He was killed at the Battle of Loos on 13 October 1915 having written 37 complete poems, including *When You See Millions of the Mouthless Dead*, composed shortly before he died.

SIEGFRIED SASSOON

Sassoon enlisted in the Sussex Yeomanry but he was commissioned into the Royal Welsh Fusiliers in May 1915 where he met Robert Graves (who wrote the autobiographical work *Goodbye to All That*, which discusses his military service). Nicknamed 'Mad Jack' because of his fearless courage, Sassoon was awarded the Military Cross in June 1916. He was wounded in April 1917 and while recovering developed a sense of anger at the authorities, believing that they were prolonging the war unnecessarily. After a letter was published in *The Times*, Sassoon narrowly escaped court-martial after Graves convinced the tribunal that he was suffering from shell-shock. While he was receiving treatment at Craiglockhart Military Hospital, Sassoon met Wilfred Owen (he arranged for Owen's works to be published after the war). When he was pronounced fit, Sassoon served in Palestine where he was again wounded. His poems, such as *The Old Huntsman* and *Counter-Attack*, expressed anti-war sentiments; he also wrote a three-part fictionalized autobiography based on his experiences.

EDMUND BLUNDEN

Blunden joined the Royal Sussex Regiment on the outbreak of the war and fought at Ypres and on the Somme where he was awarded the Military Cross. Blunden recalled his experiences in his autobiographical work, *Undertones of War*. He also produced collected editions of the work of Wilfred Owen and Ivor Gurney.

TRENCH POETRY AND SONGS

Trench poetry displayed a mixture of humour, vulgarity, contempt for the Germans or the Army's higher authorities, and a longing to be anywhere else but in the trenches. Many authors preferred to remain anonymous because of the ribald content of their poems but one of the best known was 'Woodbine Willy', the Reverend Geoffrey Kennedy MC, an Army chaplain.

The soldiers used songs to while away the hours on the march or nights in the billets behind the lines. The themes were similar to those of the poems and the following list includes a few old favourites among the troops: *It's a Long Way to Tipperary, We Are Fred Karno's Army, Good-bye-ee, Never Mind, Bombed Last Night, Hush Here Comes a Whizz-Bang, The Bells of Hell, Three German Officers Crossed the Rhine, Hanging on the Old Barbed Wire, When This Lousy War is Over, I Don't Want to Join the Army, Whiter than the Whitewash.*

PROPAGANDA AND THE WAR ARTISTS

Soon after the outbreak of the war the British government set up the British War Propaganda Bureau led by Charles Masterman and invited 25 leading British authors (including Arthur Conan Doyle, John Masefield, G.K. Chesterton, Thomas Hardy,

The village war memorial, like this one in Gargrave in the Yorkshire Dales, lists friends, brothers, fathers and sons of the local community.

Rudyard Kipling and H.G. Wells) to discuss how to promote Great Britain's interests. They agreed to contribute anonymously to propaganda pamphlets and books and these started to appear at the beginning of 1915; one of the first titles was *Report on Alleged German Outrages*, describing German atrocities against the Belgian population.

Masterman's bureau printed over 1,150 publications including the titles *To Arms, The Barbarism in Berlin, The New Army, The Battle of the Somme, England's Effort* and *When Blood is Their Argument*. The bureau also produced a 24-part history, a patriotic (and one-sided) view of the conduct of the war, written by John Buchan.

The Army was acutely aware that photographs depicting the squalid conditions at the front could seriously affect morale at home. Private cameras were banned and only official photographers were allowed to take pictures for release to the press. There was, however, a need for suitable illustrations and the first official war artist, Muirhead Bone, went to France in May 1916, producing 150 sketches over the next six months. Francis Dodd took his place and other artists, including Eric Kennington, William Orpen, Paul Nash, C.R.W. Nevinson and William Rothenstein, soon joined him; John Lavery was employed to paint pictures of the home front.

John Buchan headed a new Department of Information from February 1917, while Masterman's office continued to turn out pamphlets, books, photographs and paintings, keeping a steady flow of propaganda available for the press, publications and cinemas. The various offices of information and propaganda were grouped together under Lord Beaverbrook (owner of the *Daily Express* newspaper), who was appointed Minister of Information in March 1918. The principal officers were:

Director of Publications: Charles Masterman.
Director of Intelligence: John Buchan.
Propaganda against enemy countries: Lord Northcliffe (owner of *The Times* and the *Daily Mail*).
Propaganda in neutral countries: Robert Donald (editor of the *Daily Chronicle*).

Beaverbrook set up the British War Memorial Committee and increased the number of artists, changing their role from propaganda to creating a record of the war. Altogether 90 artists produced official work during the war.

The grave of Rifleman Strudwick who died in January 1916, aged only 15, one of hundreds of thousands of men and boys who never came home.

PRINCIPAL COMMANDERS OF THE BRITISH AND DOMINION FORCES

ALLENBY, GENERAL SIR EDMUND (1861–1936)

Allenby led the BEF's Cavalry Division during the retreat from Mons and the advance to the Aisne before becoming commander of the new Cavalry Corps during the First Battle of

General Allenby

Ypres in November 1914. After commanding V Corps during the Second Battle of Ypres, Allenby took command of Third Army in October 1915. After clashing with Field Marshal Haig over plans for the Battle of Arras in April 1917, and the subsequent failure to exploit early successes during the battle, Allenby was transferred to command the Palestine Front and took over the Egyptian Expeditionary Force in June 1917.

The advance into Palestine suited Allenby's style of command and, by concentrating on sectors in the Turkish line at Gaza, his cavalry made spectacular advances, capturing Jerusalem in December. With the help of the Arabs, Allenby forced a decisive victory at Megiddo in September 1918.

BIRDWOOD, GENERAL SIR WILLIAM (1865–1951)

Birdwood led the Australian and New Zealand Army Corps during the landing at Anzac Cove on Gallipoli. He was one of the few British senior officers to have a good working relationship with the ANZACS. He went on to lead I ANZAC Corps during the Somme and Third Ypres campaigns. Birdwood was promoted to command Fifth Army in May 1918 and led the army through the Advance to Victory during the autumn of 1918.

General Birdwood

BYNG, GENERAL SIR JULIAN (1862–1935)

Byng led 3rd Cavalry Division from the autumn of 1914 and the Cavalry Corps during

the summer of 1915. He was posted to Gallipoli in August and organized the withdrawal from Suvla Bay before returning to France to take command of the Canadian Corps. After the Canadians captured Vimy Ridge during the Arras campaign of April 1917, Byng was promoted to lead Third Army. He led the army through the Battle of Cambrai in November 1917 and the difficult days of the German Somme Offensive in March 1918. Third Army played a leading role in the Advance to Victory, advancing 60 miles between August and November.

CURRIE, LT-GEN SIR ARTHUR (1875–1933)

Currie led 2nd Canadian Brigade through the difficult days following the first gas attack at Ypres in April 1915. He was promoted to GOC 1st Canadian Division the following September and led the division in the fighting at Courcelette on the Somme in the autumn of 1916. His troops helped to capture Vimy Ridge the following April. As the first Canadian appointed commander of the Canadian Corps, Currie fought to keep his corps together until the end of the war. After

General Byng

General Currie

the horrendous battle for Passchendaele in November 1917, the Canadians led throughout the Advance to Victory, first with Fourth Army during the Battle of Amiens and then with First Army as it broke through the Hindenburg Line at Cambrai.

FRENCH, FIELD MARSHAL SIR JOHN (1852–1925)

French, a cavalry officer, was chosen to command the BEF in August 1914. He proved an uncertain and timid leader, changing from unrealistic optimism before Mons to despondency during the retreat to the Marne. French's confidence was restored by the advance to the Aisne, but he failed to cooperate effectively with the French commanders and frequently clashed with his own subordinates.

Field Marshal French

French struggled to come to terms with the static conditions of trench warfare and a series of disappointments throughout 1915 culminated in a poor performance at Loos in September 1915.

French was replaced at the end of the year and commanded GHQ Forces at Home (later GHQ Home Forces) until 1918, when he became Governor-General of Ireland.

GOUGH, GENERAL SIR HUBERT (1870–1963)

Gough led the 2nd Cavalry Division through the Battle of Messines in October 1914 before commanding 7th Division in the heavy fighting in the spring of 1915. He was promoted to lead I Corps in July and his troops had mixed success during First Army's offensive at Loos. In April 1916, Gough took command of the Reserve Corps, which expanded into the Reserve Army a few weeks later. His army took over part of Fourth Army's front on 4 July 1916 and Gough led it during the fighting on Thiepval Ridge (it was renamed Fifth Army at the end of October). Attacks during the Arras offensive in the spring of 1917 failed to break through the Hindenburg Line at Bullecourt and a combination of poor staff work and over-confidence led to Fifth Army's role in the Third Ypres battle being reduced in favour of General Plumer's pragmatic approach. Field Marshal Haig still held Gough in high regard but Fifth Army's failure to stem the German Somme Offensive in March 1918 led to Gough's dismissal.

General Gough

HAIG, FIELD MARSHAL SIR DOUGLAS (1861–1928)

Haig was serving as Director of Military Operations before taking command of I Corps in August 1914. After keeping his corps intact during the retreat to the Marne and the advance to the Aisne, Haig was put to the test when his command bore the brunt of the fighting around Ypres in October and November. He was promoted to lead First Army in December 1914. First Army had limited success at Neuve Chapelle in March and Loos in September 1915 but Haig was still promoted to lead the BEF following Field Marshal French's dismissal in December 1915 and remained in command until the end of the war. The Somme campaign in 1916 and the Third Ypres campaign in 1917 would forever associate Haig's name with attrition in Great Britain.

Field Marshal Haig

Haig's total commitment to the Western Front made him an enemy of Prime Minister Lloyd George, but he kept his post through repeated setbacks. The departure of General Robertson (the CIGS) in February 1918

weakened Haig's position and the German attacks on the Somme in March and in the Lys area in April placed him in a new role working for the new Allied supremo Marshal Foch.

The string of successful British attacks, starting at Amiens in early August and culminating in the breakthrough of the Hindenburg Line at the end of September, proved that Haig and his staff had weathered the worst to mould the British Army into a formidable fighting machine.

Haig took command of British Home Forces in 1919 and retired in 1921. He will always be a controversial figure, linked with the horrendous loss of life in the trenches of 1916 and 1917 rather than the victories of the last 100 days of the war. To some he was the leader of a successful Army but to others he was an unimaginative general who sent thousands of men to their deaths.

HAMILTON, GENERAL SIR IAN (1853–1947)

Hamilton commanded Home Forces before he was chosen by Kitchener to lead the

General Hamilton

Gallipoli campaign. After failing to take advantage of the surprise achieved in some sectors of the landings, subsequent attacks at Krithia, Anzac Cove and Suvla Bay failed due to his over-optimism and limited imagination. He was replaced in October 1915 after recommending the evacuation of Gallipoli.

HORNE, GENERAL HENRY (1861–1929)

Horne was General Haig's artillery commander during 1914 and took command of 2nd Division at the start of 1915. Despite failures at Festubert and Loos, he was promoted to lead XV Corps in Egypt in January 1916, returning to France three months later. His corps played a major part in the Battle of the Somme at Mametz and Delville Wood and, following the tank attack in September, he was again promoted this time to lead First Army. The army played a principal role in the Battle of Arras in April 1917 and held on to Givenchy and Béthune during the German Lys offensive twelve months later. Horne led the army throughout

General Horne

the Advance to Victory, advancing through Cambrai to Mons.

KITCHENER, FIELD MARSHAL HORATIO EARL (1850–1916)

An illustrious solder, Kitchener was on leave from his post as the military governor of Egypt when Prime Minister Asquith appointed him Secretary of State for War on 6 August 1914. He was one of the few men to believe that the war would not be over by Christmas 1914 and set to work mobilizing Great Britain's population for a long drawn-out conflict. His call for volunteers (and the powerful recruiting poster on which he featured) created a flood of new recruits for the Army, disrupting industry and the Army's administration, but his New Armies were to take the lion's share of the fighting after the summer of 1915.

Field Marshal Kitchener

Kitchener recognized the need to concentrate strength on the Western Front, but also diverted forces to Gallipoli and Salonika, causing friction between the politicians and the Army. He drowned on

5 June 1916 when the cruiser HMS *Hampshire*, taking him on a mission to Russia, was sunk en route.

MAUDE, GENERAL SIR F. STANLEY (1864–1917)

Maude led a brigade on the Western Front from October 1914 until he was wounded. On his recovery he commanded 13th Division at Gallipoli, transferring to Mesopotamia in March 1916. He took command of the Tigris Corps in July and the entire front a month later as the Anglo-Indian forces were being reorganized. Maude made a steady advance up the Tigris, taking Kut and then Baghdad in March 1917. Further operations secured the Euphrates, Diyala and Tigris Rivers from Turkish attacks. Maude died suddenly of cholera in Baghdad on 18 November 1917.

General Maude

General Milne

MILNE, GENERAL GEORGE (1866–1948)

After serving as an artillery officer during the early campaigns of 1914, Milne was promoted to Second Army's Major-General General Staff in February 1915. He sailed to the Balkan Front in command of the 27th Division in September 1915 and six months later became Commander-in-Chief of the forces in Salonika (British Salonika Army after January 1917). With a limited number of troops in the region and a harsh climate, there was little scope for large operations and attacks at Lake Dojran in the spring of 1917 failed. The Vardar Offensive in September 1918 routed the Bulgarian Army and, after the armistice with Turkey, Milne's troops headed to Constantinople where they remained until 1920.

General Monash

MONASH, GENERAL JOHN (1865–1931)

Monash, a civil engineer by profession and a pre-war Australian territorial militiaman, commanded 4th Australian Brigade at Gallipoli in 1915 before he was promoted to lead the new 3rd Australian Division. After successes at Messines and in the Third Ypres battle, Monash took command of the Australian Corps. His cautious but efficient leadership brought the corps successfully through the Battle of Amiens and the assault on the Hindenburg Line.

MURRAY, GENERAL SIR ARCHIBALD (1860–1945)

Murray became the BEF's Chief of Staff in August 1914 but the stressful trials of the retreat to the Marne and the First Battle of Ypres led to a breakdown at the end of the year. After recovering he joined the staff in London, gaining promotion from Deputy to Chief of the Imperial General Staff in September 1915, Murray took command of the troops stationed in Egypt and became Commander-in-Chief of the Egyptian Expeditionary Force in March 1916. Following

a slow advance towards Gaza, he was relieved after two failed attempts to take the city in the spring of 1917.

General Murray

NIXON, GENERAL SIR JOHN (1857–1921)

Nixon, an Indian Army officer, was appointed to lead the British forces in Mesopotamia in April 1915. He was instructed to advance on Baghdad by the Indian government but his over-confidence led to his forces becoming over-stretched. In the advance from Basra his tendency to overrule his field commanders at the front, while neglecting to arrange vital logistics back-up, was a recipe for disaster. The advance stalled at Ctesiphon in November and after his forces tried in vain to reach the besieged city of Kut, Nixon was relieved on the grounds of ill-health.

PLUMER, GENERAL SIR HERBERT (1857–1932)

Plumer took command of II Corps at the end of 1914 and he was promoted to lead Second Army in the Ypres Salient in May 1915. He was responsible for the Messines attack in June 1917 and played an increasing role in the Third Ypres campaign in the autumn of 1917, applying his thorough planning to the later stages of the battle.

Plumer led the Anglo-French army sent to aid Italy after the catastrophe at Caporetto in November 1917 and he returned to Second Army the following spring, in time to defend the Ypres Salient. His army joined the Advance to Victory at the end of September 1918, advancing through Courtrai.

General Rawlinson

IV Corps after they fell back to Ypres. After commanding his corps at Loos, he was promoted to command Fourth Army and led it through the drawn-out Battle of the Somme in 1916. Following a short period in charge of Second Army over the winter of 1917–18, Rawlinson was an advisor to the Supreme War Council in February and March 1918. He took over the shattered Fifth Army after Gough's dismissal at the end of March and it was renamed Fourth Army a few days later. Rawlinson's Fourth Army played a major role in the Advance to Victory, advancing over 70 miles, starting with the Amiens Offensive on 8 August and then breaking through the Hindenburg Line.

General Plumer

RAWLINSON, GENERAL SIR HENRY (1864–1925)

Rawlinson led the troops sent to defend Antwerp in October 1914, taking command of

ROBERTSON, FIELD MARSHAL SIR WILLIAM (1860–1933)

Robertson was the only man to rise from private to field marshal in the British Army. After a successful period as the BEF's Quartermaster-General during the mobile

Field Marshal Robertson

General Smith-Dorrien

warfare of 1914, Robertson was Chief of Staff to Sir John French throughout 1915. He was chosen to be the Chief of the Imperial General Staff (CIGS), as the link between the War Cabinet and the Army, when General Haig took command of the BEF at the end of the year and he supported a full commitment to the Western Front. He felt undermined when General Henry Wilson became the British representative on the Supreme War Council in November 1917 and he resigned the following February. Four months later he became Commander-in-Chief Home Forces in Great Britain.

SMITH-DORRIEN, GENERAL SIR HORACE (1858–1930)

Smith-Dorrien was given command of II Corps in August 1914 following the death of General Grierson. Smith-Dorrien's corps faced the brunt of the German attacks at Mons and Le Cateau, but he soon fell out of favour with Field Marshal French. He was promoted to lead the new Second Army in December 1914 but disagreements with French about the defence of the Ypres Salient during the German attacks in April and May 1915 led to his dismissal.

APPENDIX 2

ABBREVIATIONS

AA	Anti-Aircraft	CCRA	Corps Commander Royal Artillery
AA and QMG	Assistant Adjutant- and Quartermaster-General	CCS	Casualty Clearing Station
ADC	Aide de Camp	CE	Chief Engineer
ADMS	Assistant Director Medical Services	CEF	Canadian Expeditionary Force
		CGS	Chief of General Staff
ADOS	Assistant Director Ordnance Services	CHA	Commander Heavy Artillery
		CID	Committee of Imperial Defence
ADS	Advanced Dressing Station		
ADVS	Assistant Director Veterinary Services	CIGS	Chief of the Imperial General Staff
AFA	Army Field Artillery	CO	Commanding Officer
AIF	Australian Imperial Force	CQMS	Company Quartermaster Sergeant
ANZAC	Australian and New Zealand Army Corps		
		CRA	Commanding Royal Artillery
AOC	Army Ordnance Corps	CRE	Commanding Royal Engineers
AOD	Army Ordnance Department	CSM	Company Sergeant-Major
APO	Army Post Office		
AQMG	Assistant Quartermaster-General	DAAG	Deputy Assistant Adjutant-General
ASC	Army Service Corps	DAC	Divisional Ammunition Column
AT	Army Troops		
AVC	Army Veterinary Corps	DADMS	Deputy Assistant Director Medical Services
BAC	Brigade Ammunition Column	DAG	Deputy Adjutant-General
BGGS	Brigadier-General General Staff	DAQMG	Deputy Assistant Quartermaster-General
BGRA	Brigadier-General Royal Artillery	DA & QMG	Deputy Adjutant- and Quartermaster-General
BL	Breech-Loading (artillery piece)	DCM	Distinguished Conduct Medal
		DDMS	Deputy Director Medical Services
BRCS	British Red Cross Society		
		DDVS	Deputy Director Veterinary Services
CB	Confinement to Barracks (punishment)	DMS	Director of Medical Services

DSO	Distinguished Service Order	*POW*	Prisoner of War
		psc	Passed Staff College
EEF	Egyptian Expeditionary Force		
E&M	Electrical and Mechanical	*QF*	Quick-Firing (artillery piece)
		QMG	Quartermaster-General
FANY	First Aid Nursing Yeomanry		
FOO	Forward Observation Officer	*RAP*	Regimental Aid Post
		RFA	Royal Field Artillery
GHQ	General Headquarters	*RFC*	Royal Flying Corps
GOC	General Officer Commanding	*RGA*	Royal Garrison Artillery
		RHA	Royal Horse Artillery, and
HAR	Heavy Artillery Reserve		Reserve Heavy Artillery
HE	High Explosive	*RMLI*	Royal Marine Light Infantry
HT	Horse Transport	*RSM*	Regimental Sergeant-Major
		RTC	Reserve Training Centre
MC	Military Cross		
MDS	Main Dressing Station	*SAA*	Small Arms Ammunition
MEF	Mediterranean Expeditionary Force	*SMLE*	Short Magazine Lee-Enfield (Rifle)
MGC	Machine Gun Corps	*SR*	Special Reserve
MGGS	Major-General General Staff		
MGRA	Major-General Royal Artillery	*TF*	Territorial Force
MM	Military Medal	*TMB*	Trench Mortar Battery
MMGC	Motor Machine Gun Corps	*TR*	Training Reserve
MSM	Meritorious Service Medal		
MT	Mechanical Transport	*VAD*	Voluntary Aid Detachment
		VC	Victoria Cross
NYD	Not Yet Diagnosed (unknown medical condition)	*VO*	Veterinary Officer
NYDN	Not Yet Diagnosed Nervous (suspected shell-shock)	*WD*	War Department
		WO	War Office
		WWCS	Walking Wounded Collecting Station
OC	Officer Commanding		
OR	Other Rank		
OTC	Officer Training Corps	*YS*	Young Soldier

APPENDIX 3

SOLDIERS' SLANG

Soldiers have always used slang to communicate and the Great War produced a language of its own at the front line, often using anglicized variations of French words. The following is a short list of the words commonly used by the men:

Alleyman	A German (from the French *allemand* meaning German)
Ack Ack	Anti-aircraft artillery
Archie	Anti-aircraft fire
Ammos	Standard issue Army boots
Boko	A large quantity (from the French *beaucoup*)
Bellied	Term used to describe a tank caught on an obstacle and unable to move
Billy	Australian nickname for a cooking-pot or can
Big Bertha	Originally the German 42cm Mörser; later any German heavy artillery
Blighty	Britain, a Blighty wound was one which required evacuation home
Boche	A name for the Germans
Brass	High-ranking staff officers (also Brass Hats and Red Tabs)
Buzzer	A field telephone
Chit	A written message
Coal Box	A type of artillery shell
Crump	Shell-burst or series of explosions
Digger	An Australian soldier
Ditched	Term used to describe a bogged-down tank
Dixie	British Army camp kettle
Dud	A shell that failed to explode
Emma Gee	Machine gun (phonetic letters for MG)
Fritz	A name for the Germans
Glasshouse	A military prison or detention centre
Hun	A pejorative name for the Germans
Jack Johnson	Type of artillery shell (after a famous boxer of the time)
Kitch	Australian slang for a British soldier (from Kitchener)
Kiwi	Term used to describe a New Zealander
Old Sweat	An experienced soldier
Over the Top	To leave the fire trench and attack the enemy
Push	A large-scale attack
San fairy ann	Term of resignation – 'it doesn't matter' (from the French *ça ne fait rien*)
Sausage	Type of artillery shell
Stand To	Period when men manned the fire step in case of enemy attack
Stunt	A raid or an attack
Toc Emma	Trench mortar (phonetic letters for TM)
Tommy	Term for British soldier
Tour	Period spent in the front-line
Whizz-Bang	A type of artillery shell

BIBLIOGRAPHY

SOURCES

The Military Operations Series of official histories was printed in the 1920s and 1930s and original copies are now collectors' items. The series was compiled by Brigadier-General James Edmonds, who many consider to have censored the accounts to save reputations and future controversy. The Naval and Military Press started to reprint the series in the 1990s and the majority are now available.

Although the accounts of the battles are often brief and tedious, the technical information scattered throughout the text and the appendices is extremely useful.

Military Operations France and Belgium, 1914:
   Volume 1: *Mons, Marne, Aisne*
Military Operations France and Belgium, 1914:
   Volume 2: *Armentieres, Ypres*
Military Operations France and Belgium, 1915:
   Volume 1: *Neuve Chapelle, Ypres*
Military Operations France and Belgium, 1915:
   Volume 2: *Aubers Ridge, Festubert, Loos*
Military Operations France and Belgium, 1916:
   Volume 1: *Up to July 1*
Military Operations France and Belgium, 1916:
   Volume 2: *July 2 to December*
Military Operations France and Belgium, 1917:
   Volume 1: *Arras and Bullecourt*
Military Operations France and Belgium, 1917:
   Volume 2: *Messines and Third Ypres*
Military Operations France and Belgium, 1917:
   Volume 3: *Cambrai*

Military Operations France and Belgium, 1918:
   Volume 1: *German Somme Offensive*
Military Operations France and Belgium, 1918:
   Volume 2: *Somme continued and the Lys*
Military Operations France and Belgium, 1918:
   Volume 3: *Aisne*
Military Operations France and Belgium, 1918:
   Volume 4: *100 Days, August*
Military Operations France and Belgium, 1918:
   Volume 5: *100 Days, September*
Military Operations France and Belgium, 1918:
   Volume 6: *100 Days, October onwards*
Military Operations Gallipoli: 2 volumes
Military Operations Mesopotamia: 4 volumes
Military Operations Salonika: 2 volumes

Other important reference works are:

Bean, Charles, *The Official History of Australia in the War of 1914–1918*: 6 volumes, Angus & Robertson 1921–42, reprinted University of Queensland Press, 1980s
Becke, A.F., *Order of Battle of Divisions*, Ray Westlake Military Books, reprinted 1980s and 1990s; Volume 1: *Regular Divisions*; Volume 2A: *First Line Territorial Divisions*; Volume 2B: *Second Line Territorial Divisions*; Volume 3 and 4: *New Army Divisions*; Volume 5A: *Australian, New Zealand and Canadian Divisions*; Volume 5B: *Indian Divisions*
Bourne, John, *Who's Who in World War I*, Routledge, 2001
Chasseaud, Peter, *Topography of Armageddon: A British Trench Map Atlas of the Western Front 1914–1918*, Naval and Military Press, 1994

Ellis John & Cox, Michael, *The World War One Data Book*, Aurum, 1993

Gibson, T.A. Edwin & Ward, G. Kingsley, *Courage Remembered*, HMSO, 1989

Griffith, Paddy, *Battle Tactics of the Western Front: The British Army's Art of Attack, 1916–18*, Yale University Press, 1996

Haythornthwaite, Philip, *The World War One Source Book*, Weidenfield & Nicolson, 1996

Holmes, Richard, *Tommy: The British Soldier on the Western Front*, HarperCollins, 2004

James, Brigadier E.A., *The British Armies in France and Belgium 1914–1918, Charts showing dispositions and employment of Corps and Divisions*, Unpublished, 1954

FURTHER READING

There are hundreds of books covering all aspects of the British Army's campaigns in the First World War, many now out of print. What follows is short list of current publications:

Beckett, Ian, *The First World War: The Essential Guide to Sources in the National Archives*, The National Archives, 2002

Beckett, Ian, *Ypres: The British Army and the Battle for Flanders, 1914*, Longman, 2004

Carlyon, L.A., *Gallipoli*, Bantam, 2003

Carver, Field Marshal Lord, *The National Army Museum Book of the Turkish Front 1914–18: The Campaigns at Gallipoli, in Mesopotamia and Palestine*, Pan, 2004

Cherry, Niall, *Most Unfavourable Ground: The Battle of Loos, 1915*, Helion, 2005

Corrigan, Gordon, *Loos 1915: The Unwanted Battle*, Spellmount, 2005

Dixon, John, *Magnificent but not War: The Second Battle of Ypres 1915*, Leo Cooper, 2003

Hart, Peter, *The Somme*, Weidenfeld & Nicolson, 2005

Laffin, John, *The Agony of Gallipoli*, Sutton Publishing, 2005

Macdonald, Lyn, *Somme*, Penguin, 1993

Macdonald, Lyn, *They Called It Passchendaele* Penguin, 1993

Macdonald, Lyn, *To the Last Man: Spring 1918*, Penguin, 1999

James, Captain E.A., *Record of the Battles & Engagements of the British Armies in France & Flanders 1914–18*, Naval and Military Press, 2001 (reprint of 1924 original)

Oldham, Peter, *Pillboxes on the Western Front*, Pen and Sword, 1995

Saunders, Anthony, *Weapons of the Trench War 1914–18*, Sutton Publishing, 1999

Smithers, A.J., *New Excalibur: Development of the Tank 1909–19*, Leo Cooper, 1986

Walter, John, *Allied Small Arms of World War One*, Crowood, 2000

Winter, Denis, *Death's Men: Soldiers of the Great War*, Penguin, 1978

McWilliams, James & Steel, R. James, *Amiens 1918*, Tempus, 2004

Middlebrook, Martin, *The Kaiser's Battle*, Penguin, 1995

Middlebrook, Martin, *The First Day on the Somme*, Pen and Sword, 2002

Messenger, Charles, *Call to Arms: The British Army 1914–18*, Weidenfeld & Nicolson, 2005

Nicholls, Jonathan, *Cheerful Sacrifice: The Battle of Arras 1917*, Leo Cooper, 2005

Palmer, Alan, *Victory 1918*, Weidenfeld & Nicolson, 1999

Prior, Robin & Wilson, Trevor, *Passchendaele: The Untold Story*, Yale University Press, 2002

Prior, Robin & Wilson, Trevor, *Command on the Western Front: The Military Career of Sir Henry Rawlinson 1914–1918*, Leo Cooper, 2004

Sheffield, Gary & Bourne, John, *The Haig Diaries: The Diaries of Field Marshal Sir Douglas Haig: War Diaries and Letters 1914–1918*, Weidenfeld & Nicolson, 2005

Sheffield, Gary & Todman, Dan, *Command and Control on the Western Front: The British Army's Experience, 1914–19*, Spellmount, 2004

Travers, Tim, *The Killing Ground: The British Army, The Western Front and the Emergence of Modern War, 1900–1918*, Pen and Sword, 2003

Pen and Sword's Battleground Series includes over sixty titles dedicated to First World War actions, complete with photographs, maps and tours of the battlefield.

WEBSITES

The internet is rapidly becoming a major source for First World War material as individuals and institutions make their information available online. The following is a short list of useful sites:

A comprehensive guide to the British Army in the Great War: <www.1914-1918.net>

Australian War Memorial: <www.awm.gov.au/atwar/ww1.htm>

Canadian Libraries Database of personnel files: <www.collectionscanada.ca/archivianet/020106_e.html>

Centre for First World War Studies: <www.firstworldwar.bham.ac.uk>

Commonwealth War Graves Commission: <www.cwgc.org/cwgcinternet/search.aspx>

General information on all aspects of the First World War: <www.firstworldwar.com>

Imperial War Museum: <www.iwm.org.uk>

National Army Museum: <www.national-army-museum.ac.uk>

National Archives (Public Records Office): <www.nationalarchives.gov.uk>

Western Front Association: www.westernfront.co.uk>

The Great War Society: <www.worldwar1.com>

INDEX